Coherence
The secret science of brilliant leadership

Dr Alan Watkins

KoganPage

LONDON PHILADELPHIA NEW DELHI

Publisher's note

Every possible effort has been made to ensure that the information contained in this book is accurate at the time of going to press, and the publishers and author cannot accept responsibility for any errors or omissions, however caused. No responsibility for loss or damage occasioned to any person acting, or refraining from action, as a result of the material in this publication can be accepted by the editor, the publisher or the author.

First published in Great Britain and the United States in 2014 by Kogan Page Limited

2nd floor, 45 Gee Street	1518 Walnut Street, Suite 1100	4737/23 Ansari Road
London EC1V 3RS	Philadelphia PA 19102	Daryaganj
United Kingdom	USA	New Delhi 110002
www.koganpage.com		India

© Complete Coherence Limited, 2014

The right of Complete Coherence Limited to be identified as the author of this work has been asserted by them in accordance with the Copyright, Designs and Patents Act 1988.

ISBN   978 0 7494 7005 0
E-ISBN   978 0 7494 7006 7

British Library Cataloguing-in-Publication Data

A CIP record for this book is available from the British Library.

Library of Congress Cataloging-in-Publication Data

Watkins, Alan, 1961-
    Coherence : the secret science of brilliant leadership / Alan Watkins.
        pages cm
    ISBN 978-0-7494-7005-0 (pbk.) – ISBN 978-0-7494-7006-7 (ebook)   1. Leadership.
2. Management.   I. Title.
    HD57.7.W379 2014
    658.4'092–dc23
                                                                                            2013026093

Typeset by Graphicraft Limited, Hong Kong
Print production managed by Jellyfish
Printed and bound by CPI Group (UK) Ltd, Croydon, CR0 4YY

CONTENTS

LIST OF FIGURES

LIST OF TABLES

ACKNOWLEDGEMENTS

I normally skim past the acknowledgements in most books, so please feel free to do the same. This is really for the people mentioned here. It is so rare to be able to publicly thank the people that make our lives not only possible but also a pleasure. This bit is for all of you.

The truth is that this book has been incubating for 15 years and it has only happened now because of the incredible support of so many people.

First and foremost to my wife Sarah, with whom I have shared the highs and lows on our journey together. Your loving, welcoming smile and warm embrace sustains me. You lift my heart and soul. I love you more deeply with each passing year and I am so blessed that we found each other (thanks to Russell Symmons for that). My children, Jack, Sam, Joe and Charlie are so wonderful in so many ways; you make it easy for me to get out of bed every single day. I am proud of you all and the men that you are becoming.

I would also like to acknowledge my parents. My Dad, from whom I get my sense of humour, wit and sharpness – thank you. Your life, I know has had its challenges and your perpetual desire to meet them head on is so admirable. To my Mum who taught me, by example, the nature of compassion and kindness. Your resilience and willingness to work really hard continue to amaze me. To my sister Julia and brother Andy, I love you both. I'd also like to say thank you to Lillian and Brian. Your relationship has always been an inspiration to me.

At Complete Coherence I am privileged to have so many wonderful people to work with. Carol, what a blessing we found you just round the corner. You have been an absolute star, a rare gem and your natural chirpy nature lifts us all. Rebecca, thanks for your willingness to put up with me and your warmth with clients. Alan L, it has been a source of deep pride to see you develop so much through your commitment and application of the work. Peter, your strength, flexibility and ability to do what is right provides such a strong foundation for the business, thank you. To Diane, you are simply the best practitioner in the world and like a sister to me. Why hasn't Obama called you? Tom, thanks for bringing your considerable talents to the party and I look forward to some great times together.

To Chris P, thanks for your passion, counsel and willingness to be irreverent. Nick, your integrity and persistence is a real asset, not to mention your impressive collection of shirts. Katie, your spark, stimulation and story-telling adds something special to the mix. Georges, thanks for your loyalty; you have been with us since the early days. Zander and Orowa, I have high hopes for you both. You are both exceptional young men and give me hope for the future. I am looking forward to seeing how you both develop. Kirsty, thanks for your tireless commitment to the research agenda and ability to work without enough help from me. It has been a pleasure to see you develop since you joined. Steve B, welcome to the party; you fitted right in. Extra thanks go to Carolyn who keeps us tidy on the finances with Carol and Sarah.

A special thanks in this book must go to Louise, who was absolutely instrumental at the inception phase and in getting things off the ground and keeping us on track with Carol, Jack and Zander in support on the marketing front. A very special thanks goes to Karen, who has edited what I wrote so brilliantly. You made this dream a reality and your ability to marshal, sort, polish and enhance what I gave you was incredible. This book would simply not have happened without your help. Did I mention that this was the first of an eight-book series?

In addition to the core team above, I would like to extend a special thank you to so many clients who were prepared to provide brief case studies and bring certain aspects of the book alive. Without you I could not be me. It has been a real pleasure working with you all and great that you have been prepared to put into practice so much of what we discussed together. But watch out because we are not finished yet and there is more to share before the journey is done. I would also like to extend my gratitude to all the other clients I have worked with over the last 15 years. There have been so many wonderful conversations with both individuals and teams in many businesses, schools and sporting organizations. I hope the provision of this book will help consolidate what we have covered and set you up for the next stage.

I would also like to mention a few other special people whom I have shared part of this journey with. Kevin Murray, you have been a good friend, stood by me when things were tough, challenged my thinking and brought your own magic. Charles Fallon, you likewise have been a good friend and wise counsel at critical points on the journey. Thank you also to Angela Clow for your academic counsel, and Davide Sola for your entrepreneurial spirit. I'd also like to thank Tom and Brian at Holacracy One for stimulating my thinking and showing us a new way forward. For Pippa and Jennifer I sense a great collaboration brewing. Also a special thanks to my friends

Steve Tappin, a pioneer prepared to challenge the status quo; Hugh Lloyd Jukes, an exceptional framer of complex issues; and Ido van der Heijden, who brings a sensitivity to the shadow work that is fascinating.

Lastly I would like to thank Kogan Page and Matthew Smith in particular for being prepared to take this book on, for being flexible and taking such a straightforward approach. You have definitely made this book better.

The great performance myth

I remember sitting on the couch at home watching the last day of the British Open in July 2007. In an impressive display of golfing talent, Spaniard Sergio Garcia had taken the lead and kept it for three days. On the final day he was paired with Irishman Padraig Harrington and it was a nervy day for both players. In the end it all came down to the 18th hole. Garcia needed to sink a 10-foot putt to win but the ball lipped out; the game went to a playoff and the Irishman lifted the Claret Jug. When it was all over the legendary golf commentator Peter Alliss gave one of his customary sighs and said, 'Ahhh, It's a funny old game, golf,' as though it was a complete mystery why these things happen. At which point I was jumping up and down in front of the TV yelling that it's not a mystery at all!

Garcia had been in that position before. The year earlier in the same tournament he lost to Tiger Woods on the last day despite playing blistering golf in the previous days. On the Saturday he even shot a 29 on the front nine holes. On the last day he shot 39 on exactly the same holes. A year later, in the 2008 PGA Championship, Harrington beat him again after the wheels fell off on the final day. But it's not just Garcia. Remember Greg Norman in the 1996 Masters, Rory McIlroy's final round meltdown at the 2011 Masters or Adam Scott's spectacular demise at the 2012 British Open.

And more importantly, this drop in performance is not unique to golf or any sport for that matter and it happens in business all the time. People are consistently underperforming and making poor or sub-optimal decisions that have massive repercussions for the business – we just don't normally hear about them or get the opportunity to witness them in real time in quite such spectacular fashion. But contrary to conventional or Peter Alliss's wisdom there is nothing mysterious about the performance aberrations that plague sport or business. The reason it happens and it appears mysterious – whether on the golf course or during a new business pitch or off-site strategy session – is that we simply don't understand what's really influencing performance in the first place. It's time to set the record straight.

In order to do that properly we are going to explore a number of scientific discoveries from all the levels of the human system, including the fields of medicine, cardiology, neurophysiology, evolutionary biology, quantum physics, signal processing and systems theory as well as organizational performance, sports psychology and emotional intelligence. In examining many largely agreed upon 'facts' we will see that some astonishing conclusions become clear, conclusions that, as extraordinary as they may seem, consist of no more than pre-existing knowledge. Whilst this book exposes the secret science of brilliant leadership, it's important to understand that these scientific insights have not been kept secret deliberately; it's just that they are rarely known by the people who could benefit most from their appreciation and application. In truth, this knowledge has been around for many years, sometimes decades, but each 'part' has usually only been known in academia or reported in obscure medical or scientific journals. Very few of these key insights have made it into mainstream discussion and almost none are taught in business schools or published in business literature. And yet when we integrate these insights they lead us to a surprising conclusion about ourselves – we can be brilliant every single day. We can regain the energy we had 10 years ago, we can be much smarter, happier and healthier. We can be more successful, have much better relationships and have a greater impact on our business, our society and the world.

This journey is not for the faint hearted. Most leadership books contain one big idea and a few interesting nuggets along the way. That is not true of this book. There are several big ideas in each chapter and the nuggets are large enough and frequent enough to start a gold rush. I will introduce a vast amount of information in this book, covering topics in detail that may initially seem irrelevant. I promise you that none of it is irrelevant. Each is an important piece of the puzzle that will link up into an integrated whole. The magic occurs when all the parts are connected to provide a complete, coherent picture of who we really are, how we really function and what we are truly capable of. It is therefore essential that the 'parts' are explained in sufficient detail. This book brings together the critical business-related insights of the last 20 years so that we can finally appreciate the 'mystery' of performance once and for all. And the first of those critical insights, as we shall see, is that our brilliance all starts with the quality of our physiology.

In business or in sport it's all about results. Results are the yardstick of success and business leaders are all after the same goal – better results, greater growth, more success and increased shareholder value. The obvious place to look if we want to understand and improve our results is behaviour. What are we doing? What are the key people in our team doing? What milestones are being met, what gains are being made? And it is behaviour that is most commonly addressed by the variety of 'business solutions' put forward by consultants and coaches. The standard approach usually involves assessing what is currently happening and deciding what needs to be done differently to improve results. Unfortunately every manager already understands that knowing what needs to be done does not mean that it will get done. The answer to elevated performance does not therefore lie in behaviour alone. If we really want to improve performance and crank out our A-game every single day then we need to look deeper into what is happening on the 'inside' and not just focus on the 'outside' surface behaviours (Figure 1.1).

FIGURE 1.1   The integrated performance model

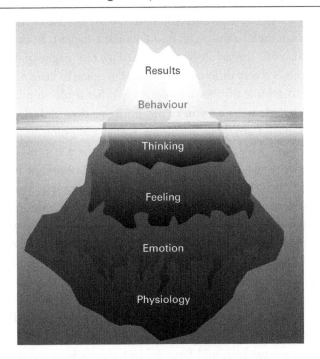

There really is no mystery to performance: our effectiveness and the results we achieve start with something much deeper in the human system than behaviour – our physiology.

It's your physiology, stupid!

During the 1992 US election Bill Clinton's campaign strategist James Carville effectively drew the American people's attention to the largely ignored but critically important topic of the economy with his campaign slogan: 'It's the Economy – stupid!' Bush Senior had failed to pull the economy out of recession and was busy fighting his campaign on other less important issues. Clinton won the election.

In the same way, many of the 'solutions' to business performance put forward by the coaching and consulting industry are ineffective or irrelevant, albeit interesting, while the real catalyst for elevated performance – physiology – is almost exclusively ignored.

Just think about it for a moment...

If we want to guarantee that people actually do the right things to deliver the results we want, we need to understand what really drives their behaviour. The answer is thinking. What we think determines what we do. So if I'm coaching a CEO and he thinks I'm an idiot or he thinks that what I'm saying is rubbish then he's not going to do what I suggest. In the same way, if I don't grab your attention in these opening few pages and make you think, 'Mm, this is a very different approach, I'm going to keep reading', then you're going to assume this book is like every other leadership book you've ever read and close it – and you're not going to do anything differently. And if you don't do anything differently you're not going to get different results. But, even if I manage to change what you think it's still not enough.

There is little doubt for example that Sergio Garcia already had a sports psychologist to help him manage his thinking. In business, you may even have employed some sort of psychometric testing to measure reasoning or analytic skills, or commissioned psychology-based coaching to help try and improve the quality of your thinking and that of your senior management team. But getting to grips with thinking isn't enough to lift performance either, because what we think or how well we think it is determined by something more fundamental in the human system – and that's how we feel.

How we feel has a very direct impact on what we think. There is, of course, a reciprocal relationship between thinking and feeling. How we think affects how we feel; and how we feel affects how we think. But in the arm wrestle between the two it is feeling that triumphs; feeling is the active ingredient that determines what we do. A salesperson may think, 'I have to make 20 more cold calls to meet my prospecting quota for the week.' But if it's Friday afternoon and they don't feel like it, what wins? Thinking or feeling? Feeling wins over thinking almost every time. Sure, we can force ourselves to follow through on tasks because we think they are important, but it's unsustainable. Consider New Year's resolutions to get fit for example. There's a mountain of evidence about the results that can be expected if we do. We know it's a smart thing to do and we may be able to use willpower to force ourselves to comply for a week or two. But sooner or later – usually sooner – most of us will stop going to the gym because we just don't feel like it!

What we feel has a far bigger impact on what we do than thinking does. If someone is anxious or stressed about something at work, does it make any difference if you tell them, 'Hey, look it will be OK – don't worry!' They are already worried and so telling them not to worry doesn't help. If anything it usually makes it worse! When Garcia started to drop shots, his feelings took over and no amount of thinking could halt or reverse that process. You can't overwrite a feeling with a thought very easily, whereas the feeling of 'worry' or 'stress' can dominate an individual's thinking all day.

So in order to change the quality of someone's thinking, so they will behave differently, improve performance and achieve better results, we actually have to change the way they feel. Every good marketer knows that. People don't buy things because they think they want them; they buy them because they feel they need them!

But how we feel is determined by something even deeper in the human system and that is raw emotion, or more accurately e-motion (energy in motion). The reason it is so hard to control or change the way we feel is because of the raw emotion that is occurring in our body without us realizing it. Telling someone not to worry is like closing the barn door when the horse has bolted. The raw energy pulsing through their body is already in transit – it's too late. And the reason this raw energy is coursing through their body in the first place is because at an even deeper level, down in the basement of the human system, is their physiology or their biological reactions and processes. So what is really driving our behaviour is our thinking. And what we think, and how well we think it, is largely determined by our feelings, which are driven by our emotions, which are made up of our physiology. And this is the real reason Sergio Garcia lost. His physiology changed; he didn't realize it, he couldn't feel it but this shift meant that he was unable to 'read the conditions', which led to poor decisions that ultimately cost him several tournaments and millions of dollars in prize money. There is no mystery. There was just a human being not functioning at his best because he didn't understand and integrate the myriad internal and external systems and processes that need to be aligned in order to consistently perform at his best.

So if it all starts with physiology, what is physiology? Physiology is just data or information streams that are occurring inside your body all the time. As you read these words your body is taking care of a million little details that keep you alive – there is constant activity. Vast streams of data are being sent and received from one body system to another in the form of electrical signals, electromagnetic signals, chemical signals, pressure, sound and heat waves. We don't have to think about this information or put it in our diary, the human body is the ultimate performance machine. It doesn't require an agenda, instruction or reminding. We don't need to micro-manage it – it just does its thing whether we are aware of it or not.

So we all have this constant traffic of physiological information flowing around our body 24/7. But very few people understand its impact and fewer still have learnt how to master this traffic and generate better-quality information flow that enables better-quality performance. And learning how to change the quality of signals in our system to deliver brilliance every day is the first skill set of Enlightened Leadership.

The performance myth explained

Even today I am constantly amazed by how often the great performance myth is peddled in ineffective albeit well-meaning attempts to improve an individual's or team's performance. All too often coaches and consultants are dishing out insightful nuggets such as, 'it's OK to be nervous before you start' or 'if you are not a bit nervous you will not perform well'. Such statements are based on the belief that we need to be 'psyched up' in order to excel. Other coaches may tell us the exact opposite and suggest that in order to perform at our best we need to be 'relaxed under pressure'.

So which is it? Before giving a major presentation to city analysts or pitching to win a large corporate account, do we need to be pumped up or do we need to be relaxed? The answer is neither because neither determines performance on the day.

When we put our 'pedal to the metal' or hit the accelerator prior to a major event, we activate our autonomic nervous system (ANS). Any effort to psych ourselves up has just engaged the primitive 'fight or flight' response. Although the result may look similar, the chemistry that drives each response is slightly different. When flight looks like the best option our system releases adrenaline or, as the Americans call it, epinephrine, which gives us a boost of energy so we can run away! In contrast, when we trigger the desire to fight our body releases adrenaline's sister, noradrenaline, which readies the body for battle.

The other main physiological response to a threat is to freeze, play dead or faint. None of which are terribly helpful in a high-pressure business setting. Nevertheless this 'relaxation response' is also often advocated by coaching professionals. Interestingly while most people have heard of adrenaline, the 'accelerator fluid', very few people have heard of the brake fluid. When we freeze or faint our body releases a chemical called acetylcholine.

So in very general terms heating our system up requires adrenaline or noradrenaline, and cooling the system down requires acetylcholine (Figure 1.2).

Performance is not about relaxation or arousal. It's not about 'chillin' out', getting 'Gee'd up', fight, flight or freezing! What really determines the quality of our output is our neuroendocrine system (NE) not our autonomic nervous system (ANS). The NE system determines the quality of our emotional experience whereas the ANS determines the degree of our arousal.

FIGURE 1.2   The assumed drivers of performance

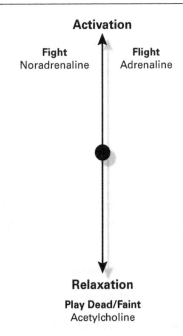

When we are on the right-hand side of the horizontal NE axis (Figure 1.3) we are said to be in a catabolic state or 'breakdown' state. This state is underpinned by the catabolic hormones, particularly cortisol, which is the body's main stress hormone. There is a strong scientific relationship between cortisol and negative emotion. For example, people with brain tumours that produce too much cortisol often get depressed. And people suffering from depression show high levels of cortisol in their brain fluid. Consequently, increased levels of cortisol are likely to induce more 'negative' emotions. High performance is extremely difficult when we feel negative. These negative emotions then increase the cortisol still further, creating a vicious cycle.

FIGURE 1.3   The real drivers of performance

Positive Emotion	Negative Emotion
DHEA	Cortisol
'Anabolic state'	'Catabolic state'

When we are on the left-hand side of the NE axis we are said to be in an anabolic state or 'build up' state. This is underpinned by a range of 'anabolic hormones', particularly dehydroepiandrosterone (DHEA). DHEA is the 'performance' or 'vitality hormone', the body's natural antidote to cortisol, and is associated with more 'positive' emotions. It is the molecule that makes testosterone in men and oestrogen in women. High performance is obviously much easier when we feel positive. These positive emotions then increase the levels of DHEA still further, creating a virtuous cycle.

Cortisol:DHEA ratio

This ratio is a widely used marker for biological aging and a high cortisol:low DHEA ratio has also been implicated in many of the most common diseases we face today:

- Obesity: cortisol increases fat on the waist.

- Diabetes: cortisol increases blood sugar.

- High blood pressure: cortisol disrupts fluid balance.

- Heart disease: cortisol increases cholesterol.

- Cancer: cortisol impairs immune function.

- Depression: cortisol promotes negative feelings.

- Senile dementia: cortisol impairs brain function.

FIGURE 1.4   The performance grid

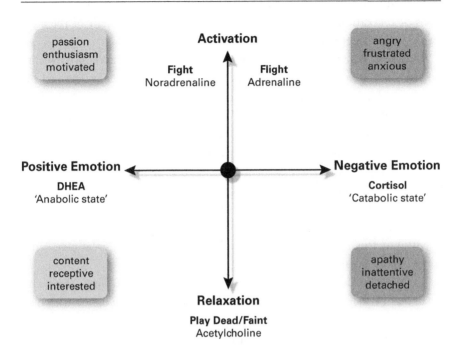

A high level of cortisol impairs many aspects of performance and consequently a business may underperform simply because the 'corporate cortisol' level is too high. Conversely, high DHEA levels underpin great performance. In fact DHEA is a banned substance in the Olympic Games because of its performance-enhancing capabilities.

If we put the vertical 'Activation' axis together with the horizontal 'State' axis we get the performance grid (Figure 1.4). The interaction of these two critical physiological systems was first described by James P Henry, while professor and emeritus professor of physiology at the University of Southern California School of Medicine in Los Angeles (Henry, 1982; Henry, Stephens and Ely, 1986).

What really matters when it comes to consistent performance is whether we are on the positive left-hand side or the negative right-hand side of the performance grid not whether we are in the activated top half or relaxed bottom half of the grid.

Too often the blanket antidote for stress and performance issues is assumed to be relaxation – or just cooling the system down and dropping into the bottom half of the grid. People are obsessed with relaxation, but again this obsession is underpinned by a universal misunderstanding of how our physiology really works. Just as there are two types of arousal –

positive arousal (states such as passion or enthusiasm: top left) and negative arousal (states such as anger or frustration: top right) – there are also two types of relaxation. It is possible to drop into the bottom half of the axis positively or negatively.

Positive relaxation is characterized by feelings such as contentment, curiosity and peacefulness whereas negative relaxation is characterized by feelings such as apathy, boredom or detachment. The problem is that when we drop into these negatively 'relaxed' states we are still running high levels of cortisol and other catabolic hormones that will seriously interfere with our health, our ability to think clearly and ultimately our performance. In fact the dangers are often exacerbated because people in these negative states tend to think that they are alright because they are 'relaxed'. They are not alright – physiologically speaking they are in real danger. At least when someone is in the top right quadrant of the performance grid, feeling angry, resentful or frustrated, they usually realize they are not in a great place and may be more inclined to do something about it.

Just because we have learnt to detach from negative feelings does not mean that the negativity has disappeared. It is still wreaking havoc with our physiology.

It is therefore essential that we are able to distinguish whether we are operating in the top right or top left of the performance grid and where our senior team is operating from. This is critical to consistently delivering best performance.

Coherence is the answer

The real secret to performance is not relaxation; it is not even motivation. It is the ability to get over to the left-hand side of the performance grid and stay there. Living on the left-hand side requires us to develop a new way of being, a state of 'coherence'. Coherence is, in essence, the biological under-pinning of what elite performers call 'the flow state' (Csikszentmihalyi, 2002): a state of maximum efficiency and super effectiveness, where body and mind are one. In flow truly remarkable things are possible. Like the stonemasons of old, coherence is the 'keystone' that locks all the pieces of Enlightened Leadership together to create an Enlightened Leader. It allows us to be at our brilliant best every single day and this book is dedicated to coherence and how to achieve it.

Conceptually, coherence is a state of 'stable variability'. All healthy systems, whether the human body, a car, a society or a business must have variability. There are two aspects of variability that are critical to the optimum functioning of the system, namely the amount of variability and the type or pattern of the variability. When a system exhibits a predictable pattern of stable variability it is a vibrant, healthy, living system. A lack of variability indicates a lack of health: brittleness, rigidity and an inability to adapt to changing conditions. Variability is therefore essential for the health of complex systems.

When architects designed the Burj Khalifa in Dubai (currently the world's tallest building standing at 829.8 metres) they needed to create a design with the right amount of variability so the building would bend in the wind. Too much variability or flexibility and it would be unstable and the people inside the building would feel seasick. Too little variability and the building would be rigid and brittle and the first serious sandstorm would destroy it.

The same is true in business – too little variability makes the business vulnerable to threats. If a leader refuses to change a strategy despite evidence it is failing or that market conditions are changing, then the business will eventually die out. If you want a reminder of the carnage a lack of variability can create, just think of the music industry's refusal to accept that their market wanted to download music instead of buying a physical product. They were so focused on stopping illegal downloads that they ignored the fact that whether someone paid for the music or not didn't alter the fact that people were using and actively seeking to get their music in a different way. Had they demonstrated greater flexibility this could have been a major cost-saving opportunity but it was missed as they chose to battle it out in the law courts instead.

At the same time, too much variability also makes the business unstable; it becomes too changeable, jumping from one new idea or new strategy to the next. Often struggling businesses become overly flexible – diversifying into new untested markets or new untested products or services in a desperate bid to find a solution to falling revenue or diminishing market share. In the 1990s for example there was a rash of big multinational mergers that involved the acquisition of businesses that had nothing to do with core strengths and almost always resulted in painful and costly divestment years later. This is the 'throw everything at the wall and let's see what sticks' approach to business, but it's costly and ineffective. Results become erratic and unpredictable because no one knows what's expected of them anymore. It is, after all, very hard to hit a moving target.

A sign of health in *all* systems from buildings to business to biology is therefore the right amount and pattern of variability. When we achieve that balance we achieve coherence. The principle of coherence is therefore a healthy amount of predictable stable variability. And physiological coherence is the platform on which complete coherence is built. When we learn how to actively manage our energy levels and recuperate properly, we have access to the right amount and pattern of energetic variability in order to deliver optimal performance. If we can learn physiological coherence through the mastery of some simple techniques that I will share in this book, then we can effectively turn the clock back to access the energy levels we experienced 10 years ago. Not only will we feel as though we have more energy, but we will use it more efficiently and recharge our batteries more effectively. In short we will feel younger (Chapter 2).

This internal physiological awareness in turn facilitates emotional coherence because we become more aware of more of our emotional data giving us access to a deeper, richer vein of emotional expression. Remember, physiology is just data or information streams. Using a musical metaphor, physiology is the individual stream of notes that are being played all the time by our bodily systems (Table 1.1).

Emotion is the integration of all those individual notes to form a tune. And feelings are the cognitive awareness of what tune our body is playing

TABLE 1.1   Types of physiological signals or 'notes'

Types of physiological signals	Examples of different bodily systems
Electrical signals (along the nerves)	**Heart**
Electromagnetic signals (field effects)	**Lungs**
Chemical signals (hormones & peptides)	**Joints**
Pressure waves (eg blood pressure, peristalsis in gut)	**Guts**
Sound waves (eg stomach rumbles, heart beats)	**Liver**
Heat waves (body heat)	**Kidneys**

at any given moment. Is your physical system playing a coherent symphony or an incoherent cacophony?

Our body is always playing a tune – 24 hours a day, 7 days a week, whether we are aware of it or not. Problems occur when we're deaf to the tune we are playing, refuse to acknowledge that we are playing any tune at all or misinterpret the tune, thinking we're playing Mozart when we're actually playing thrash metal. This is hugely important and ignorance and misdiagnosis of the repertoire of emotional 'tunes' our biological systems are currently playing can have serious consequences for our health and emotional well-being as well as the success of our business.

Physiological coherence, facilitated primarily by cardiac coherence, therefore makes emotional coherence possible. As the most powerful organ, the heart can trigger coherence in all our other bodily systems until all the biological data streams are playing a coherent tune.

When we learn to recognize and actively manage our emotions and improve our emotional literacy we have access to the right amount and pattern of emotional variability. By learning to harness emotions so that we use them constructively and appropriately instead of suppressing them or ignoring them, we develop greater emotional flexibility, intellectual capacity and maturity, and this emotional coherence also positively impacts our energy reserves. The cumulative effect of physiological and emotional coherence will positively impact our health and happiness (Chapter 3).

Physiological and emotional coherence in turn facilitates cognitive coherence and gives us consistent access to more of our cognitive ability whilst also preventing brain shut-down. You'll probably have experienced brain shut-down or seen it in others when you are in a meeting and someone gets upset or overly anxious and either freezes like a rabbit caught in headlights or starts babbling nonsense. It's caused by chaotic physiology and lack of emotional variability. Brain shut-down will be explained fully in Chapter 4 and can easily be prevented through the cumulative advantages of coherence – starting with physiology.

But preventing brain shut-down is just part of the answer when it comes to improving intellectual horsepower. Real cognitive breakthroughs and superior cognitive processing are only really possible once we expand our awareness and develop our level of maturity as adult human beings. When we do both, we have full access to the right amount and pattern of cognitive variability. We are able to think more deeply and clearly; we can apply the right type of thinking to adapt to complex and challenging problems in real time. As a result we become more creative, more innovative and better able to bring our A-game to the table every day, not just intermittently. In short, cognitive coherence makes us smarter (Chapter 4).

This collective internal coherence then facilitates a vast leap forward in performance that begins to manifest in the external world through behavioural coherence. When we add a greater understanding of the types of behaviours that develop elevated performance and we understand the mechanics of performance, we have access to the right amount and type of behavioural variability. As a result we do more of the right things, at the right time and have a wider range of behaviour open to us in our tactical arsenal, so success becomes more consistent and replicable. Or as neuroscientist John Coates suggests, 'emotion and mood ensure conscious thoughts synchronize with body to produce coherent behaviour' (Coates, 2013). Too often in business we end up doing what we've always done or we end up doing something that is not what we thought we would do. In those moments our thinking and behaviour is not congruent. And often the discrepancy is down to lack of energy, emotional upset or poor thinking. Once we gain physiological, emotional and cognitive coherence we are finally in a position to turn our attention to the key behaviours in a business that can transform results. When we do that we will become more successful (Chapter 5).

When we are unobstructed by low energy reserves, reactive, negative or suppressed emotion, fuzzy thinking or ineffective behaviour, we are more productive and more influential. When we also master people leadership we take another huge leap forward in productivity and performance because we understand what creates powerful working relationships and high-functioning teams. Coherent leaders appreciate that it's not smart to treat everyone the same because people are people; such leaders are able to adapt their interaction and approach because they have access to the right amount and type of relationship variability. When we understand what makes people tick and appreciate their motives we have far greater interpersonal flexibility, which in turn allows us to negotiate more effectively, make collectively coherent decisions and develop powerful teams and strong relationships. When we implement genuine governance up and down the business then the people in the business finally come together to deliver on a shared purpose.

Coherent leaders are individuals who demonstrate high integrity; they are people of their word who embody vast flexibility in their behaviour and interpersonal approach, which is not only absolutely critical to future-proof a business but is inspirational and the leader becomes much more influential (Chapter 6).

Coherence is the active ingredient to Enlightened Leadership and amazing things are possible when we achieve coherence in ourselves, our teams, our businesses, our industry and society as a whole.

The evolution of Enlightened Leadership

So far there have been four great ages of humanity. The first was Hunter–Gatherer society and that stage of development lasted 200,000 years. As human beings evolved, we became more sophisticated at manipulating our environment. The nomadic hunter–gatherers started to develop tools, cultivate crops and raise animals for food during the Agrarian stage of development, which lasted 10,000 years. People in small groups became more creative and cooperation and trade began. Business emerged and, as commerce grew, more and more workers were required and towns and cities developed and industry followed. This Industrial Age, which lasted about 200 years, was a period of immense creativity and invention when the world's smartest minds turned their attention to scientific understanding and innovation during the 'enlightenment'. Today we are in the post-industrial age, which is marked by service-orientated work. This stage, whose name is still being debated, is characterized by an increase in the service sector, outsourcing or increase in mechanized manufacture, technology and information. For that reason it is also sometimes known as the Information Age. This Information Age is due to last 70 years although at the time of writing (2013) we are already 55 years in.

When we view the human journey from this vantage point, the feature that really stands out is the systematic compression of time from one stage to the next. The first stage lasted 200,000 years and the stage we are in now will last about 70 years. That is a massive difference and indicates just how much our evolution is speeding up. The business world we live in today is vastly different from the environment even 20 years ago and almost unrecognizable to the corporate environment of 100 years ago. We live in a VUCA world – Volatile, Uncertain, Complex and Ambiguous – and it's changing the face of business forever.

Definition: VUCA

Volatile:	change happens rapidly and on a large scale
Uncertain:	the future cannot be predicted with any precision
Complex:	challenges are complicated by many factors and there are few single causes or solutions
Ambiguous:	little clarity on what events mean and what effect they may have

The only way we will survive is if we adapt and evolve, but in a coherent way rather than erratically lurching from one new possibility to another. The most Enlightened Leaders will be able to facilitate the growth and evolution of their businesses as quickly and as painlessly as possible because they are coherent. And they will be the real future-proofed winners of tomorrow.

The three stages of coherent evolution

American intellectual and development psychologist Ken Wilber states that there are three stages to the evolution of anything, whether that's a new product, a new market, a new idea, a new species, a new business opportunity or a new leadership framework.

Despite modern business being obsessed with improving performance, individual, team and corporate performance still remains a problem. The truth is that most modern businesses are massively sub-optimal because the individuals within them have stopped evolving. Even the best companies in the world no longer know how to grow themselves without acquisition. As a result we are almost at the end of the current road, a road paved with financial disasters, business failures, heart attacks, stress and misery. And bigger bonuses and share options are not improving the performance or easing the distress – at least not for very long. Too many senior executives already feel they are giving all they have and more and yet it still doesn't seem to be enough. It's a bruising way to live and frankly it's unsustainable. There has to be a better way and this book is the road map to that better way. In order to make the leadership journey and arrive successfully then we must appreciate and embrace the three stages of evolution, namely:

1 Emergence.

2 Differentiation.

3 Integration.

Emergence (emergent leadership)

Things must first emerge. If conditions are right, which may take months or years to achieve, people or systems will suddenly burst forward and new behaviour, products, ideas and opportunities will emerge. This is a feature of complex systems. The truth is that there are many small, often unnoticed steps prior to the emergence of the new thing before it impinges on our consciousness. But one day it's there and we notice it.

In business this can take the shape of a new product or a new marketing strategy or campaign innovation.

If we really want to leap forward we must first arrive at the point where we are at least questioning the current approach or realizing that just working harder or pushing others to work harder will not be enough. We must realize that the current system is not working. If we are doing OK, or we are comfortable, or we are not yet ill or miserable then we may not realize the game is already over. And if we don't yet realize the game is over then we are almost certainly heading for extinction. There has to be a burning platform for change. We have to be constantly questioning everything we do and have the humility to realize that we are probably wrong about a few things in order to create the conditions for something new to emerge. Let's face it, corporate history is littered with examples of over-confidence, hubris, certainty and unshakeable self-belief. The mindset that 'I am the leader and therefore I know the answers so shut up and follow' is the single biggest obstacle to progress and a one-way ticket to obsolescence.

Wilber, perhaps one of the best thinkers currently on the planet, suggests that there are two key processes in human development: 'waking up' and 'growing up'. First, we must individually and collectively 'wake up' from the delusion of control and power. In order to 'grow up' properly it is necessary to 'own up' to those parts of our nature that we dislike so we can re-integrate them. When we 'wake up' and 'grow up', this evolution alone can make a dramatic difference to how we 'show up' as a leader, which in turn can help us and our company grow up into a new, more dynamic and competitive future. If we refuse to make this personal journey then we will go the way of the dinosaurs. We must evolve. All of us, from where we are now to a more sophisticated level so we can successfully deal with the increasing levels of complexity and intensity in business. If we want to succeed long term in a VUCA world and build an enduring legacy, it's the only way. Being in a state of openness to input, receptive to new ideas even from unlikely sources, is the state of emergent leadership. Something new is emerging and change is not only possible but planned for.

Differentiation (evolving leadership)

Once something has emerged, the next major developmental stage is to differentiate this new thing from all the other similar things that exist. For example, when a new software product is launched it is vital to define its unique selling point (USP). What are the benefits of this product in relation to the other similar products in the market place? What makes the iPhone 5 better than the iPhone 4S or a Samsung Galaxy S3?

Many of the insights in this book are about differentiation and flow from the importance of this evolutionary step. Much confusion reigns when a leader or a business is unable to clearly define and differentiate an issue. A lack of definition will often lead to an imprecise solution. Just as poor diagnosis leads to poor treatment in medicine, the same is true in business. For example, if performance in one department is particularly poor and I am unable to define and differentiate the cause of this poor performance, then I will fail. If I can't tell if the problem is down to the recently installed database or the age of the servers that database was installed on, then I am likely to take the wrong course of corrective action. In business we waste vast amounts of time and money fixing the wrong problems simply because we didn't define and differentiate the problem properly in the first place.

When we move from Emerging Leadership to Evolving Leadership we are essentially, as Wilber describes, 'growing up'. Evolving Leaders are therefore very focused on differentiation and developing greater sophistication. In fact differentiation is a sign of increasing maturity. What used to work is no longer working or it's simply not working well enough. An Evolving Leader is perpetually seeking to define and redefine the agenda to drive change and build his or her own future.

Integration (Enlightened Leadership)

In order for the new thing to become really useful it must find its place in the world or integrate with what already exists, whether it is a new business or a new product. As a result integration is about context and relationship and it is vital in a complex world. It is entirely possible to break a problem down into very clearly defined smaller issues but, unless there is integration, the danger is that this leads to fragmentation or even disintegration and the problem solved may be too narrowly defined. Indeed this has been one of the prevailing problems with modern scientific medicine.

Our understanding of the human body has advanced massively over the last 150 years. For most of that time scientists and physicians have been unravelling the complexity of the human condition by systematically reducing it to ever smaller parts. This systematic reductionism has been the overriding approach to investigating human beings and it has been incredibly successful. Reductionism has shed new light on how the human body works. It has generated an enormous amount of new information, spawned whole new areas of medical research and created new languages to capture the myriad discoveries being made.

As a result of the overwhelming amount of new information generated it became impossible to keep pace with all the new data and discoveries.

So each part of the human body developed its own expert. To paraphrase comedienne Maureen Lipman, everyone became an 'ologist'.

The 'ologists' now publish their new insights in their own journals, speak in their own unique language and attend specialist conferences to share increasingly finer details about their specialism.

Physicians needed to become not just specialists but super-specialists. For example, as a cardiologist I have found it completely impossible for some time now to remain up to date even within that single discipline. If I restricted my reading to just new publications on 'chest pain' I would have to read approximately six new articles every single day.

But there have been unintended consequences of this incredible dissection and fragmentation of the human condition. In medicine we have largely mastered the emergence part of the evolutionary process and are pretty skilled at the differentiation element, but we have a long, long way to go to master integration. In fact 'integrated care' and 'interdisciplinary research' have only really emerged in the last 20 years as a concept, let alone matured as a practice. The human system is an example of a complex system, and complex systems cannot be understood simply by understanding each part of that system because the whole is always greater than the sum of the parts.

Business is also a complex system. We have become reasonably proficient at the emergence of ideas, new businesses, new products and new strategies for growth. We have broken business down so as to understand its component parts and we now have different divisions and departments. We have specialists managing those divisions whose area of expertise is limited only to that division or industry. And of course we have every type of business consultant and guru known to mankind who will supposedly fix a specific corporate ailment.

But there is very little integration. Even within the same business, divisions compete against each other; departments remain isolated and act as separate silos within the single entity. And without access to the 'whole', the parts are not greater than the sum of the parts, they are just the sum of the parts. Strategic direction and tactics become stale, new ideas are no longer new ideas, new products are no longer new products; they are simply old ideas and old products, tweaked slightly, repackaged and launched to great media fanfare. In desperation we look around at the competition, only to find they are doing the same thing: regurgitating what already exists and spending vast sums of money trying to convince their customers that it really is something new, something better or something different. And yet if you look at the companies that have truly innovated – Apple, Dyson and Sony for example – these are all disruptive innovators, and often their innovations were made possible by looking outside their industry. Sir James Dyson, for example, had the idea for the cyclone vacuum cleaner that revolutionized the industry after a trip to a saw mill.

Many modern businesses are struggling to deliver their potential to grow and deliver shareholder value. We seem to repeat the same mistakes over and over again. We work harder, we work longer, our blood pressure rises and health and happiness plummet, and yet business still struggles. We invest in learning and development and still there is little learning and minimal development. We seek to hire smarter and smarter people and pay them more and more money and still performance remains relatively unchanged. Why? Because business is stuck between emergence and differentiation; integration isn't even on the radar and we have stopped evolving as a result. Even companies that seek to expand by merger and acquisition do so because they don't know any other way to grow even though the integration of those acquisitions is traditionally exceptionally poor.

Business from this perspective is like playing poker with half a deck of cards: we are all constantly shuffling the same cards in an effort to find a new solution but unless we get access to the rest of the deck it's impossible to create the hand we know we want to play or are capable of playing because we just don't have the cards in the deck. We invest in costly mergers in an effort to access the other cards in the deck only to find we now have a duplicate set of exactly the same cards rather than the other half of the deck.

Innovation is more important now than ever before but genuine innovation is impossible without high quality differentiation and integration. The evolution of anything is an upward spiral of emergence, differentiation, integration and re-emergence. We have broken everything down so far that we are innovating from the same, often duplicated, deck that everyone else is innovating from, and as a consequence we are banging our head off the same performance wall, throwing good money after bad in a desperate attempt to unlock some new potential.

Of course, some of the more enlightened businesses have spotted the critical importance of breaking down their silos and are working more collaboratively and cross-functionally. However, most are still in the early stages of learning how to do this. Some have slipped into complex 'matrix management' practices that in truth are often a labyrinth of hierarchical relationships and power battles with people reporting to two bosses with 'dotted lines' to one boss and a 'hard line' to another. The more mature matrix structures are really attempts to crystallize the differentiation rather than actually integrate properly. In a few organizations there is effective cross-functional integration, which over time can develop into a sort of organizational fluidity. Such maturity within organizations really requires sophisticated guidance to make it work and unlock its real potential. Once leaders are able to integrate the new, differentiated knowledge and expertise about organizational models they can expand their perspective of the business landscape and start to 'grow up' into Enlightened Leaders.

On a personal level the Enlightened Leader has moved beyond differentiation and is constantly on the lookout for a more 'completely' coherent answer. They are concerned about maturation, sophistication and integration. They seek to define the next level of performance or capability and seek to identify how this can be achieved through greater integration, given the current reality. Leadership becomes a journey and Enlightened Leaders recognize their own potential to impair progress. In fact 'owning up' to this fact becomes a critical step in really 'growing up' as a leader. So having 'woken up' as Emerging Leaders and 'grown up' as Evolving Leaders we now 'own up' to become Enlightened Leaders. And that in turn determines how we 'show up'.

Integration is the real challenge we face today. The knowledge available to all of us now is staggering, so staggering in fact that it has pushed many individuals in all walks of life into specialist subjects and intellectual silos. While that is understandable, it's time to bring it all back together. It's time to integrate all the really insightful and important 'parts' of all the myriad complex systems to create a holistic understanding of business as a whole so that the whole is once again greater than the sum of the parts.

As I said earlier Enlightened Leadership is the integration of a number of scientific discoveries from disparate fields of research – most of which are not associated with highly functioning business. Many of these discoveries are common knowledge in their respective fields and they are all robustly proven. These insights have however not made their way into mainstream consciousness, and remain relatively unknown in the place where they could make the biggest positive impact – business. The 'parts' of this information are useful but what is transformational is the integration of all the information as a map to personal and collective coherence and brilliance – every day.

The Enlightened Leadership model

Since 1996 we've been working with global leaders and in that time we have become very curious about what they were paying attention to. We noticed that they were largely focused on short-term performance tasks and operational issues that were necessary to drive quarterly results. This was not surprising, considering that business leaders have to deliver results today otherwise they will be out of a job tomorrow. In fact according to McKinsey and Co the average corporate life expectancy of a modern CEO is just six years, down from 10 in 1995 and, depending on results, as low as 4.5 years (Barton, 2011; Devan, Millan and Shirke, 2005). Other sources state that 72 per cent of Fortune 500 Company CEOs survive less than five years with the median tenure just three years (Todaro, 2003). In other words, leaders can't afford to focus on anything else because it's the short term that they are predominantly judged on. Some leaders also spend quite a bit of time focused on strategic issues. A handful, particularly those that understood that culture always trumps strategy, invested some time in people issues and the organizational climate.

However, hardly any leaders spent time thinking about their own awareness or perspective, their own individual development, the quality of their own thinking or their energy levels. And not one ever thought about their physiology. This was also not that surprising. These critical but lesser known and rarely discussed aspects of effective leadership are not taught in business schools, or if they are they are skirted over in a matter of hours. They are not discussed in commerce and they rarely, if ever, appear in business journals.

We realized that the model of leadership being used by most leaders was probably incomplete. So we set out to build a more comprehensive model, one that included the imperative aspects that leaders already paid attention to but that also embraced the other equally critical issues we believed they needed to pay attention to if they wanted to deliver sustainable results and build an outstanding legacy. Put simply, we wanted to develop a model for Enlightened Leadership.

As usual the starting point was to look at the academic research that has been done investigating what anyone pays attention to. We started with the work of integral philosopher Ken Wilber and his well-known 'all quadrants all levels' (AQAL) model (Figure 1.5) (Wilber, 2001). The AQAL model represents the core of Wilber's work and is, as he describes it, 'one suggested architecture of the Kosmos' (Wilber, 2012). Without getting too technical Wilber has looked at all the maps of how the world and people work and created a map of all the other maps that essentially describes reality. This four-box 'all quadrants all levels' model sketches the inner landscape and the outer landscape of human possibilities for both the individual and the collective. As such it describes individual leaders and teams as well as the interior and exterior reality of each.

FIGURE 1.5   Ken Wilber's original AQAL model as it applies to business

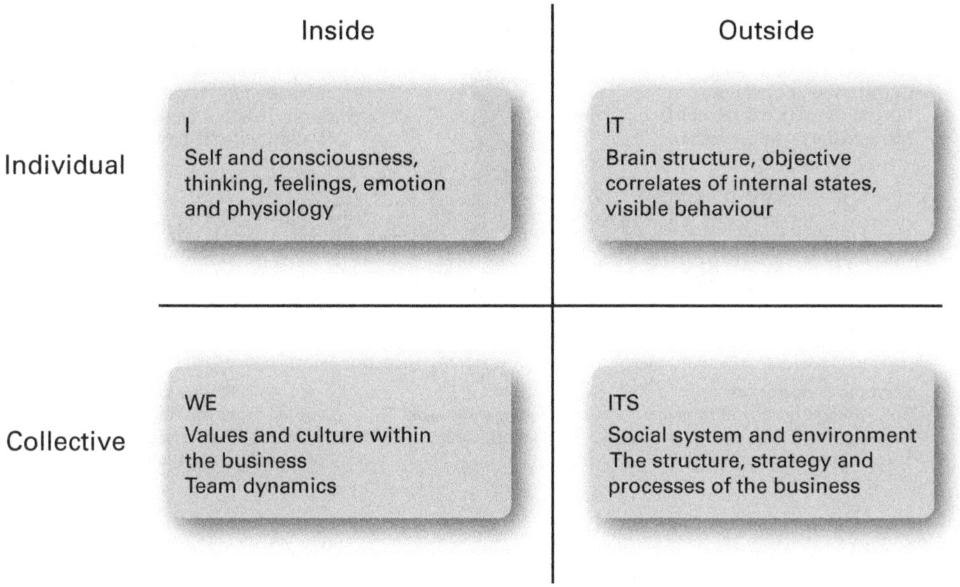

	Inside	Outside
Individual	**I** Self and consciousness, thinking, feelings, emotion and physiology	**IT** Brain structure, objective correlates of internal states, visible behaviour
Collective	**WE** Values and culture within the business Team dynamics	**ITS** Social system and environment The structure, strategy and processes of the business

Wilber's objective is to provide frameworks that will allow us to understand the complexity of the modern world and ultimately to create an integral theory that explains everything. The essence of his model is that there are three perennial perspectives that one can take in life and they are present in every moment of our day.

When a leader is in an executive meeting, the leader is thinking and feeling certain things, as are all the other individuals in the room. There is also an interpersonal element where the individuals are relating to each other well or poorly and they are almost always talking about the business – a rational objective thing in the real world.

Therefore it is possible to see the world through a rational objective lens. Wilber calls this third-person perspective the world of 'IT', meaning what 'IT' is that we need to do to make this business work. The second-person perspective he calls the world of 'WE'. This is about relationships and interpersonal dynamics. The first-person perspective is the subjective inner world of 'I'. So Wilber's AQAL model illustrates an objective world in the two right-hand quadrants of 'IT and ITs'; an upper left-hand quadrant of 'I' and a lower left-hand quadrant of 'WE'.

We adapted this model by rotating it anti-clockwise and placing the individual at the centre looking forward into their rational objective

FIGURE 1.6 The Enlightened Leadership model

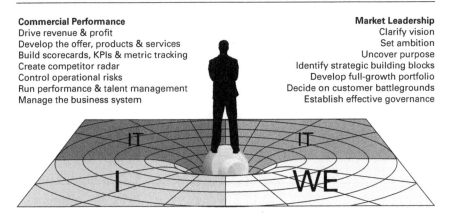

Commercial Performance
Drive revenue & profit
Develop the offer, products & services
Build scorecards, KPIs & metric tracking
Create competitor radar
Control operational risks
Run performance & talent management
Manage the business system

Market Leadership
Clarify vision
Set ambition
Uncover purpose
Identify strategic building blocks
Develop full-growth portfolio
Decide on customer battlegrounds
Establish effective governance

Personal Performance
Step-change quality of thinking
Develop boundless energy
Uncover personal purpose

People Leadership
Identify organizational 'Way' & evolve organizational culture
Develop executive fellowships & high-performing teams
Clarify personal leadership qualities

world. In doing so, we created a more commercially relevant frame that could help leaders better understand the breadth of the challenges they face. Standing at the centre of their 'gravity grid' (Figure 1.6), front left the leader is focused on short-term commercial performance issues and front right are longer-term market leadership issues. Over their left shoulder, and out of normal vision, is the inner subjective personal performance world of 'I' and over the right shoulder is the interpersonal people leadership world of 'WE'.

The reason we rotated the model and gave it a 3-D landscape is because that is how modern business leaders think about their world. Leaders stand in the centre of their own lives looking forward and they rarely see what's behind them ('I' and 'WE'). Instead they are predominantly focused on the 'IT' – and then only the short-term 'IT' – most of the time. Since 2010 I and my colleagues have successfully 'road-tested' this model with 450 global CEOs, including 70 per cent of the FTSE 100, the best CEOs in India and China plus luminaries in the Fortune 500 (Tappin and Cave, 2010; Tappin, 2012). We wanted to determine whether they were thinking about anything that is not included in this new model of leadership. They are not. As a result we share this model extensively with clients and encourage them to think about the challenges they are facing in terms of the four quadrants.

The simple reality is that if we don't realize that our efforts in the rational, objective world are built on the individual 'I' (physiology, emotions, feelings and thoughts) and that the success of what we want to build requires our connectivity at the interpersonal 'WE', then we've no solid foundation on which to build effectiveness in the solid, rational world of 'IT'. As countless failed businesses will attest, even if the strategy is brilliant and the short-term results look good, if no one trusts the leader, he or she will never unlock the discretionary effort of the workforce so the strategy will probably never get executed anyway!

To succeed in a VUCA world we must appreciate the importance and impact of all four quadrants. We've got to be self-aware, we've got to have the interpersonal skills and we've got to be building today and tomorrow. So the best leaders, and there are very few, move effortlessly between and are coherent across all four quadrants and that requires vertical development across a number of different 'lines of development'.

Vertical development and 'lines of development'

I was asked recently by the CFO of a major consultancy firm to see one of their executives. This CFO told me: 'We have a problem because we don't know whether to promote her or fire her.' When I asked the CFO to explain she said: 'The woman is one of our highest fee earners but she bullies every-one so we now have five grievance procedures related to her.'

'Don't tell me,' I said, 'you gave her a coach?'

'Well yes I did,' the CFO said rather ruefully.

'And the coach taught her some skills in how to communicate more effectively?' The CFO nodded. 'And it has just made her a more effective bully hasn't it?'

The CFO conceded that this is exactly what had happened.

This story aptly illustrates the difference between 'horizontal' and 'vertical' development. Horizontal development is really the acquisition of skills, knowledge and experience, or put more succinctly, 'learning'. These three things are very useful but they are very different from actual adult develop-ment, increased maturity or vertical development (Figure 1.7). With 'horizon-tal development' the consulting executive had just become more skilful at bullying and manipulating other people. Had she actually matured, it is likely that the bullying behaviour would have stopped as she developed greater self-awareness and an increased capacity to change unhelpful behaviour. Most leadership programmes focus on learning rather than development. Most organizational 'learning and development' departments consist of a massive amount of 'L' and a miniscule amount of 'D' (if any at all). The cutting edge of organizational performance has already acknowledged that vertical

FIGURE 1.7   Vertical and horizontal development

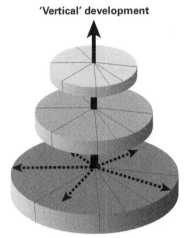

development of the leadership cadre within an organization will, perhaps, be *the* defining factor of future success.

Enlightened Leadership differentiates between horizontal and vertical development (Figure 1.7) and is based on the work of four of the eight leading developmental theorists in the world who have written extensively on the subject of adult development (Wilber, Cook-Greuter, Torbert and Kegan). Indeed, Kegan likens adult development to filling a glass with water – horizontal development is about filling the vessel while vertical development expands the glass itself (Petrie, 2011). Not only does that allow us to take on more skills, knowledge and experience but we are better able to create complex solutions because we have a broader, deeper perspective that can transform results and finally provide access to the potential everyone has been so desperate to find.

It is the integration of key insights, not normally found in business schools, which allows us to expand our perspective not just horizontally outward, through the accumulation of knowledge and experience, but vertically upward – giving us access to significantly more resources as a result.

Unlocking dormant potential

I often ask groups to assess, as a percentage of their potential, how smart, capable and productive they are. Invariably the modest will suggest around 65 per cent and the more confident will suggest 85 per cent. Based on 50 years of neuroscience the number for most people is actually around 9 per cent. As a medical doctor and neuroscientist I believe we could all access the remaining 91 per cent of our potential if we just understood how to optimize the brilliance of our entire system through learning to become much more coherent. I take an incredibly optimistic view of human beings and what we are truly capable of, particularly in relation to our minds. In truth I don't think we have really started to tap into the potential that exists in people within organizations.

I also believe that people judge themselves as already close to capacity because they are only considering the part of the iceberg that is visible above the waterline (Figure 1.8). If an individual thinks that all that they are is confined to what they do and the results they get, then it is little wonder that they imagine their capability to be around 75 per cent. If however they were able to glimpse what is invisible, hidden from view under the waterline and see the real size of their potential, they might feel very differently. At the moment, most of us, especially in business, completely ignore or disregard most of what is invisible.

I believe that the concept of coherence and Enlightened Leadership holds the key to significant transformation in business, government and society

FIGURE 1.8   Your real potential

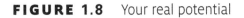

FIGURE 1.9   Lines of development

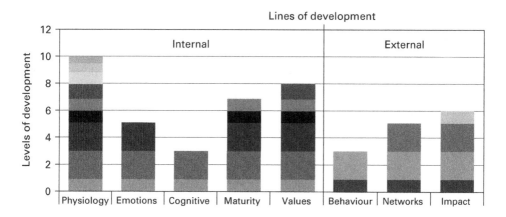

at large, because it explains performance in a whole new way and provides a commercially relevant framework for development and the skills necessary to unlock that vast reservoir of, as yet, untapped potential in ourselves and all our people. These skills finally allow individuals, teams and businesses to evolve and progress horizontally and vertically across eight separate but interconnected and cumulative lines of development (Figure 1.9). Whilst the developmental psychologists recognize various lines of development an Enlightened Leader must have sufficient altitude across all eight of these specific business-centric lines of development as a fast-track route to business transformation.

These lines of development also go further in explaining why people are so keen to underestimate their own potential for improvement. If we have no frame of reference that separates the ingredients of consistent outstanding performance, then we simply lump everything together and judge our current ability across 'one line of development', or if you like, out of 100. It is therefore easy to see why people routinely suggest they are already achieving 75 or 85 on performance. When they then realize that there are actually eight commercially relevant lines of development, they can see that the estimate that they based on 100 is actually based on a potential 800. And 75 as a percentage of 800 (9.375 per cent) is considerably lower than 75 as a percentage of 100 (75 per cent). To be honest I believe 9 per cent is generous because I have witnessed time and time again what's possible when an individual vertically develops across all eight lines (Figure 1.10). They literally become unrecognizable from the individual who began the developmental journey – they become brilliant every single day.

Plus we also assume that development is linear and that each line is equal. It's not and they are not. Development is not constant and sequential. For example, development up the maturity line is pretty straightforward as we grow from a child into an adult, but the real magic occurs when we mature as adult human beings and expand our perceptual awareness. Unlike the physical development from child to adult the maturity development from adult to mature adult is not an automatic process – it requires conscious effort and attention.

Plus not all lines of development are equal. At Complete Coherence we believe for example that the energy and emotion lines are especially important because, left undeveloped or ignored, they will actively stifle consistent high performance and success. And this is the reason why many of the initial skills of Enlightened Leadership, which I will explain in a moment, are focused on these fundamentally important lines of development. As you learn about each skill you may be tempted to dismiss it because it appears too easy or straightforward. Don't! These skills, when mastered, punch well above their weight in terms of energy, health, happiness, cognitive ability, peak performance and influence.

FIGURE 1.10   How the lines of development provide access to massive untapped resources

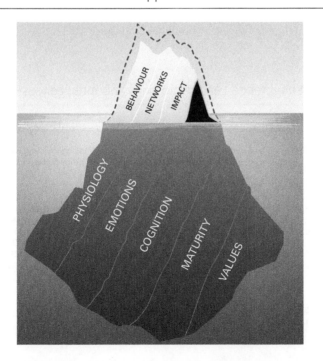

The skills and intelligences of Enlightened Leadership

Each chapter of this book builds and adds to the last and we will explore the initial skills of Enlightened Leadership necessary to build a solid foundation that will, in turn, facilitate vertical development and transform organizational performance. When we understand all the elements of the integrated performance model, why they cause the challenges they do and how to avoid those challenges, we will transform our results. When we understand all the elements of the Enlightened Leadership model, what causes problems and how to avoid those problems, then we transform our results still further. When we develop coherence at every level in all quadrants we will be on our way as an Enlightened Leader – capable of leading business into new, uncharted and profitable territory with a fraction of the angst, stress and pressure.

You may notice that there is a specific focus at this early stage on emotional mastery in the context of business success. This is not a repackaging of emotional intelligence but a new framework that packs a powerful punch. The reason these skills are so potent is that it is an area that is almost exclusively ignored in business and it offers the fastest and simplest way to elevate performance and achieve greater growth and success.

These skills build on each other from physical intelligence up through emotional intelligence to social intelligence (Figure 1.11).

FIGURE 1.11 Enlightened Leadership skills and intelligences

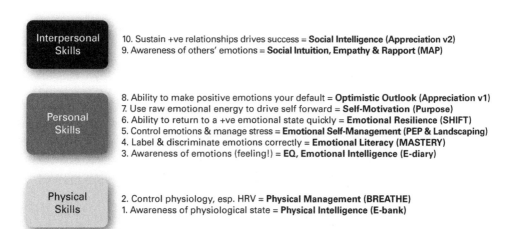

Interpersonal Skills
10. Sustain +ve relationships drives success = **Social Intelligence (Appreciation v2)**
9. Awareness of others' emotions = **Social Intuition, Empathy & Rapport (MAP)**

Personal Skills
8. Ability to make positive emotions your default = **Optimistic Outlook (Appreciation v1)**
7. Use raw emotional energy to drive self forward = **Self-Motivation (Purpose)**
6. Ability to return to a +ve emotional state quickly = **Emotional Resilience (SHIFT)**
5. Control emotions & manage stress = **Emotional Self-Management (PEP & Landscaping)**
4. Label & discriminate emotions correctly = **Emotional Literacy (MASTERY)**
3. Awareness of emotions (feeling!) = **EQ, Emotional Intelligence (E-diary)**

Physical Skills
2. Control physiology, esp. HRV = **Physical Management (BREATHE)**
1. Awareness of physiological state = **Physical Intelligence (E-bank)**

Intelligence is an important ingredient of business success. Large companies seek out the brightest graduates from the best universities and scour the land for talented individuals, but IQ is not the only type of intelligence. For example, American developmental psychologist Howard Gardner proposed the Multiple Intelligence Theory (Gardner, 1983), which initially included linguistic intelligence (word smart), logical-mathematical intelligence (logic and numbers smart), musical intelligence (music smart), bodily-kinaesthetic intelligence (body smart), spatial intelligence (picture or pattern smart), interpersonal intelligence (people smart) and intrapersonal intelligence (self-smart). Gardner suggested that the first two were highly prized in the education system through a focus on maths and language. The next three are often associated with 'the arts' and the final two are personal intelligences. Gardner later added three more intelligences to his theory, namely, naturalist intelligence (environment smart), spiritual/existential intelligence ('ultimate issues' smart) and moral intelligence (ethics and humanity smart).

In his work on emotional intelligence Daniel Goleman suggests there are five dimensions of emotional intelligence: self-awareness, self-regulation, internal motivation, empathy and social skills (Goleman, Boyatzis and McKee, 2002). Richard Davidson, Professor of Psychology and Psychiatry at the University of Wisconsin-Madison, also talks about emotional intelligence and suggests that the brain actually has structures that support six dimensions of emotional intelligence (Davidson and Begley, 2012). The six dimensions are: self-awareness; resilience, which is similar to the idea of self-regulation; attention, which is related to internal motivation; social intuition, which is related to empathy; sensitivity to context, which is related to social skills; and finally outlook, which equates to individual optimism or pessimism. The skills and intelligences of Enlightened Leadership therefore draw on academic research, embracing both Goleman and Davidson while seeking to go further through 'commercial experience' so as to create a practical framework. In our work we differentiate 10 separate but interconnected intelligences and suggest that they may be somewhat sequential, whilst also adding practical skills and techniques that can facilitate vertical development of all 10 intelligences.

The inadequacy of traditional IQ

Clearly focusing on IQ is not enough; all that happens is we recruit very smart people who often behave badly, as evidenced by the bullying executive mentioned earlier. Let's face it – smart people usually know they are smart and their hubris and superiority can often cause more problems than they solve.

When several executives at McKinsey and Co launched an initiative in the 1990s called 'War for Talent' they concluded that success in the modern world required 'the talent mindset' and their research confirmed the 'deep-seated belief that having better talent at all levels [of the organization] is how you outperform your competitors' (Michaels, Handfield-Jones and Axelrod, 2001).Considering that it was McKinsey and Co – one of the most prestigious management consulting firms in the world – who were sending this message, modern business sat up and took notice, and talent has been a central discussion in business ever since. And yet performance hasn't moved much, despite the recruitment of expensive, highly intelligent individuals. In fact if we need a reminder of the inadequacy of traditional IQ we need look no further than Enron, which was obsessed with the issue. Enron was the ultimate talent-focused business. Jeff Skilling, himself ex-McKinsey, advocated hiring the very best people from the very best schools and paying them more than even they thought they were worth. The problem of course is that the link between IQ and performance is 'distinctly underwhelming' (Gladwell, 2010).

Our view is that we should forget about talent per se and instead focus on vertical development – especially in the C-suite. When individuals consciously work on physical, personal and interpersonal intelligences so that they become more mature emotionally, cognitively and socially then genuinely astonishing results are possible – with or without talent!

Clearly, hiring great people is always going to be important but it is unrealistic to expect, in today's global talent market, that we can recruit all the people we need to grow the business. Senior recruitment is expensive, fraught with difficulty and takes a lot of time. Wouldn't it be wiser to embed a real talent development agenda deep into our organizations? One whose goal was to grow Enlightened Leaders from within our current ranks? That is the purpose of this book.

The journey to Enlightened Leadership is ultimately one of coherence and vertical maturity across multiple lines of development, from basic physical awareness to physical management through to emotional awareness and management, so we cultivate a detailed and finely differentiated appreciation for our emotions and how to use them constructively to achieve our objectives while staying energetic, healthy, happy, smart and successful at the same time. Once we have mastered these skills in ourselves we become more socially intelligent. As a result we are better able to integrate all we've learnt previously to foster and develop highly functioning working relationships inside and outside our business. Becoming much more masterful in the physical and socio-emotional lines of development can significantly accelerate progress in the other key lines that are all required if we are to embody Enlightened Leadership.

As a coherent Enlightened Leader we become like Bradley Cooper's character Eddie Mora in the movie *Limitless*. When we first meet Mora he is plagued by a serious case of writer's block and about to be kicked out of his apartment. Mora then has an accidental meeting with an old friend who gives him a dubious drug called NZT that unlocks all his untapped potential. Enlightened Leadership is the drug-free equivalent of NZT. When we have aligned and synchronized our physiology, emotions, feelings, thoughts, behaviour and relationships, we will massively elevate our results and our performance – without expending more effort, blood, sweat or tears. In fact coherence is about synchronizing yourself and your team across all eight lines of development in all four quadrants of the Enlightened Leadership model so you can consistently crank out your A-game every single day. As Enlightened Leaders we are truly limitless.

Be younger

02

Do you ever start dreaming of the weekend on the way to work on Monday morning? Do you find yourself nodding off on the couch in the evening before your kids are even in bed? Do you sometimes feel as though you've dragged yourself to the end of the week but it still takes you all of Saturday to wind down? Do you find yourself falling asleep during the day at weekends and yet never feel fully rejuvenated by the 'rest'? Have you ever woken up feeling more tired than you did when you went to sleep? Do you still recognize yourself when you look in the mirror or are you sometimes taken aback by how much you've aged? Are there days when you just feel utterly exhausted and emotionally and physically fried? If so, you're not alone.

Most of us struggle with the demands of modern life at some point or another. As human beings we only have a certain amount of energy and yet the demands on that resource seem far from finite. No matter how hard we work or how productive we are there is always more to do and this is especially true for busy professionals, senior executives or business leaders. All too often I meet leaders who are running faster and faster just to stand still.

Collectively we fantasize about our two week summer holiday, time to lie on the beach, soak up the sun and unwind. Only we are so wound up it takes a week just to uncoil! If we are lucky we then get to enjoy a couple of days of 'golden time' where we are genuinely relaxed before wasting the remaining two or three days of the holiday thinking about all that needs to be done when we return to work!

We feel increasingly burnt out and yet most executives assume it just goes with the job. Most of the time our fatigue either goes unnoticed or it manifests as irritability, increased aggressive or autocratic behaviour, excessive responsibility and, ultimately, poor commercial decision making.

With each generation, change is accelerating, the number of decisions we need to make today is significantly greater than our parents or grandparents ever had to make and the complexity and dynamism of those decisions is increasing steadily as we seek to prosper in a VUCA world. As a result too many of us endure intense pressure and live truly exhausting lives.

Time management vs energy management

In an effort to manage this challenge we have become obsessed with time. Most people feel 'time poor' and lament the fact that they 'never have enough time' and there are 'not enough hours in the day'. They yearn for more 'time to think' or 'time off'. As a result, many organizations run 'time management' courses in the mistaken belief that it is possible to 'manage time'. But time is not the problem.

The assumption is that if we could just learn to manage our time better we would be able to accomplish more in less time so we wouldn't be so exhausted. It's a logical argument but it's not accurate. The truth is, if we look back to our twenties or thirties, time was never an issue. We would work hard all day then go out for dinner and a few drinks, and then rock up to work the next day ready to do it all again. We didn't need to manage our time because we had enough energy to do everything we needed to do with plenty to spare.

Besides, we can't magic a few extra hours out of the day or convert three hours into six. There are 24 hours in every day regardless of who we are or how desperately we need a few extra. And if we are exhausted, having another week to complete the task usually doesn't help that much because we just don't have the energy to get the job done.

In today's fast-paced, complex, ever-changing world, leaders need boundless energy. We need to pour energy into our organizations, invigorate our teams and constantly enliven our stakeholders. It is a never-ending demand. When we have the energy we can get through a huge amount of work and our productivity is enormous. With energy we can achieve more in one hour than we can in 10 when we're 'running on empty'.

Perhaps the reason we are so focused on time management as opposed to energy management is because it's easier. Most of us don't manage our energy effectively simply because we don't know where our energy comes from or where it goes. We have no idea what our energy source is, never mind how to manage it! As a result we attribute energy to youth and assume that it simply diminishes as we age. And whilst it's scientifically true that from an energy perspective we peak at 25 years old and, if left unchecked, our energy levels decline at roughly 3 per cent every year after that, there are ways to turn back the clock.

No one can hold back time, but in a stressful, demanding job it is energy management not time management that will transform results. We need to learn how to manage our energy reserves properly so we can re-experience the energy and stamina of our youth.

What is energy and where does it come from?

When people talk about energy they are really referring to their ability to make effort. Our ability to make effort requires a certain degree of physiological vitality. But how can we quantify our vitality in a way that is commercially relevant? The size of our muscles does not predict our ability to keep working on a strategic issue late into the night. Our raw physical fitness may give us a slight indication but it is actually a very poor predictor of corporate capability or commercial vitality. Fortunately it is now possible to scientifically quantify the exact amount of energy or power that is currently available to us in our system. We can also objectively measure how well or how appropriately we are using that available energy.

Business needs leaders with bountiful energy reserves and great dynamism. We need to be able to show up to work and pour energy into the organization day in day out, week after week, month after month, quarter by quarter without end. We need to inspire those around us with our passion and enthusiasm for the tasks at hand. And what's more we also need an ability to renew our energy levels easily and quickly at the end of each day or week ready for the next battle. If we don't have the energy then we will never be able to crank out our A-game every day. At best our performance will be erratic.

Energy is created automatically through the physiological processes that are occurring in our body all the time – whether we are consciously aware of them or not. As mammals, human beings have the capacity to create a huge amount of raw energy, and the vast majority is created by the heart. So when I say that our physiology is at the heart of our performance I mean it metaphorically and literally!

If you ever watch *ER* or *Casualty* or any TV medical show, you will see the patient hooked up to an ECG machine and their heart rate will blip its way across the green screen in a series of peaks and troughs.

FIGURE 2.1   The different deflections in a single heart beat

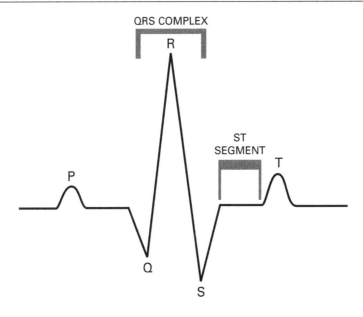

Figure 2.1 shows the different deflections in a single heart beat. This is the graphic you may be familiar with from your favourite medical dramas. But what is less well known is that the variability, pattern and flexibility of this graphic can provide a huge amount of information about the health and coherence of our physical system.

The flickering changes of direction indicated in Figure 2.1 simply reflect the direction the current takes as it navigates its way through the conducting tissue within the heart itself. As the upper chambers of the heart contract the electrical current initially moves towards the recording electrode on the front of the chest (giving rise to the P wave), then as the lower chambers of the heart contract the electrical current moves away from the recording electrode (the Q wave), and then towards it (R wave) and then away again (the S wave). The shape of the QRS complex can reveal information about the health of the main pumping chambers of the heart.

Once the heart contracts, it then relaxes to allow time for the chambers to fill back up with blood before the next contraction. Because the chemical balance in every heart cell resets, this relaxation, or 'repolarization' as it is called, also causes a deflection of the ECG needle, giving rise to the 'T' wave.

The gap between the 'S' and 'T' waves, called the 'ST segment', is used to determine whether there are any blockages in the arteries supplying the heart muscle with oxygen. If the ST segment is elevated, this suggests the patient may be having a heart attack. If the ST segment is depressed, this suggests that there is insufficient blood getting to the heart muscle and the coronary arteries may be partially blocked, which could lead to angina or chest pain.

From a medical perspective the amplitude (ie height and depth) of the component parts of the single heart beat each tell a story about the health of the heart. And considering that it is our heart that creates the vast majority of our raw energy, it's therefore essential that we understand more about the heart so we can look after it and feel younger.

The extraordinary heart

Your heart is an incredibly important and sophisticated organ. And it is important in more ways than you might imagine. It's also likely that you didn't imagine you would be reading about it in a leadership book! Chances are you've never heard about the importance of physiology in a business context and yet creating and maintaining physiological coherence can have profound effects on performance and success. And physiological coherence, or the right amount and type of physiological variability, is largely made possible through the conscious control of your heart via your breathing.

Ultimately the human body is a complex multi-directional network of interdependent systems each sending information and each affecting everything else. If we want to have the energy to consistently deliver our best we have to appreciate that complexity and understand how and when to intervene to get the best results.

Astonishing heart facts

- Your heart begins beating four weeks after conception and doesn't stop until you die.

- Your heart beats about 100,000 times each day, which equates to around 35 million times in a year, and by the time you reach 70 years old your heart will have beaten 2.5 billion times.

- Your heart does more physical work than any muscle during your lifetime.

- Grab a tennis ball and squeeze it tightly: that's how hard your heart is working every time it beats (Thomas, 1986).

In business we are so used to looking in a particular direction, through a particular lens with a particular mindset that everything else can seem unnecessary and irrelevant. Please understand I'm not sharing this information because I'm a medical doctor and I can or because it's interesting; I'm sharing it because, whilst outside the normal field of business vision, it is directly relevant to business performance and results.

The most recent and cutting-edge scientific understanding of the heart has revealed the following key insights:

- The heart is not just a pump.
- The heart is the most powerful signal generator in the human body.
- The heart has its own neural network or 'brain'.
- The heart creates hormones.

The heart is not just a pump

Medical science recognizes the prominence of the heart in human physiology, particularly its central role in the cardiovascular system. The cardiac muscle pumps blood through organs and cells over a distance of 60,000 miles, propelling five litres every 60 seconds (Thomas, 1986).

The belief that the heart is essentially just a pump is a view that only gathered momentum in the last 100 years and even then only really in the West. Prior to this the heart was revered for its wisdom – a potent reservoir of intelligence that surpasses the logical reasoning of the mind.

While modern science sought to reduce the heart to the central cog in an elaborate machine, the idea that it is so much more has been one of the strongest common threads uniting many ancient traditions and worldviews. Ancient cultures, including the Babylonians, Egyptians, Mesopotamians and Greeks, maintained that the heart was the primary organ in the human body, capable of influencing and directing emotions, morality and decision-making ability. Heart-centred views were found in Homer's *Iliad*. Aristotle believed that 'the seat of the soul and the control of voluntary movement – in fact of nervous functions in general – are to be sought in the heart' and that 'the brain is an organ of minor importance, perhaps necessary to cool the blood' (Aristotle). Hebrew, Christian, Chinese, Hindu and Islamic traditions all share the view that the heart plays a significant role in emotion and morality and respect the heart for harbouring an 'intelligence' that operates independently of, although in communication with, the brain.

However, following the birth of modern medicine, this expanded view of the heart has gradually eroded over the last 300 years. As science became increasingly reductionist and focused primarily on anatomical structure and demonstrable function, the brain was decreed to be the sole organ of conscious intelligence and appointed to a position of central importance in the human system. As a result Western thinking adopted a new paradigm and became accustomed to the concept of intellectual prowess, which translated into 'mind over matter' or 'brain over heart'.

Interestingly, many contemporary editions of various dictionaries have not been quite as ready to relinquish our initial holistic understanding of the heart and have presented us with a dual definition, a synthesis of present-day perspectives and fragments from the past:

> heart (härt), n. 1. a hollow, muscular organ that by rhythmic contractions and relaxations keeps the blood in circulation throughout the body. 2. the centre of the total personality, esp. with reference to intuition, feeling, or emotion (*Random House College Dictionary*, Revised Edition).

Common English expressions still attest to the heart's intimate involvement in conscious perceptual and emotional experience: 'Follow your heart'; 'Do it whole-heartedly'; 'Speak from the heart'; 'Be strong of heart'; 'Don't take it to heart'; 'Go deep in your heart for the answer'; 'I know in my heart...'; 'His heart wasn't in it.' This is not to minimize the role of the brain, but temper it accordingly. As the Dalai Lama said to a group of health practitioners in 1996, 'The brilliant brain sometimes creates more suffering. The smart brain must be balanced with the warm heart, the good heart, a sense of responsibility, of concern for the well-being of others.'

Fortunately, we haven't entirely shed past perspectives. Recent research, from some of the most biologically robust labs in the world is now causing us to re-evaluate these ancient beliefs and re-embrace the expanded perspective, only this time, based on science (Pereira *et al*, 2012).

In the corporate world we talk about bringing 'the heart back into business' but it is largely an idealistic concept or PR stunt rather than a literal remit. And yet it is clear that the heart is the source of a great deal of our power, wisdom and ethical insight.

The heart is the most powerful signal generator in the human body

Within the sophisticated hierarchy of the human body there are many bodily organs and sub-systems that generate their own data and subsequently transmit that information to the entire human network. Some of these organs are sending messages constantly. They literally play a tune all the time. These permanently tuneful parts of our system are called 'biological oscillators' (Strogatz, 2004). Although there are a number of biological oscillators in the human system, the best-known and most powerful biological oscillator is the heart beat produced by the heart's pacemaker cells.

The heart generates a continuous message and communicates that message to every cell in the body 24 hours a day, 365 days a year. These outgoing messages are encoded in a number of different frequency domains and are transmitted to all other bodily systems, particularly the brain. It is not so much that the heart directs the brain or the brain directs the heart; rather they are two parts of a network that is in constant dialogue, continually altering each other's information and function.

The heart is also the body's main power station with a power output of anywhere between 1 and 5 watts – considerably greater than the power output of the brain or any other system in the body (see *The Power of the Human Heart*, Muslamova, 2003) and this is largely because of something called 'autocoherence'. Autocoherence is the process whereby the heart has to synchronize the electrical charge across all of its individual cells in order to contract and pump blood. The brain doesn't pump blood so it doesn't have to synchronize its electrical activity, which is why, electrically speaking, the heart generates about 40 to 60 times more electrical power than the brain; this electrical signal can be measured, in the form of the electro-cardiogram or ECG (known as EKG in the United States), anywhere on the body (Deepu *et al*, 2012).

Perhaps more significantly the magnetic field produced by the heart is 5,000 times greater in strength than the field generated by the brain and can be detected and measured several feet away from the body, in all directions. Fur-thermore, the electromagnetic field of the heart carries information that can not only be detected in the brainwaves of other people in close proximity but also has measurable physiological effects on them (Childre and Martin, 2000).

Each heartbeat is accompanied by an electrical and electromagnetic signal that saturates every cell in the body. And the power of this signal is greater than any other signal produced by any other organ in the body. Therefore the heart's rhythmic electrical oscillations have the capacity to alter the output of all other biological oscillators.

And this is especially relevant to us because of something called 'entrainment'.

Entrainment is a term first coined by the Dutch physicist Christiaan Huygens, who in 1656 transformed timekeeping by inventing the pendu-lum clock. Before then it had only been possible to tell the time to within five minutes. Huygens' innovation in timekeeping was so impressive and so accurate that it wasn't superseded until the advent of quartz crystals almost 300 years later.

Marvelling at his incredibly smart invention, Huygens apparently noticed that all his pendulum clocks were ticking in time with each other. Even when he deliberately pushed some of the pendulums out of sync the clocks would all sync up within a few minutes. Huygens went on to describe this phenomenon as synchronization between oscillating signals, or 'entrainment'. What was actually happening was that one clock was sending its reverberation signal through the wooden case across the wooden floor to the other clock, which was then 'entrained' by that signal. In other words the signal of one clock trained the other clocks to follow its lead. Huygens also discovered that it was always the biggest pendulum in the system that dictated the synchronization. While this was an absolute revelation at the time, entrainment is now a well-understood mathematical phenomenon or fundamental principle of how the universe operates. Any complex system that has a repeating signal, pattern, beat or rhythm will always synchronize to the strongest and most powerful 'pendulum' or beat.

If you go to the theatre, one or two people will start clapping loudly and everyone else will follow. Within moments all the clapping is in sync. Female friends or family members will automatically sync their menstrual cycle. When swarms of fireflies start flashing in the night skies of southeast Asia they will synchronize in seconds (Strogatz, 2004). Shoals of fish or flocks of birds move as one to avoid predators and yet there is no collision avoidance system or air traffic control. Even clouds of electrons have been shown to synchronize. So even at a sub-atomic level systems synchronize.

Synchronization also happens in business when a powerful leader 'sets the tone' for the team, which then starts to sync to that rhythm – depending on the leader that can be very good or very bad! However, in 15 years working with executives I have rarely met a single leader who has even heard of entrainment let alone known how to harness it to drive better performance in his or her organization.

In the human body, due to the process of autocoherence the 'biggest pendulum', or the strongest and most powerful beat, comes from the heart. Remember, your heart produces 40 to 60 times more electrical power and 5,000 times more electromagnetic power than the brain, which makes it the biggest pendulum in your biological system – by far.

When we train our heart to generate a coherent signal instead of a chaotic one, it has a much greater impact on all other biological oscillators. In a coherent state the heart can cause the other oscillators to synchronize with its own rhythmic oscillations (Tiller, McCraty and Atkinson, 1996). Cardiac coherence, perfected through the practice and mastery of the skills explained later in this chapter, therefore aligns and synchronizes all our other systems to create physiological coherence that gives us greater control over our energy reserves and how we choose to utilize them.

In addition physiological coherence then facilitates emotional coherence and cognitive coherence, which means that the quality of our thinking improves. When we learn to align our own system and create coherence, we automatically help to align the systems of others, which means that the team then becomes coherent. Once we have several coherent teams at the top of an organization they become the most powerful signal in that complex system and everyone else becomes entrained and coherent around those highly functioning individuals and highly functioning teams, and that can have a profound effect on business performance.

The heart has its own neural network or 'brain'

In 1991 evidence emerged from the laboratory of John Andrew Armour MD, a leading researcher in the field of neurocardiology, that the heart has its own brain (Armour and Ardell, 1994). The nerve cells in the heart's 'brain' are identical to those found in the brain in your head. Dr Armour's research demonstrated that this brain in the heart was made up of an intricate network of several types of neurons, neurotransmitters, proteins and support cells, just like those found in the actual brain.

It had been known for many years that the heart possessed a sophisticated conducting system that was responsible for transmitting impulses from the heart's pacemaker cells to the rest of the cardiac muscle. And this conducting system enabled the synchronous contraction of the heart's pumping chambers to eject blood around the body. However, what had not been appreciated was that the heart also had a complex intrinsic nervous system sufficiently sophisticated to qualify as a 'little brain' in its own right (Arnetz and Ekman, 2008).

American neuroscientist and pharmacologist Dr Candace Pert has also presented work on neuropeptides, tiny chains of amino acids that hold the key to our emotional experiences. These neuropeptides were originally found in the brain, hence the 'neuro' prefix, but Dr Pert discovered that these tiny 'bits of brain' are floating all over the body and they are particularly prominent in the heart. Pert suggests that emotions are sophisticated frequencies or 'cellular signals that are involved in the process of translating information into physical reality, literally transforming mind into matter. Emotions are at the nexus between matter and mind, going back and forth between the two and influencing both.' We have long believed in the power of the mind over the body but the new evidence is clear – the mind does not dominate the body. The mind and body are one – hence the term Bodymind – the body is the physical space of the mind (Pert, 1997).

Our physical body is the source of a vast amount of information but we just don't listen! And yet 'without such visceral colouring we would be lost in a sea of possibilities unable to choose' (Coates, 2013). Where do gut instincts come from for example? The quick answer is the gut! Like the heart the gut also has its own 'brain' – there are about 100 million neurons in the gut! (Gershon, 1998).

All neural networks, whether in the brain, the heart or the gut, are organized as hierarchical systems. Each nerve network sends its data 'upwards' to sorting centres, called 'ganglia', where the information is processed to determine its relevance and whether it deserves further escalation. There are several layers of processing ganglia in a sophisticated neural network. Some of the larger ganglia in the human body have local decision-making capability and can execute their decisions, altering local operations without any further recourse to a 'higher authority'. So these neural networks and ganglia operate much like the CIA's listening centres, scanning electronic traffic for threats to the entire system. Research now suggests that the heart has a sophisticated neural network with several layers of ganglia or information-processing capability. This neural network can escalate its information and ultimately influence a number of aspects of the entire human system, affecting all levels of well-being: mental, emotional and physical.

From a business perspective we may pride ourselves on our commercial finesse or our ability to make smart, rational, 'head-based' decisions but it is actually biologically impossible to separate the mind and the heart. In business I believe it's time to acknowledge that our brain-based intellect actually functions by integrating data from a myriad non-cognitive knowing centres such as the heart and the gut, and this is central to our ability to decide what actions have the greatest business impact.

The heart creates hormones

The heart doesn't just generate electrical data (ECG), it generates electromagnetic, pressure and sound energy and it has recently been shown (in animals at least) that the heart also produces hormones.

Recent research has shown that the heart is an endocrine gland, informing and influencing the brain by manufacturing and secreting hormones that act as important physiological regulators for a variety of bodily processes.

In fact the heart was reclassified as part of the hormonal system in 1983 when a new hormone produced and secreted by the atria of the heart was isolated (Cantin and Genest, 1986). Now commonly referred to in the literature as ANP (atrial natriuretic peptide), this heart hormone, nicknamed the 'balance hormone', exerts its effects throughout the system.

More recently, a number of other hormones have been discovered in the heart, the most intriguing of which is oxytocin, otherwise known as the 'love hormone' or 'bonding hormone'. Oxytocin evokes feelings of contentment and calmness whilst also reducing anxiety and fear. Originally it was thought that this hormone was only produced by the pituitary gland and only in breast-feeding mothers because it helped them relax and connect more effectively with their child. Oxytocin, however, doesn't just help a mother and child bond – it helps all of us bond and is the hormone that facilitates social connections, and we all produce it in the heart as well as the pituitary gland. The heart is therefore crucial in how we relate to other people, form social bonds and develop relationships – personal and professional.

Although the heart is at the centre of our system it is not the only organ communicating information to the rest of the brain and body. Perhaps one of the most significant advances in medical thinking in the last 25 years has been the realization that every bodily system, while often capable of operating independently, must be viewed within the context of all other systems and they are constantly cross-regulating each others' function.

The rapid explosion in recent years of interdisciplinary, integrative fields of medicine acknowledges and substantiates the inseparability of mind and body. Living systems generate and process information at multiple levels, and fundamental interactions occur not only within but also across levels. We are truly vast, multi-directional information networks of communicating sub-systems, in which our mental processes, emotions and physical systems are inextricably intertwined. Every thought, attitude and emotion has a physiological consequence, and our physiological activity feeds back, in turn, to influence our thought processes, emotional reactions and behaviour.

Our research and experience at Complete Coherence also suggests that when the heart's input to the brain becomes more coherent and stable, this is associated with feelings of pleasure, hope and appreciation. Some of the skills of Enlightened Leadership are therefore designed to consciously shift chaotic heart rhythm patterns to more coherent heart rhythm patterns so as to increase energy levels, improve health and enhance brain function. We have also observed that, with practice, the incoherent albeit familiar patterns can be extinguished and replaced by new more coherent and productive patterns. When physiological coherence is extended to include emotional coherence, the new coherent rhythms become the default and the benefits start to become 'baked in' or 'hard-wired' into our system. We have taught these skills to thousands of executives and teams and they have reported significant increases in energy levels and mental clarity as well as the awareness of new sensitivities that occur when they have changed their default chaotic signal to one of cardiac coherence.

As part of our unique approach to leadership and executive development we have been quantifying the energy levels of leaders and executives in many market sectors since 1996. We have measured energy production, availability and recuperation in over 1,000 leaders through the course of a normal working day. This has been achieved by measuring the individual's heart rate for 24 hours – or more specifically their heart rate variability (HRV).

Heart rate variability (HRV)

Generally speaking most leaders are relatively poor at estimating how much energy they actually have, overestimating and underestimating in equal measure. So how do we know if our energy levels are above average or below average? How do we know if our fuel tanks are full or we're running on fumes? We may have a vague subjective sense of our own energy levels and vitality, but how accurate is that assessment really?

When working one-on-one with leaders or teams of executives we often start by objectively answering those questions. Using the sound, widely accepted metric called heart rate variability (HRV), it is now possible to determine – very accurately – how much energy a leader actually has, whether they have enough to get the job done or whether they are about to 'run out of steam'.

Essentially, energy can be measured by looking at the efficiency of our physiology or body. This isn't about physical fitness although the two are related, but rather the energetic efficiency of our physical system. Think of your body like a car and your energy reserves as the fuel. Even if you have a full tank, the way you drive your car will massively impact the efficiency of the engine. You could, for example, crawl through city traffic at 8 mph, constantly stopping and starting all the way, and you would use up your fuel very quickly. Or you could escape the city streets and cruise smoothly at 50 mph down the motorway. Not only would you travel further at 50 mph, you would use much less fuel to get to your destination and your car would not break down as quickly. The same is true of the human body.

Earlier I deconstructed an individual heart beat to explain the information inherent in that single beat, and whilst a single beat can provide some information it is actually the space between each heart beat that yields the genuinely insightful data.

Although most of us are not aware of it, our heart is beating at a slightly different pace all the time, which means that the distance between one beat and the next is constantly changing (see Figure 2.2). It is this variability or perpetual change in the interval between each individual heart beat that is measured by heart rate variability (HRV).

FIGURE 2.2   Changes in the inter-beat interval

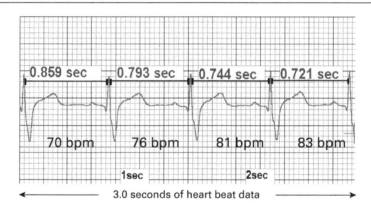

Looking at one single heart beat is the equivalent of gaining the knowledge contained in one book. Measuring HRV over a 24-hour period however is equivalent to gaining the knowledge contained in the whole library. In fact measuring HRV doesn't even look at the shape of the single heart beat; it is purely focused on measuring the variability or inter-beat interval, how that distance varies from normal beat to normal beat and what that means. Collectively this information can reveal a treasure trove of data about our energy levels and what we need to focus on to feel younger so we can consistently improve performance. Creating cardiac coherence is also central in creating complete system coherence and driving entrainment because the heart is the biggest pendulum in the system and can sync all the other biological oscillators around its own coherence.

Studying HRV is like studying the ocean – there are lots of different things happening simultaneously. For example if you watch the ocean you can see the froth on the surface of the water that is caused by wind; at the same time waves come into the beach every 10 seconds; if you look beyond the breaking surf you can see the swell out in the ocean; and all of this is going on in the context of tidal fluctuations. Watching the HRV patterns during a normal working day is very similar, and there are many different types of fluctuations caused by different underlying biological phenomena. Using some clever mathematics to deconstruct an individual's HRV recording we can then reveal the 'tides' in their human system, which in turn can illuminate some, often disturbingly accurate, insights into that person's performance without them having uttered a single word!

For example, I was working with a former England footballer and the first thing I did was measure his HRV. We arranged a meeting so we could discuss his results and I proceeded to explain to him what his HRV assessment had highlighted. In conclusion I said, 'Your main problem is you find it difficult to motivate yourself, you can't get started, but once you've decided to do something and you get into action you are totally relentless – like a dog with a bone.' He was speechless and more than a little spooked because, although my statement was spot on, we had not discussed anything, never mind any performance issues he might have. He couldn't understand how I could possibly know what I knew. I knew because his physiology was telling me.

In a business setting, we are also able to pinpoint some critical areas of concern regarding productivity and performance. Just by looking at the results obtained over a 24-hour period (Figure 2.3 and Table 2.1) we can tell whether a leader's main problem is motivation or endurance, how much energy they have, whether they are wasting energy and feel exhausted or whether they are using their energy efficiency. We can also tell if their system is breaking down or whether their body is recuperating properly. And we can even tell how much international travel they are doing and how well they are coping with it!

FIGURE 2.3   Sample of data gathered from HRV

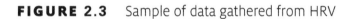
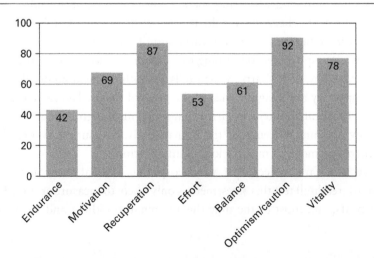

TABLE 2.1   Explanation of data gathered from HRV

Reflects	Biological basis	Measured
Endurance	Tidal hormones	24 hrs
Motivation	Autonomic nervous system	5 mins
Recuperation	Brake = acetylcholine	1–2 secs
Effort	Accelerator = adrenaline	10–30 secs
Balance	Water & temp balance	5 mins
Optimism/caution	Short-term hormones	30 mins
Vitality	Total power HRV freq	30 mins

It's important to understand that measuring HRV is not the same as getting our heart checked in a standard 'corporate medical'. When our pulse rate is taken in orthodox medicine, it is usually to determine our average heart rate or the number of beats per minute. This is usually achieved by counting the number of heart beats in 15 seconds and multiplying the result by four. But this measure ignores the fact that our heart rate changes repeatedly during those 15 seconds even though the difference is much too subtle to detect just by feeling our pulse.

For example, Figure 2.4 illustrates an average HRV recording and we can see that the number of heart beats per minute fluctuates between 60 beats per minute (bpm) and 120 bpm – there is constant variability. And yet when we get our heart checked by a doctor he or she is usually only interested in the average heart rate, not the variability. Taking an 'average heart rate' in this way is equivalent to listening to a Chopin piano concerto and saying the average key is 'F sharp', which tells us nothing meaningful about the depth, intricacy and magnificence of the piece of music. The same is true of average heart rate – it tells us virtually nothing meaningful about the depth, intricacy and magnificence of the human body. Measuring average heart rate therefore means a massive loss of information.

Even if we are subjected to a full corporate medical and complete the standard treadmill test this assessment is only likely to measure around 1,000 heart beats, and most of the time this illuminates nothing and we are told

FIGURE 2.4   Average heart rate and variations over time

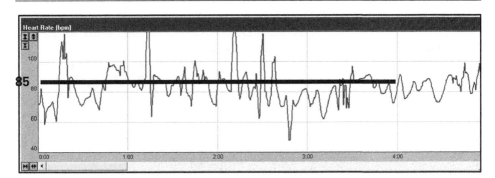

that everything is 'normal'. In a 24-hour HRV recording, around 100,000 heart beats are examined and this provides a much more detailed, sophisticated and accurate assessment, including how 'normal' the data really is.

The executive tachogram

The recording of the changes in someone's heart rate is called a 'tachogram', which means 'speed picture'. A tachogram is therefore literally a picture of how the heart rate speeds up and slows down over time.

Figure 2.5 is an example of the information generated from a simple tachogram of a busy executive. Notice that while the executive was in meetings his heart rate was fluctuating around 65 bpm. Then he left work and his heart rate leapt almost immediately as he walked quickly to the train station, reaching 105 bpm, falling slightly as he reached the station.

In the second tachogram, we can see what happens when the executive runs up an escalator. Again his heart rate nearly doubles from a steady 65 bpm to 120 bpm before dropping back to a higher resting level of 75 bpm. But then something interesting happens – he realizes he's missed his train! He's not walking fast or running up escalators and yet for the next 10 minutes his heart rate remains elevated, reaching up to 100 bpm. Being frustrated at missing his train clearly has a direct effect on his physiology, causing him to burn energy at a much higher rate than necessary for at least 10 minutes. This not only explains why people who have endured a very frustrating day come home feeling exhausted, but also illustrates the critical importance of physiological and emotional coherence on energy management.

Watching an individual's tachograms during a normal working day reveals that, for most people, the 'normal' pattern of HRV is far from a state

FIGURE 2.5   Example of executive tachogram

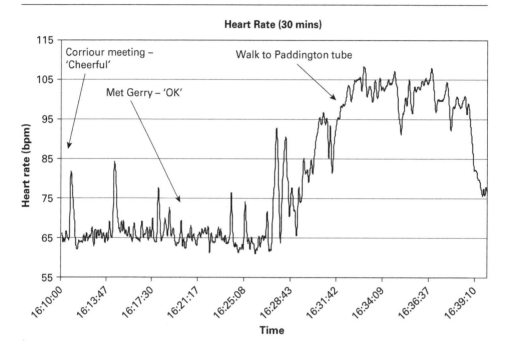

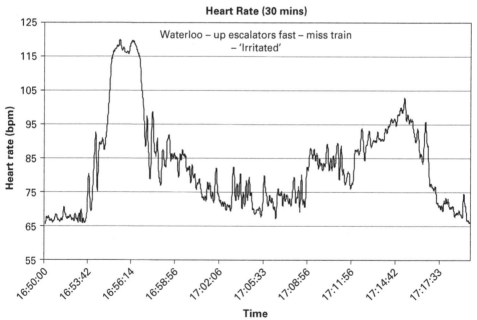

of equilibrium. In fact the normal pattern is a chaotic heart beat all day. Changes in an individual's external environment, events and situations at work, physical activity, emotional response – nearly everything we do during the course of our day results in almost instantaneous changes in our internal physiological environment.

These internal changes, in HRV and other physiological signals – of most of which are unconscious – change the way we feel, which changes the way we think, which in turn changes what we do and the results we achieve. Thus there is a bi-directional interaction of internal and external environments, both affecting each other. If we want to feel younger and positively impact results, we first need to know how much energy or fuel we have in our tanks and how well we use that available fuel. And we must get to grips with our physiology so we can turn that chaotic heart beat into a coherent heart beat. Measuring HRV is the first step in that process.

Why HRV is so important

There has been an explosion in interest regarding measuring HRV and there are now some 15,000 published scientific papers that explore the different aspects of HRV (Malik and Camm, 1995). But why is it important for a leader to know about HRV? There are three critical reasons:

- HRV can predict death and illness and reveals biological age.
- HRV quantifies energy levels and levels of dynamism.
- HRV alters brain function.

HRV can predict death and illness and reveals biological age

In 1996 the famous Hollywood film producer Don Simpson went to visit a colleague of mine, Dr Bill Stuppy. Simpson was at the time the business partner of Jerry Bruckheimer and they were famous for films like *Dangerous Minds, Beverley Hills Cop, The Rock* and *Top Gun*. It was Simpson who coined the phrase, 'you'll never work in this town again.' Simpson's doctor, John O'Dea, was seriously concerned about Simpson's health and sent him to see Bill, who measured his HRV over the course of 24 hours. It was the worst he'd ever seen so he sent a letter to John O'Dea telling him that he needed to get Simpson into hospital immediately otherwise he'd be dead within six weeks – probably on the toilet or eating a meal.

Dr O'Dea was so concerned about these findings that he sent Bill's letter on to Don Simpson with a handwritten note on the letter asking him to come in right away. Don, being the big-hitter work-hard-play-hard, take-no-prisoners kind of guy that he was, refused to accept the analysis and instead sought out a second opinion from another doctor. That doctor however only gave him a standard medical, monitoring his heart for a few minutes rather than 24 hours; it all sounded 'normal' so Simpson was sent home and told not to worry.

Six weeks after Bill wrote the letter to John O'Dea Don Simpson died on the toilet as predicted. The police found him in his bathroom. He'd been reading Oliver Stone's autobiography and his bookmark was the letter that Bill Stuppy had written saying he was going to be dead in six weeks. Bill was subsequently brought in for questioning! But as he explained to the police, 'I didn't kill him; I just told him he was going to die if he didn't get medical help.'

That's the power of HRV.

The National Maternity Hospital in Dublin has one of the lowest emergency caesarean section rates and infant mortality rates in the world. And the reason is that they pioneered what is known as the 'Active Management of Labour' and could pretty much guarantee that once an expectant mother entered the labour ward they would have a healthy baby in their hands within 12 hours. Some years ago I worked on the John Radcliffe Hospital obstetric ward in Oxford, which also adopted the Dublin approach to labour.

A key principle of this approach is the continual monitoring of the baby's heart rate during labour, paying particular attention to HRV. If we started to witness a reduction in the amount of HRV we would then stay with the mum to be, watching the baby's tachogram trace like hawks. Once a loss of HRV on the baby's tachogram has been detected, the clock will start ticking. Since 1965 it has become common obstetric practice around the world to watch a baby's HRV during labour for early signs of foetal distress, thus using HRV to predict and prevent death (Neilson and Mistry, 2000).

But HRV does not just predict foetal distress and infant mortality in labour. In 1978 Dr Graeme Sloman, an Australian physician, reported in the *Medical Journal of Australia* that it predicted adult mortality after a heart attack (Wolf *et al*, 1978). He noticed that some heart attack victims had a degree of variability while others' hearts ticked like a metronome. Those with little HRV never made it home to their family; they died right there on the ward. In this study none of the traditional risk factors such as age, cholesterol levels or smoking predicted the outcome. Since then there have been many studies that show the powerful ability of HRV to predict death from heart disease (Tsuji *et al*, 1994, 1996; Kleiger *et al*, 1987).

In 1997 Jacqueline Dekker and her colleagues discovered that HRV was capable of predicting death, not only in babies or heart attack victims but also of predicting 'all-cause mortality' (Dekker *et al*, 1997). In other words, HRV could predict the demise of anyone from any cause (Mayor and Micozzi, 2011). Strangely, HRV, which is a measure of cardiovascular flexibility, can also predict death from non-cardiovascular disease because HRV is a measure of our overall system flexibility (Gerritsen *et al*, 2001). A loss of flexibility means a brittle system unable to adapt to physiological stress. And a brittle system is likely to snap.

Clearly, the sudden collapse or even death of a senior executive is an extremely important risk in business, could completely alter succession planning and has a massive impact on a company.

In November 2011 Lloyds Banking Group CEO António Horta-Osório took six weeks' sick leave on the advice of his doctors after he was diagnosed with extreme fatigue and stress. In a world of shareholder value and quarterly results his decision to step down, albeit temporarily, wiped 4.4 per cent or a whopping £930 million off the value of Lloyds Banking Group shares (Seamark, 2011). He would have been acutely aware that his decision would cause such a reaction and it is perhaps an indication of just how close to total collapse he really was. The really sad part however is that it could have been averted. Had Horta-Osório had his HRV measured over 24 hours the warning signs would probably have been clear to see months before any real physical symptoms emerged, giving him enough time to recalibrate his physiological system and learn how to effectively manage his energy levels and recuperate properly.

Poor HRV can't be fixed with a tablet but it can be improved by embracing many of the coherence-creating skills of Enlightened Leadership, and we'll explore more of these health implications in the next chapter.

Biological age

In addition to preventing death and predicting illness, both extremely useful in and outside business, the amount of HRV can also tell us a lot about our biological age as opposed to our actual chronological age (Umetani *et al*, 1998). Without conscious intervention our HRV declines by approximately 3 per cent per year, deteriorating from our mid-twenties until we lose all variability and die. This means that if our HRV is assessed for 24 hours it is possible to tell roughly how old we are to within about one year, based on the decline in our heart rate variability.

Figures 2.6 and 2.7 illustrate the difference in HRV amplitude in two individuals with a 20 year age difference. The 60-year-old has much smaller HRV amplitude than the 40-year-old.

FIGURE 2.6   HRV amplitude in a 60-year-old

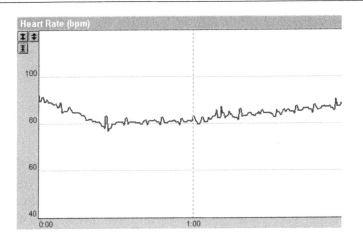

FIGURE 2.7   HRV amplitude in a 40-year-old

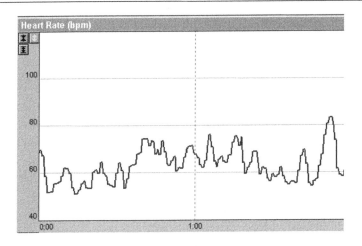

Obviously a birth certificate or pointed question could elicit someone's age, but biological age and chronological age don't always tally. Depending on how well someone has managed their energy, their true biological age as revealed by their physiology (HRV) may be considerably older than the actual number of birthdays they have had.

Have you ever wondered why prime ministers and presidents seem to age rapidly when they are in power? For example, if you look at the photos of Tony Blair as he came to power in the UK in 1997 he looked youthful and vibrant. That was 'Young Tony'. Look at photographs of him when he left power and he had aged dramatically. The same thing can be seen with Barack Obama – when he became President of the United States he was just 48 years old, he had dark hair and looked youthful and enthusiastic. At the start of his second term, just five years later, Obama looks considerably older than would be expected with the passage of so little time. Clearly being the 'most powerful man on earth' plays havoc with biological age!

Although we can't change our chronological age we can change our biological age and increase HRV with the right kind of lifestyle adjustments. It is therefore possible to improve HRV and turn back the clock through exercise, emotional self-management, omega-3 supplements and yoga (Watkins, 2011). The easiest and quickest way however is to create cardiac coherence through the breathing skills that will be explained a little later in this chapter.

HRV quantifies energy levels and levels of dynamism

Despite the huge energy demands of modern business few executives ever consider this critical resource and how to manage it appropriately. It is however very difficult to feel younger when you're exhausted all the time. In fact it's pretty much impossible.

Most senior executives and business leaders have risen up through the ranks of business in a specific field or industry over the course of many years, possibly decades. As a result they are susceptible to a double whammy as far as energy reduction is concerned. Not only are they losing 3 per cent every year from their mid-twenties onwards but, under the relentless pressure to perform and achieve consistent shareholder value, their biological systems break down faster. So they have less fuel in the tank to start with and they are not using what they do have efficiently – something that Nick Buckles, one of the most resilient CEOs in the FTSE 100, is fully aware of. Before stepping down in 2013 Nick was CEO of G4S – the largest security services provider in the world, with operations in more than 125 countries across six continents employing over 620,000 people. However in the run up to the London 2012 Olympic and Paralympic Games, G4S came under intense media criticism for their handling of the Olympic security contract and Nick had to face a government select committee. Struggling to regain his energy levels, Nick's HRV was assessed for 24 hours and although the assessment indicated he did have the reserves he needed to meet the challenges, he was not recuperating and replenishing his reserves well enough. At times, the life of any CEO can be incredibly exhausting and ensuring you have the energy to address a crisis, an acquisition failure or extremely tough market conditions is vital. Nick was able to sustain himself through incredibly difficult times using the techniques taught in this book.

In the early stages of exhaustion there is often an excessive increase in adrenaline levels and an increased activation of the sympathetic nervous system (SNS). This can go hand in hand with agitation and hyper vigilance, a picture often seen in individuals with chronic fatigue (Boneva *et al*, 2007). This type of excessive arousal can ultimately lead to sympathetic exhaustion. Senior executives and leaders who are under excessive pressure are constantly pumping adrenaline into their system and will often exhaust their adrenal glands' ability to produce sufficient adrenaline to cope with the demand. The amount of adrenaline produced by the sympathetic nervous system and the adrenal gland can also be quantified using HRV analysis. Thus HRV can be used as a marker of excessive SNS activation and ultimately adrenal exhaustion.

Furthermore HRV analysis can be used to determine whether a low level of energy in the SNS is matched by a similarly low level of energy or vitality in the counterbalancing parasympathetic nervous system (PNS). Exhaustion of the PNS as well as the SNS/adrenals is more concerning than just SNS exhaustion because it depletes our ability to make effort (SNS) and our ability to recover (PNS). The good news is that both can be improved and we can manage our energy levels so we feel years younger.

Crocodiles and wildebeests

One of the most poignant examples of the importance of HRV for energy levels and dynamism is seen when we compare mammals and reptiles and their ability to respond to a threat or rise to a challenge. Reptiles, because they are cold-blooded, do not have much HRV. They can alter their heart rate, but they can't do it quickly. In comparison, all warm-blooded mammals, including humans, have a lot of heart rate variability and burn 5–10 times more energy than reptiles (Coates, 2013). In fact, it is the high variability that makes mammals responsive and dynamic.

Imagine for a moment a situation where the world of mammals and reptiles collide – an African watering hole. On land a warm-blooded wildebeest approaches to quench his thirst. It is cautious because there are cold-blooded crocodiles in the water waiting for dinner. The wildebeest does however have a significant advantage – high variability, which means that should a crocodile attack it can increase its heart rate very quickly, generate power and rapidly get out the way. Although a crocodile can also vary its heart rate it can't do it quickly, so the crocodile only has one shot at its prey because it uses all its energy reserves making the initial attack and doesn't have the heart flexibility (or physiology) to chase the wildebeest. Reptiles just don't have the energy that mammals have and they certainly can't run marathons!

Mammals have access to more energy because they have a much greater capacity to change their heart rate (HRV). Specifically, mammals can change their adrenaline levels (the accelerator hormone) and their acetycholine levels (the brake hormone) more quickly than reptiles. This enables the wildebeest to rapidly mobilize the energy needed to escape a crocodile attack by releasing the brakes and applying the accelerator. Mammals can move from low energy to high energy repeatedly but reptiles can't because they don't have the HRV.

Think of it like a drag race. At the start of a race the driver has his feet on the accelerator and the brake. When the starting light turns green he removes the brake and the car bursts forward and then he applies the accelerator. In the same way that taking your foot off the brake in your car will make the car surge forward, the body can remove acetylcholine to achieve the same result.

Luckily for the wildebeest and all other mammals, including us, the heart muscles metabolize acetylcholine much more quickly than adrenaline, and this can provide life-saving energy until adrenaline can kick in and provide a more sustained surge in energy.

These hormonal brakes and accelerators are crucial to energy reserves and efficiency. How much energy we create is one thing; how appropriately we utilize that energy is quite another.

HRV determines our ability to respond to the challenges life throws at us. In fact this flexibility to adapt to our environment is part of what it means to be alive and dynamic. It is therefore possible to use the 'variability' of the heart's electrical signal to quantify the 'vitality' of the human system. HRV could be considered a way to measure 'aliveness'.

It is clearly imperative that business leaders learn how to effectively manage their energy so that they can deal with the increasing demands of modern business and maintain flexibility, yet most leaders never question why they are energetic one day and exhausted the next. Very few leaders know where their energy comes from, where it goes and why they feel utterly drained at the end of the week. Often the pressure is relentless, and unless we can harness our most critical resource it's also unsustainable – as António Horta-Osório, and the Lloyds shareholders, found out to their cost!

The good news is that HRV can be changed, which will in turn alter energy levels and help to turn back time. With tailored coaching we have for example been able to demonstrate an average 30 per cent increase in all HRV parameters within six months for executives in multinational corporations (Watkins *et al*, 2013).

After a very successful career at Unilever and elsewhere, Alan Brown took over as CEO at Rentokil Initial in 2007. Rentokil Initial is one of the largest business service companies in the world, with over 60,000 employees operating in over 60 countries where the brands have come to represent consistent quality of service. The challenge posed by this appointment was significant and would require a massive amount of energy. Despite being a very fit cyclist Alan, like many other CEOs, struggled to maintain his energy in the face of the draining nature of his executive responsibility. He remembers:

> I was frustrated by significant dips in my energy levels through the
> day that made it difficult to perform consistently in my work, and I was
> unsettled at home.

Intrigued by the concept of energy management and the idea that it was something he could control instead of his energy levels controlling him, Alan set out to learn and master the techniques in this book adding:

> The biggest change for me has been that I can now operate much more
> consistently throughout the day and the week. My attention span is much
> greater. I have always been able to work long hours, but the quality of that
> work was not consistently high. Today, the quality of my concentration has
> improved significantly.

You can read Alan Brown's case study at **www.coherence-book.com**.

HRV alters brain function

In addition to predicting death and illness, revealing biological age, quantifying energy levels (both amount and overall dynamism), HRV also influences brain function.

HRV can have a profound influence on your ability to think clearly, and therefore plays an absolutely critical role in business. When we learn and use the skills of Enlightened Leadership we create cardiac coherence, which in turn will give us consistent and continuous access to our very highest cognitive abilities – regardless of the external pressures or circumstances. But I'll explain this phenomenon in more detail in Chapter 4, 'Be smarter'.

How to be younger

In order to sustain performance at the very highest levels it is necessary to balance intense effort with the appropriate recuperation. It's simply not possible to keep going indefinitely.

Ironically most people accept the need for recovery time when it comes to athletics or sport, yet in the business world executives are simply expected to keep going, day in day out, year in year out. Clearly the rules of business are different from athletics or sport but learning how to manage our energy levels for maximum efficiency and recuperation can revolutionize performance. The first step toward consistently brilliant performance is therefore physiological coherence, and that means mastering the physical skills of Enlightened Leadership. Michael Drake, TNT Express's Asia Pacific Managing Director, successfully led the business through a significant period of change. TNT Express provides a wide range of express services to businesses and consumers around the world, employing over 68,000 people in more than 200 countries. In his brief case study at **www.coherence-book.com** Michael talks of the importance of acknowledging difference, embracing ambiguity and becoming more coherent to drive performance:

> [Enlightened Leadership] has helped me a great deal with linking my emotional state to my performance outcomes. As a consequence I am much more aware of how I am feeling – both mentally and physically – when I turn up 'to perform'… I am also now very aware that your emotional state is largely dependent on your physiology. Learning various techniques to help with this has been very valuable.

In order to turn back time, have more energy and feel 10 years younger, we have to become aware of and then learn to control our own physiological signals, especially our HRV. Such a step-change in our vitality is achieved first through physical intelligence, or the awareness of our physiological state. The E-bank allows us to gain a greater appreciation of what is currently adding to and draining our energy levels. Once we have cultivated a greater level of physical awareness we need to learn to control our physiology and such physical management is achieved primarily through control of our breath with the BREATHE skill.

Physiological coherence – physical intelligence: the E-bank

The first step to generating physiological coherence and energy preservation is practising the E-bank. The E-bank can help us to become aware of where we are currently using our most important resource – our energy. This is achieved by tracking the events, situation and people that drain and boost our energy and it can reveal areas of our life where we can make a significant difference, feel younger and preserve energy for only a small energetic investment.

Using the format demonstrated in Figure 2.8 below, take a moment to write down all the things, situations, events and people that increase your energy (deposits) and everything that robs you of energy (withdrawals).

FIGURE 2.8   The E-bank

Deposits	Withdrawals

Don't worry about the timeframe or when these energy transactions occurred; just make a note of everything that positively or negatively impacts your energy account. Make sure you:

- Relive the deposits as you write them down.
- Leave the withdrawals behind as you write them down.

The key benefit of this exercise is that it will give you awareness about your current energy levels and what affects those levels – either for better or for worse. Maybe you realize that the only energy boost or credit you've received in the last few days was the cuddle from your four-year-old daughter. Perhaps you realize just how debilitating your office manager, Marjorie, is to your energy levels.

Once you've created the lists, take a moment to really consider the insights that they present to you. Are there any conclusions that you can draw from these lists that will help you to better manage your energy levels? Can you spot any patterns in the timings, the people or the type of work that rob you of energy and vitality? Is there a common denominator between the experiences or events that add to your energy levels? If there are plenty of deposits and only a few withdrawals, then perhaps the withdrawals are so significant that they cancel out the deposits. For example a pending divorce can be a significant and consistent energy drain and will not be easily allevi- ated by a good night out with colleagues from work, even if you are not dealing with the divorce on a daily basis.

Go through the list and highlight the top three energy accumulators and the top three energy drains. Write down what action you can take to add more positive energy to your account or minimize the drains on your energy reserves.

Say you realize that your office manager, Marjorie, is really wearing you down. Has she always been like that or is she particularly painful just now because she's upset about the new database installation? If her negativity is related to a particular situation, then do what you can to change the situation. If she's just a pain but is actually good at her job, then you can't fire her but you could change her reporting lines so she no longer reports to you. Find a way to either resolve her negativity or reduce your expo- sure to her so she does not rob you of energy. If you are struggling to come up with a solution, the SHIFT skill explored in Chapter 4 will help.

Perhaps creating your E-bank allowed you to see a pattern? A director of a credit card company we worked with discovered a very toxic pattern when she documented her energy account in this way. What she discovered was that she was always thinking about the past. She wasted huge amounts of time and energy worrying about whether or not she made the correct decision and what she could or should have done differently. So much so, in fact, that she simply didn't have any energy left for thinking about the present or the future. Reflection is an important quality for all senior execu- tives and business leaders but she needed to extract the lesson and move on quickly.

Almost all ancient spiritual wisdom and some new (Tolle, 2005) reminds us that there is only one moment that really matters – right now. When we spend time in the past or the future we rob ourselves of life.

When we interviewed Mike Iddon, Finance Director of Tesco UK, about the benefits of Enlightened Leadership, he specifically mentioned the energy bank and how it helped him through a significant period of change:

There are things in your life that make deposits and other things that make withdrawals. Over a period of time, you need to ensure there are more deposits than withdrawals. It's a really helpful technique for thinking about your whole life, including work and home. Alan encouraged me to keep an energy bank of my deposits and withdrawals. It drives me to do more things that lead to deposits. You beat yourself up over things that go wrong, but you rarely give yourself or your team credit when things go right. The E-bank helps to redress that and it certainly helped me think differently.

Tesco is the world's second-largest retailer, employing over 520,000 people, with over 6,700 stores in 12 markets and serving millions of customers every week, and you can read the rest of Mike's case study at **www.coherence-book.com,** where he discusses the importance of finding his own purpose and meaning as a result of our coaching.

When protecting your energy levels watch out for self-criticism and self-judgement as they are particularly powerful energy drains on your system. They act like direct debits going straight out of your account on a daily basis.

Also be aware that you can put deposits in other people's E-banks just with a simple act of kindness or an encouraging word. And when you review your list of deposits and relive the positives as you write them down, this can have the same effect as compound interest. Not only did you get a boost when that event happened but reflecting on it gives you a further boost when you write it in your E-bank.

Physiological coherence – physical management: the BREATHE skill

One of the primary ways that we lose our energy is through incoherent or erratic breathing. In the same way that we use more fuel driving in the city than we do driving on the motorway, when our breathing is chaotic we use up much more energy. Coherent breathing is like motorway driving – we travel further using less fuel, and there is less wear and tear on our system so we feel younger.

When we are reactive we will, by default, have a chaotic and erratic HRV signal. Remember the tachogram of the executive who missed his train – his frustrated reaction to that event caused his heart rate to spike and he used more energy over the following 10 minutes than he needed to. Had he controlled his response to missing the train, he still would have missed the train but he wouldn't have then compounded the error by leaking valuable energy. Our job is to create a coherent HRV signal so that we become dynamically responsive instead of reactive. This can be achieved via our breathing. If we want to impact performance we must stabilize our physiology. And by far the quickest and easiest way to stabilize our physiology is to stabilize our breathing.

Just think about this for a moment... When you are surprised or shocked – what happens? When you get angry or upset – what happens? When you are relaxed – what happens? Your breathing is immediately and constantly affected by whatever is going on around you – inside and out. In order to experience many negative emotional states, it is necessary to lose control of your breath. For example, 'panic' requires an individual to breathe in a rapid, erratic and shallow way. The first thing to 'go' in a difficult situation is our ability to breathe properly. As a result, what happens is that our breathing becomes chaotic, scrambling everything from how we feel to how we think, to what we do and ultimately our behaviour and our results.

Generating a rhythmic breathing pattern creates cardiac coherence. The rhythmic changes in intrathoracic pressure caused by rhythmic breathing cause the heart rate to vary in a dynamic stable way. As our cardiac physiology becomes coherent the power output of the heart increases, and this drives other biological systems to synchronize with the heart causing physiological entrainment.

The easiest way to understand this is to imagine that the body is an orchestra. The heart is the string section of that orchestra. Within the string section there is a violin, viola, cello, double bass etc. This is the equivalent of the electrical signal, the electromagnetic, the chemical, the pressure waves, the heat waves and the sound waves. The electrical signal (HRV) that the heart generates is like the lead violin. Rhythmic breathing is our way of taking control of the biological equivalent of the lead violin. When we do that, the electrical signal the heart generates creates the equivalent of a harmonious note (Figure 2.9) instead of an erratic, chaotic 'white noise' signal (Figure 2.10). This strong coherent note from the heart in turn begins to entrain all the other physiological signals and releases a lot more power. Cardiac coherence basically means a stable, rhythmic heart rate variation and this is easily visible when we measure our HRV. The HRV pattern becomes a sine wave.

A sine wave can have various frequencies, ie the peaks and troughs can be close together or further apart. In other words your heart can be beating very quickly in a state of heightened awareness or arousal, say during an important presentation, but it is still creating a coherent signal at a high heart rate (Figure 2.11), or your heart can be beating more slowly and still be coherent, say sitting at your desk reading a report (Figure 2.12). In musical terms those frequencies are like different notes and we can train our heart to generate

FIGURE 2.9   'Coherence' seen in anabolic states

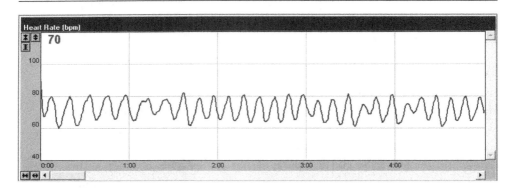

FIGURE 2.10   'Chaos' seen in catabolic states

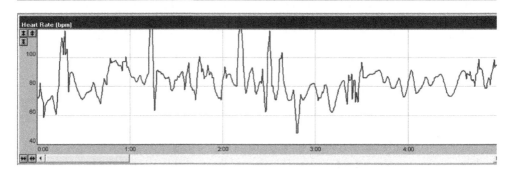

any note. So your heart can generate 'cardiac coherence' at a 10-second cycle (0.1 Hz) or a 5-second cycle (0.2 Hz) or any other frequency.

Because of entrainment, once we achieve cardiac coherence via our breathing it's much easier for the other members of the orchestra (lungs, kidneys, brain etc) to play their own coherent notes so that the whole system plays a series of coherent notes, which creates a more balanced and harmonious 'tune' and this physiological coherence then facilitates 'emotional coherence'.

The BREATHE skill

The conscious control of our breath is not a new concept; indeed many disciplines such as public speaking, playing a musical instrument, sport, yoga, martial arts and meditation all teach people the importance of correct breathing. More often than not these modalities will advocate the conscious

FIGURE 2.11   High-frequency coherence

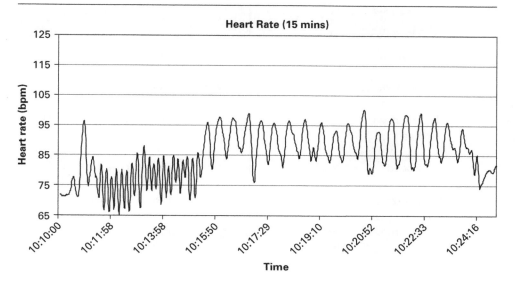

FIGURE 2.12   Low-frequency coherence

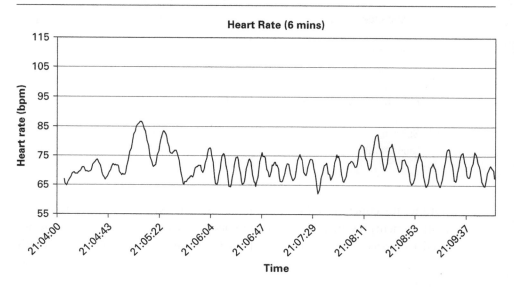

control over a number of different aspects of the breath. In total there are 12 aspects of our breathing that we can learn to control (Table 2.2).

However, when it comes to coherence the first three hold the key. Forget about speed, pattern, volume or depth. Taking a deep or large breath will do

TABLE 2.2 The 12 aspects of breath

	Parameter	Explanation	Impact
1	Rhythmicity	Fixed ratio of in:out breath	alters HRV
2	Smoothness	Even flow rate = fixed vol/sec	alters HRV
3	Focus on heart	Location of attention	promotes positive emotion
4	Speed	No. breaths per sec	alters adrenaline levels
5	Pattern	Specific ratio of in:out breath	alters CO_2 levels
6	Volume	Amount of air in a single breath	alters VO_2 max
7	Depth	Location of air in lungs	alters O_2 saturation levels
8	Entrainment	Synchronization of systems	feeling of balance
9	Resistance	To airflow in nose & mouth	can affect levels of anxiety
10	Mechanics	Use of accessory muscles	alters energy needed to breathe
11	Flow patterns	Of air around the body	alters focus of attention
12	Special techniques	eg vipassana, buteyko	varied

nothing for coherence. We can also forget about synchronizing our system (entrainment) because it's largely an unconscious process anyway. We don't need to worry about whether to breathe through our nose or our mouth (resistance and mechanics), flow patterns around the body or any other special breathing technique such as alternate nostril breathing.

Just focus on:

1 Rhythmicity – fixed ratio of in:out breath.

2 Smoothness – even flow rate, in and out.

3 Location of attention.

The single most important priority is rhythm. First we need to make our breathing rhythmic so that there is a fixed ratio between the in-breath and the out-breath. So for example you may decide to breathe in for the count of four and then breathe out for the count of six, then repeat. All that matters is that whatever ratio you choose you maintain that ratio consistently – three in three out, or four in six out, or five in five out.

There is a great deal of inherent power in rhythm – a fact not lost on sports like rowing, which is all about rhythm. I had the good fortune to work directly with the GB rowing squad going into the London Olympics in 2012. Three months before the Olympics Dr Ann Redgrave, the GB squad's medical advisor, asked me to talk to all the squad coaches to explain what else was needed to win a medal above and beyond what they were already doing. As Ann explains:

> When rowers go out to race, they leave the coaches and the support team at the landing stage around 30 to 40 minutes before the race. They go through a prepared warm up routine and then they are required to sit on the start line for up to five minutes. Once they're on the start line what happens – self-doubt can creep in. I know because it happened to me when I was competing. You sit there, you find yourself wondering what you're doing there! It's the last place you want to be. It's exciting but also a bit frightening. Crazy thoughts go through your head. Over the last few years, I've noticed this having a detrimental effect on the performance of our rowers as they leave the start line. What was needed was something to focus the attention and emotions of the rowers at the very time when they needed to do the job they had trained years for.

After the initial presentation I worked closely with eight coaches and crews in the run up to the Games. The first thing I presented to them was the importance of the BREATHE skill. For them it was particularly helpful when they were waiting nervously before the start of the race and for some rowers it made a massive difference. Six of GB's nine rowing medals came from those crews working under those coaches: three gold, two silvers and a bronze; you can read Ann's case study at **www.coherence-book.com**.

If someone was learning to row, once they were in the boat, the cox would shout 'in-out-in-out'. And the purpose of this instruction is to create rhythm. If one person is trying to put the blades in the water when someone else is taking them out then the boat won't move very well. The first step toward coherent breathing therefore is rhythm.

The second step is the smoothness of the breath. Technically we could breathe rhythmically but in a staccato 'jumpy' fashion. Coherence requires a smooth rhythm. This means we need to ensure a fixed volume of air is going in and out of our lungs per second.

Again smoothness is also critical in rowing. Once the team has been taught to get the oars in the water at the same time in a rhythmic stroke, then they must row smoothly through the water. If they put their blades in the water and pull really hard then let them drift for a second then pull really hard again, the boat will spurt forward and drift, then spurt forward again and drift again. What's needed is a smooth consistent stroke all the way through.

If you watch the GB rowers you can see that they use the same amount of power at the start of the stroke as they do at the end of the stroke. It's the same in cycling. An amateur cyclist will kick off with a really big push and then rely on momentum to bring the pedal back around so they can push down again and repeat. If you were to watch a professional such as Sir Chris Hoy or Sir Bradley Wiggins, there is a smooth consistent effort all the way round the cycle, even when they are lifting their foot up. And that generates a massive amount of force, pulling them away from less able cyclists.

And finally, the third important aspect of our breathing is our location of attention. We believe it's important to focus on our heart or the centre of our chest for three reasons:

- The heart is the main power station in the human system and generates considerably more energy than any other human organ or system.

- When we feel most chaotic and our breathing and mind are scrambled, there is usually a great deal of 'noise' in our head as we wrestle to regain control. The very act of moving our attention away from all the noise and dropping it into our body seems to be beneficial. By consciously moving our focus away from our head and into our body we facilitate faster coherence. And finally:

- When we focus on our heart or the middle of our chest we are more likely to experience a positive emotional state because the heart is where most human beings experience their positive emotion. We say 'I love my wife with all my heart', we don't say 'I love her with all my amygdala' or 'all my kneecap'. I don't love my sons with 'my anterior cingulate cortex' even though that's probably where the information registers. We feel the sensation of love in the centre of our chest. Thus when someone has a positive emotional experience it's usually felt in the centre of the chest, so consciously shifting our attention to that area can facilitate positive emotion, which in turn moves us to the positive side of the performance grid. Figure 2.13 demonstrates the impact of rhythmic and smooth, heart-focused breathing by

FIGURE 2.13 Impact of correct breathing

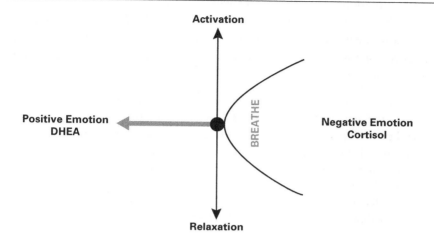

getting us to the midpoint of the grid. Ultimately the only way to get over to the left, positive side and stay there is by engaging emotions (which is the topic of the next chapter) but breathing creates the platform on which everything else – health, happiness, cognitive ability and elevated performance, success and influence – is built.

When we breathe rhythmically and smoothly we create a coherent HRV signal. This then stabilizes our physiology and creates cardiac coherence – turning our heart rate from chaos to coherence as illustrated in Figures 2.9 and 2.10. This allows us to maintain our self-control in highly charged situations, prevents our brain from shutting down and enables us to think clearly and become more perceptive. Plus it gives us a better chance to change the way we feel and, most importantly for our energy levels, coherent breathing prevents the unconscious expenditure of our most precious energy reserves.

The easiest way to remember this breathing technique is through the BREATHE acronym:

Breathe

Rhythmically

Evenly

And

Through the

Heart

Everyday.

If you control your breathing then you are in charge of your physiology. Events, situations and other people won't be able to scramble your thinking and make you reactive, which can often be disastrous for business. In his case study at **www.coherence-book.com** Michael Drake, Asia Pacific Managing Director for TNT Express, explains how he uses the BREATHE skill all the time to improve performance:

> I use the coherence techniques I've learnt on a daily basis, even outside of work. I play golf and I will do the rhythmic breathing a lot. It gets my heart rate to a level that will provide clarity of thought and help execution. It's the same before a big speech. I think about my breathing and what I'm going to do. I get my heart under control. Just the notion of taking two minutes to think about how I am feeling is beneficial... it builds confidence and, for whatever reason, I see the results in my performance. I feel calmer, more confident and focused, and all of those things can only be beneficial in terms of performance.

Complete Coherence Ltd Biofeedback Kit or iPhone app (CST mobile)

We have developed some biofeedback software, the CardioSense Trainer™ (CST), which can be used on your computer, and the CST mobile™, which is an iPhone and iPad app for when you are on the go. Using a sensor that clips on your ear at one end and plugs into your PC or phone on the other, you can see what is happening to your heart rate variability. The software also has a breath pacer that you can follow to ensure that you can actually shift your heart rate from a chaotic signal into a coherent signal. These devices are designed to help you train your breathing pattern to generate greater levels of coherence and they are especially useful at the start of the journey toward Enlightened Leadership because they provide a visual guide to what your heart is doing right now. Plus it allows you to experience just how much control you can have over your heart beat and how different it can feel when you achieve coherence.

Although we've been measuring HRV since 1996 it never ceases to amaze me how dramatic this information can be for people. I've literally seen grown men cry when they realize that they can in fact control their own response to pressure and see the immediate effect correct breathing can have on their system and how easy it is to generate coherence when you know how to do it. Suddenly, they have access to a skill that can change something they didn't think they could change.

Hierarchy of practice

So the starting point for getting your system under control is to get your breathing under control. Don't underestimate its power or how quickly the skill can desert you when you need it most. It is important therefore to practise this breathing skill. You need to gradually build up your ability to create and maintain physiological coherence in increasingly difficult situations.

Start by practising alone with your eyes closed and work up the hierarchy of practice (Figure 2.14) until you can use the technique successfully in open conflict.

Using CST and the breath pacer to guide you, you should be able to generate a coherent pattern within a couple of minutes. We have used this with children as young as three years old and people as old as 80 years with equal success. People often ask: how much should I practise? My answer is that you cannot overdose on correct breathing but do not obsess about it because the obsession will make your breathing chaotic again! Instead, simply practise whenever you remember. Use any 'dead' time you have such as waiting to board an airplane or travelling to and from work. If you find just 10 minutes a day to practise this BREATHE skill then rhythmic breathing and physiological coherence will soon become your default pattern. When it does you will discover that you are much less reactive and likely to 'fly off the handle' than you were before. And you'll have much more energy. Plus once you have your breathing under control you can start to develop your emotional coherence and get the whole orchestra playing in tune.

FIGURE 2.14   The hierarchy of breathing practice

10	Open conflict
9	Someone is <u>really</u> annoying you
8	Someone is annoying you
7	Someone is niggling you
6	You are talking back
5	You are listening
4	Someone is talking to you
3	In company Eyes Open
2	Alone Eyes Open
1	Alone Eyes Closed

Physiological coherence facilitates emotional coherence

Enlightened Leadership emerges when we develop coherence across all the various critical internal and external lines of development (Figure 2.15) – each one strengthening and facilitating the next. In this chapter we have explored the first internal line of development – physiology.

FIGURE 2.15   Lines of development

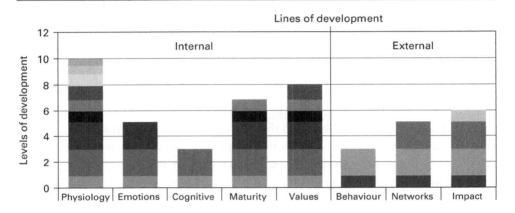

The reason we start with physiology is very simple – if we don't have enough energy it won't matter how smart our strategy is or how innovative our new ideas; they won't all be executed because we'll run out of steam. It is possible for us to have the energy levels we enjoyed 10 years ago! It is possible for us to end the day with as much energy as we had when we started and massively increase our energy levels, vitality and performance as a result. But in order to unlock our potential we must first stabilize our physiology and that is primarily achieved through correct breathing and paying attention to what adds to and drains our energy reserves.

At Complete Coherence we work with some of the best CEOs and senior executives from around the world. We measure their raw energy and energy efficiency using our Leadership Energy Profile (LEP), which consists of a 24-hour analysis of their HRV plus a salivary hormone analysis. This type of profiling is very powerful in generating highly specific insights into leadership and performance. The information generated does not form part of any standard 'corporate medical'. Most of the data gathered from the standard medical, as evidenced by the Don Simpson story, is not very helpful and is largely commercially irrelevant. The LEP is extremely commercially relevant. The HRV assessment quantifies how much energy a business leader has in his or her tank and how efficiently they are using the fuel they have. We also simultaneously assess, through salivary hormone analysis, the amount of cortisol and DHEA in their blood stream to reveal the levels of the performance hormones.

The other reason we start with physiology is that we believe there are 52 separate conversations we could have with a leader as part of their leadership development programme. The physiological profiling helps us to identify the most useful and relevant conversations for that particular leader so they get the biggest wins in the quickest time.

Certainly when energy is flagged as an issue, the executives we work with experience an average improvement of 25–30 per cent within just six months (Watkins *et al*, 2013). Considering we lose 3 per cent per year from 25 years old onward, that is equivalent to giving these leaders the energy levels they had 8–10 years ago!

By increasing our physical intelligence, we move vertically up the first line of adult development. Physiological coherence is the platform on which health, happiness, smart thinking, improved performance, better relationships and greater influence is built. Learning to be aware of our energy reserves and how to breathe properly to protect them, harness them and recuperate our energy is therefore the critical first step to complete coherence and Enlightened Leadership, and it is physiological coherence that facilitates emotional coherence, which we will explore next.

Summary of key points

If you don't remember everything in this chapter, remember this:

- Energy management is much more important than time management.
- Energy is created automatically in the body mainly by the heart, which is the body's primary power station.
- Your heart produces 40 to 60 times more electrical power and 5,000 times more electromagnetic power than the brain, which makes it by far the 'biggest pendulum' in your biological system, capable of aligning and synchronizing all other systems to create physiological coherence.

- As part of Complete Coherence's unique approach to leadership and executive development we have been quantifying the energy levels of leaders and executives in many market sectors since 1996.

- The best way to ascertain how much 'fuel' someone has in their tank and how efficiently they are using that fuel is to measure their heart rate variability (HRV) over the course of 24 hours.

- This HRV assessment, which measures the distance between each heart beat, not the beat itself, allows us to pinpoint critical areas of business performance and productivity such as endurance, motivation, recuperation, effort, balance, optimism and vitality.

- HRV is an incredibly insightful metric, which can quantify the risk of death and illness, reveal biological age, quantify energy levels and dynamism and illuminate brain function.

- It is possible to improve HRV, and creating cardiac coherence is done through the simple BREATHE technique.

- When we train our heart via correct breathing we generate a coherent signal instead of a chaotic one, which in turn increases energy levels, reduces energy wastage, improves health and enhances brain function.

- Coherent breathing is like motorway driving – we travel further, using less fuel and there is less wear and tear on our system, so we turn the clock back to gain the energy levels we had 10 years ago and feel much younger.

Be healthier and happier

03

> *Do you find it weird that health and happiness is even being discussed in a leadership book? Do you never even think about your own physical well-being unless you are feeling ill or especially run down? If you are aware of your own health do you still find it almost impossible to find the energy or motivation to do anything about it? Has your weight crept up over the years? Do you hear stories of CEO collapse, exhaustion and heart attacks thinking it will never happen to you? Do you think these incidents are rare or media exaggerations? Are you still enjoying your work or is it just a hard grind? Is the big salary really worth the pain? Do you even have time to enjoy that money or is the work relentless? Do you often wake up in the middle of the night worrying about work and unable to get back to sleep? Do you feel permanently under pressure, undervalued and stressed but simply accept it as the price you have to pay for your position? If so, you're not alone.*

In business two things happen when it comes to health and well-being – either we completely ignore it, assuming it's irrelevant to business success and performance, or we know it's important but don't have the time or inclination to do anything about it.

Commercial life is bruising, the pressure is unrelenting and yet most CEOs and business leaders do not have the time to address the health implications of their lifestyle. Most simply dismiss the stories they read such as Lloyds Banking Group CEO António Horta-Osório stepping down for six weeks' stress leave as a 'one off' or an 'exception'. They are not. The founder of JD Wetherspoon, Tim Martin, took a sudden six-month sabbatical before returning to the pub chain in April 2004 as non-executive chairman, working three days a week. Former Barclays chief executive John Varley left Barclays for one year in 1994 because he was 'feeling quite worn out' and 'needed to do something different', and Jeff Kindler of Pfizer resigned as chief executive of the US pharmaceutical giant to 'recharge [his] batteries' (Treanor, 2011).

In the last decade there have been more and more cases of people keeling over at their desks. In Japan, they even have a term for it – *karoshi*, which literally translates as 'death from overwork'. In China this phenomenon is known as *guolaosi* and countless examples of sudden death through overwork are being reported. And most disturbingly of all according to statistics published by the China Association for the Promotion of Physical Health, at least a million people in China are dying from overwork every year (Liaowang Eastern Weekly, 2006; Birchall, 2011).

Apart from the health, social and emotional cost involved, this can also be extremely detrimental to the business. If a key member of the team drops down dead or needs to take time off to recuperate following a serious illness, then clearly there are long- or short-term succession issues and the loss will be felt in the team, and on the profit and loss account. Conversely when individuals at any level are healthy and happy at work they are much more likely to unlock discretionary effort that can have a profoundly positive impact on results.

If we are not paying attention to our health then we are almost certainly eroding it. We may all think we know what to do to improve our health but it never seems quite enough to push us into consistent action. Instead our lives are characterized by coffee-laden mornings and boozy nights. Often we don't even want to speak to anyone until we've had our double espresso or macchiato hit. And at the end of the day we choose to unwind with a glass of whisky or a stiff gin and tonic. A few years ago it was 'just the one' but these days it's always two and sometimes more.

We still dream of our two weeks in the sun – if only so we can put the guilt on hold and convince ourselves that we'll get serious about the changes we know we need to make when we get home. Only they never happen. Life just keeps getting in the way.

Looking back on our life and career there were some really great experiences – pay rises, product releases, profit targets reached, promotions and bonuses that felt great at the time. But those feelings of success and euphoria never seemed to last. Whatever the achievement, time soon normalized it and the treadmill began again. Besides, happiness has no real place in modern business. But how we feel on a daily basis is not just some touchy feely idea; it is probably one of the most important factors that determine our most prized asset – our health.

There is a growing interest amongst scientists and physicians in the concept of coherence and its implications for health (Ho, Popp and Warnke, 1994). As renowned sociology and expert in stress, health and well-being Aaron Antonovsky said, 'We are coming to understand health not as the absence of disease, but rather as the process by which individuals maintain their sense of coherence (ie, sense that life is comprehensible, manageable, and meaningful) and ability to function in the face of changes in themselves and their relationships with their environment' (Antonovsky, 1987).

So what impacts health and happiness? Well, it's probably not what you think... There is now a considerable amount of scientific data showing that mismanaged emotion is the root cause. Mismanaged emotion is the 'superhighway' to disease and distress. Your emotions not only determine whether you are likely to become ill and how happy you feel but also determine whether you will do a good job and get promoted.

The three big Es

According to the adage, 'You are what you eat.' But such statements do not really recognize the profound sophistication of the human body to adapt and work with what it is given. It is amazing how well people can function despite a very poor diet. Don't get me wrong; I am a big believer in nutritional discipline and the importance of optimizing what we eat in order to enhance energy, avoid bloating and stay trim. But we can, excuse the pun, overcook the importance of food. And, for the record, taking additional nutritional supplements won't make much difference either because the body is often unable or unlikely to absorb most of their goodness anyway. Essentially, most supplements leave the body in much the same condition they went into the body so we are literally pouring money down the toilet! The gut is an incredibly complicated and interconnected ecosystem that is influenced and affected by the delicate balance of flora and fauna in our intestines, levels of circulating trace elements and the chemical balance in our system. It's unrealistic to assume that bulk-manufactured supplements will deliver the right nutrients to the right systems at the right time in the right composition to make any significant difference. Eating high-quality food is by far the best way to get the nutrients we need.

Exercise is also important and I would certainly go to the gym every day if I weren't so busy. The benefits of a regular workout are legion particularly if we are doing an exercise we love, which in my case is rowing. But there is something that in my view trumps the benefits of eating (the first 'Big E') and exercise (the second 'Big E'), and that is emotion or the third 'Big E'.

We exercise perhaps up to five times a week, if at all. We eat two or three, perhaps four times a day. Emotions, on the other hand are affecting us every second of every day. They also largely determine whether we can be bothered to exercise, and what, when and how much we eat. As psychiatrist and pioneer in the field of psychosomatic medicine Dr Franz Alexander said 'Many chronic disturbances are not caused by external, mechanical, chemical factors, or by microorganisms, but by the continual functional stress arising from the everyday life of the organism in its struggle for existence' (Alexander, 1939).

I appreciate that the idea of emotions being more important than exercise and eating may come as a bit of a surprise. Despite considerable scientific research documenting the connection between health and emotions, few business leaders take it seriously. If it's not immediately dismissed as 'new-age happy-clappy' fiction, the 'health piece' is delegated to their chief medical officer or their occupational health department. Some businesses may seek to 'tick the health box' by installing a gym or pool, and occasionally physiotherapists or gym instructors are employed, but the health and fitness of leaders and employees are largely seen as a private matter of individual choice.

Health and happiness are simply not considered commercially relevant. But surely when a high-profile leader collapses at his or her desk or needs to take extended sick leave – that's commercially relevant! When study after study proves categorically that happy, engaged employees work harder and longer, and provide significantly better customer service – that too is commercially relevant. Maybe it's time to put health and happiness on the business agenda – if for no other reason than to help unlock discretionary effort!

Health: the facts and the fiction

Most executives see health and happiness as a matter of personal choice or a conversation between them and their doctor. But are doctors the right people to turn to for guidance on health and happiness? As a medical doctor myself I can assure you that doctors are not trained in illness prevention or happiness; they are trained to treat illness and disease once it has become well established. If we want to be healthy and happy well into old age, we need to appreciate how medical thinking has changed over the years so we can separate the facts from the fiction.

Up until the mid-1940s there really wasn't that much in the way of effective medicine. If someone got toothache, pneumonia, meningitis or an STD, then they probably died from it because there were no antibiotics. As a result the biggest killer of both men and women was infectious disease. Although penicillin was discovered by Alexander Fleming in 1928 it wasn't purified and used as a mass-produced antibiotic until 1944 – during the Second World War. Antibiotics were phenomenally successful and most of what was killing us prematurely was eradicated almost overnight. A philosophy of 'the magic bullet' was born and scientific medicine started to hunt for single treatments that could eradicate complex multi-factorial diseases (Le Fanu, 1999).

For the first time in history we believed that we finally had the upper hand over disease, and the 'magic bullet' approach changed the nature of medical thinking. If we could discover a pill that could cure all these infectious diseases, then surely it was just a matter of time before we found a magic bullet for the other big killers such as heart disease and cancer. And health researchers moved en masse to find those magic bullets, initially turning their attention to heart disease, which, following the advent of readily available penicillin, had been promoted from the number two killer to the number one killer – a position it's maintained ever since (Townsend *et al*, 2012). In the developed world today, at least a third of all premature deaths, male and female, are caused by cardiovascular disease, which includes heart disease, hypertension and stroke (World Health Organization, 2011). Traditionally, women are often more concerned with breast cancer, but actually heart disease now kills up to 10 times more women than breast cancer (British Heart Foundation website; Society of Women's Health Research, nd).

The first sign of heart disease in 60 per cent of men is death (Society for Heart Attack Prevention and Eradication, 2013; News Medical, 2012). This stark statistic says much about people's ability to notice an imminent disaster. Many people are pressing on unaware of the impending doom. Doctors themselves are not necessarily any better at spotting the warning signs because they've been trained to spot symptoms, not warning signs. Traditional medical teaching rarely focuses on the anticipation of a crisis. Rather it tends to wait until the crisis has occurred and then attempt heroic intervention. Consequently, many people who suffer a heart attack simply did not see it coming, and neither did their physician. Most people believe that heart attacks or illnesses 'come out of the blue'. Of course they don't; most medical conditions have been brewing for months if not years. The main problem is we just don't see the signs or heed the signals.

In an attempt to change this so we could identify those early signs, and hopefully reduce mortality rates, the US government, specifically US health policy-makers, joined forces with the medical community to solve the mystery of heart disease by conducting a long-term research project into the causes of heart disease in an 'average' American. To do this they needed to identify 'anytown USA' that was representative of the US population (Lynch, 2000). The town they chose was Framingham.

Heart disease: the Framingham heart studies

At the time Framingham was a small, beautiful, leafy town of 28,000 working people, 20 miles from Boston. It was extremely stable socially – if someone was born in Framingham they usually lived and died there too. This was essential for the research because the study was going to monitor the health of 5,209 volunteers every two years for the next 50 years! It would have been extremely difficult to conduct this research if the subjects moved away and ended up being scattered across America. And so in 1948 a small army of medical scientists descended on the town, and research data into the causes of heart disease has been pouring out of the Framingham Heart Studies ever since. The longevity of the study and the depth of the data collected means that the findings at Framingham have influenced medical thinking in this area more than anything else – by far.

But as it turns out, Framingham was not 'anytown USA'. Because the researchers didn't know what they were looking for or what they would find, it didn't occur to them that Framingham wasn't actually representative of America. It was a small, mostly white, mostly middle-class town that enjoyed almost total employment. There was very little poverty; the divorce rate of 2 per cent was considerably lower than the national average at the time of 10 per cent. It was also incredibly socially cohesive – everyone knew everyone else in the town and there was strong social support. Framingham was – socially at least – nothing like inner city Detroit, Las Vegas or New York. And frankly, even if the researchers had realized this fact, there was absolutely no evidence to suggest these issues had any bearing on heart disease.

Ironically, the researchers had chosen a town that just happened to be naturally insulated from heart disease in the first place. As a result, the causes of heart disease in Framingham were never going to be the same as the causes of heart disease in inner city Detroit, Las Vegas, New York or just about any other large town or city in America. The researchers had inadvertently discounted a vast array of contributing factors that have struggled to become recognized as contributing factors ever since. Things like poverty, social inequality, low educational attainment, stress, social isolation, depression, anxiety and anger didn't even exist in Framingham! So of course they didn't find them.

It follows therefore that if many of the real driving forces for heart disease were absent from the research group, then what's left are the 'other', possibly less important, contributing factors for heart disease – high blood pressure, cholesterol, age, diabetes, smoking, obesity/lack of exercise, other medical conditions and family history. And it is these other 'causes' that have since been written into medical law as the 'traditional risk factors' for heart disease. The truth however is that over half of all the incidence of heart disease can't be explained by the standard physical risk factors (Rosenman, 1993). Doctors all over the world are scratching their heads because people are dying of heart disease every day even though they exhibit none of the so-called risk factors. The real reason they are dying is, largely, because of mismanaged emotions such as depression, anxiety, anger, hostility and cynicism brought on by poverty, social inequality, low educational attainment, stress and social isolation.

It wasn't that Framingham was some utopian nirvana where nothing went wrong and everyone was happy, it was just that when the inevitable knocks and bumps of life occurred the inhabitants of Framingham had strong social networks to help them through. Those types of networks are not always present in large, transient cities and these real risk factors are hugely important. Ironically Framingham inadvertently discovered the antidote for heart disease – healthy emotional management that is manifest through strong social bonds and social cohesion.

Don't get me wrong, the Framingham heart research has improved our understanding and treatment of heart disease considerably. The traditional risk factors are important but not as important as the social, educational, interpersonal or physiological factors that were almost entirely absent from Framingham.

In an effort to raise awareness of these critical but largely ignored causes of heart disease, Dr James Lynch went back and re-analysed all the data from Framingham. What he discovered was that when those original 5,209 volunteers aged between 30 and 62 were initially interviewed, the only in-formation that was gathered was medical – height, weight, blood pressure and a host of other physical factors. The researchers neglected to record any social, educational, interpersonal or physiological data at all, and yet those are the things that probably account for most of the 'inexplicable' cases of heart disease where no risk factors are present.

Whilst the Framingham Heart Studies have produced incredible insights into heart disease, they have also inadvertently caused the general public and medical professionals the world over to minimize or ignore the most important risk factors in heart disease – mismanaged emotions.

Depression

Everyone knows that smoking is bad for you and we are rightly bombarded with adverts telling us to stop smoking. Everyone knows that it is especially bad after someone's had a heart attack. In fact people are twice as likely to be dead within a year of their heart attack if they smoke. What is less well known however is that if a person is depressed after their heart attack they are four times as likely to be dead within one year (Glassman and Shapiro, 1998). But we don't see adverts telling us to 'Cheer up! Stop being so miserable – it's killing you!'

Some doctors, aware of the significant link between depression and heart attack, have sought to treat heart attack patients with anti-depressants. Whilst sensible and often brave, this hasn't always worked because the current treatment options of Cognitive Behaviour Therapy (CBT) or drugs only make a difference to some patients (Antonuccio *et al*, 1995). As a result the medical profession has often wrongly concluded that depression is not a big deal when it comes to heart disease. It is just that the current treatments don't address the root cause of depression, which is mismanaged emotion.

Depression is on the increase and according to a recent global analysis project, if current trends continue, depression will be the second greatest disease burden by the year 2020 and the first by 2030 (Murray and Lopez, 1996). It is now estimated that 350 million people globally are affected by depression (World Federation for Mental Health, 2012).

Mismanaged emotions such as worry, hopelessness, anxiety and depression are seriously toxic. The Harvard School of Public Health conducted a 20-year study on the effects of worry on 1,750 men. Researchers found that worrying about typical issues such as social conditions, health and personal finances – something most of us are familiar with – all significantly increased the risk of developing coronary heart disease (Kubzansky *et al*, 1997). In fact, hopelessness in middle-aged men is as detrimental to cardiovascular health as smoking a pack of cigarettes a day (Everson *et al*, 1997).

Anxiety, worry and panic have also been associated with diminished heart rate variability (HRV), which as you may remember from the previous chapter is a potent risk marker for heart disease and sudden cardiac death as well as 'all-cause mortality' (Dekker *et al*, 1997).

But these negative emotions are not just toxic for our physical health; they are having a considerable impact on our ability to be happy, content and fulfilled. Anxiety, hopelessness, worry, panic and even the vast majority of depression are caused primarily by our inability to regulate our own emotions. Please understand I'm not saying people who suffer from these negative emotions are making them up; I'm just saying the cause is not medical. The real problem is that, collectively, we have not been taught about emotion, how to differentiate between various emotions and how to manage them effectively. As children, when we were upset most of us were told to calm down, 'pull yourself together' and stop crying. Even if we were bursting with excitement or some other positive emotion we were told to calm down! We were never taught how to distinguish between upset and anger or anger and boredom or boredom and apathy, and even if we could tell the difference we were almost certainly not taught how to manage those emotions, take appropriate action or change the emotion.

As a result most people believe that emotion is something to be avoided or hidden. It's as though emotion is considered part of our childhood that must be shed like a beloved comfort blanket or favourite toy as part of the inevitable metamorphosis from emotional child to fully functioning adult. As a result we learn to ignore and suppress emotion and proceed into adulthood with a degree of emotional literacy that can differentiate between 'feeling good' and 'feeling bad' and little else. All the negative emotions congeal into 'bad' and all the positive emotions congeal into 'good'. If we experience more 'bad' emotion then 'good' emotion, then the 'bad' elongates into a negative mood that over time acts like grooves on an old LP record. The person then plays the same negative tune over and over again until it becomes an ingrained habit. The vast majority of people who are diagnosed with depression or anxiety disorders don't have a medical condition (yet); their record player has just got stuck playing the emotional record of anxiety or sadness and they don't know how to cut the power or change the record to something more upbeat and positive. And this is having a huge impact on individual happiness.

What's more, emotional and stress-related disorders significantly impair productivity. In one study depression was identified as the most common mental health condition, responsible for 79 per cent of all time lost at work – significantly more costly to the employer than physical disease (Burton *et al*, 1999).

Cancer

Cancer is currently the second biggest killer, responsible for about a third of all deaths in the developed world (Centers for Disease Control and Prevention, 2013). That means that heart disease and cancer collectively account for almost 70 per cent of all premature deaths! And negative emotion has been proven to drive both. Way back in 1870, Queen Victoria's physician and surgeon, Sir James Paget, stated, 'The cases are so frequent in which deep anxiety, deferred hope and disappointment are quickly followed by the growth and increase of cancer that we can hardly doubt that mental depression is a weighty addition to the other influences favouring the development of a cancerous constitution' (LeShan, 1977).

Since then the evidence has been mounting and there is now significant robust scientific data that demonstrates the clear link between psychological factors and the development of tumours (Grossarth-Maticek, 1980; Pettingale *et al*, 1981; Levy *et al*, 1988). So much so that it has been said, 'the data are now so strong that [they] can no longer be ignored by those wishing to sustain a scientific attitude towards the cancer field' (Bolletino and LeShan, 1997). There is now zero doubt that the superhighway to disease, including cancer, is mismanaged emotions.

The big questions regarding cancer have been: 'Can we predict who gets cancer?' and 'Can we predict who is then going to survive cancer?' And in most cases, the answer to both these questions is a resounding 'YES!' (Nabi *et al*, 2008).

There was, for example, a large-scale Scandinavian trial that sought to correlate emotional outlook to cancer by researching subjects in their 50s and 60s, which is the age people tend to get cancer, and cross-referencing their results to their university entrance exams. So the researchers went back to these people's university psychometric tests to see if there was anything about those people in their early 20s that would correlate to their propensity to get cancer 30 or 40 years later. Studying over 25,000 people they discovered that there was a direct correlation – those who were negative when they were 20 and who had remained perpetually negative throughout their life were the ones that were more likely to develop cancer (Eysenck, 1993).

Phychologist and the 'Father of Positive Psychology' Dr Martin Seligman and two colleagues studied members of the Harvard graduating classes of 1939 to 1944 (Goleman, 1987). Following their return from the Second World War, the men were interviewed about their war experiences and physically examined every five years. Where the post-war interviews indicated that individuals had been optimistic in college, their emotional disposition directly correlated to better health in later life. Seligman stated that, 'The men's explanatory style at age 25 predicted their health at 65,' adding 'Around age 45 the health of the pessimists started to deteriorate more quickly.' People's explanatory style impacts how they explain the inevitable ups and downs of life to themselves, which in turn influences their behaviour and performance. For example, pessimists interpret a failed exam or missed promotion as though it were a permanent reflection of their own personal failings that will infect all areas of their life. Optimists, who have greater emotional intelligence, will look at the same event or situation and see it as temporary, fixable and only confined to the area it originally affected.

If we are negative, if we feel that we can't control our destiny, if we feel put upon and internalize our frustrations instead of talking about them and finding solutions then, to quote Woody Allen, we 'will grow a tumour'. Emotional distress can influence the incidence and progression of cancer (Kiecolt-Glaser *et al*, 1985).

The locus of control

Our emotional well-being is also significantly influenced by how much control we feel in our lives. The original Whitehall Study (Marmot, 1991) conducted by principal investigator Sir Professor Michael Marmot discovered that there was a strong association between the ability to control our own destiny and mortality rates. After studying over 18,000 men working in the British Civil Service, Marmot found that the civil servants employed at the lowest grades or levels such as messengers and doorkeepers were three times more likely to die than those employed in the top grades or levels such as administrators. Even when Marmot controlled for the traditional risk factors, he found that those at the bottom of the organizational ladder were still twice as likely to die as those at the top. Whilst the stress may have been more significant at the top, those individuals also had more control over their day.

Ellen Langer, Professor of Psychology at Harvard, conducted a now famous study with colleague Judith Rodin in the 1970s that also demonstrated the connection between mortality and control. Nursing home residents were split into two groups. The first group were encouraged to find ways to make more decisions for themselves. They were for example allowed to choose a houseplant for their room and it was their responsibility to care for the plant. They could also choose when they had visitors or when they watched a movie. The idea was to encourage this group of residents to become more mindful and engage with the world and their own lives more fully. The second group did not receive these instructions and were not encouraged to do anything differently. They were given a houseplant but the nursing staff chose the plant, decided where it would sit in their room and took responsibility for watering the plant. Based on a variety of tests conducted at the start of the experiment and then again 18 months later, members from the first group were more cheerful, active and healthier. What was however more surprising was that less than half as many residents from the engaged group who could demonstrate personal control had died compared with those who had no control (Langer, 2010). Langer stated, 'The message is clear – those who do not feel in control of their lives are less successful, and less psychologically and physically healthy, than those who do feel in control.'

How this works biologically is that if someone is negative or feels as though they have limited control over their life, their body creates more cortisol and cortisol suppresses the immune system. We all, for example, generate cancer cells in our body every day but if someone is cheerful, positive and emotionally coherent most of the time, then their immune system will simply flush out those potentially problematic cancer cells as part of its normal function. This doesn't happen if someone is perpetually miserable or emotionally incoherent. Once cortisol levels have suppressed the immune system over a long period of time, the cancer cells are not adequately disposed of by the poorly functioning immune system and instead they can take hold and develop into cancer.

The emotional component is also critical for cancer survival, as evidenced by a very famous study conducted by David Spiegel and psychiatrist Fawzy I Fawzy, who recruited 86 women with advanced metastatic breast cancer of similar age. All the women received the same medical care but two-thirds were randomly assigned to group meetings of one and a half hours per week for a year. As a result these women had the opportunity to get together and talk to each other and share the difficulties they experienced firsthand, discuss their treatment, laugh and cry together through their mutually harrowing experience. The other third was the 'control' group and they only received the medical treatment.

Logic and common sense alone would suggest that those with social support probably did better – after all 'a problem shared is a problem halved.' But the results were nothing short of remarkable. The women with the social support reported less pain and lived 18 months longer than the control group, which effectively doubled their life expectancy (Watkins, 1997). So even if someone gets cancer, whether they survive or not is massively influenced by their emotional well-being and whether or not they have access to social and emotional support.

Happiness: the facts and the fiction

Whilst conceptually health and happiness may mean very different things, especially to busy executives who don't consider either terribly relevant to quarterly results, in practical daily life it's virtually impossible to separate health from happiness – the two are inextricably linked. When someone has the 'giving-up–given-up complex' (Engel, 1968) or experiences 'the emotional eclipse of the heart' (Purcell and Mulcahy, 1994), their gloomy expectation and negativity will facilitate a host of negative consequences – physically and mentally. Those that are more optimistic or are at least able to manage their emotions and use their feelings to initiate constructive action to solve their problems are almost always healthier and live longer, happier, more contented lives. That fact is unequivocal.

Interestingly, the scientific literature on the negative consequences of emotions is about 10 times larger than the evidence on the beneficial effects of positive emotions. Psychology and psychiatry, for example, are almost exclusively focused on dysfunction, studying it and treating it respectively. In fact, for decades, it was widely considered 'a career-limiting move' or academically inappropriate to research happiness or elevated performance from an emotional perspective.

Thankfully 'positive psychology' has gathered pace over the last 30 years and we now realize that we can actively alter our emotional outlook, which in turn can enhance our immune system and increase our protection and resilience against disease and illness. We also now realize that positive emotions that make us feel happy, contented and confident can be learnt, practised and incorporated into our daily lives. For years we were told that happiness and positivity were largely genetic – we were either born optimistic or we were born pessimistic. It's not true. Optimists may have won the 'cortical lottery' (Haidt, 2006) because they habitually look on the bright side and more easily find the silver linings, but this ability is open to all of us. Thanks to research giants such as Abraham Maslow, Aaron Antonovsky, James W Pennebaker, Tal Ben-Shahar, Dean Ornish, Martin Seligman and Mihaly Csikszentmihalyi amongst others, we now understand that our emotional outlook is not fixed as a permanent set point but rather that we each have a range. Whether we view the glass as half-empty or half-full can be significantly altered through emotional coherence and self-management so that we habitually operate at the top end of that emotional range.

When crisis strikes – and it does for everyone at some point in life – most people will deal with crisis in one of three main ways. They will get into action and fix the problem (active coping), reappraise the situation (engage in inner emotional and cognitive work to find the silver lining) or avoid the problem (engage in distraction tactics such as alcohol or drugs so they can forget or blunt the emotional reaction) (Carver, Scheier and Weintraub, 1989; Lazarus and Folkman, 1984).

In the 1970s Holmes and Rahe developed the stress scale as a way to correlate difficult, traumatic or stressful 'life events' so we could better understand the effects of these events on health and happiness. Of course it was also hoped that these insights would lead to a way to help people find the right coping strategy for crisis.

Holmes and Rahe found that if someone experienced several life events such as divorce, death of a loved one, redundancy or moving house, they would be more susceptible to physical illness, disease or depression. And this became medical 'fact'. But the 'evidence' that proved this 'fact' also clearly demonstrated something else... Some individuals were experiencing a great many of these major life events and yet they were not adversely affected, mentally or physically, over the longer term. Clearly it was not the life event that predicted illness but rather the way the individual responded to those events and what they made them mean.

The active ingredient is what is known as post-traumatic growth – the ability to find something positive and beneficial out of even the most difficult experiences. This is not optimism or pessimism per se, but the ability to manage emotion and manage meaning. Social psychologist Jamie Pennebaker's work has shown that the event isn't the issue; what matters is what happens after the event and what the individual makes the event mean to them as a person and their future life (Pennebaker, 1997).

When people were able to express themselves emotionally and talk about what happened within social networks or strong relationships they were largely spared the damaging effects of trauma to physical and mental well-being. (Remember this when we explore the potent impact of positive relationships for personal and professional success in Chapter 6.) Those with greater emotional coherence were also better able to put a cognitive frame around the event that allowed them to make sense of what happened and move on.

How we view the world is not set in stone. We may not always have control over situations or events but we always have control over how we interpret them, what we do about them and what we make them mean.

From a business perspective it has also been found that those who are mentally healthy and happy have a higher degree of 'vertical coherence' among their goals and aspirations (Sheldon and Kasser, 1995). In other words they have dovetailed their short-term goals into their medium-term and long-term goals so that everything they do fits together and pulls them toward a future they want. I would go so far as to extend this definition of 'vertical coherence' to include coherence within all the areas of vertical development – especially, in this context, emotions.

Vicious cycles caused by mismanaged emotions

Clearly it's not the event or situation that impacts the outcome; it's what happens emotionally as a result of those events and situations that really makes the difference between life and death, success and failure, happiness and misery. This is the distinction that is so often missing in modern medicine.

Earlier I said that the real risks of heart disease were not so much the widely publicized traditional risks of blood pressure, cholesterol, diabetes etc but the relatively unknown social, educational, interpersonal or physiological risks such as poverty, social inequality, low educational attainment, stress, social isolation, depression, anxiety and anger. These things in and of themselves won't necessarily kill us, but what these things do to our biology can.

Low educational attainment doesn't cause heart disease but it usually leads to poverty because the individual doesn't have the knowledge, skills or self-confidence to earn a decent living, and that creates poverty. But even then it's still not the poverty that is creating the heart disease; it's the fact that poverty usually creates emotional distress, worry and pressure – especially if that person has a family to support. If the poverty creates emotional incoherence in the physiology then it is probably experienced as worry, panic, anxiety and depression. The person may feel worthless, helpless and socially isolated, which further suppresses the immune system and increases cortisol levels even more, thus laying the body wide open to a host of diseases, of which heart disease and cancer are just two.

One of commonest feelings that people live with is that they are 'not enough': that they are deficient in some way or there is something lacking in the world around them. These feelings of deficiency may be personalized into 'I am not a good enough husband/wife, father/mother or friend.' Women often specialize in feeling bad about their physicality: 'I am too fat' or 'my (insert appropriate body part) is too big or too small.' Men's specialist inadequacy is often centred on their ability to provide, or their strengths and physical ability. Why don't I have a six pack, or better biceps? Many people don't feel good about themselves and lead lives of quiet desperation. Whether their backside looks big in those jeans or not is largely irrelevant; it's what that observation does to the person's physiology that screws up their health and happiness. In the same way it's not actually the chocolate cake that makes someone unhealthy, or the fact that they didn't go to the gym again this week – what's doing the most damage is the self-flagellation, guilt, self-disgust and remorse they feel after eating the chocolate cake or not going to the gym again. That's what's really doing the damage. It's important to understand that how we feel about what we're doing often has a much bigger effect on health and happiness than what we are actually doing.

Take exercise for example. One of the primary benefits of exercise is determined by the way someone feels about the exercise. If you force yourself to go to the gym but don't really enjoy it, then your body will react catabolically and you will be operating from the negative side of the performance grid. In other words your workout will be breaking your body down, not building it up. In contrast, if you love going to the gym the exercise will provoke an anabolic response and will be much more beneficial to you because you're operating from the positive side of the performance grid (Figure 3.1) and you're building your body up. In our coaching work we've seen many individuals who are exercising regularly but still have poor physiology, and when we have changed their exercise regime to incorporate routines that are much more enjoyable their physiology has improved significantly.

Remember, what we eat and how often we exercise are relevant to optimal health but they are nowhere near as relevant as we've been led to believe.

FIGURE 3.1   The performance grid

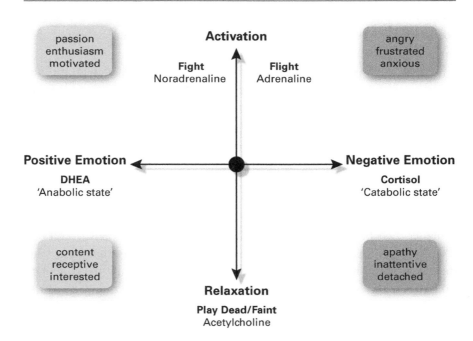

Emotion is the elephant in the room. When we understand emotion and create emotional coherence so that we can differentiate between the various emotional tunes our body is playing and behave appropriately, then our health and happiness will improve dramatically.

The simple unequivocal fact about health and happiness is that emotion is the active ingredient, and developing emotional coherence will not only make you more productive but just might save your life.

Emotions and feelings: the critical difference

Most people, including medical professionals, use the words 'emotion' and 'feeling' as interchangeable terms, believing they are essentially the same thing. They are not.

Going back to the integrated performance model (Figure 1.1) – physiology is just the raw data or the biological 'notes' that our body is playing. Emotion is the integration of all the various physiological signals or 'notes' into a tune. In contrast, a feeling is the awareness and recognition in our mind of the tune that is being played by your physical body. Or as neuroscientist Joseph LeDoux suggests, feelings are merely the 'observation' of the emotion (Coates, 2013).

These 'notes' are quite literally energy (E) in motion (e-motion). The human system is a multi-layered integrated hierarchy in a state of constant flux, with each system – heart, lungs, kidneys, liver, brain – playing a tune that contributes to the overall score of the orchestra. Our body is always playing a tune, whether we are aware of that tune or can recognize it or not. When we become aware of the tune that all our bodily systems are playing then we are 'feeling' the e-motion. Emotion is, therefore, the link between biology and behaviour – a fact not lost on Henry Maxey, CEO of Ruffer Investment Hedge Fund. Ruffer is an independent and privately-owned investment management firm employing over 160 people, with offices in London, Edinburgh and Hong Kong. When we interviewed Henry on his experiences with Enlightened Leadership he said:

> The whole profession is about perceptions... Because it's about perceptions, human behaviour plays a huge part, hence the importance of understanding the real drivers of behaviour, namely emotions. Since emotions play such a huge part in this job it's very helpful to have some understanding of them, your emotional state and how that's influencing your behaviour when you're interacting with markets.

Learning how to create greater emotional coherence has therefore been extremely valuable. Henry was one of the very few analysts to predict the credit market collapse of 2007, successfully moving his client's investments ahead of the turmoil and massively enhancing his firm's reputation and profile as a result. You can read Henry's case study at **www.coherence-book.com**.

Making the distinction between emotions and feelings may seem like semantics but it's an absolutely crucial differentiation because it suddenly resolves so much of people's misunderstanding about how we function. Moreover, differentiation is the second critical step in the evolution of anything, so if we want to develop as human beings we must elevate our ability to differentiate between different emotions, between emotions and feelings and feeling and thoughts. For us to develop as business leaders we need to improve our ability to differentiate things that are not traditionally thought of as related to business – human biology and human nature. Most of which isn't even given a cursory nod in business school. And yet the benefits of this knowledge are phenomenal. When leaders, senior executives and employees understand that emotions and feelings are completely different phenomena, it enables them to learn how to control both and ultimately build better relationships with customers and colleagues alike.

There is little doubt that some individuals have already learnt a degree of emotional 'self-control' or at least they think they have. However, such self-regulation often only extends to the control of the more obvious manifestations of body language rather than the emotional energy itself. For example, an individual may be able to conceal the fact that he is feeling angry or is desperately unhappy. He may be able to stop himself from lashing out at a colleague or bursting into tears in a meeting, but this is usually no more than gross control of body language. It might look like he's 'got his act together' but inside his body he is still experiencing the negative consequences of those negative emotional signals whether he actually feels the feeling or expresses those feelings or not. In other words it might look like he's listening to Beethoven, and he may even be able to kid himself that his body is playing Beethoven, but his physiology is still reacting to what's really going on – thrash metal at full volume.

Going back to our orchestra metaphor again, underneath the external façade of 'controlled emotions' is a vast number of individual musicians, each playing different 'notes' or sending subtle (and not so subtle) signals around the body. An examination of these uncontrolled signals can be a very revealing window on the underlying emotional state that is currently impacting the individual. Few people recognize, let alone control, the fine emotional nuances of their physiological orchestra.

And sophisticated control does not mean simply throwing a blanket over the whole orchestra; it means knowing how and when to allow the expression of each musician within the orchestra and how to bring coherence to the tune being played so as to create something genuinely astonishing. When we learn genuine control over our emotional repertoire then we alter our physiology and this can literally protect us from the illness and disease caused by mismanaged emotions. It can also protect us from poor decision making.

The business impact of conditioning

Shifts in our emotion can be triggered by the perception of anything external to us or by internal thoughts or memories. Most of what we perceive with our senses does not reach conscious awareness. We already know for example that the central nervous system is only capable of processing a tiny fraction of what it could be aware of via the five senses. The retina transmits data at 10 million bits per second, our other senses process one million bits per second and only 40 (not 40 million) bits per second reach consciousness (Coates, 2013). Our subconscious mind, ie the mind that is busy doing stuff we don't have to think about like pumping blood or digesting food, is capable of processing 20 million environmental stimuli per second versus the rather puny 40 environmental stimuli that our conscious mind is processing (Norretranders, 1998).

So not only are we privy to a vast amount of data we are never consciously aware of but, because of a process called conditioning, any one of those millions of external cues could trigger an emotion that alters our behaviour or decision making without us knowing why.

The way we respond to the world around us is largely determined by unconscious emotional programming buried deep in our brain. Our mind is 'conditioned' to respond to the external world super-fast. So we are often unaware of our own emotional triggers and we may also lack awareness of the emotion itself, making it virtually impossible to distinguish between real external data and potentially erroneous data supplied by an outdated conditioned response.

Conditioning is an automatic survival and learning mechanism that starts soon after we are born and long before we are able to speak. The purpose of this automatic response is to evaluate threats to our survival and trigger a response that keeps us alive. And it's made possible by the body's emotional early-warning system – the amygdala.

Neuroscientist Joseph LeDoux from the Center for Neural Science at New York University was one of the first academics to highlight the key role – and shortcomings – of the amygdala in decision making. It is the amygdala that is often to blame when, feeling threatened, we blurt out something stupid in a meeting or get caught off guard by a journalist. In certain situations, the old maxim 'think before you act' is actually a biological impossibility.

Before LeDoux's research it was thought that the sensory signals received via the five senses travelled first to the thalamus, where they were translated into the language of the brain. Most of the message then travelled to the neocortex so an appropriate response could be initiated. If there was an emotional component to those signals, a further signal was then passed from the neocortex to the amygdala for emotional perspective but the neocortex was considered to be the boss. We now know that this is completely incorrect.

Instead there is a neural emergency exit connecting the thalamus to the amygdala, which means that a smaller portion of the original message goes directly across a single synapse to the amygdala – bypassing the thinking brain altogether and initiating action before the rational brain even knows what's going on. This allows for a faster response when our survival may be threatened. And all this happens in a fraction of a second below conscious awareness, and what becomes an emotional trigger largely comes down to individual conditioning.

Human beings are born with only two fears – falling and loud noises. Everything else, whether that is fear of failure, fear of success, fear of death, clowns, heights or spiders, we've learnt from someone else or from experience. As we grow up, we absorb a massive amount of information largely through conditioning and there are two types of conditioned learning. If we burn our hand on a hotplate we don't ever do it again because the experience is sufficiently painful that the conditioning is immediate. Such experiences are called single-trial conditioning and, as the name would suggest, they teach us very quickly. When an experience is painful, either physically or emotionally, then we can learn that lesson with only a single exposure to the event or situation.

However, most learning is not that intense and involves 'multiple-trial learning' where we have to repeat the experience over and over again until it becomes a conditioned reflex or response. It was famous physiologist Ivan Pavlov who first discovered this innate biological response.

Working with dogs, Pavlov noticed that if he gave his dogs food while also making a sound such as blowing a whistle or ringing a bell, then over time the dogs would make an association between the two separate stimuli (being fed and the sound of the bell). With repetition it was therefore possible to get the dogs to salivate just by ringing the bell. Clearly there is no logical connection between salivating and the sound of a bell, and this highlights the often inaccurate and unsophisticated nature of the conditioning process. It matches stimuli that don't necessarily belong together and the subsequent presence of one or more of those stimuli can then trigger an emotional response that doesn't match the situation.

Part of the reason conditioning is so inaccurate is that the system is designed around survival not sophistication. A conditioned response is often blunt and can mean that we occasionally use a sledgehammer to crack a nut. Say someone ate a poisonous mushroom as a child and was violently ill for 24 hours; the conditioned response to that event would have been single exposure and the child's brain would have immediately scanned the situation to establish the characteristic of the event so as to ensure it never happened again. Even after the child grows up and learns that there are many different types of mushrooms that are tasty they probably won't ever eat mushrooms again, even if they don't remember the mushroom incident that created the conditioning in the first place. Their rational, intelligent adult brain will not be able to override the 'danger-danger' siren that is being set off by the amygdala to save them from eating a dodgy mushroom. The amygdala's mission is to detect danger. Precision decision making is the domain of the frontal cortex but the amygdala engages far faster than the frontal cortex. Plus, when we are making all these early pairings through the process of conditioning, our frontal lobes are not fully developed, which further reinforces the inaccuracy of the conditioning process.

The amygdala has a comparative function that means that it is constantly comparing current reality with all previous experience from the day we were born. So every new incident, event or situation is unconsciously compared to all the data we possess to ascertain if there is any danger. So every new client we meet, or every executive we interview for a position, will be compared to everyone in our amygdala's vast rolodex of names and events to see if there are any correlations that could spell trouble. And if it finds a match the amygdala will trigger a biological response that will cause us to get nervous, irritated or uncomfortable in some way. If we don't have a sophisticated understanding and awareness of the emotional signals created by our body, then we can miss these messages or completely misinterpret them. Neither is great. With greater emotional awareness, literacy and self-management, we are better able to avoid poor decisions based on imprecise interpretation of a conditioned response we don't remember, a response that has absolutely no real bearing on current reality. Conditioning acts like the strings on a puppet and emotion pulls the strings. The trouble is, we think we are pulling the strings based on rational, verifiable data – we're not. Without conscious intervention, a huge number of our so-called 'decisions' are actually subliminal, amygdala-based knee-jerk reactions to long-forgotten events, designed to protect us from things we are scared of or have been trained to be scared of. And it's all happening below conscious awareness.

Imagine four-year-old William has colic and doesn't sleep for more than 20 minutes at a time. This goes on for weeks on end and his parents are at the end of their tether. Exhausted and bewildered William's mother finally loses her temper one evening and screams at William, 'For God sake go to sleep!' Of course that makes William scream even louder because he feels threatened – his primary carer is angry and he senses danger to his survival. William's amygdala then springs into action and goes into situation assessment mode so that it can log all the features and characteristics of the moment for future reference so that he can avoid this type of threat in the future. For example, his amygdala might log that his mum is wearing a yellow shirt, that his favourite blanket is on the floor not in his cot and that the bedside light is on. So William's amygdala stores upset = yellow shirt = dropped blanket = light. It's pre-verbal so this isn't conscious or stored as words, but that's essentially the message.

Fast forward 50 years and William is a CEO interviewing candidates for a new commercial director position. It's late afternoon in winter and as William's secretary shows the last candidate into his office she flicks on the light and a man in a yellow shirt walks in. William immediately feels uncomfortable. What he doesn't appreciate is that his amygdala has matched 'light' and 'yellow shirt' and triggered an emotional response even though he has no conscious memory of the colic episode. Assuming William is not emotionally literate he will take an instant dislike to the candidate and dismiss him immediately and simply go through the motions of the interview. Or he will misinterpret his discomfort as something else and then justify and rationalize that initial conditioned response as 'gut instinct', 'intuition' or 'business experience'. Either way his 'decision' is not based on real data and due interview process of a viable candidate; it is based on an erroneous survival-based conditioned response created when he was four years old and feeling a bit poorly!

As bizarre as this may sound, it is happening all the time – inside and outside business. And the only thing that could rein this conditioning in and facilitate consistently better decision making is emotional awareness. Unfortunately we are so disconnected from our emotions, especially at work, that we're often not even aware of these shifts in energy. We certainly can't ascribe an accurate feeling to the emotion, which means that we almost certainly don't have the cognitive ability to ask ourselves whether the conclusion we've just jumped to is actually based on anything solid or not. This is why the emotional line of development is so important for Enlightened Leadership. It allows us to wrestle back power from the hyper-vigilant, neurotically over-protective amygdala and apply some common sense and logic to the situation so that perfectly capable candidates in yellow shirts don't get thrown out without due consideration.

In addition, it has been demonstrated that what we 'think' we are capable of is often nothing more than a conditioned response or habit (Ikai and Steinhaus, 1961). In other words, we need to learn how to tap into our innate emotional signals so we can stop jumping to erroneous conclusions based on long-forgotten events and misperceived threats. And so we can tap into our true potential instead of an outdated idea of that potential. We need to become more 'response-able' rather than reactive. We can't stop the e-motion happening (at least, not without a lot of practice) but we can learn to intervene and manage the response.

The *real* E-myths

According to Michael Gerber of *E-Myth* fame (Gerber, 1995), the E stood for Entrepreneur and he proposed that in order to be successful entrepreneurs needed to systemize their business. That's probably true but what I'm suggesting is that the real E-myths that are holding business back are the universal dismissal of E-motion as a business tool and the fact that intellect is viewed as considerably more important – especially in business.

Business is often perceived as the cool, rational pursuit of profit. In the history of commerce it's been largely a male-dominated sport and even today if you look at the statistics for women in senior roles the percentage is very small (Grant Thornton, 2012). The vast majority of businesses are still run by men. Most cultures still condition their sons to be the strong, show-no-emotion protectors who provide for the family. What we instinctively assume about business is therefore mainly dominated by our outdated and inaccurate assumptions about men. Emotion is seen as a demonstration of weakness preserved for the 'weaker sex' and is often cited as the whispered although invalid justification for why women shouldn't be in business in the first place. Men are rational, socialized from a very early age to dismiss emotion and feeling entirely – or so the story goes.

This is so ingrained into our collective psyche that if we ask a man what he feels, he will tell us what he thinks. If we ask a male CEO how he is feeling after the dismissal of a colleague for example, he will tell us how the decision was necessary and how the business is going to move forward. He often doesn't even understand the question, and if he does he is so used to ignoring and suppressing his feelings that he often has no lexicon to answer the question! The challenge for men is their lack of emotional awareness.

For women, it's slightly different because they tend to be more aware of their emotions in the first place. This awareness is facilitated by their direct experience of strong physical and emotional tides on a monthly basis. The challenge for women is therefore not lack of awareness but potentially lack of control over their emotions. Women can sometimes be more easily over-whelmed as the energy bubbles to the surface more readily, and certainly this is a widely perceived 'female' issue, especially in business. As a result men and women struggle in this endless dance where a woman's lack of control reinforces the male belief that emotions are unhelpful and the men's overt control reinforces the female belief that men lack empathy and have the emotional capacity of a stick insect. The truth however is that it is emotional mismanagement that is unhelpful, not emotions themselves, and that is true for both sexes.

Emotional suppression is every bit as toxic and unhelpful as emotional excess and over expression. Unfortunately this misdiagnosis of emotions – rather than emotional mismanagement – as the problem creates a vicious cycle where men justify their lack of awareness, fearing that if they paid attention to emotions they could become overwhelmed, lose control and make poor decisions. So they dismiss the whole topic of emotions, which then makes women even more irritated, triggering even more upset that further solidifies the unhelpful stereotypes and maintains the endless dance.

This blanket dismissal or ridicule of emotion is also further compounded by the fact that we prize cognition significantly more than emotion. For many centuries it's been intelligence, creativity and thought that has been valued above all else. Consider the intellectual transformation brought about during the Renaissance between the 14th and the 17th centuries, the Age of Enlightenment in the 17th and 18th centuries, or the New Thought Movement of the early 19th century. Thought has been king for a very long time. In business strategy, analysis, customer insight, like-for-like sales figures, process reengineering and a whole manner of other fields, rational pursuits are highly prized. Relationship dynamics, sensitivity, emotion and feelings are less explored if not taboo.

In the workplace we often hear how a certain individual is 'highly intelligent' or 'super smart'. That's a compliment. When someone is described as 'emotional' however it is never a compliment and such a statement is most often directed toward a female executive. Ironically, if a male executive does occasionally express emotion it is more often regarded in a positive light such as 'aggressive' or 'passionate'.

This supposed difference between men and women is simply not true. Every human being – male or female – has emotion. Everyone has physiology that is in a constant state of flux, and this energy in motion creates signals that are being sent continuously and simultaneously around the body across multiple biological systems. The fundamentals of the physiological reaction to the world are therefore no different between the sexes; the triggers and intensity of emotions and the degree of self-regulation vary by person, but the fact that emotions occur every second of every day is true of men and women. The only thing that is different is the weight of thousands of years of gender-based expectations that can be manifested as unhealthy biases inside and outside business. This in turn has created a mistaken belief that emotions are commercially irrelevant and do not belong in a modern business context.

Nothing could be further from the truth.

Why emotions are important in business

In 1776 Adam Smith wrote *The Wealth of Nations* – a treatise on economics and business that is still used to this day. In it Smith talks about the division of labour. Everyone in a business was to have a particular job and they did only that job. People were rewarded for doing the tasks they were assigned and punished if they didn't. Simple – and during the Industrial Revolution, very effective. But getting people to do what you want them to do is not just about reward and punishment. In fact social science has conclusively proven that reward and punishment only works for very specific types of tasks – known as algorithmic tasks. These are tasks that follow a set path to a set outcome and as such are often monotonous and boring. For everything else, known as heuristic tasks or those that require creativity, innovation and trial and error to perfect, reward and punishment do not work and can often elicit the very behaviour you are trying to stamp out (Pink, 2009). A hundred years ago most people spent most of their time doing algorithmic tasks; today technology and innovation have replaced many of those jobs and according to McKinsey and Co this type of work will account for only 30 per cent of job growth now and into the future (Johnson, Manyika and Yee, 2005).

Regardless of what we might want to believe, people are people and not machines, so treating them like machines is no longer effective. And people have emotions, so to ask them to leave their emotions at the door is like asking them to stop their heart beating while they are in the office because the noise is a little distracting. Besides, negating emotion in the work place is not commercially smart because it renders employees incapable of making good decisions, unable to work hard, unlock their discretionary effort or feel a sense of fulfilment. Plus, it facilitates terrible customer service. If we are serious about securing a commercial edge over our competitors then we really must understand how central emotions are to human functioning and the development of potential.

It was MIT management professor Douglas McGregor who really started to question this 'leave emotion at the door' approach to business back in 1960. Drawing on the work of motivation luminaries such as Harry Harlow and Abraham Maslow, McGregor refuted the notion that people, men included, were basically walking machines that needed to be programmed to do a job and kept in line. McGregor believed that the productivity and performance problems that plague business – then and now – are caused by a fundamental error in our understanding of human behaviour. He described two very different types of management – Theory X and Theory Y (McGregor, 1960). Theory X assumes people are lazy and to make them conform you need a command and control approach. Emotion has no place in Theory X and if anything is considered a show of weakness. Theory Y on the other hand assumes that work is as universal and necessary as rest and play, and when you bring people together toward a shared vision that everyone is emotionally connected to, then truly amazing things are possible. McGregor's insights, made all the more palatable because he had real leadership experience as well as a Harvard PhD in psychology, did help to shift work practices a little but for the most part Theory X is still the predominant management style in modern business. We still seem reluctant to embrace the very thing that makes us human in the first place – emotions.

I think that the biggest reason we cling on to Theory X in some form or another is because the alternative is terrifying. Theory Y requires that we break down the barriers and start really communicating with each other. It means facing the messy and unpredictable side of humanity and if we don't even appreciate our own emotions and how we feel on a daily basis, 'feelings' can seem like an alien and unfathomable black hole. It's just too hard! So instead we try to ignore the fact that business is first and foremost a collection of human beings. It's like owning a Formula One team but refusing to hire mechanics to look under the shiny red exterior!

In her case study at **www.coherence-book.com**, Orlagh Hunt, one of the best HR directors (HRD) in the FTSE, reflects on her time as Group HRD for RSA and discusses the critical importance of embracing the human element of business – and that means emotion. With a 300-year heritage, RSA is one of the world's leading multinational insurance groups, employing around 23,000 people, serving 17 million customers in around 140 countries. Talking about her time with RSA, Orlagh said:

> In theory we worked together, but our old way of operating had been all about driving individual performance. That was how our performance management and people management processes were set up. But to think bigger you need to have more collaboration and innovation and that requires different ways of working... Individually, for members of the executive team, it was very much about being open. We needed to stop the sense that you have to have all the answers just because you're in a senior position. That means being open to including more people in decision making... Moving our leadership style on in that way was very important.

And the effort paid off; by looking under the hood of the team dynamic and really seeking to understand human behaviour in a more sophisticated way, RSA achieved significant wins:

> We moved to a more human and engaging leadership style that supported the organic growth phase and teed up opportunities for us to think differently about how ambitious our strategy could be... The outcome has been that the organization moved from failing to being well respected on the FTSE. Not only that, but the organization has seen benefits in terms of significant levels of organic growth despite a difficult economic environment, world class levels of employee engagement (as measured by Gallup) and it achieved sixth place in The *Sunday Times* Best 100 Big Companies to work for scheme in 2012.

Emotions must be understood if the leadership journey is to be successfully navigated. Of course it is possible to be a powerful business figure with low levels of emotional and social intelligence (ESQ). But individuals who become more emotionally and socially intelligent will significantly improve results. Emotional mastery can:

- improve clarity of thought and ability to learn;
- improve the quality of decision making;
- improve relationships at work to avoid 'leadership by numbers';
- facilitate effective management of change;

- increase leadership presence;
- improve health and well-being;
- increase enjoyment and quality of life;
- ignite meaning, significance and purpose;
- improve motivation and resilience;
- expand sense of self.

Improve clarity of thought and ability to learn

We've all found ourselves in the middle of a heated argument saying some-thing stupid, only to think of the most brilliant comeback five minutes after the other person has stormed out the room. Unfortunately it's impossible to think of smart comebacks or great ideas when our internal emotional signals are going haywire – even if we look the picture of indifference on the outside. Whether we feel the emotion or not doesn't alter the fact that the emotion is present. And it's already impacting our clarity of thought and the outcome.

We will explore this idea in more detail in the next chapter, but ultimately chaotic physiology and turbulent emotions cause the frontal lobes to shut down. So the clear thinking that we believe we are engaged in is actually just the emotional early-warning system of the amygdala, not the neocortex. Emotion is constantly influencing our clarity of thought and ability to learn; the only real question is whether that influence is unconscious and poten-tially negative or consciously managed and positive.

There are millions of bits of information from the internal and external world that are competing to get into our conscious awareness. Unless you learn emotional mastery and self-management so that you take conscious control of that filtering process, what you become aware of will largely be determined by long-forgotten conditioning and the hyper-vigilant and over-protective amygdala. Plus it takes at least 500 milliseconds longer for the information to reach the frontal cortex and a thought to emerge than it does to activate the emotional early-warning system of the amygdala. That's why we said something stupid in the argument – our amygdala reacted before our thinking, rational frontal cortex even knew what was going on.

This process is incredibly fast. If the amygdala detects danger, real or perceived, it will send a signal to our heart and cause it to speed up. This is the 'descending loop' of the construction of a feeling. The heart rate can jump from 70 to 150 beats per minute – within one beat. This change in the energy of the heart (e-motion) is then sent back into our amygdala, the anterior

FIGURE 3.2   Construction of a feeling

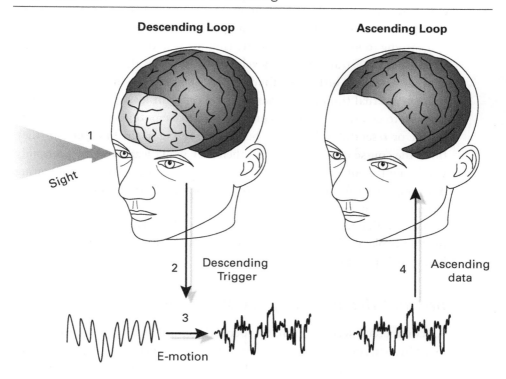

cingulate cortex, hippocampus and the motor cortex. This is the 'ascending loop' of the construction of a feeling (Figure 3.2).

In that half a second our physiology has already changed; the emotion emerged and whether we were aware of that emotion as a feeling or not it has already initiated a response that the neocortex is not yet even aware of.

This biological phenomenon means that we are all living half a second behind reality, and also explains why feeling dominates thinking and not the other way around. Feeling is faster than thought and sets the context in which thoughts even occur. Thoughts are slower and they are emergent phenomena that do not occur independently of changes in our emotion. The thought wouldn't have emerged had our physiology and emotion not changed first.

This mechanism can be useful in alerting us to danger, but without greater emotional intelligence our amygdala can become 'trigger happy' and that's not that useful in business. In fact it can be extremely costly. If we are aware of only a tiny fraction of what we could potentially be aware of, it makes sense to develop a much greater awareness of our internal data. By doing so we are able to make better decisions and accurately determine what's really commercially relevant instead of making knee-jerk emotional reactions that can pollute our thinking and hamper performance.

Learning to induce an appropriate emotional state is also key for optimal learning. In the training and development industry this is called 'learner readiness' but it is little more than common sense. If we are spending a fortune on internal training that isn't working then at least part of the reason is down to emotion. If trainees are in a negative emotional state, if they are hostile or resentful at having to be in the training in the first place or they think the course is a waste of time, then they won't learn and they certainly won't implement. When their physiology is chaotic they are generating much higher levels of the stress hormone cortisol. Cortisol is well known to inhibit learning and memory.

As an Enlightened Leader we can help to shift the emotional response of the people around us, which can improve their ability to learn and enhance their performance.

Improve the quality of decision making

All commercial success ultimately depends on the quality of decision making. Most executives, particularly male executives, believe that decisions are a logical process. You analyse the data, determine the best option and make the decision. Unfortunately this is not how decisions are actually made.

In the mid-19th century there was a breakthrough in the neuroscientific understanding of decision making, although this breakthrough wasn't fully understood until 20 years ago. It all started with Phineas Gage, who was a railway construction foreman in the United States in the 1840s (Damasio, 2000). Rather than weave the railway around a rock formation, it was easier to blast through the rock. Gage, an explosives expert, was employed for that task. The process involved drilling a hole in the rock, half filling it with gunpowder, inserting a fuse and filling the rest of the hole with sand. The sand would then be 'tamped in' very carefully with a 'tamping rod' to pack the sand and explosive in place, before finally lighting the fuse. Unfortunately, on 13 September 1848 25-year-old Gage suffered a traumatic brain injury. Momentarily distracted, he started tamping before the sand was packed in and a spark from the tamping rod ignited the gunpowder, sending the six-foot-long iron tamping rod straight through his brain to land 80 feet away. Amazingly Gage survived – conscious and talking just a few minutes after the accident (Damasio, 2006). You can see an astonishing picture of him after the accident on the Phineas Gage Wikipedia page.

Antonio Damasio has written extensively on the consequences of Gage's injury and its implications for decision making. Based on medical records at the time and brain reconstructions, Damasio suggests that the iron pole cut through his brain and disconnected the logic centres located in his frontal cortex from the emotional centres located further back including in his amygdala. Prior to the accident, the railway company that employed Gage considered him to be one of the most capable men in their business. However, after the accident his character changed completely and although he could answer basic logic problems he was unable to make decisions, or he would make decisions and abandon them almost immediately.

Gage's inability to make effective decisions led neuroscientists to realize that decision making requires emotion. In order to decide anything we have a 'feeling' first and then we simply look for rational data to support that initial feeling. So all decisions we ever make are really just feelings justified by logic. Quite simply, we can't exclude feelings from the decision-making process. Even the most hard-bitten neuroscientist will tell you that the emotional system and logical system are inseparable.

If you put this book down and find yourself saying 'that's rubbish' – then it is likely that you are having an emotional reaction to the information that is causing you to 'feel' like rejecting what is written here. Chances are you pride yourself on your logic and the mere idea that your decision making is anything other than supremely rational is offensive to you. But the fact remains, emotion is driving your decisions whether you like it or not. In fact the emotional basis of decision making in financial markets has received much attention. John Coates PhD, former Wall Street trader and now neuroscientist at Cambridge University, suggests that city traders live on instinct and operate largely below the level of conscious awareness.

At Complete Coherence we conducted a study at the European School of Management. Using the simulated trading floor, 30 MBA students were let loose with £1 million in fake money to trade shares. During the experiment each student had their biology monitored using CardioSense Trainers. The initial analysis of the data indicates that, while most of the students traded very little, there were two small cohorts that were either very successful or very unsuccessful. Preliminary evidence suggests that those that were successful and made better decision were more coherent and the people who were unsuccessful were more incoherent.

Coates looked at this same issue, although he suggested the driving force was testosterone (Coates, 2013). Our findings are entirely compatible with Coates' data. In fact we have shown in a previous study that coherence training increased DHEA levels, the precursor of testosterone (on the left-hand side of the performance grid in Figure 3.1) (Watkins and Cobain, 2013). We believe, therefore, that it isn't testosterone that is making the difference, it is coherence. Creating a coherent physiological and emotional signal can facilitate clarity of thought and better decision making in traders.

Experience, intuition, instinct and gut feeling

Many executives, unable to concede that their decisions are emotionally driven, may instead embrace the idea that their decisions are based on their 'commercial experience'. Which is ironic considering 'commercial experience' is really just emotionally laden data that is unconscious or 'preconscious' (Coates, 2013), stored in parts of their brain they don't know about, resurfacing when they are asked to make a decision today. They may not call it emotion but that is exactly what it is.

Some executives may refer to such experience as an instinct or, without even realizing, some may even call it a gut 'feeling'. Calling 'commercial experience' a gut feeling actually makes sense when you consider that there are more nerve cells in the gut than there are in the whole spinal column! Such gut feelings are, we believe, generated in the neural networks contained within what is known as the second brain in the gut (Gershon, 1998).

As with the confusion between emotions and feelings many people, including Coates, fail to discriminate between instincts and intuitions. We believe that instincts are generated in the neural networks of the gut and are predominantly driven by a desire to avoid danger and survive. They are therefore more negatively valenced and are more likely to occur when we feel fearful or threatened. Intuitions, in contrast, are quite different and may have more to do with the neural networks in and around the heart. Both types of information represent 'non-cognitive data' and can facilitate a 'knowing without knowing', a 'felt-sense' without objective data. Intuitions are more positively valenced and are more likely to occur when we are feeling more expansive and upbeat.

Both types of data, instinct and intuition, generate an output in the form of an insight – which literally means 'sight' from within. Executives are much more likely to remember their negative experiences, so their insights are more likely to be driven by their gut feelings or instincts. However, cultivating the ability to tap into our intuition could potentially make us much more insightful, as we access a different type of data – data that is positively valenced and can bring more positivity and balance to our decisions.

The rapid data-processing capabilities of instinct and intuition may be the neuroscientific underpinnings of a phenomenon called 'thin slicing'.

Thin slicing is the ability of our unconscious mind to find patterns in situations and behaviour based on very narrow slices of experience (Gladwell, 2005). However, as Nobel Prize-winner Daniel Kahneman reminds us, 'Intuition is nothing more and nothing less than recognition' and, as a result, even the mighty intuition 'cannot be trusted in the absence of stable regularities in the environment' (Kahneman, 2011). In other words, intuition can't be trusted without emotional coherence, as leader John Browett understands. After a stellar career at Tesco, as CEO at DSGi and a brief stint on the exec board of Apple, John, one of the most talented retail leaders in the UK, joined clothing and accessories brand Monsoon Accessorize as CEO and discusses the practical importance of pattern recognition and emotional coherence in his case study at **www.coherence-book.com**. Monsoon Accessorize operate 400 stores in the United Kingdom and over 1,000 throughout the world. John explains:

> There isn't a scientific way of getting to the answer for every company. You can't mechanically work through the numbers to make the right decision. You never have enough data or the right data to be able to do that. Rather you have to make educated guesses and judgements about what could be right. I use a lot of pattern recognition, but also a lot of intuition. Good intuition is really just the ability to make the right decision even without all the right data. Pattern recognition works because it can be built up from looking at many businesses and taking lots of decisions over time. It is also helpful to boil down the issues to a small number of areas where you can focus judgement. Sometimes, even if you are not certain about a decision, action will give you more information to then work out what to do. It's not about absolute rights and wrongs, but about what you learn from the decisions you make. It's about feeling your way.

Improve relationships at work to avoid 'leadership by numbers'

Commercial success is critically dependent on the ability to build good-quality relationships with anyone – even if you don't like them. And it is emotion that affects the quality of those relationships. The ability to establish and sustain positive connections is the very basis of social intelligence, which we will discuss in more detail in Chapter 6.

I remember working with one CEO and I asked him to tell me about a time in his life when he felt really passionate about something. He sat in silence for a full minute before saying, 'No I can't think of anything.' Somewhat surprised that he couldn't remember a single moment in his life where he felt passionate, I asked him to tell me what was the commonest emotion he did feel. Again he sat in silence thinking for a minute before replying, 'Even-tempered?' He was one of the least emotionally expressive executives I have ever worked with and it was immediately clear why he was having trouble motivating his leadership team.

His lack of emotional expression meant that his people found him almost impossible to read. Executives would come out of a meeting with him never really sure whether he was in support of their plan or thought it was dreadful. He also found it difficult to engage the workforce, let alone inspire them. He was a seasoned and competent manager, but as a leader he struggled and ultimately it cost him his job.

Good leaders use emotion, because that's what motivates people. Emotion inspires others and creates engagement. A lack of emotional intelligence can mean that you end up building relationships in a formulaic way – a sort of 'leadership by numbers'.

Facilitate effective management of change

Following the collapse of the Northern Rock building society in the UK, a number of financial institutions sought to refinance their position in various ways, by rights issues, further debt financing or other manoeuvres. Not long after Northern Rock's demise in the late summer of 2007 and before the credit crisis really hit in 2008, I attended an event where the key speaker was the CEO of a major UK bank who proceeded to explain his views on the current economic situation. He made a very safe speech, giving little away and saying nothing particularly insightful or incisive. However, he did say one thing that troubled me – 'no one could have really predicted the size and scale of the problem' that global markets were facing at the time.

If no one could see the size and scale of the crisis, then surely the problem was one of perceptual awareness? If an organization cannot see a problem before it hits them then that organization is effectively operating blind. And if it is operating blind then it will not see the next problem coming, or the one after that or the one after that. I approached the CEO and offered to work with him and his team to expand that awareness so that wouldn't happen and they could anticipate future threats effectively. He listened politely but rejected my offer. Six weeks later the financial crisis had worsened, the CEO had not anticipated the scale of the impact on his own organization and he was out of a job.

This CEO is really no different from many others, and I could list numerous other examples of exactly the same phenomenon. In truth few leaders would have accepted my offer to help the top team enhance the quality of their thinking. Most CEOs are not trained in neuroscience, and perceptual awareness as a topic is not something that is currently taught in business school.

However, surely one of the many lessons of the 2008 global economic meltdown is that leaders need to be much better at predicting and proactively managing change? There is no such thing as 'business as usual' in the 21st century. The pace of change is phenomenal. We live in VUCA world. Most leaders know this but few have studied the principles and dynamics of change in any great detail and many don't know how to consistently manage complex and dynamic change effectively (Berman, 2010).

No business stays the same for very long and survives. But the process of change is an emotional roller-coaster. Swiss-American psychiatrist Elisabeth Kübler-Ross proposed the five stages of grief that someone goes through when they learn of their own or a loved one's impending death. She suggested those stages were denial, anger, bargaining, depression and acceptance. Her model has since been expanded and is widely used in business to explain the emotional transition that occurs around any type of change, from new IT implementation to new management to strategic direction to new product line (Figure 3.3). Everyone goes through an emotional roller-coaster when they encounter change of any type. It follows therefore that if you want to manage change properly then you need to properly manage human emotion.

FIGURE 3.3   The change curve

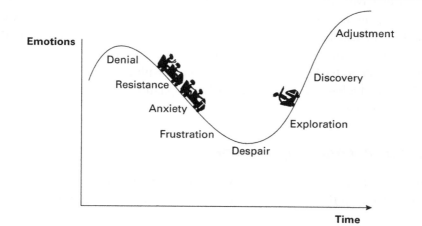

When CEOs or senior executives lead their people through change they are usually further ahead on the change curve than their troops. Leaders should have a greater perceptual awareness of what's ahead, what needs to be done and why. So the leader may have fully explored the suggested change and feel certain that it will result in significant positive benefits for the people in the business and the bottom line. But the troops, who have not been privy to all the information, are probably still not convinced about the merit or need for the change.

The leader is effectively saying, 'Come on in; the water is lovely' and the troops are standing at the side, clutching their towels, not sure they even want to get their feet wet! If leaders don't understand that emotionally they are in a different place from their people then the team will think the leader unrealistically optimistic or delusional, and leaders won't be able to get the followers to come into the change process with an open mind. Threatening them or bribing them is not the answer. Instead leaders need enough emotional flexibility to be able to go back along the change curve to an emotional position that is not so far ahead of the troops so they can encourage them, address their fears and help them to take the necessary forward steps.

When the troops are in a state of anxiety at the top of the down slope, they need strong leadership and encouragement to reassure them it's going to be OK. But then once they dive in, they can often feel even worse about the change and are now angry for trusting the leader in the first place. So the leader needs to provide even stronger support, to get in the trenches with the troops so they can feel inspired to keep going into discovery, adjustment and implementation.

Coherent Enlightened Leaders will therefore not only recognize that the troops are in an emotionally different place from them, which is itself a skill, but will have sufficient emotional flexibility to offer different emotional input depending on where the team is on the roller-coaster of change. And the Enlightened Leader will change his or her emotional state rather than expect others to change their emotional state. The leader knows that if s/he doesn't go back and emotionally connect with the troops they will not follow, or the best s/he can hope for is compliance rather than acceptance and integration.

Increase leadership presence

Most people have seen those reality TV cop shows where the officer is in the helicopter with the heat-sensitive camera tracking the criminal on the run.

Clearly we radiate heat energy and it is detectable some distance away. But we don't just radiate heat. We also radiate a wide variety of other streams of physiological data. So much so that we now have equipment that allows us to measure ECG without actually touching the patient. In fact the heart's electrical or electromagnetic energy radiates up to 50 ft off the body (Figure 3.4).

Consequently, emotion has a huge impact on leadership presence because other people can feel the emotion or energy radiating from the leader. The energetic impact that a leader has on a team can create an effective 'stress footprint'. In environmentally sensitive times we are all conscious of the carbon footprint our businesses leave behind, but what about the emotional 'stress footprint' that leaders leave behind following a meeting or de-brief session? With emotional flexibility we can control our stress footprint and leave either a trail of optimism and productivity in our wake or one of fear and uncertainty. Radiated biological energy is contagious and some people have a stronger biological signature than others.

There are stories for example of how people could feel the leadership presence or energy of Bill Clinton as soon as he entered a room, even if they couldn't physically see him. His energy was actually coming into the room about 10 ft before he arrived! Anyone who has done any amount of group or team coaching will also testify to the fact that the 'energy in the room' fluctuates significantly at different times of the day. In a particularly tense meeting we can often 'cut the atmosphere with a knife', and what we are sensing is radiated physiological data or e-motion.

FIGURE 3.4   Schematic of the heart's electromagnetic field

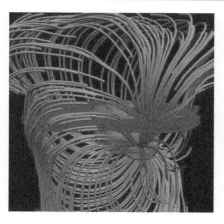 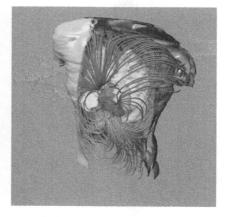

SOURCE: Taken from University of Utah Computing Dept web site

I have had the pleasure of working closely with Adrian Brown, Chief Executive of RSA UK and Western Europe. Ade is one of the most relentlessly positive and energetic CEOs I have met in 15 years and his passion is the core of his leadership:

> Energy and passion are skills and resources a leader should use as tools to make them a better leader. However to maximize your effectiveness you need to understand the impact you are having. The upside is easy to see: your energy, enthusiasm and passion rub off on those around you. You can sense them being carried along on your wave of excitement, you will create followers who follow you because they believe in you... However, as with most strengths there are dangers for energetic passionate people. When your energy drops, maybe only to that of an 'average' person, that can cause ripples of speculation! 'There must be something wrong', 'something bad is about to happen.' People around you are aware of your energy and when it drops it can have unintended consequences. So with your natural resource comes a responsibility. You have to be aware of its impact on others and, most importantly, take time to re-energize.

You can read Ade's brief case study at **www.coherence-book.com**, where he details how coherence has helped him and his team.

When we are in different emotional states we radiate different types of energy. It has been suggested that when we are in a negative emotional state we radiate much more chaotic energetic patterns than when we are in a positive emotional state. The energetic field created by people in a positive emotional state is thought to resemble a pure toroid (Figure 3.5).

FIGURE 3.5   Heart's E-magnetic field in different emotional states

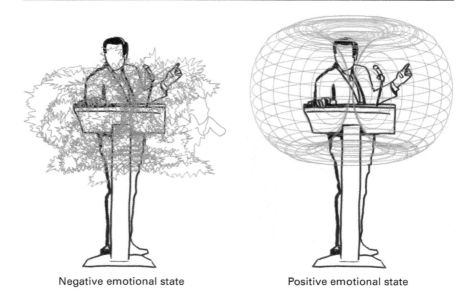

Negative emotional state   Positive emotional state

At Complete Coherence, we believe that the e-motional state that we generate underpins leadership presence. Enlightened Leaders are at the 'heart' of their team or business. As such they are potentially the 'most powerful pendulum' in the organizational system and can entrain all the other senior leaders in their system to create a coherent leadership force within the organization. With the right degree of emotional flexibility, these leaders can choose to set the emotional rhythm of their team. When they enter a meeting and they've been able to consciously choose a constructive emotional tempo, then everyone around them will begin to sync to that beat. Remember, the most powerful force in the system – positive or negative – sets the rhythm, and Enlightened Leaders ensure that they are the most powerful force. Armed with greater emotional flexibility the leader will be healthier and happier and will start to actually change the rhythm or beat of their team to increase productivity and coherence. That's powerful leadership.

Improve health and well-being

One of the greatest benefits of learning how to manage our emotions is the positive impact this can have on our health and well-being. Mismanaged emotions are the superhighway to disease. People say, 'If you haven't got your health you haven't got anything' and yet they will work incredibly long hours and in unhealthy ways in order to stockpile money and build their pension pot. I have seen many leaders ruin their health in the pursuit of money, and ironically they then spend all their money trying to regain their health. Or worse still they die before they get to their pension anyway.

If we mismanage our emotions our health and well-being will suffer. Ironic when many business executives think emotions are irrelevant in the first place! And yet the thing they have spent a lifetime ignoring will end up killing them.

Increase enjoyment and quality of life

If we really want to have a great life we have to feel like we're having a great time. We've got to really enjoy it. And when we boil it all down, our ability to enjoy our life comes down to our ability to access our emotions and feel the feelings.

Enjoyment and quality of life does not come from things, it comes from experiences. Again this is ironic, considering that so many of us strive to accumulate material possessions. Even if we buy a beautiful car like an Aston Martin DB9, the novelty soon wears off. The positive feelings we get from things like a new car, new house or a new outfit are transient at best. Spending money on experiences, especially ones that involve other people we care about, is what often creates enjoyment and a high quality of life for most people. Why? Because those experiences create positive emotion and make us feel good. The positive effects from these experiences are more meaningful and they also last longer (Landau, 2009).

Even though we know that money can't buy happiness, many of us are still driven to accumulate it. Perhaps this is because we just don't know what else will make us happy, so we decide it's better to focus on the money just in case it does buy us happiness after all. In an effort to quantify just how much money it would actually take to buy happiness, Daniel Kahneman and colleagues from Princeton studied the data from over 450,000 randomly selected US residents. The magic number, it would appear, is $75,000 or just under £50,000. What is especially interesting is that any happiness advantage conferred by money stops at $75,000 (Kahneman and Deaton, 2010). Considering that most senior executives of most companies in the Western world will already earn considerably more than $75,000, it seems a little strange that we continue to strive for more and more money even when we already know that once we have a little more than 'enough' we have achieved all the money-based happiness that we can. And for those that are not currently earning the equivalent of $75,000, be assured there are better ways to ensure health and happiness regardless of the pay check.

Material possessions – even really cool ones like a DB9 – are simply not big enough or meaningful enough to provide us with unending happiness. The minute we scratch the lovely new car, the allure begins to fade until it's just another car. In the end happiness is a habit. It's a way of being, and whether we are born with our glass half empty or half full we can all learn to be happier by practising the emotion of happiness.

It's also worth noting that happiness across societies is actually more dependent on the discrepancy between incomes than on a particular income figure. In other words, when there is a huge gap between the rich and the poor, then the society is significantly less happy than if that gap is low or 'reasonable'. As senior executive salaries have escalated in relation to lower-level employees, it's easy to see how that has had a negative impact on the 'society' of the business. When executives are earning a hundred times more than their average employee, engagement and performance can plummet within the business. So once again emotion is important for business.

Ignite meaning, significance and purpose

Feelings give meaning to our experiences. If we don't feel a sense of elation when we have achieved a target or goal, then it is likely that we consider the experience pretty meaningless. If we climb to the top of Mount Everest and think, 'Huh' rather than 'WOW', then what's the point? If we bring the project in on budget ahead of schedule and we're not ecstatically punching the air about it, then why did we bother doing it? If we don't feel something as a result of the things we do – meeting targets, launching a new product, completing a successful IPO etc – then they are all meaningless experiences. What we feel about a person, situation or accomplishment is what gives life meaning.

It is often this absence of meaning that triggers the 'mid-life crisis'. I've seen countless individuals who have faithfully followed the corporate rules and religiously climbed the corporate ladder, only to 'arrive' in the C-suite and wonder, 'Is this it?' The sense of victory or achievement they felt sure they would experience doesn't materialize or if it does it is so transient that it's almost non-existent. The very nature of the meaning of our own existence requires us to feel something. We have to be sensing that biological data or emotion so we can feel the emotion, otherwise life becomes very bland.

If you speak to people who have lost their sense of smell, for example, they often become quite depressed because their food tastes of nothing and all the pleasure of eating disappears. Smell is one of the most evocative senses we have – you smell cut grass and immediately you are transported back to childhood playing cricket on the village green. The reason is that there is only one neuron between the receptor at the back of our nose and the emotional network in the base of our brain. So there's a very high-speed link between the sense and the experience. If we can't feel the variability of life's experiences everything just runs together and becomes a bland treadmill. Emotions are the seasoning, spices and condiments that give our experiences flavour and meaning.

Improve motivation and resilience

The word motivation comes from the Latin word 'movere', which means 'to move'. Emotion comes from the Latin word 'emovere', which means 'to move out'. So the core of motivation is emotion. Motivation is literally the process of changing the internal energy.

As I said earlier, business has been getting motivation wrong for decades. In one study psychologist Edward Deci along with two colleagues went back over 30 years of research, assessing 128 experiments on motivation and concluding that, 'tangible rewards tend to have a substantially negative effect on intrinsic motivation.' The long-term damage caused by offering short-term rewards is one of the most robustly proven findings in social science and yet it is continually ignored (Kohn, 1993).

Reward and punishment have repeatedly been shown to reduce creativity, diminish results, inhibit good behaviour and foster bad behaviour (Pink, 2009; Ariely *et al*, 2005; London School of Economics, 2009). And yet business on the whole still seems reluctant to embrace a more sophisticated view.

The only genuinely sustainable motivation is internal or intrinsic motivation. We have to create the energy to take action ourselves – shift our own internal energy so we become self-motivated. Every business leader dreams of running a highly motivated team. Even better when that team is highly self-motivated so the leader doesn't have to keep micro-managing them, kicking them up the backside or offering them loads of cash to come in early or work late – they want to because they are excited and engaged in their work. When we have 'fire in our belly' it's just an emotion. So if we want to engage our team we have to engage their emotions.

Expand sense of self

If there is one overriding insight that could be gleaned from most leadership books it's to 'be yourself', often referred to as authenticity. While this is perfectly correct the problem is that few of us have a sophisticated understanding of what 'self' really is. Most leaders have spent very little time studying how their 'self' is constructed, what it means, so how could they really know if they are being authentic? The most knowledgeable researchers in the world, who have been studying the nature of the 'self' for thousands of years, are probably those who have been engaged in what are called the 'contemplative sciences'. Business leaders can learn a great deal about authenticity from the contemplative practitioners such as the Tibetans, although the wisdom and insights are not confined to any one particular tradition or denomination.

One of the critical insights from the research that has been conducted into the 'self' is that our sense of self is directly related to our emotions. So when someone is in a negative emotional state, their sense of self shrinks and contracts and sometimes they may apologize to those around them, saying things like, 'Hey, sorry about yesterday; I wasn't myself.' Conversely when someone is in a positive emotional state it feels as though the 'larger more expansive' version of themselves showed up. Our sense of 'self' therefore expands and contracts as our emotional state changes.

What we now understand about this construct of self is that self, consciousness and emotions evolved together (Figure 3.6), so when we collapse emotions into a negative congealed mess, or we ignore this essential strand of human existence, our sense of self also collapses and a smaller 'you' shows up. Conversely when we are in a positive expanded emotional state, the real 'you' – the bigger, more expansive, more creative, smarter 'you' – shows up and consciousness expands too.

FIGURE 3.6   The evolution of consciousness, emotions and the self

The evolution of awareness and consciousness

When we understand how consciousness evolved we are better able to fully appreciate the inextricable link between emotion and thought. Consciousness is important because it makes it possible for us to know what it is like to be something. We are, after all, human beings not human doings. And like most things, consciousness evolved to confer a specific survival advantage that has allowed us to be an extremely successful species. The more sophisticated the consciousness, or ability to be aware, the greater the success – and human beings have, by far, the most sophisticated consciousness of all animals. And all this was made possible because of emotion. Consciousness does not exist in a vacuum. It evolved out of something – and that something was emotion. Therefore the very origins of human existence as we recognize it today are rooted in emotion, and consequently consciousness and emotion are welded together.

In order to survive and prosper, living beings needed to map their external world using their sensory apparatus so they could successfully navigate their way around it. However, creating maps was not enough. What was really required to allow the species to evolve and survive more easily was a way to view and manipulate several maps simultaneously. Consciousness is that ability. Professor Sir Roger Penrose, Professor of Mathematics at Oxford, and Professor Stuart Hameroff, Professor of Anaesthesiology at Arizona State University, have suggested that consciousness emerges when an organism has a neural network of 20,000 neurons – which is about the level of an earthworm (Hameroff and Penrose, 2003). Granted an earthworm is not aware of much, but it is aware.

The second quantum leap forward in consciousness occurred when living things became aware of themselves. This required a map of the external world and a map of the inner world too. This ability to map the internal world changed everything because it is at the heart of human consciousness. Internal mapping differed from external mapping in one very critical way. Internal maps don't change very much. If you look up from this book and look to your right you will see an external map or picture of your surroundings, if you turn your head to the left that external map will immediately change – you'll see a different picture. Your internal map, however, hardly flinched.

Our internal map is assembled from the information being fed into our brain about blood pressure, oxygen levels, water balance, pH and numerous other pieces of physiological data critical to internal stability. This afferent information arrives in many forms – electrical, electromagnetic or chemical – and establishes a stable baseline against which all other information is compared. Most of these biological parameters are very tightly controlled. For example, changing the pH level in our system from 7.4 to 6.9 would probably be fatal, so there is very little wiggle room in these internal maps, especially compared with the external maps.

This small, and often overlooked, fact had a huge impact on the destiny of mankind. In particular it spawned the evolution of the self in human beings. The self is the thing that is not changing in comparison to the rapidly changing external world. The self can observe the external world and know that it is not that. In short, consciousness became aware of itself and constructed a sense of 'self'. This self was therefore born out of the ability to closely map the internal world, and it evolved out of the physiology and emotion data, which is why the sense of self changes when the emotion changes and consciousness changes (Table 3.1).

What makes human consciousness different from an earthworm or a honey bee is the degree and sophistication of our consciousness and our ability to distinguish the vast range and subtlety of emotional experience.

TABLE 3.1 The relationship between physiology, emotions, feelings and consciousness

Level	Function
Consciousness	Is the awareness of the 'maps' of the interior and exterior world. Such map making confers survival advantage. These maps are created by the manipulation of images of both landscapes. The interior maps are much more stable integrations of physiological data streams (e-motions) and these arise in consciousness as feelings. From the 'map of the self' arises the knowing that it is 'me' forming the plan, manipulating it and having the feelings.
Feeling	E-motions converted into images/symbols to represent the internal world for conscious apprehension and subjective interpretation.
Emotions	Complex stereotyped patterns of information from multiple sources to prepare internal state and drive for action.
Physiology	Simple stereotyped streams of information from single systems for the regulation of biological meaning.

How to be healthier and happier

In Chapter 1, I introduced the 10 initial skills of Enlightened Leadership that facilitate vertical development (Figure 1.11). In our work we believe that it is the emotion line of development that holds most senior executives and leaders back. Therefore the majority of the initial skills that you will learn throughout this book are focused on emotional skills. It is however important to understand that emotional coherence is much more than the basics of 'emotional intelligence' that many managers and leaders are already familiar with. The reason people don't effectively manage their emotions is that they don't know how to, and that's partly where this book comes in. Changing neurocircuitry and 'patterned responses' requires an individual to lay down new emotional circuits, patterns and experiences and that's called 'practice'.

In Chapter 2 we covered the physical skills. Now it's time for some of the personal skills of Enlightened Leadership. Specifically, the E-diary enhances emotional intelligence or awareness and MASTERY develops greater emotional literacy, while PEP and Landscaping facilitate emotional self-management. Each of these skills builds upon the last. Emotional intelligence therefore builds on physical management, and that is why breathing is such an important platform on which to build complete coherence.

Most negative emotional states involve some sort of disordered breathing pattern. For example, if someone is frustrated their breathing tends to be a series of mini breath holds or what are known as 'glottic stops'. If they just replace that particular pattern with smooth, rhythmic breathing they can stop the frustration in its tracks. The breath hold is a vital ingredient in the 'cake' we bake called frustration. In the same way that a chocolate cake ceases to be a chocolate cake if we remove the chocolate, frustration ceases to be experienced as frustration when we remove the disordered breathing pattern. The same is true of panic, anxiety or anger – all of which are accompanied by a particular chaotic breathing pattern.

So rather than wasting time trying to rationalize your way out of negative emotion by telling someone (or yourself) that 'everything will be OK', just have them take some smooth, rhythmic breaths while focusing on the centre of their chest and the anxiety or frustration will melt away. It's such a powerful technique and it's so simple. My wife and I taught our youngest son this skill when he was just three years old!

The BREATHE skill in the last chapter is specifically designed to stabilize our physiology and create a coherent electrical signal from our heart. If we are in the right-hand side of the performance grid experiencing apathy, anger or frustration, then just taking some time to engage in smooth, rhythmic

FIGURE 3.7 Impact of correct breathing

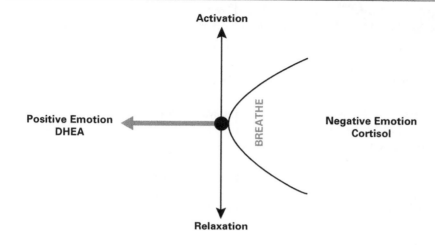

breathing while focusing on our heart will move us to the midpoint of the performance grid (Figure 3.7).

Breathing is absolutely critical in getting us to a neutral emotional position while shutting off our access to negative emotional states. The real benefits however are experienced when we move into the left-hand positive side of the performance grid and stay there. And that's what the next few skills are designed to facilitate.

Emotional coherence – emotional intelligence: the E-diary

If we want to occupy the positive side of the performance grid and stay there, then we first need to develop our emotional intelligence. When we boil it all down, intelligence is just awareness. If the government has intelligence of al-Qaeda, then they are aware of the organization and know what it is doing, but that's all. In the same way emotional intelligence is really just the process of cultivating awareness of our emotions. After all we can't use emotions or do something about them if we don't know what they are and what they are doing!

It has been suggested that there are only two opposing emotional states, love and fear, and all other states are variations and modifications of these two (Walsch, 1998). Some scientists have expanded that view slightly by arguing that there are only eight primary emotions (Plutchik, 1967). In the same way that we can mix primary colours together to get all the other

TABLE 3.2   Primary and secondary emotions

Primary emotions	Secondary emotions
Sadness	Sadness + Loss of Control = Hopelessness
Disgust	Disgust + Anger = Contempt
Anger	Anger + Betrayal = Rage
Anticipation	Anticipation + Joy = Optimism
Joy	Joy + Acceptance = Appreciation
Acceptance	Acceptance + Fear = Submission
Fear	Fear + Surprise = Awe
Surprise	Suprise + Sadness = Disappointment

colours of the rainbow these primary emotions then mix together to give rise to all the other secondary emotions (Table 3.2).

At Complete Coherence we believe that human beings cluster different emotional states in the same way they cluster or categorize music. Where some people would only ever listen to classical music, others prefer dance tunes or opera while still others enjoy a wide eclectic mix. The most important aspect for health, happiness and performance is not the individual emotion but whether we tend to cluster around positive or negative emotions on the performance grid. Unfortunately most of us don't really know what emotions we feel on a daily basis, so emotional intelligence is the critical first step in changing that.

One way of developing our emotional awareness is to keep track of exactly what emotions we feel over the course of several weeks. This can be achieved by keeping an E-diary.

- In your diary insert a column on the left-hand side of each day.
- During meetings or during the course of your day, simply jot down any emotional states you notice and make a note of the feeling you are aware of as a result.

- At the end of the day take a moment to consider how many different emotions you noticed as a feeling.

- How many are positive?

- How many are negative?

When I work with executives and encourage them to keep an E-diary I often get them started by asking them to make a note of the emotions they have been aware of in the last 24 hours. What is always interesting is what they focus on and how many they identify.

Once they have got over the 'this is silly' moment, most executives or business leaders will immediately start with their negative feelings. I'll ask them a few minutes later how they are getting on, they then review their list and realize they've got six negative feelings and no positive feelings. Quickly they will then rack their brain for a few 'token' positive emotions to add to the list!

Unfortunately, most people are much more aware of their negative emotions than they are of their positive ones. I think there are two reasons for that. First, evolution has equipped us with the super-efficient amygdala whose sole purpose is to spot threats, not opportunities. Plus we are socialized to believe there is not enough to go around, which makes the amygdala even more nervous that we will miss out. As children we play musical chairs – run as fast as you can and then when the music stops push everyone out the way and secure a seat, because otherwise you're a loser. Our primary focus therefore is to move away from the bad stuff of life rather than being pulled toward the good stuff.

That said, even with our ingrained awareness of the negative, most executives will still only recognize around 12 emotions that they feel. That is a pretty impoverished repertoire when we know that there are at least 34,000 distinguishable feelings (Goleman and Dalai Lama, 2004). Granted there are only around 3–4,000 words to describe specific emotions or feelings in the English language so if we wanted to differentiate all 34,000 we would need a combination of words, but nonetheless only being able to identify 12 different emotions on a regular basis is very poor.

With an impoverished emotional palette we simply don't have the emotional vocabulary to describe most of the emotions we feel and we don't appreciate the important nuances between similar emotional states.

For example, I remember coaching a young golfer a few years ago and I started to explain to him the importance of sustained positive emotion. He replied 'but I play some of my best golf when I'm angry.' I suggested that this was almost certainly not the case. He was probably 'extremely determined' rather than angry and just couldn't tell the difference. I reminded him that if he was really angry he would probably want to hit someone with his club rather than take his determination out on the ball, which is what he'd been doing. Helping him to understand the difference between these two highly activated states helped him get into the correct performance state when he was in competitive situations.

The point is we just don't pay attention to the data that our body is providing us; add to that the fact that we don't have the lexicon to describe them or the confidence to express them and it's hardly a surprise that most people's emotional palette is extremely limited. Knowing just 12 distinguishable emotions is the equivalent of barely being able to tell the difference between red wine and coffee. Learning to distinguish even half the emotions listed in Tables 3.3 and 3.4 would massively increase our emotional literacy and enable us to connect much more effectively with those around us.

The first step is to take the time to make a note of the emotions we currently feel so that we can bring them into conscious awareness. After all we can't change or utilize something we don't know we have.

TABLE 3.3   List of a sample of 76 positive emotions

Affectionate	Excited	Inspired
Amused	Flexible	Jolly
Brave	Focused	Joyful
Clever	Funny	Kind
Creative	Gentle	Likable
Competent	Grateful	Lovable
Curious	Happy	Loving
Delighted	Helpful	Mellow
Determined	Heroic	Neutral
Dreamy	Humorous	Nice
Eager	Important	Noble
Efficient	Innocent	Open
Enthusiastic	Interested	Organized

TABLE 3.3 *continued*

Overjoyed	Relaxed	Tender
Passionate	Respected	Thankful
Peaceful	Respectful	Thoughtful
Playful	Responsible	Tranquil
Pleased	Satisfied	Treasured
Precious	Secure	Trustworthy
Proud	Sensitive	Understanding
Qualified	Smart	Understood
Quick	Sophisticated	Unique
Quiet	Special	Valued
Radiant	Stoic	Warm-hearted
Rational	Strong	
Ready	Successful	

TABLE 3.4   List of a sample of 80 negative emotions

Angry	Furious	Lonely
Annoyed	Grumpy	Mad
Anxious	Guilty	Mean
Ashamed	Hateful	Mischievous
Bored	Helpless	Miserable
Bothered	Homesick	Mournful
Confused	Hopeless	Muddled
Depressed	Hurt	Nasty
Disappointed	Intolerant	Negative
Embarrassed	Insecure	Nervous
Forgetful	Irritable	Offended
Frightened	Jealous	On-guard
Frustrated	Lazy	Oppressed

TABLE 3.4 *continued*

Overcome	Small	Uncertain
Overwhelmed	Stressed	Unhappy
Perplexed	Stuck	Unyielding
Puzzled	Stunned	Upset
Quarrelsome	Surprised	Vexed
Rejected	Talkative	Volatile
Relentless	Threatened	Wacky
Restricted	Timid	Weird
Run-down	Tired	Whimsical
Sad	Tortured	Wild
Scared	Traumatized	Wilful
Shocked	Troubled	Withdrawn
Shy	Unavailable	Worried
Silly	Unbalanced	

Emotional coherence – emotional literacy: MASTERY

Simply noticing a feeling isn't enough, however, because noticing a feeling doesn't mean we are able to tell exactly what emotion it is that we are feeling. Once we have started to notice the number and variety of emotions we experience, using the E-diary, the next step is to cultivate emotional literacy or the ability to distinguish between different (and similar) emotions and accurately label each one.

Remember, this ability to differentiate is a sign of development and it is crucial in our evolution toward integration, coherence and Enlightened Leadership.

The skill for emotional literacy is MASTERY.

Think about MASTERY like a wine-tasting course. Expert wine tasters with a highly sensitive palette can distinguish between a chardonnay and a chablis, even between different types of chardonnay, noting which country it came from, what year it was made, what grape was used and even the type of soil the grape was grown in.

Wine experts are not born with that knowledge; instead they train their palette so that they can distinguish one wine from another with an ever-increasing degree of sophistication. And it is possible to do the same thing with our emotions.

It is important to be able to discriminate our feelings for two reasons:

- *Access.* If we know the exact 'features' of a particular feeling that we are trying to recreate and know exactly how we experience it in our body, then we have conscious access to that emotion. And if we have conscious access to it instead of just haphazard, unpredictable unconscious access to it, then we can turn that emotion 'on' when we need it. For example, confidence is a potent emotion that impacts performance negatively or positively. If we don't know what confidence is as an experience and have no appreciation for how it feels in our body, then we don't have access to it. If on the other hand we have developed emotional literacy and have practised the emotional MASTERY skill, then we will understand how to actually re-create a state of confidence whenever we need it, whether in a tennis final or in front of the shareholders.

- *Action.* The purpose of emotion is to provoke action and every emotion is designed to provoke a different action. As such, emotions have distinct survival advantages. If, however, we are unable to differentiate which emotion we are feeling, then it is highly likely that we will select the wrong action for the situation we're faced with. For example, when we see a grizzly bear, it triggers an emotion (our heart rate becomes erratic, our palms become sweaty etc) and we feel fear. The fear is designed to provoke an action, ie running away, which will hopefully save our life. That's the purpose of the fear. If we don't feel the fear or misinterpret the emotional signal as confusion, then we are likely to remain immobilized for too long and get attacked!

Similarly in a meeting, if we can't tell the difference between frustration and disappointment, then we are much more likely to take the wrong action. The purpose of disappointment is to provoke us to step back so as to evaluate the situation more closely. The purpose of frustration is to step forward and overcome the stumbling blocks. If we can't tell the difference then some-times we will step forward when we should have stepped back and become reflective, and vice versa.

The simple truth is that most of us don't have a clue how we are really feeling at any moment and even if we do we are unable to accurately tell the difference between those emotions – especially those that are similar to each other. If we can't distinguish between emotions then we have no emotional literacy and our health, happiness and performance will suffer as a result.

The MASTERY skill is therefore a technique to build our emotional repertoire so we can tell the differences between the emotional data we are privy to. You may for example know the intellectual difference between frustration and disappointment but MASTERY teaches us to recognize the difference in our body so we can differentiate between the emotional states as an experience.

The MASTERY skill

When someone attends a wine-tasting course they are given a glass of wine and asked to describe it. At first, assuming the learners didn't know much about wine, they probably wouldn't know what to say other than, 'it's white' or 'it's red'. Their teacher would then lead them through a process to deepen their observation and appreciation of the wine by asking pertinent questions to elicit more detailed descriptions. With practice the budding wine aficionados would soon begin to surprise themselves as they describe the wine in terms far more sophisticated than 'white' or 'red'. Before long they would be able to accurately describe the colour of the wine, how it smells and how it tastes. Developing emotional literacy follows the same process by providing a structure to describe our emotions in greater and greater depth.

The MASTERY process

1 Sit in a comfortable position, close your eyes and BREATHE.
2 Simply notice what emotion exists in your body right now.
3 If you are not feeling a distinct emotion, try triggering an emotion through the use of music, a memory or a picture/vision.
4 Once you have identified the emotion, give it a label or word that you think best captures it. Write that word down.
5 It actually doesn't matter if the label you choose to describe what you feel is accurate or not at this stage. What matters is that you familiarize yourself with that emotion.
6 Explore the features of the emotion within your body. How does the energy feel? What is the location of the emotion in your body? What is the size of the emotion? What colour is the emotion? What sound does the emotion make? What is the emotion's temperature? What is its intensity?
7 Moving on to the movement features, take a moment to describe how the emotion moves through your body. Does it stop at your skin or does it radiate off your body?
8 And finally, does the emotion have any special features?
9 Make a note of any insights that may have surfaced during the process.

When people first hear about this process, it always seems weird, especially to seasoned business leaders and senior executives. No one thinks that emotion has a colour or a temperature or a location, and yet once people get over their initial scepticism and run through the MASTERY process using the MASTERY worksheet (Figure 3.8), they are usually very surprised to realize that the emotion does have a colour and a size etc. Very often, the experience is a revelation!

Consistent practice of this MASTERY skill has also been shown to produce significant and sustained biological improvements over time. By learning how to convert something that is normally an entirely subjective inner experience into an objective, observable and repeatable one, we can build resilience, improve energy levels, happiness, fulfilment and enhance effectiveness. The more we understand the subtlety of our inner experience the more we will be able to control the very thing that drives our own and other people's behaviour.

FIGURE 3.8   MASTERY worksheet

Label

Basic Features	Location	
	Size	
	Colour	
	Sound	
	Temperature	
	Intensity	
Movement Features	How it moves through your body	
	How it moves off your body	
Special Features		

MASTERY in action

I remember coaching a real 'alpha male' executive and he really put some effort into seeing if he could in fact master a specific emotion that he felt he wanted more of in his life. He chose to study 'contentment'. After he felt he had mastered contentment, I asked him to describe his experience of it to me. I will always remember his response. He said, 'Contentment is a small glowing ember at the base of my heart, its red-golden and it's oozing through my chest and my arms and into my legs and I glow like the Ready Brek Kid and it purrs like a Cheshire cat.' His description was so beautiful and vivid that I actually started to feel his contentment; he had actually infected me with it! (And in case you don't already know, Ready Brek is a sort of porridge-like breakfast cereal that enjoyed a very successful advertising campaign. In the ad a child who had Ready Brek for his breakfast was seen with a full body halo around him all through the day.)

Whenever this executive was frustrated or irritated in a meeting or with one of his staff, he was able to turn on contentment as an antidote because he had practised the MASTERY skill.

MASTERY allows us to build up a database of the emotions we experience the most, work out the distinctions between similar emotions, and consciously build up a repertoire of positive emotions we would like to feel more often. In Chapter 4 we'll explore the SHIFT skill, which allows us to consciously move from a negative emotion to a positive emotion at will. This is also an extremely powerful skill but it's only possible once we've mastered some positive states to move into.

Emotional coherence – emotional self-management: positive energy practice (PEP) and landscaping

I've lost count of the number of times I've taught the MASTERY skill to business executives, reminded them that it can transform their daily experience, and returned to check in with them a month later only to hear they were unable to find the time to practise. The people I work with are leaders of large global companies and they are usually beyond busy, so I fully appreciate that the idea of learning new skills that require practice is not terribly appealing. Clearly, what was needed was a way to help executives practise without it feeling like practice. So I came up with a cunning plan to help them bake the transformational practices of Enlightened Leadership into their life without actually practising, and that's where PEP comes in.

Positive energy practice (PEP)

We may not always realize it, but we don't actually make that many conscious decisions in a working day. If we look at our life, we are largely repeating a series of daily habits or rituals. These rituals populate our day from our 'breakfast ritual' to our 'driving to work ritual' to our 'meeting ritual' to our 'winding down ritual'. In fact most of our day is highly structured and these rituals tend to occur in what I call the 'transition points' – the space between activities where we are transitioning from activity A to activity B.

For example, the first ritual we all have is the 'getting up ritual' that signals the transition from horizontal rest to vertical action. Everyone has a morning ritual although few are really that aware of it. Some people wake up to the alarm and some don't. Some of the people who wake up to the alarm will get up as soon as it goes off, others will hit the snooze – some will hit it once, some twice or more. Some leap out of bed, some swing their legs over and sit up in the bed, stretch and push their feet into their slippers before padding to the bathroom. Some go to the bathroom and others go straight to the kitchen to put the kettle on and then go back to the bathroom. When we start to think about it, most people can identify between three and ten steps in their 'getting up ritual'. The idea behind PEP is to identify the rituals that we already engage in and enhance them with Positive Energy Practice (P-E-P).

So for example in our 'getting up ritual' we would do what we always do, but include an additional step that involves feeling a positive emotion such as appreciation. PEP therefore encourages us to insert a few seconds into an existing ritual so we practise positive emotions and perceive for ourselves how they can change our experiences. Instead of hitting snooze and going back to sleep we might choose to take a few moments in bed to feel warm appreciation for the fact that we are alive or that our partner is next to us or that we have our health or it's a sunny day outside. So for just 30 seconds we feel appreciation, and then get on with the rest of our ritual as normal. Psychologist Sonja Lyubomirsky from the University of California studied 'happiness boosters' and found that those who found the time to consciously count their blessing – even just once a week – significantly increased their overall satisfaction with life over a six-week period (Wallis, 2005).

When my wife Sarah and I were in India for three months in our 20s I distinctly remember getting to Kathmandu and experiencing a warm shower for the first time in three months. I can't tell you the joy I experienced from the warm water. It was a real golden nugget of positivity and I remember thinking at the time: 'I must save this experience; it can help me in the future.' Today part of my 'getting up ritual' is to have a shower and when I am in the shower I spend 30 seconds to a minute where I just relive that amazing moment of sheer joy. As a result every day of my life starts with 30 seconds of appreciation and a minute of sheer joy. It's a great way to start the day.

Similarly I remember coaching an executive to identify his 'car ritual'. Initially he didn't have a clue what I was talking about but as I asked him questions it soon emerged that he did actually have a car ritual: open the car with the beeper – open the door with right hand – get in, sit down – put the key in the ignition – turn the engine on – put his seat belt on – turn on Radio 4 – drive to work. Once the ritual was identified I got him to do exactly the same but for the first five minutes of his 30-minute journey he was to listen to his favourite CD instead of Radio 4. While listening to his favourite music he was then to rehearse the feeling of exhilaration and sing at the top of his voice! He noted that five minutes into his journey there was a physical landmark that would remind him to stop his PEP and tune into Radio 4, turn on his phone and carry on to work as normal.

This executive was dubious to put it mildly but he did it nonetheless. For five minutes every morning he rehearsed exhilaration. What surprised him however was that this little and simple practice meant that he began to arrive at work feeling energized and optimistic, which in turn had a positive impact on his day and the people around him.

TABLE 3.5   Examples of PEPs

	Ritual/routine	PEP the ritual
1	Getting up	APPRECIATION (30 secs)
2	Shower	JOY (2 mins)
3	Breakfast	GRATITUDE (30 secs)
4	Traffic Lights	PATIENCE (45 secs)
5	Sitting in Chair	STABILITY (20 secs)
6		
7		
8		
9		
10		
11		

The best way to incorporate PEPs into your day is to identify your rituals around transition points and enhance them by rehearsing an emotion for 30 seconds to a few minutes.

Landscaping

In addition to experiencing more positive emotions throughout our day with a PEP plan, it can also help to engage in formal times of practice so as to embed the positive emotion into our life. The best way to do this is to 'landscape' our week (Table 3.6). Landscaping is about identifying where we can get the most bang for our practice buck.

Imagine your diary is like a half-full bucket of water. The time you can dedicate to practising emotional self-regulation are the rocks (> 5 minutes), pebbles (2–5 minutes) and sand (< 2 minutes) that you need to add to your bucket in any week. You only have space for a certain amount of practice, otherwise your bucket will overflow and you won't do any. So the best way to landscape your week is to put in the big chunks of practice where you really need them, say just before a really tough meeting. That way you will be in the best possible emotional state prior to the meeting so your practice immediately provides a practical real-world benefit to your day. Depending on the space you have left in your bucket, you would then landscape in the pebbles around events that were not so critical and then finally trickle in a few handfuls of sand where you were practising for under two minutes as and when you can.

For example you might have a board meeting on Friday – that's a really important meeting so you might want to spend 10 minutes before that meeting getting into the right frame of mind and emotional state. You might have a weekly meeting with your department heads that is important but nowhere near as important as the board meeting, so it might only require a few minutes of pre-meeting emotional preparation. By landscaping your week you factor in a little extra time before each activity, depending on the importance or significance of that activity, and it can really help if you make your PA complicit in this plan.

Landscaping is a tool that acknowledges that you are already busy while encouraging you to incorporate the practice into your normal business day rather than some hypothetical situation. That way you can experience the benefits of emotional self-regulation in situations that really matter to you.

This approach also allows us to recuperate and refresh ourselves as we go through the week rather than having to rely on weekends or holidays to recover. Practice thereby becomes part of the way we operate, unconscious competence is established and the benefits accumulate.

TABLE 3.6   Landscape your week

	Morning	Afternoon	Evening
Mon			
Tues			
Wed			
Thurs			
Fri			
Sat			
Sun			

Emotional coherence facilitates cognitive coherence

Enlightened Leadership emerges when we develop coherence across all the various critical internal and external lines of development (Figure 3.9) – each one strengthening and facilitating the next. In this chapter we have explored the second internal line of development – emotions.

FIGURE 3.9   Lines of development

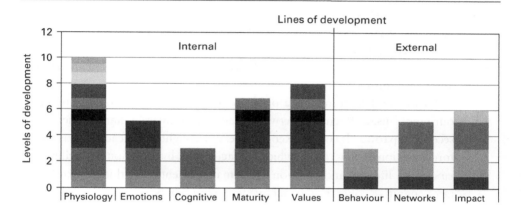

In business the emotional line of development is ignored or considered irrelevant. This is a mistake and robs us of a massive amount of data, energy and cognitive ability. It is, however, easy to understand the reluctance of senior leaders to embrace emotion. For a start many of the diagnostic tools available to measure emotion are cumbersome. They rarely provide information that can be acted upon at a managerial level. In an attempt to overcome these limitations we developed the Emotional and Social IQ Profile (ESQ). The ESQ gives a leader a sense of the emotional state of the employee base. For example, if a leader can establish that 72 per cent of his senior team or managerial team feel tired or exhausted often or most of the time, then clearly that is impacting results and needs to be addressed. The ESQ questionnaire therefore provides leaders with meaningful data about the level of energy, emotional negativity and emotional positivity in the workforce. It also quantifies the levels of stress in the workforce because the GHQ12 is also embedded into the ESQ. The GHQ12 is the most widely used and highly validated stress assessment instrument in the world. There are also additional questions in the ESQ that assess the current level of emotional awareness, emotional literacy and emotional self-management within the business or team.

We are only consciously aware of a tiny fraction of what we could be aware of, which means we have a choice. We can ignore emotion and let our negatively biased amygdala decide what information squeezes through into our conscious awareness, or we can master our emotions and take charge of that process. We may not be able to change the difficult situations we find ourselves in but we can change how we process them, and that is largely done through emotional self-regulation. How we feel is actually a choice; we can choose to rehearse happiness, gratitude and appreciation or we can choose to practise upset, anger and frustration. Such an insight is not new, happiness is essentially a habit (Maltz, 1960). The skills in this chapter allow us to become much more familiar with our emotions and the MASTERY, PEP and landscaping skills provide a methodology for turning happiness and health into a habit.

Health and happiness are only possible when we learn to appreciate our emotions, differentiate between them and ultimately manage them. The second step towards complete coherence and Enlightened Leadership is therefore emotional coherence, which is facilitated by emotional intelligence, emotional literacy and emotional self-management. And this in turn facilitates cognitive coherence, which we will explore next.

Summary of key points

If you don't remember everything in this chapter, remember this:

- Health and happiness are relevant to business because they reduce absenteeism, increase employee engagement, diminish the risk of unexpected succession and improve productivity throughout the company.

- Mismanaged emotion is the superhighway to disease and distress. There is now a mountain of evidence linking prolonged negative emotion to heart disease, cancer, stroke and depression.

- Emotion is significantly more important to health and happiness than exercise or what you eat.

- Emotion is just a composite of physiological data. A feeling is the conscious awareness or observation of that composite data; therefore everyone has emotion: male, female, young and old.

- Even if people look calm on the outside and have learnt how to ignore or suppress their feelings, that does not mean they are coherent on the inside. The emotional data may still be chaotic and it is this emotional chaos that is so toxic for mental and physical health.

- The real E-myths that are holding business back are the universal dismissal of (E)motion as a business tool and the fact that intellect is viewed as considerably more important – especially in business.

- In business we think we are making rational logical choices based on verifiable data and intelligent thought. Without emotional management what is actually happening is that our emotionally-driven amygdala is initiating a subliminal knee-jerk reaction based on long-forgotten conditioning designed to protect us from external threats.

- Emotional mastery is critical in business because it improves clarity of thought, ability to learn, decision making, relationships at work, effective management of change, leadership presence, health and well-being, enjoyment and quality of life, meaning, significance and purpose, motivation and resilience and facilitates an expanded sense of self.

- Emotional coherence is created by developing emotional intelligence or awareness (E-diary), greater emotional literacy (MASTERY) and emotional self-management (PEP and Landscaping).

Be smarter

04

"Have you ever had the experience of being in an important meeting when you suddenly go blank, forgetting everything you've rehearsed? Have you ever nipped out of the office to get something and been so distracted that you've stopped dead in your tracks while you try to remember what you had nipped out for? Have you ever needed to focus on a certain task and project but found it impossible to think straight? Do you find that some days you are 'on fire' and other days you couldn't come up with a good idea if your life depended on it? Are you tired of telling your people to 'think outside the box' even though you're not sure where the box is or what's outside it? Have you ever made decisions or barked out orders that you later regret? Do you ever wonder if your anger or volatility are negatively affecting your decision making but have no idea how to change it? If so, you're not alone.

Most of us have had the experience of reading a book or business report and ended up having to read the same page over and over again because it's just not sinking in. In business we are called upon to adapt constantly in response to changing market conditions, changing economies, industries, legislation, changing technology and the ever more sophisticated demands of our customers. We need to come up with new, great ideas only sometimes we can't come up with any idea, never mind a great one! And why is it we can never think of that smart comment or comeback in the middle of an argument? Why do seemingly smart people occasionally blurt out something completely inappropriate or inane in a meeting? Sometimes they don't even seem to notice, sometimes they even look quite pleased with themselves, as though they have impressed themselves with their contribution.

How could very successful businessman Gerald Ratner, CEO at the time of a major British jewellery business, make such a catastrophic error of judgement in his speech at the Institute of Directors in 1991? His comments are now so famous that 'doing a Ratner' has entered business vernacular and for good reason. In a last minute attempt to inject some humour into his speech Ratner said, 'We also do cut-glass sherry decanters complete with six glasses on a silver-plated tray that your butler can serve drinks on – all for £4.95. People say, "How can you sell this for such a low price?" I say, "Because it's total crap."' As if that wasn't bad enough he then went on to talk about some of the earrings his cut-price jewellery empire stocked, adding they were, 'cheaper than an M&S [Marks & Spencer] prawn sandwich but probably wouldn't last as long'. Ratner's inappropriate remarks wiped an estimated £500 million off the share value of the company and he was forced to resign.

Or what about some of the bizarre answers given by contestants on TV quiz shows like *The Weakest Link* or *Family Fortunes*. The contestants are usually intelligent, articulate individuals yet after a frosty stare from compere Anne Robinson their brains turn to jelly – 'In traffic, what "j" is where two roads meet?' Answer: 'Jool carriageway.' Under the lights and pressure of *Family Fortunes* contestants have also been known to come out with a few classics – 'We asked 100 people to name something you put in a jacket potato.' Answer: 'Jam!' Or, 'We asked 100 people to name something blue.' Answer: 'My jumper!'

Growing a business requires clarity of thought, or at least better thinking than the competition. But the content and the quality of our consciousness is determined by our physiology. This chapter explores what drives thinking, both the content (ie WHAT we think) and the quality (ie HOW WELL we think it). We will discover that our physiology doesn't just impact on our energy levels, health and happiness but also our ability to think and clearly articulate our point of view – a fact not lost on G4S's former CEO Nick Buckles, who was able to use his mastery of many of the techniques in this book to deliver a much more coherent performance the second time he faced the Home Affairs Select Committee investigation. He notes that:

> [the techniques] helped me to project myself better and, as a result, I was better able to get the key points across... and to be more positive and to channel energy away from being apologetic. I focused on what we had done to rectify the problems, without being arrogant. In this kind of situation, if you show any fear it is very easy to allow others to take control of the situation.

Companies need people who can think high-quality thoughts on a consistent basis. They need innovators, able to generate great ideas, spot opportunities and define the things that provide a competitive advantage. Without innovation and really smart thinking, executives just come up with the same ideas, strategies and products that someone else has already thought of. If we look at the companies that dominate their markets, like Apple, they employ the best thinkers available, capable of disruptive innovation. So the way we really get ahead and stay ahead is to become smarter than everyone else. And that starts with physiology.

The DIY lobotomy

Under pressure people don't think straight. Everyone has experienced this at some point or another. Most of us can remember going through the pressure of exams for example. Endless hours of revision can evaporate the moment we turn over the question paper and the stress causes our brain to shut down – we experience a Do-It-Yourself (DIY) lobotomy.

Two hundred thousand years ago when humans first stood up, brain shut-down under pressure gave us a distinct survival advantage. When our ancestors were wandering across the savannah and they encountered a lion, they didn't need clever thinking. If they stood in front of the lion musing on whether the lion was fully grown or whether it looked hungry then they would probably have been killed. So in an emergency, human beings evolved a mechanism for shutting down all the clever thinking parts of the brain to leave only two options: fight/flight (adrenaline driven) or play dead (acetylcholine driven). In the face of real danger our brain goes binary to save our life.

The problem is that here we are 200,000 years later still using the same mechanism. We are using 200,000-year-old software and we've never had an upgrade. We don't meet lions on the savannah anymore. We meet each other. We meet demanding bosses, difficult colleagues, agitated partners and angry customers. They are the lions of today. But our brain doesn't distinguish a difficult boss or colleague from the predator of primitive times, causing a DIY lobotomy just as effectively as the lion ever did.

And to make matters worse, once our brain has shut down we often don't even realize it, because we don't have enough remaining perceptual awareness to notice we've lobotomized ourselves. We think we are still functioning well when in fact we have lost focus, drifted off the point, become confused or even started to babble incoherently. Because of the pressure that we are now under every day at work, many people are wandering around corporate offices the world over with a partial, or in some cases almost complete, self-induced lobotomy that is massively impacting their cognitive ability and therefore their performance.

Clearly this is not career enhancing. Stupidity may have saved our life once upon a time but now it impairs our success and our ability to deliver results. And it's not always easy to tell who has been lobotomized – particularly when it's you! Unfortunately once we have triggered our own lobotomy we can't think our way out of it. To stop self-inflicted brain shut-down we must control physiology.

What we often fail to appreciate is that the thoughts we think don't happen in a vacuum. There isn't a series of bubbles coming out of our head like in the comic books. Our thoughts occur in the context of our physiology. When we think, our heart is always beating, our guts are always digesting, our muscles are always moving, and these physiological signals can have a profound effect on what we think and how well we think it.

This is why it is so imperative to build coherence from the ground up, starting with physiology, because without physiological coherence emotional coherence is almost impossible and without emotional coherence consistent, high-quality thinking is also much more difficult.

When people make mistakes, be it in an exam, in a shareholder meeting or when being interviewed by a journalist, we usually shrug our shoulders and dismiss this phenomenon with a statement such as 'these things happen' or it was 'human error' as though such phenomena are unavoidable, or worse, normal or acceptable. They may be common but they are completely avoidable.

Many senior executives try to minimize the possibility of making stupid blunders by putting themselves under stress ahead of time in the mistaken belief that this may stop the blunder from happening. It won't. The biology is too powerful. Practising a speech is of course helpful, but it is not enough to stop us going blank when we get a tricky question from an analyst during the Q and A at the end. No matter how much we have practised we are still susceptible to brain shut-down if our brain goes binary under the pressure.

With hindsight we have all made decisions or taken action that we later find utterly bewildering. But it's not bewildering if we understand what's actually happening. The human brain is constantly getting a signal from all the bodily systems but particularly from the heart via the vagus nerve. When we are under pressure our heart rate variability (HRV) becomes super-chaotic, which causes 'cortical inhibition', and the frontal lobes of the brain shut down (Figure 4.1).

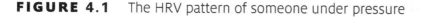

FIGURE 4.1   The HRV pattern of someone under pressure

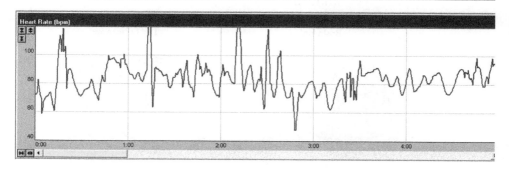

I demonstrated this in a TEDx talk I did in 2012 (**http://www.youtube.com/ watch?v=q06YlWCR2Js?v=q06YlWCR2Js**). My brave volunteer Neil came up on stage and I attached a small clip to his earlobe to measure his HRV, which was then displayed on a big screen behind him. Initially Neil's heart rate was pretty normal at about 75 bpm. But then I asked him to perform a maths challenge. I gave him a number and all he had to do was subtract three from that number and give me the new answer and then subtract three again. Pretty straightforward, especially as Neil assured me that he was 'quite good' at maths. Interestingly as soon as he said 'quite good' his heart rate spiked, which indicated he perhaps wasn't as confident as he was telling me. I started him at 300 and immediately he set off well, '297', '294'. Then I started to feed him the wrong answers and he soon became flustered and his heart rate was going crazy on the screen behind him. Neil himself still looked calm and confident but his brain stopped working because I had put him under pressure that caused his heart rate to become chaotic and initiate a DIY lobotomy. In a matter of a few seconds I had shut Neil's brain down and a normally smart person became dumb.

Neil didn't want this to happen – it just happened. And for the record he still looked composed and confident. So when you call an emergency crisis meeting to deal with a breaking news story or a faulty product and are reassured that your senior team appear composed and rational – don't be. If you were to attach an HRV clip to their ear, their physiology would probably tell a very different story. Just because someone looks composed and calm on the outside does not mean they are composed and calm on the inside. And if their HRV is totally erratic then what's really happening is your people have lobotomized themselves under the pressure of the crisis and you don't even realize it!

FIGURE 4.2   Schematic for the effect of physiology on brain function

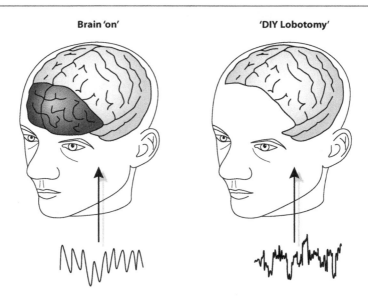

When we cut off access to our frontal lobes through a chaotic HRV (Figure 4.2) we can experience many of the same shortfalls – albeit temporarily. The frontal lobes are the 'executive part' of our brain that gives us greater cognitive resources than our Neanderthal ancestors. Losing frontal lobe function therefore takes us back to very primitive function and capabilities.

A chaotic signal from the heart:

- impairs perceptual awareness;
- reduces mental clarity;
- reduces creativity;
- impairs problem solving;
- reduces the ability to make effective decisions.

A coherent signal from the heart:

- enhances clarity;
- enhances creativity;
- enhances reaction speed;
- enhances thinking and decision making.

The evolution of the brain

In the 1950s neurologist Paul MacLean proposed that we did not have one brain but that we actually had three. Expanding on the work of James Papez, MacLean hypothesized that we have three layers of brain, each a direct response to evolutionary requirements representing the stages of human development. He called this the 'triune brain' and stated that the three brains operate like three interconnected biological computers, each with its own special intelligence, its own subjectivity, its own sense of time and space and its own memory (MacLean, 1990).

The three brains in order of evolutionary appearance are referred to as:

1 Reptilian.

2 Limbic or midbrain.

3 Neocortex.

Prior to MacLean's research, science had assumed that the most highly evolved part of the brain, the neocortex, was in charge. MacLean showed this was not the case and that the emotional control centres that make up the limbic system were actually more powerful.

Just very briefly, the reptilian part of the brain is the oldest. Physiologically it consists of the brain stem, medulla, pons, cerebellum, mesencephalon and the oldest basal nuclei – the globus pallidus and the olfactory bulbs. It is responsible for coordination, unconscious perception of movement and spatial orientation, and body movement.

The limbic system is the middle layer of the brain, which evolved over the top of the reptilian brain. It is also known as the mammalian brain because it's most highly evolved in mammals. The midbrain is concerned with the 'four Fs' – fight, flight, feeding and fornication – and it's the home of our autonomic nervous system. Physiologically it includes the hypothalamus, hippocampus, the anterior cingulate cortex and the amygdala (which we explored in the last chapter). The amygdala (Latin for almond-shaped; there are two, one on each side of the brain) has been the focus of intensive research. The amygdala has been called the 'fear centre' and is associated with emotional memory. When the frontal lobes shut down, several authors have referred to this as the amygdala 'hijacking' the neocortex. This is not strictly true. The amygdala doesn't take over the frontal lobes under pressure; it's just that the frontal lobes stop working and we can't think straight. Nevertheless the limbic system has vast interconnections with the neocortex, which means that brain function is neither purely limbic nor purely cortical but a mixture of both, as evidenced by conditioning.

And finally, the neocortex is the most recent layer of the brain, evolving over the limbic brain. The neocortex makes up two-thirds of the total brain mass and is responsible for the higher cognitive functions that distinguish human beings from many other species. It is home to free will and is what allows us to think, learn and rationalize. MacLean referred to the neocortex as 'the mother of invention and father of abstract thought'.

The neocortex is divided into two hemispheres, right and left, and across each hemisphere there are four regions known as lobes: the frontal lobes, parietal lobe, temporal lobe and occipital lobe. As a quick guide, the frontal lobes, which are affected when heart rate is chaotic and we can't think straight, are responsible for intentional action and our ability to focus our attention. The reason we can sometimes be 'lost for words' when under pressure is because volitional language is also directed from the frontal lobes and the chaotic cardiac signal of the heart can make it next to impossible to access it properly. The parietal lobe is responsible for sensory perception. The temporal lobe is responsible for audio perception and the occipital lobe is responsible for visual perception (Dispenza, 2007).

In order to fully appreciate the importance of frontal lobe function and the need to avoid a functional DIY lobotomy in a business setting, it's worth exploring what happens to people when they suffer a head injury in a car crash and damage their frontal lobes. Functional frontal lobe shut-down can produce many of the same problems that occur in real frontal lobe damage following a car accident. Specifically frontal lobe damage can result in:

- severely impaired planning and organization capabilities;

- increased risk-taking behaviour;

- more aggressive and antisocial behaviour;

- disrupted timelines and sequencing;

- impaired attention shifting leading to perseverance with faulty answers;

- impaired working memory;

- the inability to inhibit responses – an individual will tend to become socially inappropriate.

FIGURE 4.3   Brain development: level of connectivity at 0–2 years

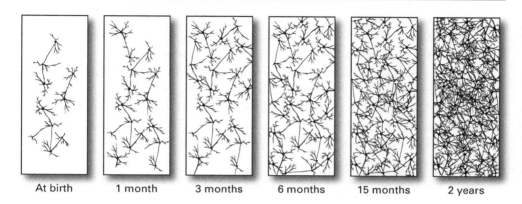

At birth   1 month   3 months   6 months   15 months   2 years

The three layers of the brain develop in order of age. During development from the embryo to the foetus the reptilian brain is formed first, then the limbic system and finally the neocortex. At birth the first two layers of the brain are almost fully developed whereas the neocortex is not (Figure 4.3).

MacLean assumed that the neocortex simply overrides the mammalian and reptilian brain, but it's actually a two-way street and the reptilian and mammalian brain can also inhibit the function of the neocortex. So if we want to get the most out of our 'smart' neocortex we must understand how the relationships between the different evolutionary layers of the brain really work. The subtlety and sophistication of these interactions is in fact central to understanding how executives make decisions and also what ultimately drives behaviour and our ability to make meaning.

One of the world's leading experts on the subtle and dynamic relationships within the human brain is neurophysiologist Karl Pribram. His research over the last 50 years is so groundbreaking that most neuroscientists are still coming to terms with it today. Pribram developed a theory that was able to explain the brain's incredible data storage capability. This theory also goes right to the heart of what may cause smart executives to make stupid calls and also of what enables some of the most advanced functions of the human mind.

The holographic brain

In the early 1940s Pribram became interested in the idea of where memory was stored. At the time the prevailing scientific view was that memories were stored like files in a filing cabinet somewhere in the brain and it was just a matter of time before the boffins discovered where that filing cabinet was located. But in 1946 Pribram went to work with eminent neuro-psychologist Karl Lashley, who had also been investigating the location of memory. What they discovered completely changed our understanding of how the brain works. Lashley had performed a series of experiments where he had taught rats to run a maze. Then he surgically removed parts of a rat's brain to see if it could still remember how to run the maze. The experiment was then repeated over and over again until the rat had lost most of its brain mass and yet it could still run the maze. The rats did become clumsier and it sometimes took them longer to run the maze but their memory of the maze was not impaired in any way.

Pribram was fascinated by these results. If memories were stored in filing cabinets in the brain but you removed all the locations where the filing cabinets could be and the rats could still remember how to run the maze, then memory was clearly not stored in a specific location in the brain. Plus the sheer volume of memory that a person must accumulate in a lifetime would have required millions of filing cabinets, and how was it even possible to store that volume of data in the six inches between our ears?

Pribram felt sure that memory was somehow distributed through the brain and 'pulled down' when needed by some sort of mechanism he didn't understand. In 1948 he went to work at Yale but continued to be puzzled by this phenomenon, especially as he studied patients who had lost portions of their brain and yet their memories were not impaired. But again he couldn't figure out how this was possible. Then, as Pribram read an article in the mid-1960s documenting the first construction of a hologram, he suddenly became very excited. What if the brain was holographic in nature? (Talbot, 1991).

Pribram discovered that one of the most interesting things about a hologram is that if we cut a hologram of say, an apple, in half we don't have two halves of an apple; rather we have two holograms of the complete apple. If we then cut those two halves in half we would get four complete apples. And this phenomenon continues with every cut providing increasingly small yet complete apples. This occurs because a hologram is actually a phenomenal data-compression system, so even when we half the hologram we still have enough information to reconstruct the entire apple.

If we look at a real holographic plate containing the data of an apple we don't actually see an apple. Instead we see what's known as 'interference' in the shape of lots of concentric overlapping circles. Think of it like the ripples that occur when a pebble is dropped into water – the pebble creates lots of

FIGURE 4.4   Schematic of hologram construction

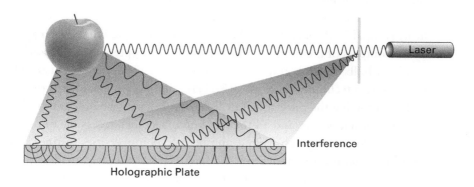

Holographic Plate

concentric circles that move out from the place the pebble was dropped. If two pebbles are dropped into a pond at the same time, one from the right hand and the other from the left hand then two series of concentric circles that will pass through each other are created. Those waves that move out from the pebble and cross each other are known as the 'interference pattern'. Any type of wave can create an interference pattern: waves in water, light waves or radio waves. If you looked at a holographic plate – that's what you'd see (Figure 4.4).

If we shine a light through the interference pattern – the apple magically reappears. But not just any light. If we shone a light bulb through a holographic plate we would not see the hologram; we might see something emerge but it would be very poor quality. However if we shone the pure, coherent light of a laser through a holographic plate, the hologram of the apple would appear, so clear and perfect we would feel as though we could reach out and take a bite.

This holographic property would not only account for the fact that memory didn't seem to be situated in any particular location of the brain and was distributed equally throughout the brain. It also explained how it's possible to store so much information. It didn't matter that the physical brain was removed from the rats because the information was still stored in the interference patterns in what was left of the brain, and from even a fraction of the original information it was possible to recreate the entire data set or memory. Memories or information are not stored in mental filing cabinets at all; they are compressed, like zipped files on our computer. The file will only decompress to give us access to that memory or information when the right 'light' is shone through the plate.

But what has all this to do with our ability to make decisions or the fact that under pressure we give ourselves a DIY lobotomy? At Complete Coherence we believe that the heart plays a critical role within the human system. The heart is capable of generating a chaotic, incoherent signal that, when applied to the contents of the brain, is about as potent as applying the diffused light of a light bulb to a holographic plate. If however we develop cardiac coherence, using a technique such as BREATHE, outlined in Chapter 1, then it is akin to applying the pure coherent light of a laser to the holographic plate and all of what we are and all that we know becomes accessible to us.

In fact recent research from a number of US universities testifies to the distributed nature of innovative thinking. This research provides a more precisely nuanced explanation for how innovation actually happens in the brain involving a number of different brain centres. The evidence suggests that just prior to the apprehension of a new idea by the frontal lobes a burst of alpha activity inhibits the visual data coming out of the occipital lobes (Kounios et al, 2006). This 'cognitive blink' is followed by a burst of gamma activity in the right superior temporal lobe (Ellamil et al, 2012). The right superior temporal lobe, through its much greater level of connectivity compared with the left, co-opts several other brain regions to contribute data that is necessary for the creation of a new idea. This information is submitted to the frontal lobes. Functional magnetic resonance imaging studies suggest that, rather than a huge burst of diffuse frontal lobe activity, there is a quieter, more focused activation of the frontal lobes (Jung et al, 2009). This supports the idea that focused coherent activation may be at play, rather than there being the prefrontal shut-down suggested by some authors (Limb and Braun, 2008). Such coherent activation allows the frontal lobes to access information that was previously unconscious or lost in the noise or diffuse interference.

The power of a coherent signal

When we are angry or feeling under pressure, our erratic, unpredictable and chaotic heart signal (HRV) travels up the vagus nerve and hits the 'holographic plate' of the brain, but because the 'light' is chaotic we don't get full access to the information stored holographically in the brain. If that signal is coherent however then, even in intensely pressurized situations, we can keep our frontal lobes turned on and maintain access to the smartest parts of our brain. When we generate coherent signals from all our bodily systems more of the time then our thinking becomes clearer, we become much more perceptive, more innovative and we have far greater access to all of our innate cleverness regardless of how tough the market conditions are. In short, we can become brilliant every day and give ourselves a massive competitive advantage.

All our memories, all the information we've accumulated, the knowledge and experience we've gathered is not stored in mental filing cabinets; it's stored as interference patterns in our brain and it is the physiological signals from our body, especially our heart, that may hold the key to whether we can access that information or not.

Some people have even suggested that creating a coherent signal may even allow us to tap into collective consciousness or the wisdom of crowds (Talbot, 1991). What's clear is that it is the quality of our physiology and our emotions that determines the quality of our thinking, not the other way around.

When we experience the DIY lobotomy or seem to have taken a 'stupid pill', it's not because we've suddenly become stupid; it's because we are trying to access our intelligence by candle light! If we try to view the hologram by shining a candle light through the holographic plate we won't see anything but the interference patterns. But all we need to do to convert the candle to a laser is to stabilize our system through smooth rhythmic breathing and become emotionally literate enough to recognize and manage the emotional signals circulating through our body at any given moment. That's why the signal from our body to our brain is critical in giving us access to what is in our brain.

Have you ever wondered where a good idea was two seconds before you had it? It was already in your mind, circling like an aeroplane waiting to land. When it comes to cognitive ability, creativity and problem solving, the problem is rarely that we can't think of the idea or solution; it's that we can't land it. When we change the physiological conditions, suddenly the things that we couldn't quite retrieve or access or tap into suddenly start landing like airplanes on the main runway at Heathrow airport. When we are 'on fire', metaphorically speaking, ideas are flowing easily and we're on a roll, planes are landing every couple of minutes. What I think is happening physiologically is that we are creating a coherent physiological state that's facilitating our very best thinking.

The development of maturity

The primary task in front of us if we really want to be smarter is to 'wake up' and 'grow up'. Physiological and emotional coherence will certainly facilitate a significant improvement in cognitive function and ability, but if we are to make a quantum leap then vertical development of adult maturity is the only way. If we are to prosper and genuinely thrive in a VUCA world, we need to expand our awareness and maturity so as to raise the calibre of leadership exponentially – Shaun Usmar, one of the most energetic and innovative financial leaders I've ever worked with, is clear on the importance of leadership. Reflecting on Enlightened Leadership and his time as Chief Financial Officer for Xstrata Nickel – the world's fourth largest nickel producer – Shaun explains:

> We put aside lots of time to help mostly inexperienced managers and vice presidents who had grown up in technical functional roles to think more broadly. We would dedicate half a day or a full day to work through scenarios. We also broadened out the attendees and included people who were not necessarily the most senior, but who had good promise or something to contribute to a particular part of the discussion. Having worked through those scenarios, our people had the ability to think through what might happen or what course of action or decision we might need to take when things got tough... We used very different thinking and tried to challenge each other, not to be destructive but to get people to stretch their thinking. We worked on helping them to think from a broader, macro perspective and to understand how decisions interrelated and how their decision could impact on the whole business. The most senior people at the centre don't have the monopoly on brains. We discovered that if you combine challenging discussions with decent models and data then you can make profound changes... We entered the financial crisis in the upper third quartile on costs in our industry, but we exited in the lower second quartile – we had leapfrogged the competition.

You can read Shaun's full case study at **www.coherence-book.com**.

In the last chapter we explored how consciousness emerged and how that emergence is inextricably entwined with emotion and our sense of self. But awareness or even self-awareness is not simply an on/off phenomenon; there are many levels and degrees of sophistication that we must evolve through. The way that we think and lead an organization is fundamentally altered by the level of consciousness, awareness or maturity we operate from at any given time. These levels literally transform our ability to succeed (Rooke and Torbert, 2005).

Everyone understands that children go through key stages of development – physically, emotionally, cognitively and morally. These stages are often visible and very obvious. Most of us, as parents or aunts or uncles, have witnessed this development first hand. Infants wake up to the world around them and figure out their place in that world as they physically grow up.

When most human beings reach the level of development of the average 14-year-old they have most of the necessary skills and capabilities they require to function in an adult world. In most cases there is no 'burning platform' or strong need for them to develop further. A few years later, they leave school or university and believe they've finished their development. But in reality they've just completed one stage of development. The next stage is where the real magic happens. Once we reach physical maturity – that's when the really important adult development work should begin. It is this internal, invisible work that is critical to vertical development and holds the key to unlocking the vast reservoir of human potential.

Adult development is an invitation to become more sophisticated, not just physically but energetically, emotionally and mentally. This vertical development facilitates a broader, deeper, more mature perspective. When we expand our awareness in this way it can radically alter behaviour and results, not to mention health and well-being.

Most corporate training or leadership programmes focus on horizontal development or the acquisition of knowledge, skills and experience. Although worthwhile, horizontal development creates incremental shifts at best and does not result in much expanded awareness or increased maturity. Just because someone looks 'all grown up' on the outside doesn't mean they are 'all grown up' on the inside. Remember the successful female executive from Chapter 1 who was given additional horizontal development; because she hadn't woken up to the world around her and grown up as an adult human being, the horizontal development just made her a more sophisticated manipulator. She was the same person, just more knowledgeable at how to get her own way. That's not helpful.

The horizontal development journey is just the beginning – it gets us to the starting line not the finish line. The vertical development journey is the real journey and it can create quantum leaps in development that can immeasurably expand capacity, creativity and productivity. And yet most organizations are blissfully unaware of the significant academic literature on adult development. Most companies have not yet realized that the future of their businesses and their leaders fundamentally depends on their ability to develop vertically.

When it comes to adult development and maturity there have been many significant contributions, from the early days of Piaget (1972), Kohlberg (1981) and Loevinger (L-Xufn Hy, Loevinger and Le Xuan Hy, 1996) to luminaries such as Ken Wilber, Susanne Cook-Greuter, William Torbert and Clare Graves. Each describes the vertical evolution of maturity and adult development from a slightly different perspective (Table 4.1). Wilber, whom we'll unpack

TABLE 4.1 Comparison of key adult development frameworks

Wilber's self-awareness	Graves's spiral dynamics[1]	Cook-Greuter's ego development[2]	Torbert's action logic[3]	World view	World % Pop[4]
10 Non-dual					
9 Pure awareness					
8 Unity in duality		Unitive (6)	Ironist (<1%)	Post-post conv. Cosmocentric	
7 Pure being (walk the walk)	Harmonizing TIER 2 Turquoise (1%)	Magician (5/6)	Alchemist (2%)	Post conventional Worldcentric	10%
6 Integrated self (walk the talk)	Integrative TIER 2 Yellow (12%)	Strategist (5)	Strategist (4%)		
5 Transpersonal self (talk the walk)	Inclusive TIER 1 Green (10%)	Pluralist (4/5)	Individualist (10%)		
	Individualistic TIER 1 Orange (34%)	Achiever (4)	Achiever (30%)	Conventional Ethnocentric	75%
		Expert (3/4)	Expert (38%)		
	Absolutist TIER 1 Blue (19%)	Conformist (3)	Diplomat (12%)		
4 Concrete self (talk the talk)	Egocentric TIER 1 Red (24%)	Self-protective (2/3)	Opportunist (5%)	Pre-conventional Egocentric	10%
3 Concrete self	Magical TIER 1 Purple (5%)	Impulsive (2)	Impulsive (<1%)	Pre-Egoic	
2 Emotional self	Instinctive TIER 1 Beige (0%)	Undifferentiated			
1 Physical self					

in a moment, looks at the evolution of awareness or consciousness of self. This is especially useful when considering how to be smarter and how to elevate our own personal levels of maturity. Cook-Greuter takes the perspective of ego development, which is similar to self and helps to explain maturity. Torbert's 'Action Logics' look at how those stages play out in business; this can be especially insightful when looking at behaviour and will be explored in more detail in the next chapter. And finally Graves's model of 'Spiral Dynamics', which will be explored in more depth in Chapter 6, is especially relevant to individual and collective values and explains how businesses and cultures evolve. See Table for 4.1 for comparisons.

These models offer us clear and elegant frameworks for understanding some profound truths and insights into how life works. Or as Graves puts it, their purpose is to illustrate:

> that the psychology of the mature human being is [an] unfolding, emergent, oscillating spiralling process marked by progressive subordination of older, lower-order behaviour systems to newer, higher-order systems as an individual's existential problems change. Each successive stage, wave, or level of existence is a stage through which people pass on their way to other states of being. When the human is centralized in one stage of existence, he or she has a psychology which is particular to that state. His or her feelings, motivations, ethics and values, biochemistry, degree of neurological activation, learning systems... conceptions of and preferences for management, education, economics, and political theory and practice are all appropriate to that state (Graves, 1981).

Regardless of which academic theorist we adhere to or which aspect of vertical development fires our imagination, there are various processes that will or can occur in the transition from one level to the next. As Goethe once said, 'Progress has not followed a straight ascending line, but a spiral with rhythms of progress and retrogression, of evolution and dissolution' (Phipps, 2012).

Behavioural scientists have also confirmed Goethe's original insight. Progress is almost always followed by faltering, stagnation or regression (Prochaska, Norcross and Diclemente, 1994). The early stages of each new level are unstable so they can feel uncomfortable and unfamiliar. So being clear about the different stages of vertical maturity can help to stabilize each new level so that additional transformational development is possible and regression is avoided.

The process of moving through the levels involves:

1 Differentiation: understanding how this stage differs from the previous stage.

2 Integration: internalizing the learning of this new stage.

3 Consolidation: increasing comfort and identification with the stage.

4 Realization: something's missing and becoming restless with the status quo.

5 Transformation: moving into the next stage.

6 Regression: backslide to previous level if proper consolidation doesn't occur.

The rules of adult development

In addition to the process of evolution through the levels, all of these vertical development theories share the following 'rules'. These rules or observations are the 'physics of vertical development' and none of us escape their gravity (Cook-Greuter, 2004):

- Adult development describes how human potential evolves towards increased sophistication, deeper understanding and greater wisdom, facilitating greater potential for effectiveness but not necessarily greater success.

- Adult development follows a logical sequence of stages like the levels of a computer game. We can't skip a level, and if we haven't fully gathered what we need at a new stage we may need to go back, retrace our steps and properly consolidate the learning of one level in order to be successful at the next.

- As we move from one level to the next the challenges we face become more complex; they evolve from static single issues to dynamic multi-dimensional issues. We evolve from an ego centric perspective to socio centric (embracing the 'tribe', 'family', 'team' or 'organization' we are bonded to) to world centric (where global concerns and planetary dynamics become central).

- Later stages can only be reached by successfully overcoming the trials and tribulations of early stages. Once we have successfully completed the challenges inherent in the early stages we take that learning with us and it becomes part of our skill set that we can then access at later more complex stages.

- Each new stage transcends and includes the previous stage, like a series of nested Russian dolls. When a child learns to run s/he does not lose the ability to walk. In the same way, the knowledge we accumulate at each level remains part of our experience.

- Each later stage provides the possibility of greater functioning in all previous levels because our abilities are more mature, differentiated and integrated. We are less attached to any one particular perspective and can change or adapt much more easily, providing the potential to drive successful transformation of our organization or life.

- As we mature through each successive stage, what we notice and what we pay attention to changes. Therefore what we are able to talk about, explain and impact also expands. Our ability to influence a wider world increases but that doesn't mean we always will. It means we are able to if we choose.

- As we mature up each level, our defensiveness diminishes and our freedom to act increases. Our tolerance for ambiguity increases and our fascination with diversity and ability to work with that diversity also improves. We become more reflective, less reactive, more responsive, more sensitive and less troubled. We become more skilful in our interactions.

- Someone at a later stage can understand the issues facing someone at an earlier stage, but an earlier stage traveller has no way of conceptualizing the challenges or thought processes of someone at a later stage. This represents a critical disconnect and is the reason behind much of the confusion and disharmony in business. It is always the responsibility of the more sophisticated person to adapt to the less sophisticated person since they are the only one that really can.

- The ascent through the stages of maturity occurs as a result of the interaction between individuals and their environment. If a leader is comfortable at a certain level there is no reason for further ascent. Most people do not develop unless there is a reason to do so, and unfortunately this often means they are in pain or confusion. Development can only really be guided by someone who has ascended beyond the current level and who understand the demands of the journey. Many may offer to guide our ascent but very few can take us to the mountain top.

- No matter how much we develop, our wisdom is inevitably incomplete and always somewhat constrained by our maturity, the happenstance of our birth and the way that we have been socialized.

To succeed in a volatile, uncertain, complex and ambiguous world, leaders will need to develop more sophisticated, systematic thinking. They will need to master collaboration and effective change management, and these are all abilities that only start to become really sophisticated at Level 6 and above (see Table 4.2). Unfortunately, Torbert reported in the *Harvard Business Review* that a whopping 85 per cent of leaders are currently operating just at that level or below (Rooke and Torbert, 2005). A little over half of all leaders (55 per cent) are currently operating at a level of sophistication that is insufficient if their business is to prosper today and into the future. Although this probably goes some way to explain the levels of stress in modern business, it can all be changed with genuine vertical development.

Our level of maturity or awareness is therefore fundamental to our ability to be smarter because it effectively creates a lens through which we view and interact with the world. The truth is that most people are completely unaware that they are looking at the world from one rigid perspective through one particular lens that is determined by their own individual level of maturity. Only once we 'wake up' to that fact can we truly 'grow up' and mature.

Think of it like a fish swimming in water. The fish has no idea it's even in water and yet its entire life is determined and dictated by the water. Its very existence depends on the water. Human beings are the same, in that we are swimming around in our own particular pool of consciousness or maturity and we assume that everyone else is swimming in the same pool and seeing the same things, thinking the same things and viewing the world in exactly the same way. We're not.

What we experience and think about, and the depth and breadth of those thoughts, is very much dependent therefore on what pool we are swimming in. It can therefore be extremely helpful to understand what pool we are in or what level of consciousness or maturity we are currently operating from, so we can understand where we are (if we don't know where we are then we are lost) and appreciate the next step of our evolutionary journey of vertical development.

The 10 stages of consciousness

Living things may become consciously aware of their environment at the level of 20,000 neurons (Hameroff and Penrose, 2003) but as human beings we have 7 billion neurons in our head, not to mention the neural networks elsewhere in the body. Such a network is capable of extremely sophisticated consciousness and human beings are therefore capable of developing vertically up 10 distinct levels (Table 4.2) (Wilber, 2001).

TABLE 4.2   The 10 stages of consciousness

Level of awareness	Average age of first bloom	Key characteristics
10. Non-dual		Same as 9 but with an evolutionary spin; vast transcendent blissful emptiness, immediacy, pure presence.
9. Pure awareness		Pure awareness, direct experience where 'observer' has gone, transcends subject–object relationship, transcends time, space and concepts of such. 'Formless union'. Tinged with bliss.
8. Unity in duality		Experience of 'divine' union, 'oneness' with an object (God, golf ball, lover), but subject and object remain. Can foster an obsession with the focus of the 'union'. Duality as there is a witness observing the union.
7. Pure being (walk the walk)		More consistent 'being' state, with nourishing personal presence, phenomenal energy and powers of concentration, incredible selflessness. Experienced by others as a 'spiritual person'.
6. Integrated self (walk the talk)		Major development work completed, emotional baggage resolved and 'shadow' integrated.
5. Transpersonal self (talk the walk)	11–15 yrs and many adults	Interior world opens up properly for the first time. Thinking about thinking emerges, abstraction and algebra become possible.
4. Concrete self (talk the talk)	7–11 yrs and most adults	Clearly recognizable 'consciousness' or awareness. Engagement with the material world. Rules and roles drive behaviour (cf The Matrix).

TABLE 4.2 *continued*

Level of awareness	Average age of first bloom	Key characteristics
3. Conceptual self	3–6 yrs	Three-dimensional representation of the world. Language is the main gain here and the ability to label the world.
2. Emotional self	2–3 yrs	Two-dimensional, emotions give depth to experience. Formal self-identity starts to emerge based in how 'I' feel. And 'I' may feel different things from 'you'.
1. Physical self	~1 yr	One-dimensional, experience dominated by physical needs and driven by physiology. Realization that 'I' am separate from 'you'.

A number of leaders who have started to develop their self-awareness and have started to reflect on the quality of their own thinking have found new meaning in the 1999 movie *The Matrix*. The Warchowski brothers, who wrote this sci-fi trilogy, were big fans of the anime genre, and while the film works as a basic boys' 'shoot 'em up' action movie it is also an insightful commentary on human consciousness. Computer hacker Neo, played by Keanu Reeves, discovers a reference to the Matrix in computer code and seeks out the answers. By way of messages on his computer screen he is encouraged to 'Wake Up Neo' and follow a 'white rabbit', itself a reference to Lewis Caroll's *Alice in Wonderland* story on altered states of consciousness. Eventually Neo meets Morpheus who offers him the choice between a red and a blue pill. Choosing the red pill, he then becomes aware of a deeper 'unseen' reality – billions of people connected to a machine that is harvesting their energy while they experience a simulated virtual reality. Each of these individuals effectively chose the blue pill and they believe they are walking around, talking to friends and living a normal, fun life. But it's all really an illusion and Neo sees the truth because he chose the red pill.

As human beings develop they experience something similar, because at each stage of development we feel sure that we are experiencing reality as it really is. We're not; we're experiencing reality from that level of consciousness only. If we want to massively shift our thinking into a totally different dimension of depth, perception and insight, then we must understand consciousness and actively develop consciousness so we expand our awareness beyond the ordinary. When we vertically develop our awareness we are able to tap into an extreme competitive advantage. With each level we expand our perception still further, making us smarter and smarter and finally giving us access to the ideas and innovation outside that famous box everyone (even those in *The Matrix*) is talking about! As we develop we see more of what's really going on, and with that knowledge comes power to change the game.

Below is a brief description of each of the 10 levels Wilber has described.

Level 1 consciousness: the physical self

The first level in conscious evolution is the development of the physical self. This normally occurs within the first year of life when an infant bites his thumb and bites his blanket and realizes that biting his thumb hurts and biting his blanket doesn't! The first level of conscious awareness is therefore rooted in physical sensation. 'I am the thing that hurts when I bite it.' Prior to this there is no 'self' and there is little discrimination of an external world or other people. It is all just 'me'. Even at this first level of consciousness the world is still pretty one-dimensional and awareness of anything other than physical needs and bodily functions is largely absent. This stage is grounded in physiology.

The emergence of the physical 'self' is beautifully illustrated when you put a baby in front of a mirror. Before they have developed a sense of their own physical existence they will look at their own image and not realize they are looking at themselves. It is always a very special moment to witness the first awaking of self. Initially there is indifference then confusion, after a while the baby will move and see the same movement reflected back to them, then a moment of recognition lights up their face as they finally realize the person they are looking at is 'me'.

Level 2 consciousness: the emotional self

Once the physical self becomes stabilized and recognizes itself as separate from others then, sometime in the second year, the emotional self also starts to emerge as separate, although these early stages may vary in when they blossom. At this stage infants begin to realize that they are not only physically separate from others but that they may not be experiencing the same emotions as others. For example, children may be bawling their eyes out in frustration at having their needs thwarted by their parents and be completely baffled as to why their parents are not also crying at the injustice of it all.

Prior to this differentiation children do not really make a distinction between their emotional needs and the emotional needs of others. So an infant would think, 'If I'm hungry the world must be hungry.' So they shout and complain because they can't understand why we would not be satisfying their hunger. This phase has often been referred to as the 'terrible twos' because of the tantrums that occur in an attempt to control the environment and have their needs met. However, it is really only a developmental stage.

At this early stage, because of the lack of separation, infants are emotionally contagious. They easily spark each other into tears or laughter and they are also easily influenced by the mood of the adults around them. They are incredibly egocentric as they want their emotional needs met.

Once this separation begins, however, they realize that their self-map does not match their map of others, particularly in relation to emotions. When this emotional self develops, suddenly the world has more depth; it has become two-dimensional. Entering this second dimension is a magical time for children. There is as yet no real responsibility and no great understanding of what makes the world work. They are physically and emotionally separate entities from the world around them but their thinking is still magical – to a child of this age the clouds seem to follow them.

Level 3 consciousness: the conceptual self

Once a child is two to three years old the evolution of the self takes a third step. Here consciousness starts to use language, images, symbols and concepts to represent the world, and this stage often lasts until the child is about six years old.

Children acquire words at a phenomenal rate during these early years; roughly six new words a day are absorbed. They start to label everything and this helps them navigate their world. They develop feelings as the emotions previously experienced are represented conceptually and start to be consciously appreciated as belonging to them. The world becomes three-dimensional and the thinking moves from magical to mythical – they know that they can't order the world around (magical) but someone can (mythical). This can be a little frightening as a child realizes that s/he is no longer in charge of the world; someone else is. Nightmares can start to occur. At this stage feelings are central.

Level 4 consciousness: the concrete self

At the fourth level of consciousness, as most people would recognize it, both self-consciousness and consciousness of the self start to emerge. The three-dimensional world becomes much more concrete. There are rules and regulations that govern the world and these must be followed. Children often become much more conformist and develop a belief in 'right' and 'wrong'. They start to rehearse various social scripts as a way of learning the social rules or ways of behaving. There is a strong need to belong and children succumb to peer pressure and herd mentality. Rationality and 'self-talk' begin as we become much more sophisticated in justifying our behaviour. This stage normally starts to develop at five or six years old and continues to eight or nine years old.

This is the first level where there is some, albeit limited, sophistication in the thinking. It is also the level that Einstein refers to when he suggested that human beings are boxed in by the boundary conditions of their thinking. Level four consciousness is where the box that boxes us in is created, and unfortunately this is where the journey ends for many people as they live out their days in this concrete three-dimensional world, with rules and regulations to be followed or ignored. There is a degree of consciousness of self at this level, but life is very concrete and materialistic. It's about working out the rules and following them, doing a good job; taking care of needs and 'getting through' is the primary objective. The recipe for life at this stage of consciousness is:

HAVE

DO

BE

So, 'If I have enough money, I will be able to do what I want and then I will be happy.' Or 'If I have enough time, I will be able to do my job and I will be successful.' Or 'If I did not have parents on my case all the time I would have the freedom to do the things I like doing and then I would be less trouble.' There are many versions of this recipe.

Most of us have encountered plenty of people in businesses who are still operating from this level of maturity. They are following the rules laid down by their industry, company or boss, and most of the time they conform to those rules without question or they deliberately 'break the rules' to operate 'out of the box', which ironically has itself become a rule for how to operate!

People may be 40 years old on the outside but on the inside they may developmentally be still operating at a much younger level. Perhaps you've witnessed managers behaving like children in an attempt to assert their own egocentric needs. This is really a combination of a Level 3 desire to have needs met fuelled by an egocentric rule that 'I am the boss so I should be able to satisfy my needs.' Playground behaviour such as bullying can also occur when a manager has not grown beyond this level. This is the level of *The Matrix* where the manager has swallowed the blue pill. We think we know how the game is played and we are following the rules, largely unaware that we are following the rules. We may be breaking the rules but in a way that also still stays within the confines of the rules for rule breaking. At this level leaders are not really awake or able to appreciate that there is something going on, a more sophisticated version of reality, although in almost every case executives at this level already believe they are aware.

It's worth pointing out however that Einstein also said that you can't solve a problem from the same level of consciousness that created it. When people get stuck at Level 4 consciousness it's almost impossible to find new, creative and innovative solutions to challenges because they can't exit the level of consciousness that created the problem in the first place – they literally can't think outside the box.

At Level 4 individuals are said to 'talk the talk'. They are talking about stuff but it's not necessarily the right stuff or appropriate stuff and they are certainly not doing anything about that stuff.

Level 5 consciousness: the transpersonal self

Between the ages of 9 and 14 the individual starts to become aware that something else is going on, and as a result there are various sub-stages to this level.

In the swampy foothills of the fifth level the tribal, ethnocentric herd mentality of the third dimension collapses. There is a realization that it is no longer just about 'me'. Individual awareness becomes more 'transpersonal' and the ability to think about thinking emerges. The frontal lobes and nerve tracts have become fully myelinated, which allows high-speed 'broadband' connections within the frontal cortex and with other brain regions. This drives more sophisticated thinking and abstraction becomes possible. As a result children can learn algebra.

If you ask an eight-year-old child '4B=16, what does "B" equal?' they will look at you with baffled amusement. Ask a 12-year-old and they can hold the 'B' in abstraction while they resolve the relationship between '4' and '16'. Once they realize that the answer is 'x4' then they retrieve the 'B' from abstraction to generate the answer 'B=x4'.

These new cognitive functions cause the interior world to open up for the first time. As such, a fourth dimension is accessed. Self-reflection becomes possible, even desirable. This is a watershed moment because the physical world is no longer three-dimensional, as it at first appeared. There is a realization that it is possible to transcend the concrete rules and roles, that there is more to life than following the roles laid down by other people, generations or society. The ability to judge and criticize comes to the fore, so individuals at this level initially become very critical, judgemental and intolerant of both themselves and others.

This angst may remind you of another stage within this level – the teen-age years! A surge in curiosity about how the world really works means that teenagers think more. No longer constrained by solely meeting their own egocentric needs, they start to question the rules and test the bound-aries. This is often a source of significant parent–teenager conflict. A battle of wills often ensues as smart teenagers start to realize that the rule book given to them by their parents is almost exclusively fabricated and arbitrary. At this stage the teenager has bitten off a corner of the red pill and is begin-ning to see the world as it really is. The battles on rules, roles and teenage identity can rage on for years, particularly if neither side realizes that this is a normal developmental stage not a game of 'chicken'.

Regardless of who wins that particular battle, when the young adult leaves home they encounter a much more powerful parent called 'society', which imposes its own rules: 'get a job', 'get a qualification', 'get married', 'earn money', 'have kids', 'be a good citizen'. The inability to break free of this omnipotent 'parent' often causes despondency and hopelessness that pushes the young adult back into Level 4 consciousness and the concrete world. Effectively they fail to fully consume the red pill and instead unwit-tingly choose the blue pill and the course of least resistance. They conform, follow the masses, assume safety in numbers and slavishly follow societal conventions and social norms. The alternative is often too scary so they become unconscious again, 'forget' the glimpses of reality they were privy to and plug back into the Matrix.

For those who have dropped back down into the concrete self, life can become very stereotypical as the rules and roles take control once again.

It is during the transpersonal that we are invited to pull back the veil and think about the nature of thought. What is it? Where do thoughts come from? What determines what we think and what determines how well we think it? The quality of our thoughts is not just dependent on our know-ledge and experience and our access to that data; it is also dependent on the content of our consciousness or how aware we are.

Waking up – the disease of meaning

The conformity of Level 4 is however often interspersed by glimpses of transpersonal stage awareness. If our life is just not conforming to some set of rules, be they societal, organizational or some alternative group, then we may have entered the trials and tribulations of the lower fifth trans-personal level. The first sign that we have entered this new level is that we feel uncomfortable. The world is no longer safe or secure or as stable as we thought it was. Something is wrong but we don't know what it is. Unfortunately, being slightly out of our comfort zone is insufficient to wake most people up.

If the individual is really lucky something happens to fully waken them or shock them from the slumber of their concrete world. Most often this is a personal crisis in the form of a loss such as the loss of a job, the loss of a marriage, the loss of a loved one, the loss of purpose or the loss of self-esteem through a period of depression. This usually occurs in mid-life and the crisis marks the entry into the 'disease of meaning'. Individuals then start to realize that they have been following a set of rules and playing certain roles for decades on the implicit 'understanding' that it would yield a certain reward. Only the health, wealth and happiness they were 'promised' didn't materialize!

When inflicted with the disease of meaning, people ask themselves, 'What's the point?' They feel despondent because they kept their side of the bargain. They believe they have been a dutiful husband/wife, father/mother, leader, worker, friend and colleague and it still didn't work out. They feel cheated. After all they played their part – they followed the rules but the reward never arrived or if it did it wasn't nearly as good as they were led to believe! I have seen this sense of injustice so often in business. It often occurs during a merger or acquisition where one side feels they have been hard done by or when one side isn't 'playing by the rules'. It also occurs when someone is suddenly made redundant after 25 years of loyal service. They didn't quite make it to the board and were then just cast aside. It often comes as a terrible shock that they could be treated this way, because they never even considered that their organization would be so callous and inhumane. And yet we hear stories all the time of people being marched out of the building by security guards as soon as they become surplus to the new requirements regardless of how long they have been working for the company.

Not everyone catches the disease of meaning through an acute crisis; for some it creeps up on them as a growing sense of dissatisfaction and a recognition that something's not working. At this stage people feel as though their life has not turned out as they expected it would, that somehow they are missing out on something. Sometimes the pain of this realization can be very sharp indeed. In religious terms this sub-stage is often referred to as purgatory or 'hell on earth'.

Many people spend their life stuck in this 'meaningless' swamp of early transpersonal awareness without realizing that it's just a developmental stage. Instead of moving on to higher levels of consciousness, they wrongly believe it's something they have to live with and set out on a quest to dull the pain. The two most popular strategies to dull the pain are:

- anaesthetic;
- distraction.

Anaesthetizing the pain usually takes the form of excessive alcohol or drug consumptions – prescription or otherwise. Alcohol is especially popular with busy executives, who frequently get by with a glass of wine or whisky every lunch time or every evening.

The range of distraction strategies and games that people play to avoid facing the issue of meaning are numerous. The commonest example of the 'mid-life crisis' is having an affair. During the excitement of deception or the act of physical intimacy, individuals may be distracted from the perceived lack of real meaning in their life. Unfortunately affairs end or the novelty wears off and the pain returns, only now it's amplified by remorse and guilt. And repeated or multiple simultaneous affairs don't solve the problem either.

Materialism is another common distraction strategy. When you are roaring around in a new Ferrari you are too exhilarated to consider the deeper meaning of life and why you are doing what you are doing. For a few weeks your life may actually take on new meaning as you tend to your beloved car, driving fast and showing off to colleagues, family and friends. But again, it soon wears off, the car is dented or scratched and you get used to the speed and envious looks. Before long it's just another car and the disease of meaning has flared up again. Spending money on any major purchase or shopping until you literally can't carry another bag is another common distraction strategy that delivers nothing more than a temporary balm and an inflated credit card bill.

Obsessive exercise is another beautiful distraction strategy, where executives turn into 'gym bunnies' obsessed with the 'body beautiful'. When they are 'feeling the burn' on the stair-master they do not have to think about meaning. Unfortunately the preoccupation with exercise wears off too and the disease of meaning returns.

All these strategies are seeking to find meaning using the Have, Do, Be recipe and they just don't work. The only real solution is to fully wake up and start growing up the levels of consciousness.

At some point the pain of the mid-life crisis becomes very intense; often this is necessary in order to facilitate a breakthrough. People hit 'rock bottom' and enter a very dark phase; they appreciate that their life isn't working and perhaps most importantly that nobody is coming to help. There is no white knight charging in on a majestic steed to save the day.

This is the most important moment in any life. When we finally realize that our parents aren't going to fix it, our boss isn't going to fix it, society or the government aren't going to fix it and that it's down to us to fix it – we finally take ownership, we evolve and we expand our awareness and our potential exponentially. At this stage individuals are forced to turn their attention from the outside to the inside. They finally realize that the blame and recrimination they have directed toward other people, situations or events has not helped to change the situation. It has kept them stuck in the meaninglessness of purgatory, and so they finally let go of the idea that someone else is to blame and look inside. As they do they swallow the red pill they ignored 20 years earlier and finally unplug from the Matrix. This is what Joseph Campbell (2012) called 'crossing the threshold' – the liberating realization that the move from ignorance to enlightenment is down to us and us alone. Just as I am responsible for my personal growth and vertical development, you are responsible for your personal growth and vertical development.

At Level 5 individuals are said to 'talk the walk'. People at the early stage of this level have read a few books, attended a few courses, they may be saying things like, 'Well of course we all have to be more emotionally intelligent.' But really they have 'aboutism': ie they know 'about' the subject they are discussing. Unfortunately they are not actually that emotionally intelligent because they have not internalized the knowledge. All they've done is regurgitated a few industry buzz words or some latest offering from the HBR or management journals so they can look like they know what they are talking about. Usually in these situations a few well-directed questions can highlight that there is no deeper intellectual understanding, they have not converted the knowledge into wisdom (Kaipa and Radjou, 2013) and put the knowledge into practice in their lives, despite their protestations that they have.

Level 6 consciousness: the integrated self

Moving on to the sixth level requires considerable effort and personal development. The upper reaches of Level 5 are consumed by the need to do some serious personal vertical development. This may take many forms. In the early days of the upper reaches of Level 5 the individual may start to read personal development books, explore religion or take classes in psychology, yoga and philosophy as they try to figure out what will make them happy and what they want to do with their life. For some it's not as ordered or structured as courses or books, but rather just a growing awareness of their own behaviour, a matter of having time to reflect on their life, the decisions they've made and why they made them. Some business executives take a career break or a sabbatical. If this is just another distraction strategy little may be gained, but if there is genuine insight there may be developmental progress. Critical to reaching the sixth level of awareness is the ability to own up to our own unhelpful patterns or the dark side of our nature. It can be as simple as recognizing when we were wrong and owning those errors. But to really make it to Level 6 there has to be a deeper understanding of why those errors occurred and how to prevent them occurring in the future. This is often called 'shadow work' (Bly, 2001). It involves working on those aspects of ourselves that are not easy to see, let alone address and ultimately heal.

But there are real dangers in the personal development journey of the upper fifth level. There are many dead ends, there are many guides who tempt us with promises of the 'summit', but they can't actually take us there as they have not done the journey themselves. Many executive coaches would argue that they don't need to have made the journey in order to be an effective guide, and whilst that may be true for the time management of some operational component it is not true of the personal vertical development journey. Remember the rule cited earlier: 'Someone at a later stage can understand the issues facing someone at an earlier stage, but an earlier stage traveller has no way of conceptualizing the challenges or thought processes of someone at a later stage.' If an executive is already at a later stage than the coach who is coaching him or her, then the coach will have no way of conceptualizing the challenges and thought processes of the executive and so is totally unable to help that executive move up to an even more sophisticated level. As a result, few people make it out of the forest of the upper fifth level of consciousness because there are very few guides or executive coaches who can actually help us get out.

I have witnessed many people who have been stuck in the forest of personal development for 20 or 30 years. They are still attending all manner of courses and, sadly, they are still unpleasant to their spouse or themselves. In order to exit this stage, the development has to actually work. The individual actually has to change, to transcend the patterns of the old and become an integrated human being. At this level the individual is no longer constrained by the scars of the past; they are aware of all aspects of self, good and bad, and have taken ownership of those traits. They have healed themselves and are free to make different choices, instead of being locked into reactive behaviours driven by early life conditioning.

In the conditioning example in the last chapter, had William transcended to Level 6 consciousness or above and achieved physiological and emotional coherence he would not have reacted to the interview candidate in the yellow shirt without knowing why. Instead his frontal lobes would have been fully 'on', allowing him to draw on all his skills, knowledge and experience to assess the candidate's suitability and find the right person for the role.

At Level 6 consciousness the individual ceases to be a victim and realizes that there is no merit in allowing other people to control their emotions. This can be an incredibly joyful and liberating experience because we come to appreciate that we really do have free will and it is not just a trite sound bite from the personal development industry.

Demonstrating Level 6 awareness, Eleanor Roosevelt once said, 'No one can make you feel inferior without your consent' (Roosevelt, 1960). As explained in the previous chapter we can't control what others do or what they say but we can always control what we make those things mean. Without this expanded awareness or emotional self-management, we are at the mercy of other people and their actions and reactions. When someone says something hurtful, they've behaved badly; it is therefore their issue, not ours. If we choose to feel upset about that, then we punish ourselves for someone else's transgression. That doesn't make sense. If we have the power to create the upset we also have the power to 'un-create' it, or even better just not to create it in the first place.

When we don't appreciate our own free will at a deep level we give people we don't even know, or people we don't like or respect, permission to ruin our entire day. And knowing what you now know about emotions and how toxic negative emotions can be for your health, are you really going to let someone else fur up your arteries? When we realize we don't have to give that permission and that if someone behaves badly it's their issue and not ours, then we have achieved ownership and emotional sovereignty. Life never improves and we will never be content for an enduring period of time until we take that ownership and master emotional sovereignty. At Level 6 there is complete ownership of all aspects of 'self'.

This moment of ownership is a paradigmatic shift – the clumsy caterpillar has transformed into the butterfly capable of flying above the crowd. When we cross the threshold, we leave the world as we knew it behind. Of course, it doesn't stop our children or other people from behaving badly, but we can choose how we feel about it.

Austrian neurologist and psychiatrist Victor Frankl talks about this moment during his experience in a Nazi concentration camp (Frankl, 1959). The Nazis took everything from him, including his wife, brother, parents and his life's work – a manuscript that had been sewn into the lining of his jacket. He experienced unspeakable horror and a daily struggle to survive, but he also realized that they could not take his self-esteem or his ability to choose how to feel about what was happening. When Frankl was eventually liberated by the Americans in 1945 he wrote *Man's Search for Meaning* and developed a type of existential therapy that helped millions of people to find meaning in their own lives – regardless of the challenges they faced.

As I said in the last chapter, if we want to be responsible human beings, we have to learn to be response-able; in other words to be able to respond rather than to react. We choose the response – as opposed to victimhood. Or as Frankl said, 'Between stimulus and response, there is a space. In that space is our power to choose our response. In our response lies our growth and our freedom.'

At Level 6 individuals are said to 'walk the talk'. These people start to convert 'aboutism' into action by putting the things they read about or know about into practice. In other words they are not just talking about being compassionate, they are compassionate. But they are not necessarily compassionate all the time. Like anyone else they have good days and bad days, although they are often aware of the bad days and can self-correct much more rapidly.

Level 7 consciousness: pure being

Individuals at this level have dealt with all their baggage so that they are a living example of what they've learnt. There is a warm radiance to these people. They have a nourishing personal presence, phenomenal energy and powers of concentration as well as incredible selflessness.

This is the way people describe meeting the Dalai Lama for example. I remember talking to Matthieu Ricard, the Dalai Lama's right-hand man in Europe, and he was talking about witnessing the difference between the queue going in and the queue coming out from seeing the Dalai Lama. Going in, people were full of their own importance and preening themselves, adjusting their ties or brushing their hair – all fluffed up in their finery. And they'd all come out in tears. His Holiness just melted them.

I experienced this myself when I and a colleague of mine spent an evening with Matthieu and his mum in their tiny little house in the Dordogne. We were conducting a research study with Tibetan monks and looking specifically at their physiology when they were in different types of meditative states

(Watkins, Young and Barrow, 2013). Matthieu's mum had also converted to Tibetan Buddhism and is also a brilliant painter in her own right. So there we were sitting in their little, humble home chatting around the table. After about 30 minutes I realized I was talking to two of the most spiritually important people on the planet and we were getting on like a house on fire. Both Matthieu and his mum were so utterly unconcerned with their own importance and it really emphasized one of the key personal qualities of this level – selflessness.

Nelson Mandela is another powerful example of Level 7 consciousness. He too has a nourishing personal presence and selflessness that is beguiling. When Mandela was having his 90th birthday celebrations a host of celebrities and international dignitaries flew in from all over the world for a photo. Mandela patiently and graciously went through the motions of doing what everyone else wanted although it probably wasn't actually what he wanted. The story goes that when it was all over he turned to the photographer who had been taking pictures all day and asked him if he would like a photo. To Mandela the photographer was no more or no less important than the people who had been visiting all day. But Mandela wasn't always this selfless or gracious. When he went to prison he was an angry man, yet he emerged after 27 years an extraordinary mediator, philosopher and president-in-waiting. He could have emerged even angrier but instead he did the personal development soul-searching work necessary to evolve as a human being.

The Dalai Lama and Nelson Mandela are two extreme examples but Level 7 consciousness can also be experienced with less well-known individuals who are non-judgemental, incredibly perceptive and loving. When we meet these people it can feel as though they really 'get' us – they see the warts and all and it's OK; all that exists is a profound loving empathy without criticism. That's what happens to the people in the queue to see the Dalai Lama. They feel understood and appreciated just for who they are and the energetic boost this creates can sustain them for weeks if not years!

And finally because these individuals have actually evolved and developed as human beings, not just physically from childhood to adulthood, they have incredible energy levels because they are not draining their energy tanks with frustrations, judgement and negative emotion. Their mind is no longer fogged up and they don't lobotomize themselves, so they demonstrate crystal clarity and impressive powers of concentration.

At Level 7 individuals are said to 'walk the walk'. These people have fully integrated the knowledge and personal growth they've accumulated and are living expressions of whom they seek to be. They are for example compassionate virtually all the time, not just now and then.

Level 8 consciousness: unity in duality

Unity in duality used to be considered as the ultimate state of conscious-ness. In the East it was called 'classical nirvana' – the ultimate destination of the spiritual journey when the student has achieved a joyful union with the 'divine'.

Many people will have experienced a glimpse of unity at some point of their life. Where and how that glimpse is experienced can alter their life forever because it can profoundly influence what they become interested in. It might for example occur as the person looks at the magnificence of the Grand Canyon. In that moment of awe their ego disappears and they merge with the Grand Canyon. Often these nature-induced experiences can feel semi-spiritual and can ignite a passion for the environment.

Others experience this moment of unity through sport. The reason some people become obsessed with golf, for example, is because they experienced the 'perfect shot', one moment where they struck the ball so perfectly in the sweet spot that they merged with the ball and become 'one with the ball'. This blissful glimpse was so moving that they then spend the rest of their golfing life trying to recreate that moment of unity. The same happens in all sports – the perfect backhand in tennis, the perfect strike in football or the killer wave in surfing.

For others, they experience moments of unity in church and people will describe it as 'seeing the face of God' so they become devout Christians, Muslims or Hindus – or whatever denomination they experienced unity in.

The vast majority of people on the planet have however never experi-enced unity in any other form than during sex. Individuals literally forget themselves at the peak of orgasm, which is one of the key reasons why sex becomes the primary and most powerful motivator for human beings – because it's the only time they ever experience unity.

But all of these experiences are not a pure unity. They are a unity in duality. So there is a realization that even if we have experienced unity it's not complete unity because there is an internal observer, observing the unity experience. As soon as we label an experience we separate ourselves from that experience. The person looking at the Grand Canyon can feel unity for a moment but as soon as s/he mentally or verbally acknowledges the magnificence of that spectacle s/he immediately creates duality in the unity by splitting the observer from the observed – subjective (I) is separate from objective (Grand Canyon).

Even at Level 8 consciousness it can be difficult to describe the experi-ence, but we know if we have experienced it. And that is definitely the case at Level 9.

Level 9 consciousness: pure awareness

Any attempt to describe Level 9 awareness immediately drops us into Level 8 because we become the observer observing again. So to really understand these higher levels we have to physically experience them because it's a bit difficult to capture them with the rational mind.

But let's have a go. Pure awareness: the Tibetans call it nothingness or emptiness, which frightens a lot of people. Vast blue sky: so there is no longer an observer observing; there is just the experience of 'formless union'. There is not someone noticing that they are looking at the Grand Canyon, just the individual and the Grand Canyon in a formless union that transcends the subject–object relationship. When someone experiences Level 9 they also transcend time and space: ie they start to realize that time is a construct and there is no time. Space too is infinite, there are no boundaries to space and the person is connected to the entire universe – a universe without end. There isn't an observer making this observation; there is just the experience of it.

'I' stops being in here and 'everything else' out there – it's all one. Pure awareness is a first-hand experience that we are all that is. It's a massively expanded state of consciousness.

When we are in Level 9 the good/bad, right/wrong, black/white, up/down duality of life is seen for what it really is – an artificial construction of lower levels of consciousness. There is no duality, no right, no wrong – it just is.

The ramifications of this viewpoint were driven home to me when I watched an episode of *Life on Earth* and the brilliant David Attenborough explained that if we shrink the evolution of the planet and all living things into one year, living organisms didn't emerge until August. At the beginning of November back-boned creatures emerged and left the water to colonize the land. By the beginning of December those back-boned creatures broke their dependence on water and by the middle of the same month they could generate heat in their body and the scales turned to feathers. On 25th December the dinosaurs disappeared and mammals and furry animals emerged. In the early morning of the 31st December apes arrived and human beings arrived two minutes before midnight (Attenborough, 1979).

Surely, it's difficult to get terribly upset about anything when we realize that human beings have been around for about two minutes! But Level 9 is not really about knowing that fact intellectually but experiencing it in our body. To say that we are in our infancy in terms of human development would be a vast understatement and yet we strut around thinking we've got the whole world all figured out. We haven't.

When seen from this perspective, the slights, upsets, challenges, disasters and traumas – large and small – are just tides of stuff. At pure awareness we cease to have preferences and transcend dualistic concepts of good/bad, right/wrong, etc. They are all just lesser conscious states to help us interpret the world, but actually the world is much more expanded and is all those things. It's everything. This is a blissful state of being. It's not someone observing the bliss, it's just bliss – a vast space with a tinge of blissful delight. This does not mean we cannot make a choice; we still can, but the way we perceive choices is completely different.

Level 10 consciousness: non-dual

This is very similar to Level 9 consciousness only Level 10 also has an evolutionary spin. When an individual transcends time and space, it's not as if they cease to exist. There is still a desk, an office and they can still see themselves in the mirror. But the relationship to the notion of desk, office and self is completely different – we are those things and see those things and experience those things, but we are also not those things.

In Level 10 it's still pure awareness but the universe is evolving so it's not just static being; it's being in motion. There is momentum and things are changing and evolving all the time so the awareness is in motion.

Where are you?

A preliminary indication of what level individuals are at can be gauged when they read the above descriptions. The minute an individual thinks, 'What the hell is this guy talking about?' is a pretty good indication that they operate at one or two levels before that level!

If you are resting in your garden and you notice a line of ants carrying a leaf back to base, you see the ants and understand what the ants are doing because you see the scene from a bigger, broader and more expanded perspective. The ants on the other hand are oblivious to you. They are busy with their task and they simply don't have the perspective to appreciate that they are being watched. Even if you could speak 'ant' and tell them that you were watching them, they would still not understand what you were talking about because they don't have the necessary frame of reference. Their experience of human beings is usually short-lived, as they are stood on or their tasks are interrupted in some way, but even if you decided to flick the leaf away they wouldn't understand what had happened. We can't understand the stages beyond our own development any more than the ant can understand you watching him and his mates carrying the leaf. If you have reached one of the upper levels of maturity (which means you definitely didn't deliberately stand on the ants and probably didn't flick the leaf away either) then you can understand all the levels of maturity that you evolved through on your way to your current level but someone on a lower level can't understand someone on a higher level.

Everyone on the planet can relate to all the levels up to Level 5 because all adults have made the physical development that coincides with that journey. Most adults therefore reach Level 5 without any thought or consideration on their part – it just happens by virtue of the passing years. Most drop back into Level 4 and others get stuck in the foothills of Level 5 forever, never finding enough motivation to engage in genuine vertical development.

These people may have a conceptual understanding of higher levels of consciousness but no real experience of them. They may get glimpses or realize there is something very special and different about the Dalai Lama or Nelson Mandela but they don't recognize those qualities in themselves. In truth very few people experientially understand beyond Level 8. What really matters in the context of adult development and maturity, however, is that we appreciate that adults develop differently from children and that a certain amount of effort and self-reflection is required to develop maturity, which can in turn transform thinking, behaviour and therefore results.

These maturity models are not a competition or an assessment of bad, better, best. The ant is no better or worse than a human being – just different, operating at different levels of awareness. A monkey is no better than a rock – just different, operating at different levels of awareness. A rock is still very useful in the right situation – if you want to break a coconut for example, a rock is considerably more useful than a monkey.

The same is true of people. These levels of maturity and adult development are not bad, better, best – their merit is in giving human beings a framework for development rather than a tool for comparison. They simply relate to the various ways human beings gain wisdom and maturity and make meaning. Each stage of maturity is more comprehensive, with increasing levels of differentiation that in turn allow an individual to deal more effectively with elevating levels of complexity from baby to adolescent to adult to mature adult. The self-centred life of an infant is, after all, considerably less complicated than the life of a global CEO.

At Complete Coherence we work with CEOs and business leaders to unlock the potential from vertical development, using a number of assessment processes and tailored coaching programmes. One of the most profound metrics for helping leaders assess their current location and where they could progress to is the Leadership Maturity Profile (LMP). The LMP uses Susanne Cook-Greuter's sentence-completion questionnaire to measure maturity – the most rigorously developed, tested, unbiased and reliable stage measure currently in existence. Unlike many questionnaires it's not possible to 'fix' or 'game' the right answers to the questions, because there are no right answers to the questions. Nonetheless the LMP provides leaders with an accurate insight into their own leadership maturity and personal integration and that of their individual team members. When leaders know the characteristics and behaviours associated with each level of adult maturity and how they manifest in business, much of the dysfunction in modern business is immediately explained. The LMP allows the leader to locate their own and their team's collective centre of gravity for personal and group maturity. This indicates where individuals operate from normally, where they can fall back to under pressure and where their opportunity for greatest growth lies. As a result the LMP often explains individual performance short-falls, why a team isn't working as well as it might or why it seems to be stuck in a destructive or unhelpful holding pattern and, perhaps most importantly, what to do about it.

Whose rules are they anyway?

Transformations of consciousness or awareness that alter an individual's world view or perspective are infinitely more powerful than the accumulation of more skills, knowledge and experience. It is these transformations that elevate thinking to a whole new level. Marcel Proust clearly understood vertical development when he said, 'The real voyage of discovery consists not in seeking new landscapes, but in having new eyes.' When we see the world through new eyes, the world itself is changed, and this awakening changes our interpretations, experiences, thoughts, feelings, behaviour and results.

What we therefore must appreciate is that our experience of the world, and specifically business, may be nothing more than the result of following a very sophisticated set of rules about the nature of business, and we are in fact stuck in concrete consciousness. These rules may lead us to believe that 'it's a dog-eat-dog world', and 'every man for himself', you need to 'muscle your way to the top', 'it's about shareholder return.' The list of 'rules' on how to successfully run a company, team or division is endless and most executives subscribe to them even though no one really knows where they came from, who wrote them or when they were created. And these rules are very rarely questioned. As soon as leaders reach the 'C-suite' they quickly learn all the rules of the C-suite and behave accordingly. It takes a huge amount of leadership to pull back and say, 'Hang on a minute, what rules are we following and are they the best rules for this company?'

For example Paul Poleman, CEO of Unilever, took a step back and stopped reporting quarterly to the City because he believed it was distorting behaviour in the company. He realized that his senior team were spending a huge amount of time producing documents to keep the City happy instead of developing the business to make the customers happy. He effectively stopped playing by that rule because it didn't serve his business. That was an act of Enlightened Leadership that took courage and a willingness to break out of the Matrix.

The truth is the stereotypes are not working. Based on the evidence, executives the world over are reaching middle age burnt out and miserable; they don't know their partners anymore and rarely see their kids. They've followed a set of rules and live firmly rooted in the concrete awareness, only to discover that the promised rewards did not materialize. They've worked their hearts out (sometimes literally) only to learn the 'promise' never really materializes. The rewards didn't come, or if they came they also came at a huge personal cost either through the loss of important relationships with their family and friends or the loss of their health.

If we as a species have only been around for a couple of minutes in the context of all life on earth, then surely it's realistic to consider that as a species we've not finished evolving. We may have physically grown into adults, we have clearly mastered the accumulation of information, knowledge, skills and experience (horizontal development) but we have barely begun our vertical development journey. If we don't first wake up to that reality then there may be very little growing up and meaningful progress in our lifetime.

And the only way we can do that is to push through the transpersonal swamps so we can learn what happiness is really about and how to live a life of service. We need to grow up to the realization that the rules don't always deliver what they promised. Part of growing up is owning up to our 'shadow' or the unhelpful, destructive and unpleasant behaviours we have previously engaged in. When someone owns up to their shadow and really integrates that healing on the inside, that will always influence how that individual then shows up on the outside, in the world.

Anyone can show up as a powerful executive, full of their own importance, overly assertive and plugged into the Matrix. They can follow a set of rules blissfully unaware of that fact because everyone else is also playing to the same rules. Such executives are probably unconscious – going through the motions. If such leaders realize that they must find a new way so as to elevate performance and function more effectively in a fast-moving world, then they begin to 'wake up'. Once they are permanently awake they begin to 'show up' differently. As their own personal development journey unfolds and they 'grow up', they begin to 'show up' very differently. And if they 'grow up' and really 'own up' to their previous unhelpful behaviour and tactics, embrace all that they are and genuinely change themselves, then they become Enlightened Leaders capable of having a profound impact.

Enlightened Leaders show up differently. They cultivate the ability to really think, and pull back from the day-to-day short-termism of modern business. They cultivate the ability to pull back the veil and really question the corporate rules, culture and myths and ask the hard questions, and they are willing to go against the grain if that position serves the long-term good of the business, society and the planet.

The influence of values on thinking

One of the key internal lines of development that alter and impact smart thinking is personal values. Values will be unpacked in much more detail in Chapter 6 because not only do they influence what we think about but they significantly alter our relationships and the way we interact with others.

One of the critical principles that underpin Enlightened Leadership across all lines of development is the need and drive toward greater and greater differentiation. Differentiation is the critical middle step necessary for evolution of anything, and business is certainly no exception. In fact one of the reasons I believe that business gets into so much trouble or fails to live up to its highest potential is that we collectively have not refined our ability to differentiate within the lexicon of business itself. If we asked a hundred senior leaders the difference between vision and mission or mission and ambition or ambition and purpose we would get a hundred different answers or interpretations. If we asked a different hundred leaders the difference between values and beliefs or beliefs and attitudes or attitudes and culture we would get the same variety of answers.

Some years ago I was asked by one of the big five global consultancies to talk at their values day. They shut their London office for a day and 400 people attended the event to discuss culture and values. I asked the group in a breakout session, 'What are the values in this company?' No one answered. I said that I assumed as no one answered they must have no values, but then someone responded by saying that the company had six values. The person who spoke up was the leader of the London office. The overriding value of that company was evident in the reaction to my question – it was fear. No one wanted to speak before he did. The first true value in that system was fear. Then when the leader of the London office told me of the values of their organization, three were behaviours, two were instructions and one was an operational standard; not a single one of what they thought were their 'values' was actually a value. This was pretty disconcerting considering this consultancy advised other organizations on values.

There is no doubt in my mind that this is a fundamental part of the problem. We can't have an educated and productive conversation about anything unless we are all clear that we are actually talking about the same thing. If two people are talking about wine for example and one only has the differentiation capability to tell white from red and red from rosé while the other could tell everything from country of origin to the altitude the grape was grown at as well as the type of grape, then the conversation will be pretty short and unproductive. The discrepancy between the level and quality of thinking in this conversation will however be very clear to both parties within about two minutes because the expert will start using specific wine-based terminology to describe his or her experience. The same is not true in business because most senior leaders already use the business lexicon fluently; it's just that the definition of the specific words and phrases has never been really nailed down and collectively agreed upon – even within MBA circles and business schools!

The result is two people can be having a conversation about values or vision, each thinking the other person's definition is exactly the same as theirs. Unfortunately, unless they've asked the question it's almost certainly not the same and this creates unnecessary frustration and confusion in business. To help alleviate this confusion we have created nine different definitions of internal phenomena that influence thinking, behaviour, results and our ability to connect and function with others. A huge amount of time is wasted in business because of our collective inability to discriminate between the following terms and agree a universally understood meaning.

Values

While values and beliefs are both clusters of thinking and feeling, the degree of thought and feeling varies in each. A value is a feeling or quality that is defined by a thought or principle. So in the yin/yang symbol in Figure 4.5, the pearl in the value 'oyster' is a feeling (F) that is then wrapped or defined by a thought (T).

FIGURE 4.5 Composition of a value and a belief

Values are a feeling and the wrapping is the thought or the principles that define that feeling. So we might go into a company and notice they have a list of aspirational values on the wall that talk of honesty and integrity. And yet if we go into the business and wander around or work there for a week or so, we quickly realize the real values bear no resemblance to the list on the wall.

Anyone who visited Enron before its spectacular fall from grace would have discovered that Enron had a 'Vision and Values' statement proclaiming Respect, Integrity, Communication and Excellence. Apparently Respect included the following detail: 'We treat others as we would like to be treated ourselves. We do not tolerate abusive or disrespectful treatment. Ruthlessness, callousness, and arrogance don't belong here' (Christensen, Allworth and Dillon, 2012).

When forest fires shut down a major transmission line into California, cutting power supplies and raising prices, Enron energy traders celebrated and were caught on tape saying, 'Burn, baby, burn. That's a beautiful thing' (Elkind and McLean, 2003). Clearly, the Enron traders didn't get the memo about Respect, Integrity, Communication or Excellence!

Belief

A belief is the opposite of a value, in that a belief is a thought or idea that is powered by emotion. So again in the yin/yang symbol in Figure 4.5, the pearl in the belief 'oyster' is a thought that is then wrapped and powered by emotion.

So for example two people may have the thought: 'Women should stay in the home.' For one it's a really emotive issue and that person expresses the view vocally and passionately. That's a powerful belief because the emotion that is driving it is powerful. The second person may also have that thought but is not emotionally attached to it; there is no energy around that belief, so it's either a very weak belief or it's not a belief at all, depending on the intensity of the emotion. It's the same thought in both cases, but what alters the intensity in each person is the emotional charge that wraps around the thought and converts it into a belief.

Both values and beliefs represent an evolution of complexity. Thoughts and feelings are quite easy to change but when they are combined to create values and beliefs they are harder to change.

Attitudes

An attitude is a collection of values and beliefs that determine the way an individual sees things, thinks, reacts and behaves.

Attitudes represent a cluster of values and beliefs (Figure 4.6), and as such they are more complex and sophisticated than a value or a belief, and consequently they are even harder to change.

FIGURE 4.6   Composition of an attitude

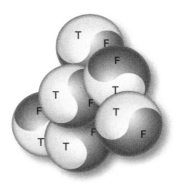

Culture

Culture is the collective attitudes within a group (Figure 4.7), team or organization, and they manifest in:

- Customs: traditional practices that may be honoured, not necessarily repetitive.
- Rituals: repetitive behaviours that are baked into the system.
- Symbols: stylized conceptual totems representing an aspect of culture.
- Dogmas, myths: unchallenged and unspoken beliefs within a system.
- Metaphors: stylized stories used to reflect culture.
- Stories: key binding narrative of culture.

FIGURE 4.7   Composition of culture

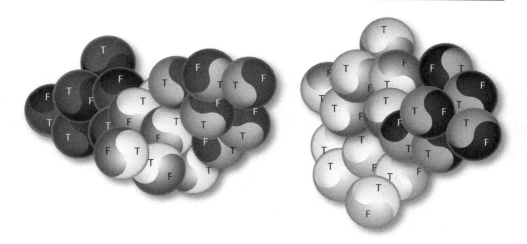

The reason that some of these things are increasingly difficult to change, especially in business, is their complexity. Changing the way a senior leader thinks and feels about a colleague is one thing; changing the values and beliefs that a senior leader holds about his colleague is another. Changing the leader's attitude to the senior colleague is even harder, and changing the culture of the team or business within which the senior colleague functions is even harder still. Culture is not only a collection of customs, rituals and so forth, it is a collection of disparate and often competing attitudes, values, beliefs, thoughts and feelings! No wonder it poses so many challenges for business leaders.

In his case study detailed in full at **www.coherence-book.com**, Matt Simister, one of the rising stars of retail and Food Sourcing Director of Tesco, discusses the importance of culture and its ability to derail even the best business innovations. Talking about the initiative he led to centralize food purchasing within Tesco, Matt concedes,

'In the end, the business rationale for change was compelling – it was likely to be the people and the fiercely decentralized, functionally driven culture of the business that would get in the way.'

Using an Enlightened Leadership approach and some of the tools discussed in more detail in Chapter 5, Matt did however make serious progress:

Not only did Alan help me to apply more rationality to the stakeholder mapping and influencing process, but he also helped me put much more emotion into the story telling. My thinking and communication became clearer and more effective. Gradually the concept of consolidating our supply capability started to be seen as a key enabler in helping us to meet customer needs in an increasingly dynamic, multi-channel world.

How to be smarter

Good-quality thinking is critical in any business; new ideas, new products, creative problem solving, the ability to see the future before it arrives and adapt accordingly are all cognitive functions that offer a vast opportunity for strategic advantage and growth.

I'm incredibly optimistic about human potential because I know that once we get control of our physiology, appreciate emotion and integrate it into our commercial experience whilst also managing it to avoid the DIY lobotomy, expand our consciousness and develop our level of maturity, we will finally realize that we are significantly more complex, more sophisticated and more capable than we have been led to believe.

Building on the physical skills outlined in Chapter 1 and the personal skills of Chapter 2, the next step toward smarter thinking and consistently brilliant performance is cognitive coherence. Cognitive coherence is facilitated by changing the energy within your system to unlock greater perceptual awareness, and this can be done using the SHIFT skill. In his case study at **www.coherence-book.com**, John Browett, CEO of Monsoon Accessorize, discusses the importance of combining the rational with the human side of business, stating:

> In business, you're dealing with people and people aren't rational machines. You may not make what is technically the perfect decision because you know it will cause more problems that it would solve. Instead perhaps there will be another solution that everyone is happy with and that gets you 80 per cent of the way there... If you're really cold and calculating, people won't like you, and being liked in business is helpful. That's not to say you shy away from difficult decisions, but you reserve them for a time when it really matters. Taking people with you is critical... In the end, it's like water flowing in a river; if you do the right thing, there's only one direction it's going to go.

The SHIFT skill facilitates productive interaction and cooperation, as John reiterates:

> Your little thinker, the little ego inside you, can be nervous, worried and unhappy. It is for me most of the time. So learning to operate from a position of inner peace and calmness is transformational. In a transcendent state you are going to be more capable of helping people. I can think of so many examples where I've been able to put myself into that state and it has been incredibly helpful and powerful.

Cognitive coherence – emotional resilience: the SHIFT skill

How do we develop a new level of thinking? Imagine someone is in the middle of writing an important report or tricky e-mail and they get stuck on how best to phrase a critical point or argument. What do people do to come up with a new idea? Some people stop and go for a coffee. Others may go out for a walk to clear their head. Some will delay making a decision so they can sleep on it. Some prefer to exercise, and in the gym the new idea may appear. Some listen to music, have a glass of wine or phone a friend. All of these techniques work sometimes, which is why they are still widely used and recommended. However, they do not work every time. They are hit and miss solutions. Plus, perhaps most importantly, they can't all be done at work and they can't all be done in the heat of the moment. If we are in the middle of a board meeting we can't nip out for a five-mile run or dismiss everyone until we've slept on it, or start pouring the whisky at 10 am. But if we look at why these techniques work, on the occasions when they do work, we discover something interesting – a common active ingredient. From this analysis the SHIFT skill was born.

The SHIFT process

Work through the following instructions:

1 First describe an area in your life or work that is currently challenging you. Write down the associated:
   - thoughts;
   - feelings;
   - current behaviour.

2 Once you have made a note of your thoughts, feelings and behaviour, work through the shift process. SHIFT is an acronym and the process takes you through each stage as follows:
   - Stop everything that you are doing and simply shift your attention to your...
   - Heart, breathe through this area of your chest to...
   - Induce a positive emotion.
   - Feel it in your body, enjoy how it moves through your body for a good 40 seconds or so and allow it to...
   - Turn the brain back on. Notice your insights and write them at the bottom of the page.

How did it go? Do you see a difference in what you wrote at the top of the page and the bottom of the page? Did your perception of the issue change or shift? What did you learn?

I will try and explain how the SHIFT process works. Say for example you've got to write a letter to an employee and it's awkward and you don't know how to phrase the letter. It may be that you've already agonized over it for 30 minutes and you still can't get the words right.

Shifting your attention

The first thing to do in any problem is stop what you're doing and shift (S) your attention. If you are struggling with the e-mail for example, you may get up and move away from the keyboard and move your attention to something else. You might shift your attention by going for a coffee, a walk, a cigarette, calling a friend, counting to 10, exercising, doing something else – anything else. All these techniques result in the same thing – your shifting your attention from the issue to something else.

Inducing a positive emotion

This conscious shift in your attention may, if you're lucky, induce (I) a positive emotion. When going for a walk you may notice the beauty of a tree, a certain way the light hits the pavement, the gentle breeze on your skin, the far-off laughter of people enjoying themselves. When you phone a friend they may lift your spirits by recounting an amusing story of their own woes. When you sip your macchiato you may experience the simple pleasure of a good warm drink. Again all of these different experiences are helpful because they induce a positive emotion.

Feel it in your body

It's not enough that the emotion has changed; you have to really feel the change in energy and feel (F) the positive emotion in your body. The more you can feel the feeling, the joy, the connection, the more you can sustain that energetic state, the more your physiology changes and this physiological change will affect your brain function.

Turn the brain back on

So as you feel the feeling, you shift into a state of biological coherence and your thinking shifts too; your brain turns (T) back on. And once you've turned your brain back on you will have far greater access to your cognitive capabilities and a new thought or perspective will emerge.

You will no doubt already have experienced this process in action. Perhaps you were confused about how to fix a problem. You had been stewing over it for days and then one evening an old friend calls and this exchange shifts your attention away from the problem. You end up laughing about a shared memory and as you put the phone down, smile plastered across your face, you suddenly have an epiphany that solves your problem. This was no coincidence or accident; it was simply the predictable consequence of shifting your emotional state from a negative to a positive state.

As I explained, SHIFT is an acronym, so you may have noticed that the explanation above misses out the H. The missing ingredient is to engage the heart (H). If we breathe smoothly and rhythmically while focusing on our heart in the way I explained in Chapter 2, then we rely only on ourselves. And we can do this anytime, anywhere. Remember our heart is the location of most of our positive emotions, so paying attention to our heart will help to induce a positive emotion (I). Once we have 'hold' of that positive emotion we need to feel (F) the emotion in our body, which will in turn switch our brain back on (T) – giving us answers we could not access only a few minutes earlier.

This process allows us to shift from a negative emotion to any one of the positive emotions that we've mastered through the emotional MASTERY skill from the previous chapter. Just like the executive who learnt to shift to contentment to improve his business decisions, we can also shift into a helpful and constructive emotional state that will give us access to our full cognitive capacity and drive cognitive coherence.

Once we have embodied the new positive state and held on to it for 30 seconds, we will then get access to new insights. After just 30 seconds we can then go back to the challenge we were facing and write down any new ideas or insights that emerge.

This exercise is often very revealing for people because they can immediately see the difference between the initial explanation of the challenge and the insights that follow once emotional coherence has been achieved – even for as little as 30 seconds. The solution they have access to now seems simple and obvious, but without coherence it was obscured by a negative emotional state. The fact is, human beings are brilliant and we already know the answers to almost all our problems. It's just that we can't access those answers until we SHIFT out of a negative state and into a positive one.

Collect positive emotions

Having developed emotional literacy, we may now be very familiar with 15 or so different positive emotions. The MASTERY skill helps us to be increasingly familiar with the biological landscape of those positive emotions. Think of these positive emotional states as different outfits that can be worn at different times for different occasions. No one in their right mind would go to an important function in their shorts and slippers, so why would we consider going to an important meeting frustrated or angry?

Or think of these different emotions as different CDs in your music collection. If someone was feeling upset about the state of their marriage it wouldn't be helpful to listen to power ballads, and they are not going to be in a constructive emotional state to fix the problems if they listen to thrash metal all day long! They need to change the record. Break the negative emotional state by listening to more inspiring, positive upbeat music and they will get access to more of their own intelligence and creativity so they can solve the challenges they face.

Emotional MASTERY adds to our collection of positive emotions so we can SHIFT into that emotion when we need it rather than just hoping it shows up. Of course it's not enough to have the positive CD – we need to play it. This means that we need to practise shifting from the emotional state that we are in to a more positive, constructive emotional state.

We will always experience emotional triggers in our daily life. We will still feel irritated and frustrated and angry, but these emotional skills mean that we are finally in control of how we respond. If we are aware of our negative emotional state, we will have the emotional flexibility to step back for a moment and re-adjust our state so we can move forward confidently in the right direction.

The good news is that we already shift emotional states very easily. If you are frustrated, for example after a particularly pointless meeting, you may get in your car to drive to see a client. As you are listening to the radio your favourite song comes on and you turn up the volume, singing along at the top of your voice. By the time the song has finished you are feeling completely different and you have a smile on your face. The music just shifted your emotional state. Or perhaps you get a letter from your boss informing you of a large bonus – that shifts your emotional state into de-light. Then you realize the letter isn't addressed to you and you shift again, only this time you feel offended. You are constantly shifting your emotional state – you're just not currently doing it consciously. At the moment you are at the mercy of external events, people and situations that will shift your emotional state whether you want them to or not.

What we need to do is take back control so that we decide what we feel, not our boss or our partner or our kids or our clients or our colleagues. Shifting emotional state itself is not difficult; doing it deliberately when we need to does however require practice.

FIGURE 4.8   Lines of development

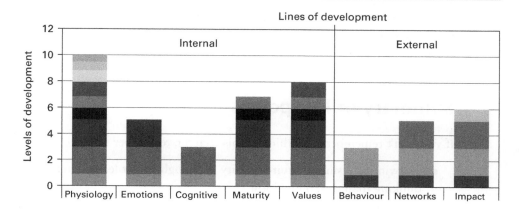

Cognitive coherence facilitates behavioural coherence

Enlightened Leadership emerges when we develop coherence across all the various critical internal and external lines of development (Figure 4.8) – each one strengthening and facilitating the next. In this chapter we have explored the last three internal lines of development – cognition, maturity and values.

Companies succeed or fail based on their collective awareness and on their ability to consistently access the very best thinking possible. Business needs to foster the ability, particularly within the C-suite, to come up with better answers to commercial challenges than their competitors; they need to be more creative and more innovative and they need to expand their perceptual awareness because that is what ultimately differentiates the winners from the losers.

The cumulative benefit of access to more energy and better energy utilization, emotional intelligence and literacy combined with vertically developed cognitive ability and maturity can have a profound impact on the quality of thought and, ultimately, business success. Being smarter is only possible when we systematically improve all internal lines of development. Each line builds on and facilitates the next. The emotional MASTERY skill provides us with emotional resilience, a quality that can massively impact performance and bottom line results. When applied, emotional MASTERY can ensure that we have permanent access to our frontal lobes! When we also expand our awareness and understand our values, then we facilitate cognitive coherence. Physiological coherence facilitates emotional coherence, which facilitates cognitive coherence, and cognitive coherence facilitates behavioural coherence, which we will explore next.

Summary of key points

If you don't remember everything in this chapter, remember this:

- Growing a business requires clarity of thought, or at least better thinking than the competition.

- Smart thinking requires us to be able to access higher-quality content (or what we think) and work it more effectively (how well we think it through).

- In an emergency or when under pressure our brain goes binary and we can experience a DIY lobotomy. This is an evolutionary mechanism that shuts down all the clever thinking parts of the brain to leave only two options: fight/flight (adrenaline driven) or play dead (acetylcholine driven).

- The only way to keep our brain 'on', under pressure or otherwise, is to develop physiological and emotional coherence, especially cardiac coherence.

- When we create cardiac coherence through smooth, rhythmic heart-focused breathing, the coherent signal from the heart travels up the vagus nerve and liberates our very best thinking. The coherent HRV acts like a laser on a holographic plate and we gain access to the smartest parts of our brain and all that is stored in it.

- While physiological and emotional coherence will certainly facilitate a significant improvement in cognitive function, it is vertical development or adult maturity that can transform results.

- Our primary function is to 'wake up' and 'grow up'.

- Without a 'burning platform' for personal growth, most people stop developing once they become fully grown adults. Physical development from child to adult is however only one stage of the adult development process. Adult to mature adult is the second stage and where all the real magic lies.

- Over half of all leaders are currently operating with insufficient awareness or maturity to survive and prosper in the VUCA world.

- The only way to vertically develop awareness and maturity is to do the personal work and practise. But the rewards are significant and unlock a vast reservoir of potential.

- The quality of our thoughts is very much dependent on our emotions and emotional self-regulation. The SHIFT skills allow us to move from a negative emotion to a positive one at will so we can access our very best thinking when we need it most.

Notes for Table 4.1

1   The percentages denote the distribution of middle to senior executives in largely multinational corporations in our database (n = ~1,700) who have completed our Leadership Values Profile™ (LVP). We do not assess Beige on the assumption that executives have evolved past this level. The seniority of these leaders has led to a much higher percentage of leaders scoring in the second tier (Yellow and Turquoise) compared to Graves and others' global estimates (12 per cent in our database versus ~1 per cent in others)

2   The numbers in brackets denote Cook-Greuter's stages of adult development. She considers that there are six main stages and some of them are intermediary between more well established stages.

3   The percentages denote the number of managers identified at each level from an Action Logic research sample as reported in *Seven Transformations of Leadership* by David Rooke and William R Torbert (Harvard Business Review).

4   Denotes the average percentage (merging multiple author estimates) of people within each tier.

Be successful 05

Do you ever wonder why you bother with annual performance appraisals because you seem to be saying the exact same thing year after year? Have you wondered why your team don't quite do what was agreed, even when you feel you made things absolutely clear? Are you frequently confused by the behaviour displayed by key personnel? Have you ever spent a small fortune recruiting the best and the brightest talent you can find, only to be disappointed with a lack of transformation, growth or new ideas they bring? Are you frustrated by the lack of execution in the business? Is there a constant discrepancy between what is supposed to get done and what actually gets done? Are you confused at the inconsistency of performance or output in your business? If so, you're not alone.

We have been taught that success is the ultimate prize – the final destination. All our life we've been encouraged to play by the rules, get a good education and march relentlessly up the corporate ladder. We work hard, put in long hours, and if we are lucky, smart or both we 'arrive'. But during it all performance seems erratic. We recruit expensive talent to unlock performance but it doesn't always work. We incentivize, we coax, we remind and we threaten but performance remains hit and miss. We hire performance gurus and consultants to unlock the secrets but still nothing much changes.

Even when we know that something isn't working we stick to the same course, because often we just don't know what else to try. If we look at the banking crisis for example, there is now a mountain of robust evidence that proves that the bonus culture is toxic (Ariely, 2008, 2010). It doesn't work and it caused or at least massively contributed to the biggest financial collapse since the Great Depression, and yet as soon as the dust settles it's 'business as usual' for banking. To paraphrase Einstein, we are insane – blindly doing the same thing and expecting a different result. As a consequence there are many well-informed individuals who believe that the next financial crisis is just around the corner (Taleb, 2007; Martin, 2011).

Performance anxiety!

The purpose of doing anything is to generate better results: better results for yourself, your team, your family or better results for your organization. If we want to generate better business performance, physical performance, relationship performance or academic performance, we need to make the right behavioural choices. So it all starts with behaviour. This is why large sections of society, be they business, education, health or crime prevention, put so much emphasis on behaviour (and correcting behaviour) because we believe that behaviour determines the results we get in life.

As a result, the 20th century has been completely preoccupied with behaviour. If performance and results are not as good as we hoped, then behaviour is almost always considered the 'problem' that needs fixing. This seems like a logical argument; after all, what we do determines the results we get. But if results are still inconsistent and performance is still erratic then something is clearly missing from our understanding of what drives behaviour in the first place.

In working with global CEOs and leaders since 1996 one thing that has become very apparent is that most executives can perform really well sometimes, but being brilliant every day is much more difficult. In sport this is often referred to as a 'loss of form'. As Sergio Garcia and many other sportsmen and women have discovered, this loss of form is thought to be something of a mystery. It is accepted as a normal cyclical part of elevated performance that just has to be tolerated because it can't be controlled. And certainly if we don't know how we are producing our brilliance, then delivering it day in day out, week in week out is obviously going to be elusive, maybe even impossible.

If we only focus on behaviour we will experience a variance in the results and we may never know why. Achieving sustainable, consistently brilliant results therefore requires a much more sophisticated approach. It requires us to look underneath the behaviours to what is really driving them, namely what we think, what we feel and the amount of energy we have at any given time. And that's what the previous three chapters have focused on.

In unpacking all the levels of the human system of physiology ('Be younger'), emotions and feelings ('Be healthier and happier') and thinking ('Be smarter') and exploring how they interact, we can begin to appreciate why performance and results are often so difficult to predict and why they seem so arbitrary and mysterious.

These insights also allow us to make sense of some of the more unfortunate business phenomena and their inherent dysfunction.

The boss who demands results

A client of mine, let's call him Trevor, was the head of an international business unit in an organization going through a period of significant change. An internal reorganization meant that Trevor was now reporting to a new boss, we'll call him George. George was a very seasoned, widely respected main board member of a well-known multinational organization. George's own role had recently been extended to give him greater accountability for a much larger piece of the business. An emergency meeting was scheduled between George and his new extended team of senior executives to review the budgets that each executive, including Trevor, had submitted to him the week before. Trevor was expecting to hear George's views on how they were going to improve the performance and some directional statements about how George saw his expanded remit and what that would mean for each member of the executive team.

It was clear from the outset that the team was in for a rocky ride. George arrived with a face like thunder. He slung the budget documents back to each of the executives like a teacher returning failed term papers to poorly performing students. Virtually everyone in the room got an 'F'. The boss then proceeded to dissect each person's numbers in front of the rest of the team, picking holes in the cost base, ridiculing the margins and attacking what he saw as a lack of ambition or ability in the sales projections. After a gut-wrenching hour of George extracting all manner of bullets from the spreadsheets and firing them at virtually everyone in the room George said:

> Frankly your performance is useless. We pay you folks an awful lot of money to deliver results and your numbers are a mess, they don't add up and they are just not good enough. You all need to redo the work and come back to me with a number that I can take to the board at the end of the month. I don't care how you do it, I just want you to improve the numbers. You've got a week.

Unfortunately such leadership behaviour is not unusual. Leaders are accountable for delivering results, and this relentless pressure often results in aggressive behaviour and an excessive focus on financial data to the exclusion of all else. Sadly, similar exchanges between leaders and their teams occur thousands of times a day in corporate meeting rooms around the world.

The coach who doesn't coach

I encountered the exact same phenomenon in the world of sport. A Premiership footballer I know was taken aside by the first-team coach during pre-season training. He was told, 'OK, what I need from you this season is more goals. Your main priority is to score more often and I want you to focus on that.' When the player asked, not unreasonably, if the coach had any views on how he might actually score more goals the coach replied: 'It doesn't matter how you score them so long as you do.'

The coach worked every day with the team on various moves on the pitch, set-pieces and tactics; collectively they worked hard on fitness and there was a good camaraderie in the squad. But the sum total of the input to the striker on an individual basis was that single conversation. The player was so disappointed by the lack of sophistication in seeking to actually help him become a better player that he started to fear that he would not develop as a player at the club.

The above examples are typical of the approach many companies and their leaders take to the issue of performance. Whilst there may be a preoccupation with results there is very little discussion, support or coaching about how the required results might be achieved. Asking for better performance, or even demanding better performance, will not necessarily deliver better performance. That is only possible when we appreciate the elements that contribute to elevated performance and systematically bring those elements under conscious control.

Performance appraisal

Most managers have already realized that changing people's behaviour is not easy and that people do not necessarily do the right thing even when they are told what the right thing is – a reality that becomes painfully apparent when they do their team members' annual 'performance review'. The conversation typically focuses on their direct reports' behaviour and fluxes between what the employees did in the previous year that was good and what they did that was not so good. The manager then encourages his/her reports to do more of the former and less of the latter. There is an assumption that this conversation will actually be helpful. Often it makes little difference. The reason that performance reviews often have limited impact is that the way employees react after the review is not based on whether they know what is expected of them; it is based on what they think and feel about what has been said in the review and what is expected of them.

For many companies the performance appraisal process is nothing short of a debacle. I remember speaking to one client who reported that her annual appraisal had been conducted as an informal chat between the courses of the in-flight meal on a business trip to Europe. She was shocked to hear, at the end of the flight, that her appraisal process had been completed successfully. She was unaware that it had even started.

Even the slightly better examples, where the boss had taken the trouble to gather 360° feedback, often ended up being a discouraging review of what the employee had not done well over the past 12 months. If anything was said about what they had done well, it was normally glossed over and the focus returned to what needed to be done differently, ie what new behaviours were required to improve performance.

Unfortunately, most leaders attempt to improve performance by focusing on what someone is doing wrong and what behaviour needs to change. But we already know that making someone change their behaviour is very difficult and behaviour change is rarely sustained (Buckingham and Coffman, 1999). In addition, as we'll explore in more detail later in this chapter, correcting the wrong behaviour never produces success, it only stops failure. So the obsession with behaviour seems a little misguided!

In order to ensure that the results are delivered, leaders will often try to enforce certain behaviours by way of authority or micro-management. It is, of course, possible to get people to do what we want them to do while we are standing over them and checking up on them. But what happens when we leave? Chances are our people will do what they want to do and may even do the exact opposite of what we want just to annoy us!

Obsession with results

In modern business and life in general, results, particularly financial results, are the primary measure of worth. This obsession has created several unintended consequences born of the ethos that no achievement or advancement is ever enough.

The World is Not Enough may be the title of a James Bond movie but this notion is also deeply embedded into our personal and professional lives and it goes a long way in explaining our obsession with performance and results. As Mike Iddon – Finance Director for Tesco UK and one of the most perceptive FDs in the FTSE – explains in his case study at **www.coherence-book.com**, this 'not enough' mindset can have serious negative consequences on teams and the business:

> [Delivering] bad news creates a drop in energy levels. I felt it too. I was almost taking the blame for any missed figures myself. With new framing, we delivered a more positive contribution and could start to figure out why the numbers were as they were. This has an effect on the energy levels in the team, but it also changed the belief structure. People had previously lived with a 'not enough' mindset; their emotional state was very much aligned with the day-to-day performance of the business. A change in this perspective helped us towards a goal of more self-belief.

As Mike and many of us experience on a day-to-day basis, we have to get more, we have to be more. There is now a relentless, restless drive for more, bigger, better, higher, faster, stronger; this pervades many lives and many businesses. Growth is the goal, and volume, size and scale are the main markers of greatness. Quality, value and meaning are subordinate. Bigger is better and the bar is set higher and higher. Cheaper is rarely challenged as a commercial target. If we are not delivering cheaper, bigger, more for less, we are not performing well enough, are somehow deficient or 'not enough'.

The first thought on waking up for many busy executives is: 'I didn't get enough sleep.' This is replaced by other thoughts and feelings of insufficiency: 'there aren't enough hours in the day'; 'I am not earning enough money or being paid enough'; or 'my career is not progressing fast enough.' A common fear of many is that they will be 'found out' and they are 'not good enough, smart enough or able enough' to do the job they are doing (Brown, 2013).

The mindset of 'lack' may relate to a leader's team or organization: 'I can't find good enough people'; 'my team isn't skilled enough'; or 'this organization isn't ambitious enough.' The thinking may relate to customers: 'there aren't enough customers'; or 'the customers aren't loyal enough.' Even people we might think of as very successful often aren't satisfied. A very successful businessperson might frequently think their business should be more profitable, or growing more quickly and earning more money.

Business can, particularly in tough economic times, become a grown-up version of musical chairs. Executives can become very focused on securing their slice of limited resources. So everyone keeps busy doing their thing, wondering when the music might stop and if they will need to shove others out the way to ensure their corporate survival and provide for their families. The rules of the game have changed, which now means that leaders often fight to get to the top, cling on there for a few years while they 'build their stash', only to be fired when they can't deliver the excessive promises they themselves had almost been encouraged to make in order to secure the position in the first place.

Because the pecuniary prize of reaching the C-suite is now so great it can, even in the most saintly organizations, foster a culture of greed and aggression as well as an erosion in humanity.

For example, I recently spoke to a very senior executive who had given 20 years' loyal service to one company and had created a world-leading business unit in her area. Unfortunately she refused to play the politics that were rife at the top of this particular organization, as they are in many companies. So when a new boss was appointed over her, she shared her thoughts about him with him after being encouraged to do so in a poorly facilitated 'team away-day'. A couple of weeks later she was summoned to the boss's office, informed she was surplus to requirements and told she would be escorted from the building.

When she asked if she could go back to her office to 'get her things', she was told she could not. When she asked what she should say when her PA called her to ask where she was, her boss said she should 'not answer the phone'. In fact the boss said: 'We want your phone too.' And, the group HR Director sat with the boss throughout this entire exchange and said nothing.

When we hear such stories we wonder what has happened to the humanity of the people dishing out such news. We seem to have created a system that is set up to promote aggressiveness and hubris instead of teamwork and elevated collective performance. There is little doubt that our overt obsession with results has fuelled this 'never enough' mentality which in turn has contributed to the erosion of humanity and the creation of a culture of greed and entitlement so often experienced in modern business and society as a whole (Rowland, 2012).

And the really disheartening part to all this is that the 'not enough' mindset actually renders the results irrelevant, because no matter how great the growth or how amazing the like-for-like results – they will never be enough. Plus, to make matters worse, our obsession with results doesn't actually work! Our singular focus on behaviour and results isn't actually improving behaviour and results. In fact it's often making them worse. The only way to deliver a sustainable improvement in results is to have a much deeper understanding of the real drivers of performance and what impairs it.

Optimizing performance

In 1908 two scientists called conducted a series of experiments with 'dancing mice' (Yerkes and Dodson, 1908). They put mice under pressure and assessed how well they performed. This was achieved by heating the floor of their cage (hence 'dancing mice') to see how this affected their ability to perform. Yerkes and Dodson were able to demonstrate a clear and definitive relationship between pressure and performance that has stood the test of time. Since then, this relationship has also been verified for people, computers, complex systems and corporations – as well as mice.

This is not really surprising, and when asked to describe the relationship between pressure and performance most people can accurately describe how one affects the other. Most people know that pressure improves performance up to a point and then impairs it (Figure 5.1), and yet few managers, leaders or organizations apply these lessons to their own lives, teams or companies.

We all need some pressure or 'stress' in our lives in order to perform well. This is why many of us work well to deadlines. This is the healthy 'upslope' of the performance curve and it is often referred to as 'good stress'. However, if we become overloaded with an increasing number of tasks, conflicting deadlines and escalating pressure, eventually we will 'peak' and find our limit. The top of the performance curve or 'peak' forms an apex because most of us can pinpoint when we are working at our peak. This is our 'peak performance' and represents the physical limits to how much we can do in one day.

FIGURE 5.1 Pressure–performance curve

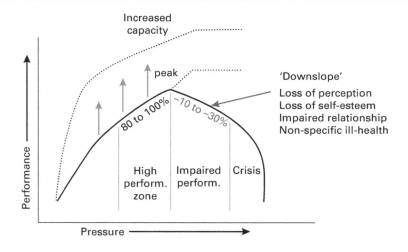

So if we're working flat out at or near our peak and somebody asks us to do an additional task, our performance cannot improve any further. All that happens is the pressure increases and performance declines.

When we are overloaded, (or we overload others), performance doesn't plateau, it actually gets worse. We might think our performance is tracking upward along the first dotted line in Figure 5.1 but it's not. We have crossed a threshold and entered what we call the 'downslope'. In the early days of impaired performance we may not even notice that we are starting to underperform, partly because the gap between what we intend to do and what we are actually doing is small. In fact most people don't know that their performance has become impaired until they are a significant way down the downslope.

Of course, once we realize there's a gap between our actual performance and our expected performance that often makes us feel dreadful and pushes us further down the downslope.

Getting the balance right

Underperformance in any organization is due either to insufficient pressure or, much more commonly, too much pressure. Unfortunately the commonest organizational response to poor performance is to 'flog it harder', ie increase the pressure and demand even more by putting more pressure into the system or onto the person. This approach simply exacerbates the problem and drives the individual or team towards failure even faster.

It is therefore vital that we all understand where we are on the perform-ance curve and how to get the balance right, for both ourselves and our people. Too much pressure results in impaired performance and too little pressure results in sub-optimal performance. Most people in organizations live their life on the downslope because there is too much pressure in the system.

Part of the problem is that in business we demand, '110 per cent or 120 per cent effort'. People who make such demands are simply revealing how little they know about performance. It's not possible to deliver a 120 per cent effort and such exhortations ultimately do nothing but perpetuate the 'not enough' mentality.

Any athlete will tell us that it is impossible to perform continuously at 100 per cent. Most elite athletes work on the healthy side of the perform-ance curve at 80–85 per cent of maximum capacity. This is what enables them to raise their game for competition. Leaders, senior executives and teams need to be doing the same – leaving some spare capacity for a crisis or a busy time of year.

If we put too much pressure on ourselves or our team then our perform-ance will tail off until eventually we can't perform at all. Often this can happen when there is just too much on someone's plate and too many equally important competing priorities. As a result one of the most pro-ductive leadership interventions is to narrow the focus by clarifying and simplifying everything. Warwick Brady, the COO of Europe's leading airline easyJet, used this approach to transform easyJet's performance and improve employee morale. EasyJet is Europe's leading airline, operating on over 600 routes across 30 countries and serving around 59 million passengers annually. The company employs over 8,000 people, including 2,000 pilots and 4,500 cabin crew, and has a fleet of over 200 aircraft and as Warwick explains:

> Day-to-day delivery was poor, customer service was low and the business was struggling to control costs. This all culminated in a collapse of performance in summer 2010. The number of easyJet planes arriving on time dropped to around 40 per cent. Gatwick Airport published the league table of airline on time performance (OTP) and easyJet came out below Air Zimbabwe – a fact shared with the wider world when Ryanair, a main competitor, used it as a headline in a national newspaper advertisement... The company was not in good shape. I stepped into the COO role in October 2010. What I found was a team of people who had worked really hard for three to four years with little to show for it. For many it had become embarrassing to work for easyJet – performance was poor and everyone knew it... I had a lot to sort out. Despite the apparent scale of the turnaround required, I decided we needed to really focus and fix just one thing: OTP. We needed to keep safety where it was, but essentially we had to fix OTP, that's it, nothing else. The only way to achieve that goal was to work together as a team on that single focus... It worked. Within six months, we had stabilized the operation... Within 12 months we had not only fixed the problem, we had become number one in the industry for OTP. We had fixed the core. Our customers could trust that we would get them to their destination on time. Our crews could trust that they would be able to get home on time after their shifts. Today my top team is predominantly made up of the same people as it was back in the dark days. We went from being the worst-performing airline to being the best. Now the team is well respected and operating like a well-oiled machine. All of this was down to the singular focus on OTP and our teamwork.

Having achieved such a dramatic turnaround in performance, his team have gone further still by implementing a step-change to their meeting process, focus and discipline. This included reviewing all non-critical projects and literally stopping work to enable other projects to really succeed. Getting executives to stop doing things was quite a performance breakthrough. Warwick explains how that was achieved in his case study detailed at **www.coherence-book.com**. Chris Hope, Warwick's Head of Operational

Strategy, also provides details of how the team moved beyond an operational focus to implement better quality governance within the team.

When it comes to performance there really is no need to overcomplicate the agenda. When a leader reduces the pressure the performance will often improve immediately without any other intervention being required. Therefore one of the most important responsibilities of a leader is to keep it simple and keep it clear. Getting the balance of pressure right is absolutely crucial for any leaders who are interested in increasing their own, their team and their organization's results.

Living on the downslope

What happens to many individuals and teams is that they slip onto the downslope and don't even realize they are on the wrong side of the performance curve. In fact many leaders don't notice anything is wrong until things reach a crisis point.

This inability to step in early enough is particularly dramatic in healthcare systems, where we often chart the downward progress of an individual and wait until their health has collapsed before we intervene. Intervening after things have imploded or failed is much harder and more expensive, and the patient takes a lot longer to recover. It would be much wiser to intervene at the beginning of the downslope when things are more easily reversed. This highlights a fundamental principle – if we want to get things working properly, early detection of underperformance or 'loss of form' is crucial. If action is only taken once the system has failed then it will be extremely costly and recovery may even be impossible.

The more perceptive we are, the sooner impaired performance will become apparent and the sooner we are able to step in and reverse the trend. Without that expanded perception and awareness of the performance curve we will simply drive harder and shout louder, which often brings about the very thing we are trying to avoid. When we ramp up the pressure we simply accelerate and accentuate the loss of form, which can in turn create real performance and safety problems. If left unchecked, the highly pressurized individual will slide all the way down the downslope toward serious health issues and breakdown. So if we don't want to keel over at our desks, have a heart attack or stroke and we don't want any of our team to suffer the same fate, then we must appreciate the signs and signals of the performance curve and remove pressure instead of adding to it.

There are several key signs and signals that can tell us if we, or our people, have been tipped from peak performance into the downslope. The first is loss of perception. Most people don't even realize they're on the downslope.

In fact when challenged they normally deny there is anything wrong. They just don't see their predicament. Remember the bank CEO I referred to in Chapter 3, who refused to believe there was anything wrong with his ability to foresee the financial crisis and lost his job as a result. The reality was that a number of economists told the G7 leaders that the financial tsunami was coming but leaders in the industry either didn't understand or didn't want to believe it (Lewis, 2010).

There are also valid and relevant neuroscientific reasons why there is a loss of perception, as discussed in the previous chapter. When we are under pressure, the physiological signals generated in our body – particularly from our heart – create an incoherent signal that causes a DIY lobotomy. Unfortunately, without access to our frontal lobes and the full depth and breadth of our own intelligence and cognitive ability, our perceptual awareness is seriously impaired. In addition to a loss of perception there is often a loss of self-esteem and irritability, and all this can lead to impaired relationships.

Another tell-tale sign of the downslope is non-specific ill health. People on the downslope may wonder if they should 'go to a doctor'. Unfortunately doctors are trained to spot pathology and the early detection of dysfunction or instability before pathology occurs is not really part of their training. As a result the doctor will often dismiss the symptoms because there is nothing 'specifically' wrong.

Actually it is these non-specific things that doctors should all be paying much more attention to. These are the early warning signs of a destabilized system and the precursors for major disease and ill-health. When things are just mildly dysfunctional and we're not quite sure what is wrong that's exactly when we should be paying the most attention, because these are the early and highly reversible signs of poor performance and ill-health.

Left unchecked, more obvious psychological issues such as depression, dissatisfaction, frustration, pessimism, agitation and demotivation start to occur. These create behavioural problems in the workforce, poor relationships at work, excessive union issues, reduced productivity, impaired or absent creativity, increased aggressiveness, impatience or indifference. Ultimately the non-specific health issues such as low energy, poor sleep and weight gain will give way to more obvious conditions such as heart problems, high blood pressure and infections. The increased consumption of pills and alcohol is also a clue that we are on the downslope.

In addition to the impairment of individual performance and health, there are organizational costs to being on the downslope. At the team level, poor system health would be indicated by poor interpersonal dynamics and frequent ego battles. At the business unit level, poor health could be indicated

FIGURE 5.2   Individual impact of excess pressure

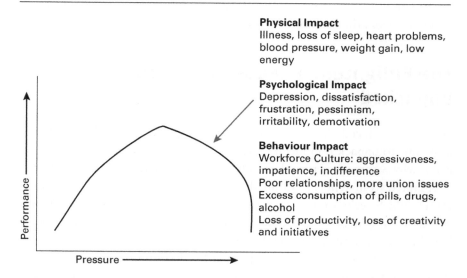

Physical Impact
Illness, loss of sleep, heart problems, blood pressure, weight gain, low energy

Psychological Impact
Depression, dissatisfaction, frustration, pessimism, irritability, demotivation

Behaviour Impact
Workforce Culture: aggressiveness, impatience, indifference
Poor relationships, more union issues
Excess consumption of pills, drugs, alcohol
Loss of productivity, loss of creativity and initiatives

by an unhelpful culture. At an organizational level, it would manifest itself as tribal behaviour and turf wars (Figure 5.2).

Absenteeism is likely to rise because people are demotivated. This can drift into long-term absenteeism and ultimately increased compensation claims against the business for ill-health or injuries at work. Such activity also has indirect costs in terms of salary replacement and increased head count required to cover the absence. Staff engagement can be stubbornly resistant to change leading to perpetually sub-optimal performance (Figure 5.3).

FIGURE 5.3   Organizational impact of excess pressure

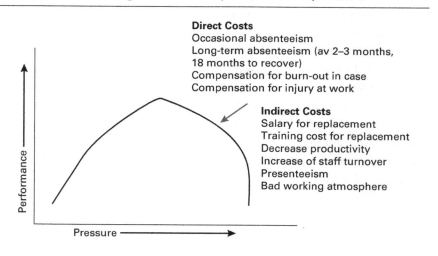

Direct Costs
Occasional absenteeism
Long-term absenteeism (av 2–3 months, 18 months to recover)
Compensation for burn-out in case
Compensation for injury at work

Indirect Costs
Salary for replacement
Training cost for replacement
Decrease productivity
Increase of staff turnover
Presenteeism
Bad working atmosphere

If we want to increase our own or our organization's performance we will need to increase our own and other people's capacity. This can only be done effectively from the healthy side of the performance curve.

The Enlightened Leadership model unpacked

Having introduced the Enlightened Leadership model in Chapter 1, it's now time to unpack it in much more detail because it is this model that explains why we are not getting the results we want, despite our very best efforts.

Adapted from Wilber's 'all quadrants all levels' (AQAL) model (Wilber, 2001), which seeks to map how the world and the individuals in it really work, the Enlightened Leadership (Figure 5.4) model focused exclusively on how business and the people within business work.

Like the AQAL model, the Enlightened Leadership model describes how there are three perennial perspectives that a leader can take, and they are present in every moment of every day. The third-person perspective is the objective, rational world of 'IT', ie what 'IT' is that we need to do to make this business work. The second-person perspective refers to the interpersonal world of 'WE', ie how 'WE' relate to each other in a way that impacts how the business performs. And finally the first-person perspective is the subjective inner world of 'I', ie what 'I' think and feel about the business and the people that impacts how well the business works.

In order to make the model more business and commercially relevant we simply rotated Wilber's AQAL model anti-clockwise and placed the individual at the centre, looking forward into their rational objective world. By doing so, leaders can immediately see their business landscape depicted in a practical and powerful intellectual framework that can help them better understand the breadth of the challenges they face.

The simple reality of modern business is that we stand in the centre of our own life looking forward, and the reason we are not getting the results we want despite our best efforts is because we rarely see what's behind us ('I' and 'WE'). Instead we are predominantly focused on the 'IT' – especially the short-term 'IT', which takes up anywhere between 80 and 95 per cent of our time. And unless we realize that our efforts in the rational, objective world are built on 'I' (physiology, emotions, feelings and thoughts) and that the success of what we want to build requires our connectivity at the interpersonal 'WE', then there is no solid foundation on which to build outstanding effectiveness in the solid, rational world.

FIGURE 5.4   The Enlightened Leadership model

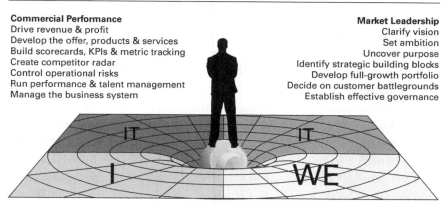

Commercial Performance
Drive revenue & profit
Develop the offer, products & services
Build scorecards, KPIs & metric tracking
Create competitor radar
Control operational risks
Run performance & talent management
Manage the business system

Market Leadership
Clarify vision
Set ambition
Uncover purpose
Identify strategic building blocks
Develop full-growth portfolio
Decide on customer battlegrounds
Establish effective governance

Personal Performance
Step-change quality of thinking
Develop boundless energy
Uncover personal purpose

People Leadership
Identify organizational 'Way' & evolve organizational culture
Develop executive fellowships & high-performing teams
Clarify personal leadership qualities

As I write this in 2013, the game of business is set up to demand almost exclusive attention on the short-term 'IT' in the drive for quarterly results and shareholder value. Leaders may, if time permits, also focus intermittently on strategic issues. And while many may appreciate the importance of 'WE', understanding the relevance of culture, values and relationships and doing something effective about them are often two very different things.

And as for 'I', very few leaders spend any time thinking about their own awareness or their own individual development, the quality of their own thinking or their energy levels. And virtually no one ever thinks about their physiology, other than to notice they are exhausted. These perspectives are rarely discussed in business; they are almost never taught in business schools and hardly ever appear in management and leadership journals. And yet, at Complete Coherence we believe that it is the long-term 'IT', the interpersonal 'WE' and the 'I' that hold the key to business transformation and rewriting the rules of business.

To be an Enlightened Leader we have to be aware of and develop in all four quadrants simultaneously. We must cultivate our self-awareness; we have to develop much better interpersonal skills and we need to build the business for today and tomorrow. There are very few leaders who are outstanding in all four quadrants. The handful of truly world-class leaders are characterized by their ability to move effortlessly between, and be coherent across, all of the following four quadrants.

Personal performance: the subjective, inner world of 'I'

If I was to summarize virtually all leadership books into one phrase it would be: 'Be yourself.' Whilst it is true that the leadership journey starts with 'I', it is also true that most leaders have not studied and do not have a detailed understanding of what 'I' or the self really is. So whilst leaders might understand intellectually the notion of authenticity, very few, through lack of time or inclination, spend any time reflecting on the 'I' quadrant or thinking about who the person is that is turning up each day to do the doing.

As I said earlier, this isn't that surprising considering that leaders are almost entirely focused on looking forward and they rarely look back over their left shoulder to the inner personal world of 'I'. Leaders are therefore encouraged to be themselves but given no time or intellectual framework to even consider who they are and what really makes them tick.

Much of what we have covered so far – physiology, emotion, feeling and thinking – seeks to provide that necessary intellectual framework so as to foster a much more sophisticated appreciation of what's really driving leadership behaviour and personal performance in the 'I' quadrant.

People leadership: the interpersonal world of 'WE'

Behind the leader's right shoulder is the interpersonal world of 'WE' – which will be discussed in greater detail in the next chapter. Obviously, successful leadership requires followership, so how a leader interacts with others is critical.

People interactions occur at three levels of scale for every leader – one-to-all, one-to-many and one-to-one. At the highest level the leader is the single biggest determinant of organizational values and culture (one-to-all.) The leader's impact (or otherwise) is then determined by their ability to work effectively through the executive teams around them (one-to-many). The ability to build and bind teams together is therefore critical to organizational success, yet working their way up through the commercial, financial, operational, marketing or legal 'ranks' doesn't necessarily train a leader in the ability to build and bind teams successfully. It is often simply assumed that a leader can do this, will work it out or it's left to chance. Finally, a leader's ability to develop and nurture productive relationships with staff and stakeholders is also vital (one-to-one). How a leader shows up with every person they encounter determines their personal leadership brand and influence. Most leaders have not spent much time thinking about their own personal leadership qualities, their personal brand or how genuinely influential they are.

Both 'I' and 'WE' are aspects of reality that are not usually that visible. Most business leaders don't consider the invisible internal aspects of 'I' and don't think that much about 'WE' because they are fully committed to the visible, external and objective world of 'IT' – the business. So despite many leaders claiming that 'people are our most important asset' they focus most of their time and attention on operations and finance.

I asked a CEO recently: 'If people are your most important asset why don't you spend most of your time with your Human Resource Director (HRD)?' 'Well,' he responded, 'Because the guy is an idiot!' This is a classic example of actions speaking louder than words. If that same CEO thought his Finance Director or his COO was an idiot they wouldn't survive five minutes because finance and operations are seen as absolutely vital to success. The fact that he thought his HRD was an idiot and the guy still had a job demonstrated very clearly just how important he really considered the people agenda to be.

When we interviewed Nick Warren, one of the boldest and most innovative HR specialists in mining and Head of Development for First Quantum Minerals Ltd, he explained what's really possible when people leadership is considered important. First, Quantum Minerals is an established and rapidly growing mining and metals company producing copper, nickel, gold, zinc and platinum group metals across several mines worldwide, and as Nick explains:

> We've really committed to people development in a practical way. We wanted it to become a normal part of our culture. A few years ago we started a graduate programme, which is not unusual in itself, but the real reason we did it was to give people-management responsibility to every manager in the organization. Each manager now has at least one graduate that they need to develop. While the graduates come with academic qualifications, they need to be developed and the managers take up that responsibility. Initially there was some resistance, but the managers soon saw the benefits of developing talent within their team and it has resulted in managers not just developing their graduates but other employees as well. In this way, we're building a culture of people development.

Market leadership: the future world of 'IT'

Driving an international business is very complex and intensely pressurized, so most leaders spend their time looking forward and only forward. Our top right quadrant, or front, forward-facing right, is the long-term 'IT' (see Figure 5.4). Here the leader is focused on 'what' 'IT' is that needs to be done, and the emphasis is on the future and how to create the future. Even though business leaders the world over know that the long-term picture is important, few get out of the 'weeds' of the day-to-day so they can focus on the other three quadrants. However, the greatest businesses spend just as much time building the future as they do managing the present.

As I already mentioned in Chapter 1, most businesses struggle to build their own future because they have not clearly differentiated the key concepts in the top right quadrant. In the absence of detailed training in strategic thinking, many companies outsource this to a strategy house that then delivers some detailed market analysis and some commercial options. As a result, the internal strategic thinking capability in many organizations remains underdeveloped or largely absent. The lack of high-quality strategic thinking or a strategic development process has a knock-on effect impairing growth and innovation. Insufficient detail on the scale of the ambition can make it very difficult for the CEO to make effective calls at pace, especially when those speedy decisions require a sense of urgency to be injected into the organization. The absence of an effectively articulated purpose can set in stone intractably low levels of employee engagement. A poorly defined vision confuses the customer and adds to the low engagement levels internally. Finally, massively inefficient governance dramatically slows down decision making and burns a huge amount of executive time in laborious meetings that don't take the organizational performance forward.

Quality focus on all these areas of market leadership can create 'clear blue water' between your business and your competitors. So despite there probably being more competitive advantage to be had in the upper right quadrant than the upper left, many leaders find it immensely difficult to stay focused on anything other than the immediate and the short term. This problem is exacerbated by the volatile market conditions that create uncertainty and more insecurity.

Commercial performance: the here and now world of 'IT'

This quadrant is concerned only with the short-term 'IT' of money, profit, costs, product, service, marketing, business model, performance management systems, like-for-like sales comparisons and success metrics. The short-term 'IT' is purely focused on today and the quarter-by-quarter battle. We've talked to over 450 global CEOs and it's clear they spend most of their waking hours consumed by thoughts of 'what' 'IT' is that needs to be done now.

Short-term results are absolutely critical, not just for an individual career but because if leaders don't deliver today then they won't get permission to even explore the potential that lies dormant in the other three quadrants. The irony of this scenario is that the big commercial wins are virtually all to be found in those other three quadrants. It is, after all, difficult to out-perform the competition just by having a tighter grip on the day-to-day metrics. But getting really tight cost control, driving down suppliers and squeezing the operation for maximum efficiency, measured via a myriad operational metrics, KPIs and 'steering wheels', is the standard combination a CEO employs to try and deliver shareholder returns.

While such a grip will always be necessary in the absence of activity in the other quadrants, it often creates a dry business seeking to grind out a result. Such organizations are often not that exciting to be part of, and over the long term morale suffers, talent becomes increasingly difficult to attract and keep, leading positions are eroded and eminence is lost.

Leaders need to focus on building a business system that works in-dependently of their own efforts. If they do not free themselves from the day-to-day operational focus, then they are probably just managing the business, not leading it. So the challenge for most leaders is getting out of the tyranny of 'today'. The simple reality is that until leaders start to make themselves redundant in that top left-hand quadrant it is very difficult to effectively lead the business.

Enlightened Leadership only really emerges when leaders operate co-herently in all four quadrants (Figure 5.5).

FIGURE 5.5 Current incoherent leadership vs coherent Enlightened Leadership

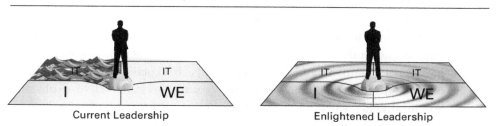

Current Leadership   Enlightened Leadership

Leading in a VUCA World

Making the transition from managing the business to genuinely leading the business by not managing it is a very difficult step for most leaders. The comfort zone for many is to continue to focus on task and driving the short-term result. Management is mainly about the top left-hand quadrant whereas leadership is really about the other three quadrants. Management is about doing, whereas leadership is more about being. And who you are being often comes down to maturity. It will therefore come as little surprise that one of the key lines of development for an Enlightened Leader is maturity. Research has shown that leadership maturity can predict the ability to drive organizational transformation (Rooke and Torbert, 2005). There are a number of academics who have written and researched adult maturity and they have identified a number of stages of adult development. However, like so many of the insights shared in this book, adult development theory has until recently largely remained in the ivory towers of academia and has not made the transition into the places where those insights could really make a difference.

One of the most widely used descriptions of adult development, which we explored in detail in Chapter 4, is Ken Wilber's 'integral frame', which describes the 10-stage evolution of the self. Other academics such as Susanne Cook-Greuter, Robert Kegan, Bill Torbert and Elliot Jacques have also all described different aspects of adult development. The research of each of these academics has something very useful to offer leadership development and yet it is surprising how few HR directors or leadership 'experts' have even heard of, let alone studied, their work.

Kegan, for example, provides some very valuable insights on the relationship between subject (the world of 'I') and object (the world of 'IT') and how this impacts the way we create our own destiny.

Of all the academics involved in this area Cook-Greuter, who has spent 45 years researching ego maturity, offers some extremely valuable insights into how this plays out in organizations. Her work provides a useful theoretical explanation for boardroom battles, the 'political manoeuvring' that so often occurs at the top of organizations and can distract leaders from building a great company and delivering results. It explains why leaders keep coming up with the same set of answers to the same set of problems. Specifically, her work adds real value and deepens our understanding of Wilber's description by providing greater differentiation of the transpersonal level by defining three additional stages of development within this level. These additional distinctions go right to the heart of the leadership debate and why so many leaders struggle with the VUCA challenge.

Bill Torbert explores adult maturity from the perspective of what drives action (called Action Logic) in a business setting. His descriptions of how the various stages play out in business are perhaps the most immediately recognizable to leaders. Torbert and Cook-Greuter have collaborated extensively in bringing this incredibly insightful topic into the business domain. The labels Torbert uses to describe the levels of maturity, especially the three critical ones identified as being the 'centre of gravity' for most businesses, are a little more accessible than Cook-Greuter's descriptors.

We will largely use Torbert's labels with some minor modifications to try and make the key levels more comprehensible. Torbert identifies the three key levels seen in business as Expert, Achiever and Individualist.

Maturity theory is a slowly emerging but profoundly insightful and practical framework for understanding much of the dysfunction within modern business (Table 5.1). As I said in the previous chapter, when leaders understand the characteristics and behaviours associated with each level of adult maturity and how that manifests in business, they are often immediately able to identify the maturity level of the other people in their team. As a result the maturity frame can often shine a light on why their team isn't working well or why it may be stuck and, perhaps most importantly, what to do about it.

The majority of academics writing about adult maturity largely agree that the most important step-change waiting to occur in the development of leaders globally is the leap from the 'conventional perspective' to the 'post-conventional perspective'. Leaders who approach the world from a conventional perspective, which according to Torbert is at least 68 per cent of all leaders (Rooke and Torbert, 2005), are focused on knowledge. In contrast post-conventional leaders are starting to differentiate and understand the critical difference between knowledge and wisdom (Kaipa and Radjou, 2013). I don't just mean this as an intellectual distinction but in terms of how it plays out for their organization and their organization's role in the world.

Torbert described how the conventional-level leaders have been promoted up through the ranks by being very proficient in a particular set of skills, but this proficiency did not automatically equip them to lead a business. And considering that the vast majority of learning and development (L and D) in any business is predominantly focused on the L with no real D, these individuals find themselves in 'over their heads' (Kegan and Lahey, 2009). And that is not good for either the individual or the business.

Conventional leaders like to know more and do more. As they move up the three levels of conventional thinking they develop an increasing ability to differentiate, and this is a sign of their development. They like to predict, measure and explain the world. This enables them to see ahead and they also like to look back in time to discover patterns, rules and laws at play. They notice more and appreciate more pieces of the puzzle, and this is what enables them to succeed.

In contrast to conventional leaders post-conventional leaders like to strip away illusions and see a deeper reality. As they move up the three levels of post-conventional thinking they develop an increasing ability to integrate the knowledge and wisdom they have accumulated, which is in and of itself a sign of their development. They prefer to approach issues without a preconceived idea of the answer. They take a much more holistic dynamic-system approach and like to see deep within, around and beneath the issue rather than just examining the preceding context and the future possibilities. They are particularly keen to flush out hidden assumptions in thinking and explore the interplay between breadth and depth.

TABLE 5.1   The levels of leadership maturity

Descriptor	Level
10. Unitive	Post-Post-Conventional
9. Magician	Post-Conventional
8. Integrator	Post-Conventional
7. Individualist	Post-Conventional
6. Achiever	Conventional
5. Expert	Conventional
4. Conformist	Conventional
3. Self-serving	Pre-Conventional
2. Impulsive	Pre-Conventional
1. Undifferentiated	Pre-Conventional

Many leaders have had no reason to focus on their own vertical development as most have achieved a certain degree of success without doing so. However, more and more realize they can't continue to succeed in a VUCA world just by doing what they have always done. An increasing number of leaders are therefore starting to 'wake up' to the possibility that they need to consider their own development as central not only to their personal success but to their business success too.

Whilst the various developmental academics may look at their subject from different perspectives with different nuances, what they all agree on is that most leaders in business operate from 'Achiever' or below. There are clearly leaders who have a more expansive perspective and greater maturity, but the current 'centre of gravity' or collective 'central tendency' (Cook-Greuter, 2004), is that some 85 per cent of current leadership, is hovering between Level 5 and Level 6 (Table 5.1) (Rooke and Torbert, 2005). And the effects of that are being painfully felt in the world today. For example, one of the main reasons that the world is still in financial turmoil is because of the predominance of non-enlightened thinking at Level 6 or below. This may also be one of the main reasons why leaders are struggling to grow their business in any other way but by mergers and acquisitions (Martin, 2011). And it's probably at least partially to blame for the worrying number of exhausted executives who are keeling over at their desks, or who are on to their second or third marriage.

We need to evolve. We need vertical development. And we need new ways to lead business that will work now and into the future. We need Enlightened Leadership.

Building the future through Enlightened Leadership

In a VUCA world, the challenge of the future can make even the biggest multi-national obsolete in a matter of years. In his case study at **www.coherence-book.com**, Thras Moraitis, probably one of the most perceptive and sophisticated executives I have ever worked with, talks about Enlightened Leadership and the need for momentum. Reflecting on his time as Head of Strategy for Xstrata – one of the world's largest mining and metals companies, operating in more than 20 countries and employing more than 70,000 people globally – Thras suggests that momentum is one of the critical components in building a successful organization. He adds:

> Conviction is crucial, because it creates momentum. Organizations of all types need momentum. Someone said to me once about my career: 'Tread water long enough and eventually you sink.' The same applies to organizations. You may feel you are doing well and making money, but if you're not creating momentum in the direction of your conviction then eventually the organization ossifies. You need to keep the momentum, not just for the organization itself, but also for the people working there, so that they feel they're going somewhere.

In order to future-proof organizations it is vital that companies accurately differentiate five key pieces of corporate thinking within the top right-hand quadrant of the Enlightened Leadership model (Figure 5.4):

1 Vision.

2 Ambition.

3 Purpose.

4 Strategy.

5 Governance.

Many organizations confuse vision with strategy, ambition with purpose, and very few possess the high-quality governance processes required to handle the complexity they are facing. Without mergers and acquisitions businesses struggle to grow. In addition to being unsure how to grow, many organizations are either unclear what their true purpose is – why they do what they do – or it is poorly articulated. There may be some detailed thinking around strategy but it is often imprecise and it is rarely connected to a full spectrum growth agenda. As I said earlier, few organizations have a clear sense of the future battlegrounds where they will engage their customers more effectively than their competitors and can execute their strategy, and most have not yet developed high-quality governance. Building clear, high-quality answers in all these areas at every level of the organization can set the stage for sustained success well into the future.

We believe that many of the problems that occur in business occur because of poor differentiation of the very concepts that organizations are wrestling with. This can be especially critical following an acquisition, as CFO Shaun Usmar found out at Xstrata Nickel. In his case study at **www.coherence-book.com**, he explains:

> In one recent acquisition the first thing we had to do was to make sure we
> were all working off the same basic information. People had varied information
> sources and would use similar terminology, but would mean different things.
> This resulted in some people double or triple counting things and that leads to
> poor decisions. We had to spend time as a senior team getting rid of the noise
> that can be created by people questioning data. That process took a couple of
> years in the mid-2000s, but it ended up being a crucial step to our future success.

I see this all the time in the work we do with multinationals. For example, we met with an executive board that had been struggling with employee engagement for two years. Within the board it was apparent that there were very different views about what engagement even was, let alone why it was important, how to measure it effectively and, of course, how to increase it. Remember, evolution is only really possible when we can accurately differentiate between one idea or concept and another, and it is a vital precursor for integration and ultimately growth.

When differentiation is poor the business will struggle to evolve. In order to effectively create a prosperous future, elevate performance and deliver results year in year out, a business needs to have universally understood clarity around its key business terms. It may sound like semantics but clarity around these terms is critical because it influences decision making (or lack thereof), productivity and results. When everyone has the same understanding of the terms so often used in business, then it becomes much easier to increase organizational efficiency and effectiveness.

Vision and ambition

When an executive team is asked where their business is going, the most immediate response is: 'Oh we've done all that, vision, strategy and purpose stuff.' In fairness, the best companies have clarified some of their directional strategic bets, but many have not. Few have linked their strategic bets to a clearly articulated vision of what the world might look like if the strategy was fully delivered. And even fewer understand the difference between ambition and purpose.

For example, in the mining sector Rio Tinto's vision is: 'to be the leading global mining and metals company' (Rio Tinto, 2013). Unfortunately their competitor Anglo American says virtually the same: 'Our aim is to be the leading global mining company' (Anglo American, 2013a). A third mining company BHP Billiton states that: 'We are a leading global resources company' (BHP Billiton, 2013). None of these are visions. They are all extremely unimaginative ambition statements and they are virtually identical to each other.

When we look at the same three companies' statements about their corporate purpose they are again equally indistinguishable. Anglo says: 'We are committed to delivering operational excellence in a safe and responsible way, adding value for investors, employees, governments and the communities in which we operate' (Anglo American, 2013b). Rio says: 'Our core objective is to maximize total shareholder return by sustainably finding, developing, mining and processing natural resources' (Rio Tinto, 2012), and BHP says: 'Our corporate objective is to create long-term value through the discovery, development and conversion of natural resources, and the provision of innovative customer- and market-focused solutions' (BHP Billiton, 2010). The Anglo statement is a statement of strategic intent with some hint at purpose. It is not a strategy or an ambition or a fully-fledged statement of purpose or vision. The Rio statement is part purpose (why they exist, ie for 'shareholder return') and part a description of what they do, which is not a strategy, ambition, vision or purpose. The BHP 'purpose' is likewise a statement of what they do, not why they do it (their purpose).

Vision

Just to clarify, vision is a picture of the future desired destination or what the world will look and feel like as a result of our corporate efforts. It's not necessarily a fully achievable state but describes our aspiration or dream.

Ambition

Ambition on the other hand is a rational (head) statement about the size, scale, reach, market share or capitalization of the business in the future. Ambition describes how big we want to be (it's a numbers thing), the level of profitability, the number of offices, geographic footprint, EBITDA etc.

Purpose

Many of the businesses I have encountered since 1996 have been somewhat unclear about the concept of organizational purpose. I recently had a FTSE board member tell me that he did not see the purpose of having a purpose! In contrast, a multinational business reached out to us for help with their purpose saying: 'We know what we do, how we do it and where we are going in the future; what we are unsure of is why we do it.' They were also aware enough to know that the answer to the 'why' question was not 'shareholder return'.

A good organizational purpose is an emotional (heart) statement that is able to drive engagement and unlock discretionary effort. It can help define why an employee works for us rather than our competitors. It is the boiled-down essence of employer brand and our employer (not employee) value proposition. In defining our organizational purpose, it can help to differentiate it slightly for the key stakeholders of the business such as customers, employees and shareholder/city analysts.

Purpose is the beating heart of our business; it drives the business forward and draws customers to us. When Apple started, Steve Jobs and Steve Wozniak believed that technology was not just for business and that it should be beautiful and perfect – inside and out. Their 'why' was around creating elegant, intuitive and beautiful products that made life easier and more fun. Their guiding 'why' is the reason people queue down the street to get their latest Apple product and are happy to pay significantly more than competitor products to get it. Customers buy into the 'why' and people buy Apple because Apple exists to make beautiful things (Sinek, 2011).

Strategy

Virtually every company has done significant thinking around its strategy; however an awful lot of what is included in a company's 'strategy document' is not actually strategy. Our strategy is how we're going to get to the destination described by the vision and ambition. It describes how we're going to achieve our purpose.

One of the common failures in strategic thinking is a lack of differentiation in organizational strategy. For example, many organizations suggest that a key aspect of their strategy is that they are going to become customer-centric. Such statements may be correct but they do not distinguish that company from its competitors. What is required is to identify the unique thing about our approach to customers that sets us apart from others. What is it about the way we treat and deal with customers that gives us a competitive advantage and sets us on a different path, providing us with a distinct direction?

Normally it is the combination of a number of strategic 'building blocks' that when coherently integrated provides that advantage. One strategic building block may give us a small edge. When that is combined with the second, third, fourth and fifth building blocks we can create 'clear blue water' between our company and our competitors. We create market leadership. Despite some truly brilliant analytic work done by the various big 'strategy houses', it is interesting to witness the struggle most organizations have in defining a differentiated strategy. Much of this is down to insufficient training in how to think strategically. Many executives are very skilled in operational thinking, but creating difference, setting the business apart – that is a completely separate ability. There are a number of ways to develop much better strategic thinking. Focusing on the differentiated strategic building blocks that will give us an advantage, as outlined above, is one way.

Another way to develop strategic thinking is to understand how to create a completely new game, or what has been called a 'blue ocean strategy' (Kim and Mauborgne, 2005) where a business innovates into areas where there are no competitors. A blue ocean strategy is about innovating customer value and creating a new demand where there is no one currently operating. Companies like Sony, Apple and many of the social media giants have successfully adopted blue ocean strategies. This approach is very different to the more familiar red ocean strategy, where businesses are effectively fighting it out in a competitive 'blood bath', slashing prices and aggressively managing margins.

Finally, a third option would be to unpack ways of creating the future, and here there are a number of specific innovation techniques that can be brought to bear on developing a winning strategy (Christensen, 1997).

Governance

Corporate governance is a much talked about topic, particularly in light of corporate finance scandals and the recent banking crisis. Just before the millennium a corporate landscape of readily available cash and low interest rates fuelled a rapid escalation of tech firm stock prices. The prevailing mindset was that of a 'quick buck'. This contributed not only to the dot com crash of 2000 but also to a rash of corporate financing scandals such as WorldCom, Enron and Tyco. As a response to all this failure of governance the Sarbanes–Oxley Act (SOX) was introduced in 2002 in an attempt to significantly beef up corporate governance and stop financial misreporting driven by greed-fuelled executive excess. Sadly SOX failed to stop the next wave of governance malpractice and just eight years later we witnessed an even more spectacular greed-fuelled failure in the corporate world, driven by banking excesses. Some authors have suggested that we have still not learnt the lessons of 2008 and a catastrophic governance failure could happen a third time in the very near future (Martin, 2011).

In our experience most multinationals see corporate governance as a set of regulatory compliance committees and practices. Most claim that they have very sophisticated governance mechanisms in place. In fairness, they often do have robust compliance processes. But compliance or operational oversight must be differentiated from effective corporate governance. True corporate governance requires a series of detailed and robust mechanisms and processes that then drive much greater organizational efficiency, improve the quality of decision making on the complex issues, and identify and enforce precise accountabilities and greater strategic and operational alignment. How that can be achieved will be discussed in more detail in the next chapter.

Enlightened Leadership requires discipline in all the above areas – vision, ambition, purpose, strategy and governance. But each needs addressing separately. Once we gain clarity around these key business principles, we can turn our attention to the types of behaviour that consistently elevate performance across the business.

Performance-driving behaviours

Over the last three decades, the popularity of leadership competency models or behavioural frameworks has grown to the point where virtually every organization has its own framework. Given the impact that leaders have on the organization, and specifically what these leaders actually do and the behaviour they exhibit, this makes good sense. However, despite investing huge amounts of time and money on the quest to find and develop better leaders, many organizations have been severely disappointed at the lack of results this approach has delivered. Many experts believe that the assumptions behind competency models are problematic (Hollenbeck, McCall and Silzer, 2006). Indeed, recent research suggests that many experts in the field believe leadership competencies are deeply flawed, which certainly raises questions as to their practical and commercial relevance (Cockerill, Schroder and Hunt, 1993).

So where does this leave organizations that are understandably keen to proactively develop the behaviours of the leaders they so desperately need? Thankfully, there has been a significant amount of academic research into identifying the behaviours that drive organizational results, and well-developed methods for applying this are available (Schroder, 1989; Cockerill, 1989a, 1989b).

The behaviours that really matter

Effective leadership clearly requires a focus on leadership behaviour, but the primary challenge is to know what behaviour to focus on. There are thousands of potential behaviours a leader could demonstrate that could improve commercial performance, but which behaviours really matter? Which behaviours drive performance improvement? Which behaviours are genuinely commercially relevant?

Harry Schroder from the University of Florida and Tony Cockerill from the London School of Economics have identified an approach that avoids all the problems with competency frameworks (Cockerill, 1989a; Cockerill, Schroder and Hunt, 1993). This was because they started with the right question: namely, what behaviours will leaders need to use to deliver high performance in a complex and dynamic environment? They then studied businesses that were experiencing a huge number of unpredictable changes (large and small), ie dynamic environments, as well as organizations that were experiencing many different types of changes, ie complex environments, so as to pinpoint the behaviours that really matter and their practical applications.

FIGURE 5.6   The impact of a VUCA world on corporate performance

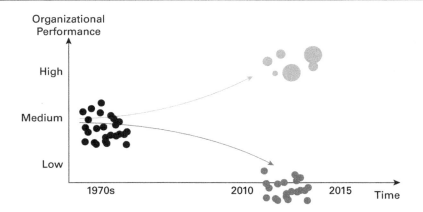

In contrast to the business world of the 1970s, where things did not change that much and were relatively predictable, in the modern VUCA world organizations can be split between those that have found a way to thrive and those that have not (Figure 5.6).

Schroder and Cockerill's research (Schroder, 1989; Cockerill, 1989b) found that when they studied people from initial idea through to successful implementation there were 12 key leadership behaviours that determine organizational success. All leaders must convert ideas into profitable action. The only difference between success and failure is how proficient each leader is within each of the 12 behaviours. In other words there are five levels of competency within each behaviour, ranging from a 'Limitation' to a 'Strategic Strength'. The more successful, senior and influential a leader is the more behaviours he or she exhibits as a 'Strength' or 'Strategic Strength'.

At Complete Coherence we therefore profile leaders using the Leadership Behaviour Profile (LBP-360), which provides leaders with an accurate insight into individual and team behavioural strengths. This provides us with a map for further development so that individuals and teams can become much more efficient and productive.

This profile will assess an individual across the 12 performance-driving behaviours and illuminate what level of competency that individual currently demonstrates for each behaviour (Figure 5.7). If a behaviour is identified as a 'Limitation', then the leader inhibits the behaviour in a way that is eroding business performance. If a behaviour is identified as 'Undeveloped', the

FIGURE 5.7   Level of competency within each behaviour

Strategic Strength	You consistently use the behaviour with high impact, AND you promote its use by others through systems or culture.	
Strength	You consistently use the behaviour with high impact to create a broad or long-term outcome.	
	Developing Strength	You use the behaviour consistently to add value and you may also use it occasionally with higher impact.
Adding Value	You use the behaviour at a basic level to add value to the short-term situation, but this is not yet consistent.	
Undeveloped	You do not use the behaviour, or use it very rarely.	
Limitation	You exhibit some significant negative behaviour which erodes performance.	

© Complete Coherence Ltd

leader either doesn't currently use the behaviour or uses it very rarely. Most leaders will have one or two 'Undeveloped' behaviours. If a behaviour is identified as 'Adding Value', then the leader is already using that behaviour at a basic level to add value to the business, but not consistently. Most leaders have three or four behaviours that are 'Adding Value'.

If a behaviour is identified as a 'Strength', then the leader is consistently using that behaviour in the business to great effect. The leader is making a considerable impact on the long-term outcome of the business through that behaviour. A sub-category of 'Strength' is 'Developing Strength', which indicates that the leader is using the behaviour consistently to add value but is not yet using it consistently to create a significant impact in the business. Most leaders have four or five 'Strengths' or 'Developing Strengths'.

Finally a behaviour is identified as a 'Strategic Strength' if the leader is consistently using the behaviour with high impact *and* is baking that behavioural strength into the business through the coaching of other people, implementation of systems or cultural change. It is possible, by comparing a leader's behaviours to a global benchmark, to separate directors from CEOs and global CEOs by the number of 'Strategic Strengths' that a leader exhibits in their business.

By identifying the current proficiency within these key behaviours, a leader and his or her executive team are able to home in, individually and collectively, on specific areas for development. Instead of wasting valuable time and money on blanket 'leadership training' or 'professional development' programmes, these insights effectively provide a very tight brief for leadership coaching with the sole aim of elevating behaviours that are currently 'Adding Value' to 'Strengths', and where appropriate 'Strengths' to 'Strategic

Strengths'. Massive improvements in individual and team performance are therefore possible with relatively minimal effort.

The 12 performance-driving behaviours

The 12 behaviours that Schroder and Cockerill's research identified can be organized into four distinct sequential clusters with three behaviours in each, as illustrated by Figures 5.8 and 5.9.

FIGURE 5.8   The four performance-enhancing behavioural clusters

TASK	PEOPLE
IMAGINE	INVOLVE
Gathering Information Forming Concepts Conceptual Flexing	Empathic Connecting Facilitating Interaction Developing People
IMPLEMENT	IGNITE
Being Proactive Continuous Improving Building Customer Value	Influencing Others Building Confidence Communicating Clearly

First behavioural cluster: Imagine

The Imagine cluster describes all the behaviours that leaders need to do in order to gather together all the facts and information they will need to progress an idea or complete a task successfully. There are three behaviours that are critical in the imagine step:

1 Gathering information: how well does the individual seek out the information they need to move the task forward?

2 Forming concepts: how well is the individual able to marshal the ideas and information gathered into a workable commercial concept?

3 Conceptual flexing: how well is the individual able to develop multiple ideas and not become overly stuck on one?

Second behavioural cluster: Involve

Once someone has completed the Imagine step and developed some workable concepts, the individual must involve others and engage them in the process or task. There are three behaviours that are critical in the Involve step:

- Empathic connecting: how well does the individual really listen to other people's perspectives and get their 'buy in' to the concept in question?

- Facilitating interaction: how well does the individual support and facilitate genuine interaction and build a coherent team idea?

- Developing people: how able is the individual to support the development of other people so as to ensure success?

Third behavioural cluster: Ignite

Once the concept has been developed and others are engaged and able to deliver it, other people need to be inspired to get into action. There are three behaviours that are critical in the Ignite step:

- Influencing others: how well does the individual influence and engage the other people necessary for success?

- Building confidence: how well does the individual inspire and build confidence in the idea or task, and in themselves and others?

- Communicating clearly: how clearly does the individual communicate with other people involved in the idea or task?

Fourth behavioural cluster: Implement

Once everyone is on board with the idea or task the final stage is implementation. There are three behaviours that are critical in the Implementation stage:

- Being proactive: how proactive is the individual in making things happen?

- Continuously improving: how focused is the individual on continuously improving or fine-tuning the idea or task to ensure elevated business performance?

- Building customer value: how focused is the individual on building customer value around the idea or task?

More detail regarding the variance of output within the 12 behaviours can be seen in Figures 5.9 and 5.10

FIGURE 5.9   Varience of output within Imagine and Involve

IMAGINE

Gathering Information

SS	Implements a system or strategy for collecting and disseminating information on an ongoing basis. Creates a value for research and knowledge gathering.
S	Looks for information from outside the situation being considered. Searches 'outside' the situation, gets a better, wider, richer diagnosis of what's going on.
AV	Actively searches for information about the task in hand. May search deeply. Collects enough information to gain an understanding of the situation being considered.
UD	Limited research that fails to collect data from main categories of information. Clarifies what is already known or stated, but does no original research. Collects information but it's not relevant to the task. Does nothing with the information.
L	Does not look for information. Makes assumptions based on existing info. Prevents others from collecting information. Distorts, rejects, ignores or denies information presented to them.

Forming Concepts

SS	Implements processes or strategies to encourage the evolution of ideas and to support others' efforts to generate ideas.
S	Links information about apparently different topics to form powerful diagnostic concepts, visions, solutions. Links in information from wider environment to make better sense of the situation.
AV	Forms ideas, judgements, conclusions from the information available. Concepts focus on or are associated with the task in hand.
UD	Repeats others' concepts, but does not generate own. Can organize and categorize info, but not use it to explain a situation.
L	Squashes others' ideas before they've had a chance to flourish. Recycles old concepts which may no longer be relevant.

Conceptual Flexing

SS	Implements processes or strategies to encourage flexible thinking in others.
S	Compares the pros and cons of at least two viable options simultaneously.
AV	Suggests or uses at least two viable options or solutions. Suggests at least two possible diagnoses for a situation. States the perspectives of at least two other parties. Options held 'in parallel' not 'in series'.
UD	Does not consider alternatives or options simultaneously.
L	Takes up just one plan or solution. Will not consider or acknowledge alternatives or other viewpoints.

INVOLVE

Empathic Connecting

SS	Creates environment where people feel valued for speaking honestly and openly, and are encouraged to air their true ideas and beliefs.
S	Tests own understanding of another's ideas by reflecting back what has been heard. Shares own feelings to encourage others to do so.
AV	Seeks to understand another's viewpoint, beliefs or opinion by asking open-ended, non-judgemental questions.
UD	Listens. Acknowledges others' contributions.
L	Closes down others' contributions: interrupts, talks over, finishes others' sentences, shows lack of value for others' opinions or beliefs. Interrogates others to verbally 'corner' them.

Facilitating Interaction

SS	Creates process or strategy to encourage cross-boundary thinking and working. Creates a value for open team interaction.
S	Facilitates dialogue until contributions of two or more team members' ideas have been cohered into a true 'team idea', not one owned by one individual.
AV	Invites others to contribute. Identifies links or themes between team members' contributions. Facilitates to make sure everyone understands links.
UD	May contribute, but does not facilitate.
L	Shuts down contribution of others, eg imposes premature consensus, hogs the stage and won't give others air time. Stops others interacting.

Developing People

SS	Implements a strategy or process to cultivate learning and development throughout the unit, eg sets up training, coaching or mentoring programme, or actively develops an open feedback culture. Sets up a system to give others ongoing opportunities to develop, eg cross-functional exchange programme.
S	Takes personal responsibility for individuals' development, eg coaching or mentoring them. Gives others challenging, stretching projects to develop them. Gives constructive feedback.
AV	Sends people on training courses to develop their skills. Supports others' efforts to develop themselves.
UD	Recognizes the need for development, but does nothing about it.
L	Squashes, ignores or denies others' attempts to develop. Uses training as a punishment. Refuses to recognize the need for constructive feedback.

FIGURE 5.10 Variance of output withing Ignite and Implement

IGNITE

Influencing Others

SS	Forms win–win alliances with other organizations, eg JVs, strategic alliances to achieve joint goals. Fosters climate which values shared interests, mutual cooperation and win–win rather than domination, imposition or win–lose.
S	Forms win–win alliances with others by citing how a proposal can achieve mutually beneficial aims.
AV	Aims to persuade others by citing advantages and benefits of an idea, proposal, product etc.
UD	Presents own proposal with no effort to persuade others to buy in.
L	Shoots down others' proposals to give own idea credibility. May use coercion or threats.

Building Confidence

SS	Creates processes or tools to boost morale and confidence of all.
S	Builds confidence of others in themselves, the company or the success of a project by making statements to build hope & optimism. Celebrates success.
AV	Speaks in a self-assured, confident way so that own position is clear to others. Makes decisions when required. Makes and expresses difficult or unpopular decisions. Holds own ground when challenged.
UD	Changes own mind without need, avoids making a decision when needed, hesitates and shows doubts, creates uncertainty.
L	Expresses own lack of confidence in project or company. Refuses to deal with contentious or difficult issues. Creates climate of pessimism.

Communicating Clearly

SS	Creates communications strategies to promote the business unit's values, messages and profile to external and internal audiences. Creates value for excellence in communication.
S	Makes communication more memorable using tools such as analogies, humour, compelling momentum, gestures, surprises and visual aids.
AV	Verbal communication is clear, well-structured and easily understood.
UD	Communication is impaired eg by mumbling, low volume, poor eye contact, strong accent or other distracting habit.
L	Communication is very difficult to understand eg due to high speed, impenetrable structure or rambling.

IMPLEMENT

Being Proactive

SS	Implements strategies to train, empower and encourage others to take the initiative and drive change.
S	Removes bureaucracy and red tape to allow freedom of action (within accepted parameters) and scope to take initiative. Eg redesigns job roles to allow greater freedom to act.
AV	Puts together effective action plans with phases, assigned roles and responsibilities. Identifies sequences and phases of a project.
UD	Responds to others' suggestions and plans.
L	Resists and/or stops others taking action if it breaks rules or is not 'what is normally done round here.' Will not allow others or self to take action or responsibility if it means going outside own job role boundaries.

Continuous Improvement

SS	Builds a culture that values performance measurement and makes measurement part of everyday language. Measures are aligned to corporate goals. Eg sets up balanced business scorecard throughout the company.
S	Sets interconnected goals, targets or measures to improve performance. Regularly reviews against indicators at milestones.
AV	Sets a goal, target or measure to monitor or raise performance. Takes action to improve performance.
UD	Talks about improving, monitoring or measuring performance – but takes no action. Believes things are fine as they are.
L	Sets goals or targets that are irrelevant to customer or improvement of performance. Prevents others' taking action to improve things.

Building Customer Value

SS	Creates a strategy or process to put customers front of mind all the time for employees across the organization. Eg change organizational structure, new business processes, rewards.
S	Implements an initiative (a set of interconnected actions) to improve value for more than one customers on an on-going basis. Eg makes measures more customer-focused.
AV	Takes a one-off action to rectify or improve some aspect of customer service, with a short-term effect.
UD	Talks about improving customer service, but takes no action.
L	Denies need to or refuses to make changes for the customer. Reinforces internal focus, ignoring customer perspective. Prevents or undermines others taking action for the customer.

It is worth pointing out that in the original research Schroder and Cockerill only identified 11 behaviours. The model, often known as the High Performance Managerial Competencies framework (HPMC), is the most widely used basis for leadership behavioural assessment globally. However, there was so much push-back from corporations about the lack of customer focus that they added a 12th behaviour focused on customer value, even though their opinion was that customer value is a mindset not behaviour.

This research enables us to focus only on these 12 behaviours, because these are the ones that really make a commercial difference and have the capacity to transform results. Plus this research has been independently validated in several separate studies (Figure 5.11), including Ohio State Leadership Studies (Stogdill and Coons, 1957), Harvard, Michigan (Katz, MacCoby and Morse, 1950), Princeton Strategy Research, the Transformational Leadership Study (Bass, 1999), Florida Council on Education Management (FCEM) Competency Research (Croghan and Lake, 1984) as well as Professor Richard Boyatzis' Study for the American Management Association (1982).

When fully present at the 'Strength' or 'Strategic Strength' level, these behaviours will provide a competitive advantage in that they enable leaders, teams and organizations to perform at outstanding levels in a VUCA world.

FIGURE 5.11   Identification of leadership behaviour framework

	Ohio State	Michigan State	Harvard	Princeton	Transform-ational	FCEM	Boyatzis
Gathering information			✓	✓		✓	
Forming concepts			✓	✓	✓	✓	✓
Conceptual flexing				✓		✓	
Empathic connecting	✓	✓	✓	✓	✓	✓	✓
Facilitating interaction	✓	✓	✓				✓
Developing people		✓					
Influencing others					✓	✓	✓
Building confidence					✓		✓
Communicating clearly							✓
Being proactive	✓	✓				✓	✓
Continuously improving		✓				✓	✓
Building customer value		✓				✓	✓

This framework allows us to assess individuals and teams and to identify strengths and weakness within both. Using the global benchmark in Figure 5.12, which is based on data from 55,000 executives, we can identify areas for improvement across a team so that individually and collectively the capacity of the team can develop.

For example, we can look at the global benchmarks and identify that effective managers exhibit three of these performance-driving behaviours at the 'Strength' level. However if a manager wishes to develop into an effective director (vice president or VP in US terms) or chief executive (SVP), he or she must develop the 'Strengths' and 'Developing Strengths' further and convert them into 'Strategic Strengths'. Based on the global benchmark, if that leader wishes to perform at a global or group CEO level then 4 of the 12 behaviours must be demonstrated at the 'Strategic Strength' level.

These insights are invaluable and allow us to identify gaps in individual development and the development of a team that can then direct learning and development initiatives. Instead of throwing everything at the learning and development wall and hoping that something sticks, we can address very specific issues highlighted through the Leadership Behaviour Profile (LBP-360) to provide tailored coaching for each member of the executive team.

Every individual has their own unique strengths, which means that leaders usually excel in four or five of these behaviours. Exceptional leaders however are also defined by the fact that they do not demonstrate any 'Limitation' or 'Underdeveloped' behaviours. In other words they do not demonstrate negative use of a particular behaviour, which means that their impact on the organization is consistently positive.

This is not about turning weaknesses into strengths; it's about highlighting the behaviours where we are already 'Adding Value' or operating at the 'Strength' level and taking active steps to develop those behaviours further so more of them become 'Strategic Strengths'. Operating at the 'Strategic Strength' level means that we bake the very best of our leadership into the business, thereby creating a leadership legacy.

If you look at Virgin for example, Richard Branson baked 'fun' into his businesses, and even though he's no longer directly involved with many of these businesses they have maintained a 'fun' culture. That's legacy leadership. The best leaders will always look to convert a personal strength into a strategic business strength so that it stays with the business whether the leader moves on or not.

Understanding the 12 behaviours also enables us to identify our weaker behaviours or any behaviour that is being exhibited in an unhelpful way.

FIGURE 5.12 The leadership behaviour global benchmark

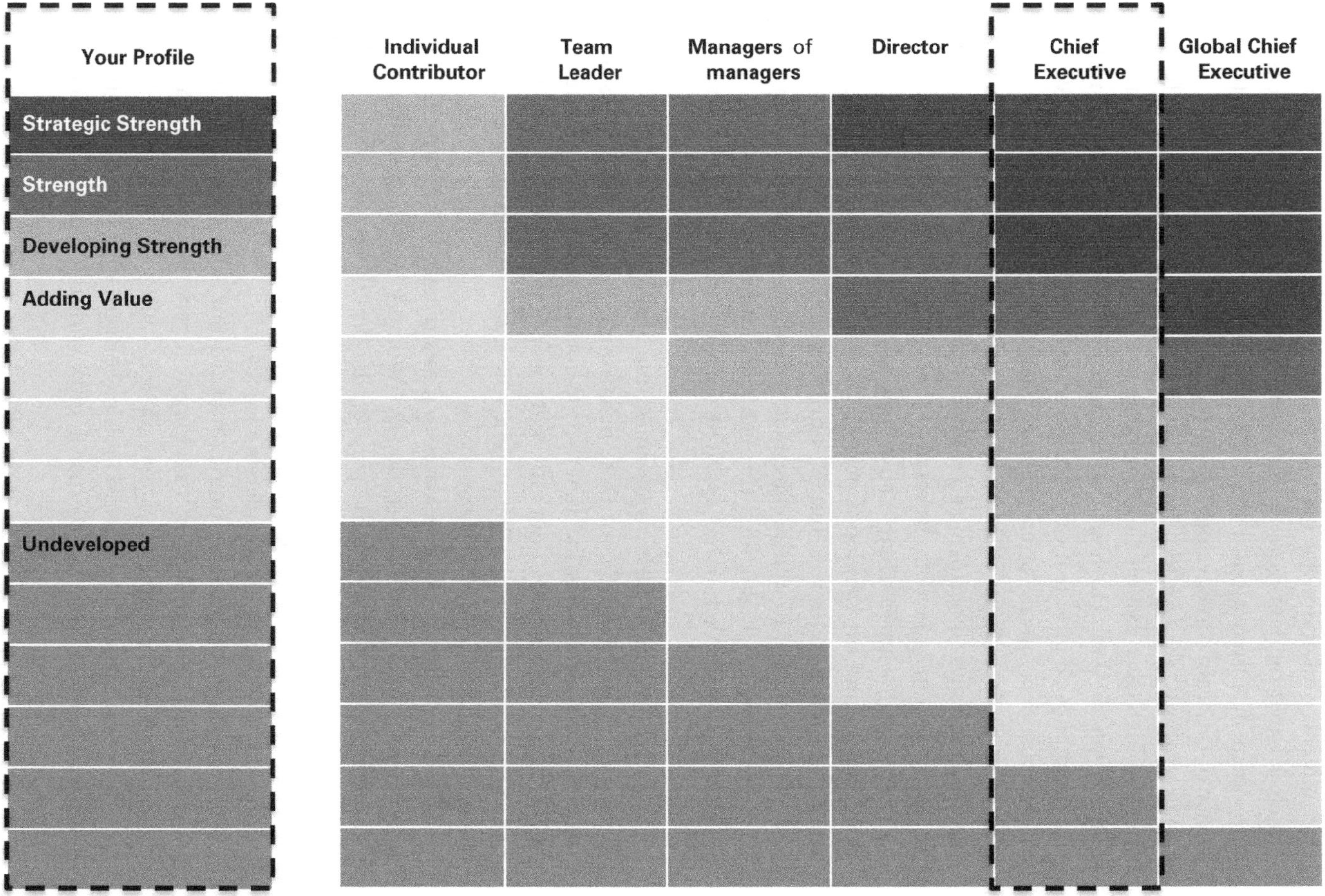

For example, if we identify a 'Limitation', that behaviour is almost certainly holding us back in our career.

The reality of human nature is that we will never turn all our limitations into strengths. It's not possible. Instead, focus on elevating the 'Limitations' just enough so that they stop being a hindrance to your personal and collective performance. Once we've done that we are better able to switch our focus to the behaviours that are currently 'Adding Value' or 'Strengths' and use our time to elevate those still higher. The reason this makes sense is because we already know that talent (strength) takes about 10,000 hours to emerge (Ericsson, Krampe and Tesch-Römer, 1993). Neurologist Daniel Levitin stated, 'The emerging picture from [various] studies is that ten thousand hours of practise is required to achieve the level of mastery associated with being a world-class expert – in anything' (Levitin, 2006). Having sought to discover the existence of innate ability over the course of 150 years, research now concludes that there is no such thing as natural talent (Colvin, 2010). Instead it is the predictable emergence of a skill following a considerable amount of deliberate practice. Elevating performance in behaviours where we are already 'Adding Value' or 'Strengths' is therefore much easier and much faster because we've probably already clocked up a considerable amount of time in these areas.

Knowing where you and your people are in terms of these 12 performance-driving behaviours can transform results and direct learning and development within the entire business (Figure 5.13).

FIGURE 5.13   The development ladder

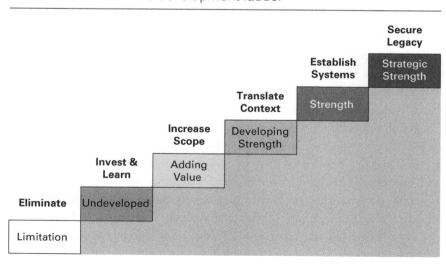

How to be *more* successful

As most leaders know, if we want to change the result and be more successful we ultimately need to change behaviour. However, even when we know the behaviours that actually drive an increase in organizational performance, it's not enough to actually deliver better performance. We still need the motivation to change and the optimistic belief that change is actually possible. So in order to drive consistently brilliant performance and behavioural coherence we need to master the last two personal skills of Enlightened Leadership.

Building on the emotional resilience of the previous chapter we need to step-change our motivation for behavioural change, and one of the best ways to do this is to identify our personal purpose. In addition, sustaining that behavioural change requires us to develop an optimistic outlook. This can be achieved by cultivating the art of appreciation.

Behavioural coherence – self-motivation: identify your personal purpose

The phenomenal pressure experienced by leaders and the punishing hours they work have often led me to wonder why they do it. When things become really difficult, many even wonder themselves. What is most interesting is that when I then ask these leaders this simple question, most are stumped for an answer.

Understanding our personal purpose is critical in enabling us to keep going when times are tough. Identifying our purpose is also at the heart of being fulfilled and learning to live in the here-and-now. When we are really clear about what really drives us and why we do what we do, then we don't need to tie ourselves in knots about the past or the future. We don't need to second-guess every decision or ruminate endlessly over various options or choices. Once we know our purpose, everything becomes simpler because every course of action is either taking us closer to that purpose or further away from it. When we know where we are going it's much easier to stay on track and make the right decisions quickly.

Working with a trained developmental coach can help you to uncover your purpose in a few hours of skilled exploration and discovery. When we work with executives, the question of purpose frequently comes up. Do they know why they do what they do, or are they simply going through the motions, following a set of corporate rules, playing different roles and just doing a job?

Clay Christensen, the Kim B Clark Professor at Harvard Business School, suggests that often:

we pick our jobs for the wrong reasons and then we settle for them. We begin to accept that it's not realistic to do something we truly love for a living. Too many of us who start down the path to compromise will never make it back. Considering the fact that you'll likely spend more of your waking hours at your job than in any other part of your life, it's a compromise that will always eat away at you (Christensen, Allworth and Dillon, 2012).

Yale psychologist Amy Wrzesniewski has spent many years studying how what we believe about our work affects our performance in that work (Achor, 2007). She found that everyone operates from one of three 'work orientations' or mindsets about work. Everyone therefore sees their work as either a job, a career or a calling. Unsurprisingly, those with a job tend to be motivated by the money alone. Those with a career may enjoy the money but they work for personal fulfilment and self-actualization. And finally, those who consider their work a calling would do it whether they were paid or not!

When someone is passionate about something, the 'work' becomes a source of energy and the more they work the more energy they have. This is why identifying purpose and motivation is so important because it can help to transform a 'job' into a 'career' or 'calling'. What was a little surprising was that Wrzesniewski found the three orientations within every profession she studied – from surgeons with a job to janitors with a calling! In every case, however, those who considered their work a career or calling worked harder and longer, and were more productive, healthier and happier than those with a job. Meaningful work – whatever that means to you – is good for the soul. However, very few people fall into blissful fulfilment in a profession that suits them perfectly. Most of us need to take conscious steps to uncover our purpose so we can actively uncover what I call the Shirley Bassey syndrome.

If you've ever seen Shirley Bassey sing, it's crystal clear she loves what she does, she comes alive on stage, and just happens to get paid lots of money to do what she would probably do for free! Shirley Bassey has a calling. That's what we should all be aiming for because when we are living 'on purpose' and tapping into our innate motivation, energy and fulfilment are never a problem.

In order to help you to uncover your life purpose, take a moment to consider these questions:

- What was the first decision you made as an adult and why?
- Think about critical moments of choice in your life – why did you go left rather than right? What was it about that choice that attracted you?

- Look for threads that unite your moments of choice. These moments of choice are clues that can help you uncover your purpose.

- What was the greatest day of your life (excluding your wedding day) – when you were most fulfilled, when you were absolutely loving what you were doing and where were you at that time?

- What is the greatest compliment or greatest insult someone could give you? (Both can also provide clues to help you discover your purpose.)

- Think about both the tragic and the magic – the high points of your life are magic, low points of your life are tragic. These experiences also give you clues to your purpose. Try to identify a consistent pattern, and that will help you understand your core purpose.

Our purpose will almost always have something to do with strengths we already possess, so take the time to consider what those are or might be. Certainly the LBP-360 highlights existing strengths that may help shed light on your purpose.

Most highly successful individuals are not well rounded, they are 'spikey'. In other words they have developed a small number of unique talents that they leverage to maximum effect. These talents are almost always something that they yearn to do, learn to do easily and love to do, or that bring fulfilment and that they do with ease. Often it is this last characteristic that can throw us off the scent of our purpose. Because most people use their talents effortlessly they are often not aware of them, so they wrongly assume that it's nothing special, not difficult or that everyone can do it. Actually it is often perceived as special and difficult by everyone other than the person who has that talent!

I believe it is possible to boil what we are really about at our core down to two, three or four words. The first word is 'I'. Once purpose has been discovered our life can start to make sense. Your purpose has been guiding you whether you realize it or not. A skilled developmental coach can bring what is unconscious into your awareness, and help you uncover your core purpose, which is about you and not the people around you.

As Steve Jobs so rightly pointed out, 'The only way to be truly satisfied is to do what you believe is great work. And the only way to do great work is to love what you do. If you haven't found it yet, keep looking. Don't settle' (Christensen, Allworth and Dillon, 2012). Joseph Campbell, the great scholar of myth and mythology also suggests that the route to fulfilment and happiness is to 'follow your bliss', adding:

If you follow your bliss, you put yourself on a kind of track that has been there all the while, waiting for you, and the life that you ought to be living is the one you are living. Wherever you are – if you are following your bliss, you are enjoying that refreshment, that life within you, all the time (Campbell and Moyers, 1988).

Meaning, do what you are here to do, live according to your purpose. As with all matters of the heart, when you actually uncover your real core purpose you'll know it. It often feels like you've 'come home'.

Behavioural coherence – optimistic outlook: the appreciation skill

The second critical element to driving behavioural change is cultivating a belief that change is indeed possible. Children have no problem believing they can change their behaviour but unfortunately such optimism is usually knocked out of us by the time we reach adulthood.

If we strip back this optimistic childhood belief we uncover something absolutely critical to behavioural change, and that is the ability to learn. In the absence of an ability to learn, behavioural change is very difficult. What is more, when we delve deeper to discover what really drives a child's innate ability to learn we discover something even more fundamental, and that is that learning requires us to appreciate the new. It is this that children are remarkably good at. They have open curious minds and can appreciate the simplest of things.

Most children are natural learners; their curiosity makes them soak up information like a bone-dry sponge soaks up water. And it's almost effort-less. For example, by the time a child is five he or she will have mastered 6,000 words and can operate 1,000 rules of grammar (Attenborough, 1979).

But then we go to school and it is often slowly squeezed out of us as we are told to 'sit down and keep quiet' as the teacher pours information into our heads. We are rewarded for outcome not effort and are taught very early on that failure is unacceptable. As a result we get to adulthood thinking we've made it and don't need to learn anything else, or feeling uncomfortable at the idea of learning something new in case we fail or look foolish.

Extensive studies into success and achievement have found that it is not abilities or talent that determine success but whether we approach our goals from a fixed or growth mindset (Dweck, 2007). As the name would suggest, a person with a fixed mindset believes that what they were born with is basically what they have. If their parents were intelligent then they will be intelligent, and if not then there isn't that much they can do to change that. Someone with a growth mindset on the other hand assumes that what they start with in terms of genetics and upbringing is the start line not the finish line, and that they have the power to improve anything. As children we have a growth mindset. We try, fail and try again. But over time it becomes more and more fixed until eventually we forget how to learn something new.

This pinpoints one of the fundamental problems for behaviour change, namely that most adults are very poor at learning. They have to hear something seven times before they 'land' the learning. We fail to appreciate what we are taught, so we need to be taught the same thing over and over again. Some people constantly repeat the same error without any reflection and improvement. When we close ourselves off from learning and life then we are not receptive to new information or perspectives, which merely amplifies the problem and keeps us stuck in outdated and unhelpful thinking – a point not lost on William James when he said, 'A great many people think they are thinking when they are merely rearranging their prejudices.'

I believe that the best way to foster a growth mindset and develop an optimistic outlook is to practise the art of appreciation. When we appreciate everything – the good days and the bad – and convert every experience into a learning experience, then we open ourselves up to life and can become wise much more quickly. This boils down to a simple phrase:

In order to appreciate what we learn we must first learn to appreciate.

Of all the 17,000 plus positive emotions, appreciation is one of the most powerful because it allows us to wake up every morning and see the world afresh. People get attached to various viewpoints and beliefs about themselves and others that make it impossible to wake up with fresh eyes and see their world anew, so they merely 'rearrange their prejudices'.

The appreciation skill is therefore about learning how to cultivate the state of appreciation as a default emotion. When we do, we see each day as a fresh and exciting opportunity for growth, learning and changing our behaviour or options.

The appreciation skill: your brand

Most people are their own worst critics and have spent years judging themselves and creating a belief structure that they are, in some way, not enough. As an antidote to this tendency, which drains energy, limits growth and interferes with creativity and innovation, it can help to develop the ability to appreciate ourselves.

This may sound simple, it may even sound silly, but it doesn't come naturally to most people. Ask someone what they dislike about themselves and they can often talk for several minutes. Ask them what they appreciate and you'll be met with confused silence or a list of bravado-based statements that don't really ring true.

To make this exercise easier think about what you appreciate about yourself across six distinct areas (Table 5.2):

- Mentally: what do you appreciate about your mental prowess?

- Emotionally: what do you appreciate about yourself emotionally?

- Physically: what physical attributes or abilities do you appreciate about yourself?

- Socially: what do you appreciate about your social skills and how you interact with others?

- Professionally: what do you appreciate about your professional skills and capacity?

- Spiritually: what do you appreciate about yourself spiritually or ethically?

So on greater consideration you may realize that you appreciate that you are mentally thoughtful and quick-witted. You might appreciate that you are professionally 'dedicated' or that you are physically fit because you exercise regularly.

It might also help for you to know that no one will ever see this list. It's simply a private stock take of the things you sincerely appreciate about yourself. Once you've written the things that really mean something to you, convert the list to bullet points and make a note of them on a credit card-sized piece of paper (Table 5.3). You could even laminate it if you were feeling particularly creative. If anyone finds it, it won't make any sense to them but you can bring it out of your wallet or handbag and look at it every day.

The idea is that even if you've had a really bad day, you can take a moment to look at your list as you go home at night and you can remind yourself that you're still 'dedicated'. What you appreciate about yourself doesn't change because of the ups and downs of life. You don't stop being thoughtful; you may demonstrate an alternate behaviour now and again but that doesn't mean you are not thoughtful most of the time. You might have behaved like an idiot shouting at your partner, but you can still appreciate that you are 'empathetic and loyal' more often than not. You may have used your 'quick wit' in an unhelpful and hurtful way but you didn't stop being quick witted. And, you can still appreciate that quality.

TABLE 5.2   The appreciation table

Mentally	Physically	Professionally
Emotionally	**Socially**	**Spiritually**

TABLE 5.3 Example of appreciation list

M:	Thoughtful/quick-witted
E:	ESQ/empathetic
Ph:	Fit/boundless energy
P:	Dedicated/loyal
S:	Adaptable/funny
Sp:	Philosophical

Psychologist Sonja Lyubomirsky from the University of California at Riverside found that people who took the time to count their blessings, even just once a week, significantly increased their overall satisfaction with life (Lyubomirsky, 2007). Psychologist Robert Emmons from the Davis campus of the same university also found that gratitude (which is a sibling from the same family of emotions as appreciation) improved physical health, increased energy levels, and for patients with neuromuscular disease relieved pain and fatigue. Emmons added, 'The ones who benefited most tended to elaborate more and have a wider span of things they're grateful for' (Wallis, 2005).

The reason this skill is so important and so powerful is that people spend vast amounts of time in self-judgement and self-criticism. These types of personally directed negative emotions do not facilitate clear and creative thinking. Plus they are the hallmark of mismanaged emotions and, as explored in Chapter 3, are extremely toxic to our health and happiness. Many of us have a natural drive to succeed, but when that spills over into excessive concern about our own performance it can and does contribute to ill-health. One 10-year study of over 10,000 managers and professionals suggested that those characterized as 'perfectionists' were 75 per cent more likely to have health issues, including cardiovascular problems (Rosch, 1995).

We simply must learn to appreciate what we are instead of berating ourselves over what we are not. Forgiveness is not something we give to others, it's a gift we give to ourselves. When we truly forgive someone (and ourselves) we release the unhelpful energy or emotional charge from our body. As a result that negative energy no longer wreaks havoc with our health, thinking or performance. We don't forgive someone to let them off the hook – we forgive them to let ourselves off the hook (Dowrick, 1997).

I was reminded of just how powerful this idea is when I was asked by a friend to help his wife. She had become so anxious that she was almost agoraphobic. She grew up with a toxic mother who constantly criticized her and made her feel awful. She became perpetually anxious and found it almost impossible to leave the house. She left home at 16, finally breaking free of her mother's negative influence. Since the age of 19 she'd had little to do with her mother. When I worked with her she was 40 years old. She had spent most of her adult life physically away from her mother and yet her mother's influence continued to affect her every single day. Her mother on the other hand was totally unaffected by this situation. The only life being ruined was the 40-year-old daughter's.

BUT, she has a choice. We all have a choice. Bad things happen to many people. The choice is whether we let them define us for the rest of our life or we choose to forgive and start to appreciate our good points.

All too often we are our own worst critics. We're not kind to ourselves and we don't care for ourselves. Being kind is not all about a having a massage or playing a round of golf; that's just addressing the surface! The real point is dealing with how we feel and think about ourselves every moment of the day. The appreciation skill breaks that negative and dysfunctional pattern of self-criticism and self-judgement so we can use our energy more constructively and foster an optimistic outlook. Cultivating the art of appreciation creates a different emotional default. If we learn to appreciate, then we are much more likely to be able to appreciate what we learn. If we can appreciate what we learn then we are much more likely to be able to change our behaviour. We see other options, we feel good about ourselves and this optimism enables us to make different choices.

Behavioural coherence facilitates relationship coherence

Enlightened Leadership emerges when we develop coherence across all the various critical internal and external lines of development (Figure 5.14) – each one strengthening and facilitating the next. In this chapter we have explored the first external line of development – behaviour. Business leaders and managers are obsessed with behaviour because they believe that it is

FIGURE 5.14 Lines of development

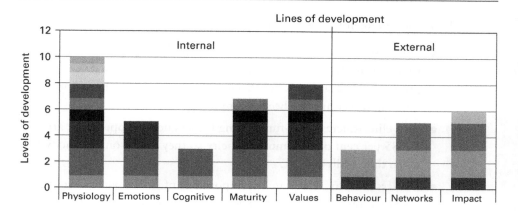

behaviour that drives performance. But there are internal lines of development that need to be understood and strengthened first, otherwise any effort to improve performance will falter.

However, once we have developed the internal lines of development then we can truly create behavioural coherence and elevate performance. When we reach this level, we do what we say we are going to do, we walk our talk. We don't find ourselves going against our own better judgement and we don't wonder why we did certain things. What we think is in perfect alignment with what we do, and that in turn has far greater influence on others.

Behavioural coherence is also facilitated by a clear understanding of our strengths across the 12 performance-driving leadership behaviours. Most people will instinctively know where their strengths lie. For those interested in a more definitive insight, the Leadership Behaviour Profile (LBP-360) can provide leaders with an accurate insight into individual and group strengths. The LBP can isolate areas for further development so that individuals, teams and the business as a whole can become more efficient and productive.

For decades we have been told repeatedly that success is the final destination. Achievement is the goal and yet there is a growing realization that perhaps there is something bigger and better that includes success but facilitates a different, more rewarding type of success. I believe that new finishing line is influence and the ability to foster powerful influential relationships inside and outside the workplace. And that's what we'll explore in Chapter 6.

Summary of key points

If you don't remember everything in this chapter, remember this:

- Our obsession with performance isn't actually improving it because we don't understand the performance curve. A certain amount of pressure (good stress) is beneficial and can improve output. Too much however and we become unproductive.

- Like elite athletes, high-functioning leaders need to operate at around 80–85 per cent of maximum capacity so they leave some capacity for when they really need it.

- Leaders need to appreciate the importance of performance across all four quadrants of the Enlightened Leadership model. Specifically in relation to behaviour, leaders must extricate themselves from the weeds of day-to-day short-term management and direct more of their attention to the long-term leadership of the business.

- What we do in business and the decisions we make are also fundamentally influenced by leadership maturity. Maturity theory is a slowly emerging but profoundly insightful framework for understanding much of the dysfunction within modern business.

- This topic is especially critical when we consider that the majority of academics writing about adult maturity agree that some 85 per cent of current leaders do not have the maturity, awareness or perspective to successfully lead their businesses in a VUCA world.

- In order to future-proof our organizations in this dynamic, competitive environment, it is also vital that companies accurately differentiate five key pieces of corporate thinking: Vision, Ambition, Purpose, Strategy and Governance. Whilst everyone in business believes they 'know' what these terms mean, the definitions vary from one person to the next, which in turn wastes time and causes a huge amount of confusion.

- Once we gain clarity around these key business principles, we can turn our attention to the types of behaviour that consistently elevate performance across the business – the 12 performance-driving behaviours.

- Based on rigorous research we now understand the behaviours that really matter when it comes to improving performance and results.

- At Complete Coherence we can now assess leaders and their teams against these behaviours, identifying whether an individual demonstrates that behaviour as 'Undeveloped' all the way up a scale of competency to 'Strategic Strength'.

- By identifying the current proficiency within these key behaviours a leader and his or her executive team are able to home in, individually and collectively, on specific areas for development that can massively improve performance with relatively minimal effort.

- As most leaders know, if we want to change the result and be more successful we ultimately need to change behaviour. Knowing something and implementing something are, however, two different things. We still need the motivation to change and the optimistic belief that change is actually possible.

- Consistently brilliant performance and behavioural coherence is therefore facilitated by mastering the last two personal skills of Enlightened Leadership – identifying your purpose and fostering an optimistic outlook.

Be influential

"*Have you noticed how incredibly difficult it is to change corporate culture? Do you often feel that some of your people are simply going through the motions and coasting along most of the time? Do you think people listen to you? Do you think they 'get' you? Do you feel accepted by others at work or do you feel judged and misunderstood? Have you ever been passed over for promotion and didn't know why? Have you ever embarked on a merger or acquisition only to be deeply disappointed with the results? Did the venture only seem to double your worries rather than fix the ones it was designed to solve? Have you ever wondered why it seems so hard to unlock the discretionary effort or improve employee engagement? Do you find that you have brilliant individuals in your team but they do not work together well? Are you on to your second or third marriage? Are the people you work with a mystery to you? Do you find the people management side of business challenging and tedious? If so, you're not alone.*

Most of us have experienced power struggles at work at some point or another. Most of us have worked in an environment that lacked leadership – where people were too busy bickering with each other, engaged in 'turf wars' and back stabbing instead of providing the team or organization with any real direction. Petty boardroom squabbles and point scoring are common business practice and yet they actively inhibit performance.

We can spend 20 years working with someone, attend their retirement party and then realize we don't actually know anything meaningful about them. The people we spend most of our lives with are virtual strangers. Business executives tell themselves that their business is customer-centric or customer-focused, yet if you walk into most shops or listen to customer conversations you'll realize we pay scant attention to the needs of the human beings our corporations are set up to serve. We can be rude and dismissive, lacking in warmth and genuine care.

We understand the importance of relationships and social connections but we have no idea how they really work. In business there is a huge industry around employee engagement, looking for ways to build productive working relationships and develop trust and camaraderie that can transform results. But the vast majority of it makes little difference. Employee satisfaction and engagement is not great in most businesses; in many businesses the majority of the workforce are not deeply engaged and see their work as just a job. If they didn't need the money most would not turn up. As employees, executives and leaders, often we don't feel seen and rarely feel heard, validated or valued at work. We often feel we can't really say what we would like to say, be who we really would like to be and bring all of ourselves to work. Our diversity is not always honoured or appreciated. Instead many of us simply homogenize to fit in and begin the disengagement process.

Most people's experience of professional relationships is patchy at best because we were never really taught how to build and sustain productive working relationships. The frustrating part of business – any business – is the people, because we don't all think, feel or act in the same way. We are by our nature beautifully complicated human beings.

And yet people, and specifically the relationships we have with those people, also hold the key to phenomenal success and elevated performance over the long term – a fact acknowledged by Nobel Prize-winning economists Gary Becker, George Stigler and Milton Friedman, who all believed that modern economics fails to adequately account for human interactions, motivation and behaviour in a business setting (Csikszentmihalyi, 2002).

It's the people in a business that make the culture, for example, and it is cultural differences that are the top of the list when it comes to merger and acquisition failures. A merger may look good on paper but when both organizations have even slightly different cultures it is almost certainly doomed to fail. Apparently companies spend more than $2 trillion on acquisitions every year. Yet study after study puts the failure rate of mergers and acquisitions somewhere between 70 and 90 per cent (Christensen *et al*, 2011).

When we fail to understand or appreciate the impact of individual and collective differences, we can end up steamrollering the changes through but that doesn't work. When no attention is paid to the people involved and the relationships they have and how they will change, then people simply disengage. But if we take the time to understand what makes people tick and engage with them as individuals rather than just employees, then we can unlock discretionary effort and amazing things are possible. If we don't, then our mergers and acquisitions will continue to fail, our work teams will continue to function poorly and we will not bake success into our businesses.

But relationships are not just a work issue. Relationships in all their forms are the single hardest thing that we do as human beings. Interfacing with a computer is far easier than interfacing with a person in a face-to-face setting. Why do you think online 'relationships' where individuals never actually meet, or websites where millions of people create avatars and live out an imaginary alternate life online without any real connection, are on the increase?

For many senior executives and business leaders, the only family member that seems genuinely happy to see them is their dog. In fact if it wasn't for their enthusiastic pet wagging his tail and the fact that they wiped their feet on a doormat that says 'welcome home', they wouldn't feel welcomed at all. Many senior executives and leaders have already experienced at least one divorce. They spend so much time at work or thinking about work that relationships with their partner, family and friends are almost non-existent or simply break down, often with far-reaching consequences. When it comes to love and intimacy – felt and shared – renowned physician Dean Ornish states: 'I am not aware of any other factor in medicine – not diet, not smoking, not exercise, not stress, not genetics, not drugs, not surgery – that has a greater impact on our quality of life, incidence of illness, and premature death from all causes' (Ornish, 1998).

Relationships are critical to everything we do in life. They are the ultimate prize in life. Success without connections – colleagues, friends and family – to share it with can often feel hollow and unfulfilling. That's why this chapter has been positioned after success. We need a new finishing line when it comes to measuring achievement that includes but transcends material success. Success is no longer enough, we need to build strong, enduring and productive relationships inside and outside work in order to live full, happy, healthy and successful lives. And the only way to do that, the only way we can truly transform business is to transform our ability to develop and maintain influential relationships.

Relationships are difficult

If you consider the number of people who have limited or no contact with their family, broken or neglected friendships, or the modern divorce rate, it's pretty obvious that relationships are not easy. They may be simple, but they are not easy and there are many reasons for that.

As human beings we need to belong. Remember in Chapter 3 I said that we are born with two fears – loud noises and falling; everything else we learn. One of the deepest and most profound things we learn is our dependency on other people. As babies we are essentially helpless and we rely on care-givers for longer than any other species. This of course makes us vulnerable and we develop a fear of abandonment that never really disappears.

This fear is baked in early in the first few days and weeks of our lives. When our mother is present, we see her eyes and feel reassured. But as soon as she puts us down in our cot and leaves the room we cry. When she comes back and we see her eyes again we stop crying, and so it goes on. This response is an emotional survival response triggered by the ever vigilant amygdala whose primary function is to alert us to danger and keep us alive. Clearly we could die if our mother or other primary carer left us for too long, so we develop a fear of abandonment. This fear is a very powerful driver of adult behaviour and explains why we are social animals. Essentially human beings are driven to belong to a group; we instinctively reach out to form protective relationships as a conditioned response to our early emotional programming. Often we are scared of being on our own, although very few leaders would admit to that.

These emotional drivers exist even if we are lucky enough to have been brought up in a stable and loving home. They are hardwired into our brains. This is why solitary confinement is universally used as a punishment or method of torture. We don't function well on our own and extended periods of isolation can play havoc with our physical and mental health.

We all know instinctively that if we want to make someone's life very unpleasant we ostracize them. This dynamic is often present in business teams where new members are added but unwelcome. No one talks to the new member and they feel increasingly isolated until finally they leave because the strain of disconnection is so great it triggered their unconscious fear of abandonment. Connection is almost on the same survival level as food and water. We need each other to survive and prosper – inside and outside business.

We already know that if we have great working relationships with our peers and colleagues, we will unlock discretionary effort and work will be significantly more enjoyable. We also know that great relationships are the catalyst for greater influence and the ability to make a more positive impact on the business. We know that great relationships with our customers will almost always translate into greater profit, growth and increased success – currently the Holy Grail in terms of business output. But for most of us what creates a great relationship is a complete mystery.

The reason relationships are so difficult is that when it comes to communication we have only ever been taught half the formula. As for trust we talk about it all the time as a concept, but we've never deconstructed trust to understand the component parts necessary for healthy, productive and fulfilling relationships – personally or professionally.

Since great relationship skills don't come naturally to many leaders, the basic principles of good human interaction need to be taught. We don't learn these things at school. In business there's a whole industry dedicated to teaching the fundamentals of human connectivity through communication skills courses or rapport-building courses, but unfortunately most don't improve relationships. Something is clearly not right when individuals aged 30 years and more are having to attend courses to learn how to communicate. And it's no better with trust – in business we routinely dedicate whole days to the phenomenon of trust and trust building. Why? Because we've never been taught how to build it, how it's lost or how to get it back!

Relationships of all types are the hardest thing we do as human beings. Add the fact that CEOs or senior leaders are usually extremely complex individuals and relationships automatically become even harder. Very few leaders have qualifications or have done any significant study of psychology or human development; some aren't even interested. Most leaders are highly individualistic and not naturally people-centric. Leaders are usually task-orientated, not people-orientated, and given that most corporate leaders are men there may not be a natural affinity for relating, connecting and social intelligence. Leaders are not taught and rarely study relationships as a phenomenon because they are too busy mired in the day-to-day quarter-on-quarter results. Lack of time, coupled with the fact that we all live in a world increasingly driven toward instant gratification, also means that leaders often fall back on fast, superficial methods of 'communication' such as e-mail, company-wide bulletins, video presentations, PowerPoint etc instead of detailed telephone discussions or face-to-face interaction that explore the dynamics of how well we interact.

And the ironic part of all this is that once leaders reach a certain level of seniority within an organization, their ongoing success at that level and beyond is almost all about relationships and not technical competency. It's as if the rules of the game that helped leaders rise up the corporate ladder – ie high technical competence and minimal focus on people – are immediately inverted on entry to the C-suite. At a certain level of seniority success becomes all about high-competency people skills and much less about technical ability.

Despite needing each other and wanting to form meaningful connections, most leaders and busy executives have little idea how to create such connections, and they are promoted into the C-suite only to find that the skills that prompted those promotions are almost obsolete. It comes as a shock to many that they are poorly equipped for the demands of people leadership.

Ultimately relationship failure comes down to two things: poor communication and low levels of trust.

Poor communication

Sit two people opposite each other and a huge amount of information is exchanged: words, tone, body language, pheromones, heat, energetic signature and a host of biological signals, including electrical, sound and electromagnetic signals. Interestingly most of that exchange is still happening even if we don't speak. And yet we are not students of this information exchange. We don't pay attention to it. Even if we do pay attention we often still don't understand it.

Effective communication has two basic aspects: transmission and reception. We are, however, only ever taught half the formula. As children growing up, we are taught transmission – our parents correct us: 'You can't say "more better", it's just "better".' They help us to understand the correct tense, pronunciation and grammar. We are taught about using the right word and the power of metaphors etc, and over time we become masterful at transmission. But we don't get trained in reception or how to receive information. Our parents rarely gave us instructions and then asked us to repeat those instructions back to them to make sure we understood them. They just say, 'Are you listening?' Or, 'Listen will you!'

Little people then grow up into big people, believing that listening is simply 'waiting to speak'. To most people listening is the moment before they say something. So when someone is sitting quietly in a business meeting we think they're listening, but they're usually not. Instead, what they are actually doing is thinking about what they are going to say next. There is little or no reception going on. This is why people constantly talk at cross-purposes. We see this in game shows like *Family Fortunes* where one member of a team will give an answer and it will be wrong and then the next member of the same team will give exactly the same answer. They were not listening to what was being said because they were so busy thinking about what they would say. This happens all the time in business, but we just don't realize it. We ask someone to do something and they seem to agree with the request and look confident, and then we see what they've done to it bears almost no resemblance to what we actually asked for – at least not in our mind. For all we know they were probably thinking about their credit card bill and only actually caught the tail end of our request. Most people are very poor at listening to each other. It's not deliberate or malicious or unprofessional; it's just that most of us have never been taught how.

Our parents and teachers told us to listen all the time but they never actually told us how to listen. We never received training or coaching in how to get it right. Consequently our level of connectivity is very superficial; we haven't really heard each other so there is little chance that we really understood each other.

Genuine communication is about both the transmission and receipt of meaning. Unfortunately the training that leaders or executives often receive on communication occurs at what I call Level 1 or Level 2. The real value of most communication is at the deeper Level 3 – the meaning level. Since most people get stuck at Level 1 or 2, the message never truly lands as it was intended.

The first level of communication is what is often discussed in mainstream communications workshops and includes a focus on the words, tone and body language of the message. Back in 1972 Albert Mehrabian, Professor Emeritus of Psychology at UCLA, proposed that when it comes to effective communication, the actual words used in the communication account for only 7 per cent of what we understand. The rest is made up of 38 per cent vocal tonality and 55 per cent body language (Mehrabian, 1972). These component parts of Level 1 communication are often referred to as the '3 Vs' for Verbal, Vocal and Visual.

We are able to gauge far more from the tone that someone uses and their body language than we can from the words they use, and it is tonality and body language that help us to go behind the words to understand the content of the message.

Although this research is extremely widely known, I am still surprised by how many people don't realize just how little the words they actually say influence the message that is transmitted.

We often know this instinctively, and have usually experienced it many times in business. If for example we ask a member of staff to stay late, they may say 'yes, that's fine', but it's crystal clear from their tonality and body language that it's not actually fine at all and they would probably rather do just about anything than stay late.

The influence of tonality and body language in effective transmission is the reason why face-to-face is always better than phone, and phone is always better than e-mail. E-mail is a pretty poor medium when it comes to effective communication, particularly on sensitive or subtle subjects. In an e-mail it is incredibly easy to misinterpret meaning and jump to all sorts of conclusions because we only have 7 per cent of the intended message. This is why people often use emoticons to try and inject some tonality into the basic message and assist accurate interpretation.

But the real gold in communication actually occurs when we seek to establish what someone means (Level 3) rather than what they say (Level 1) or what they think or feel (Level 2). The meaning level is also the domain of genuine influence. When a leader can get behind the words, tonality and body language of an interaction and accurately understand what that individual really means – sometimes clarifying a point that the individual isn't fully cognizant of until that moment – the individual can finally feel validated and heard. And making another human being feel heard is such a rare occurrence in most workplaces that it can be extremely motivating.

Often leaders mistakenly believe that their job is to give people answers. Managers and senior executives come into their office and tell them stuff, but those communications are usually only partially true. The leader's real job is to get underneath the words, tonality and body language to discover the truth and what that truth means. We all too often take conversations at face value, jump to conclusions and offer up a ready-made, albeit wrong, solution.

Instead we need to pull back, get to the truth, uncover the meaning and guide our people to the right solution. Ian Cheshire, Group Chief Executive of Kingfisher and one of the most sophisticated CEOs in Europe, is a strong believer in this approach. Kingfisher is Europe's largest home improvement retailer, employing 78,000 people. The company operates over 1,000 stores in 8 countries and nearly 6 million customers shop in one of those stores every week. When we interviewed Ian on Enlightened Leadership he said,

> 'It is fascinating to me that people who reach a certain level of seniority feel they have to know all the answers.'

A naturally empathetic person, Ian added:

> I pay attention and unlock things within what others are saying. I go deeper than the words. In terms of external stakeholders and managing relationships with the city, the first thing to say is that you have to have the right numbers. No amount of clever arrangements will disguise the numbers. Moving beyond the numbers, there is an odd intersect in the world of public companies, between shareholders, analysts and the press. There are mutually reinforcing pressures at work there and I observed two things. Firstly, you have to get out and put yourself about. You need to spend time understanding the motivations of the shareholders, analysts and the press. You need to understand their way of looking at the world, but you must show up as yourself. You can't do this with spin. You have to be authentic. If you don't know what their view of the world is, then you can't frame a message for them.

Ian explains the benefits of harnessing collective wisdom and uncovering the meaning behind the words in his case study at **www.coherence-book.com**.

True leadership requires us to get beneath the surface, beyond the gesture and even beyond what people think and feel to get to the meaning: why has this union rep come in and threatened to call a strike? Why is this customer so angry when we think we've done a good job? If we can't get to the truth we end up solving the wrong problem. And we solve the wrong problem because we are much too focused on the words, tonality and body language of any communication.

The only way to get to the meaning is to learn the other half of the communication formula. We need to get much, much better at reception. Again we already know this and so we send our people on active listening courses or rapport-building courses. But many of them don't work either. If anything these courses can make someone more sophisticated at not listening! It's all artificial: relationship by numbers – nod three times, repeat the phrase, 'I hear what you are saying...'; or when the person you are talking to leans in, you lean in; or when they cross their leg, you cross your leg! It's insincere, it looks ridiculous at times, and the very best outcome is that it allows people to get better at faking communication.

We can create better relationships but only if we dispense with the superficial and seek to go beyond the words, tone and body language so we can access meaning and create more authentic connections with others that facilitate genuine listening and genuine reception. The good news is that it's not a difficult skill to learn. It literally takes five minutes to learn the MAP skill, which we'll cover later in the chapter, and yet it can have a very profound effect on communication and the quality of all of our connections in all walks of life.

Insufficient trust

Trust is absolutely central to team development. Like listening, it is a profoundly simple concept but it is not present in teams to any great degree mainly because, like communication, we have never really been taught the component parts of trust or even stopped to consider how trust is created or lost. If we want stronger, more productive and more influential relationships then it stands to reason that we need to unpack trust.

There are two types of orientation to the very notion of trust (Figure 6.1). There are 'trust givers' who naturally trust people immediately at the first meeting. They tend to be slightly more secure and less cautious due to their upbringing. This type of upfront trust is then either validated or gets eroded over time. When the relationship works they claim that they were 'right to trust them'. If the relationship doesn't work and trust erodes over time, the trust giver ends up disappointed in the other person. As trust erodes it can reach a critical point where trust suddenly collapses (the 'hero to zero' phenomenon). The 'trust-giving' orientation is much more commonly seen with people we have hired ourselves. Relationships or even companies that operate in this mode tend to be more empowering, with more autonomy, but often the goals are less clear.

The second orientation is present in 'trust earners' where an individual does not naturally trust others and instead trust must be earned and accumulated over time. This type of orientation is seen in people who may have been taught to be more cautious. Their starting point is to be wary and they do not naturally trust until the other person has proven worthy of it. Once trust is earned they can be 'loyal lifers'. This mode is more common if you don't know the person at all when you inherit a team. Relationships or companies that operate in this mode tend to be more performance driven with more controls, checks and fear, but on the upside what is required is usually much clearer.

In our work we often spend a significant amount of time exploring the issue with leaders and senior leadership teams. We suggest that TRUST can be seen as an acronym for Taking Responsibility for Understanding Someone else's Traits. The central concept within trust is therefore understanding. If leaders want to increase the levels of trust in their organizations they must take responsibility for building that understanding. And the thing they must understand is the other person's traits. But how is this done in practice?

In working with leadership teams all over the world since 1996, we discovered that understanding someone else's traits requires us to spend some quality time with the other person to build a personal connection. It also requires us to understand their motives, their working style and why they

FIGURE 6.1 Trust orientation – 'trust givers' or 'trust earners'

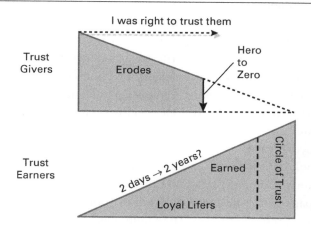

may sometimes fail to deliver on their promises. Thus we discovered there were four key elements to the 'Trust Recipe', and these are independent of culture or geography. Knowing this recipe can significantly fast-track results and performance, as Warwick Brady, COO of easyJet, explains in his case study at **www.coherence-book.com**. So if leaders want to increase the level of trust in their relationships, their teams or their organizations they need to focus on one or all of these elements:

- Personal connection: in order to trust someone and develop a strong relationship, we need to spend time with that person, connecting with them.

- Understand motives: it is very difficult to trust someone if you are suspicious of where they are coming from and why they are behaving in a certain way.

- Consistent delivery: it is vital that people consistently deliver on their promise and do what they say they will do.

- Working style: finally, if the way that a person works is very different from our own, then this alone can impair the ability to build trust, because we find it difficult to resonate with them.

Personal connection

Connection requires time. For people to trust each other they need to spend quality time together, and that usually means face-to-face time. It is certainly very difficult to develop strong bonds without at least some face-to-face time.

We live in the most technologically connected time in human history. We now communicate with each other via internet, smart phone, e-mail, intranet, Skype, Viber, Facetime – the list is endless. As a result we have been lulled into a false sense of security because we think we are connected. But these connections are not necessarily trust-building ones. If anything the constant hum of technology has made us less connected and more isolated, because when it comes to genuine relationship building and the development of trust there is no substitute for time spent in each other's company.

Just because a customer 'liked' our corporate Facebook page doesn't mean they actually trust us! Just because we have 1,000 Twitter followers or 500 Facebook friends doesn't mean we are well connected, as evidenced by the tragic story of Simone Black. On Christmas Day 2011, she posted on her Facebook page: 'Took all my pills, be dead soon, bye bye everyone.' The people who did respond only did so to taunt her, encourage her, criticize her or argue amongst themselves. Sadly she died from an overdose on Boxing Day – Simone Black had 1,048 'friends' on Facebook (McVeight, 2011).

It can make a substantial difference to the quality of our personal connection with someone if we have met their family or we understand a little about their life story and what formed them. When working with executive teams, we will often run an exercise that allows people to share some details of what it was like for them growing up and how this shaped the way they see the world now. We have heard some truly remarkable stories of incredible suffering and hardship around the world, and creating an environment where it is safe for leaders to show some vulnerability can transform the level of trust within a team.

Smart phones, tablets, corporate intranets, the internet, video conferencing, even the humble e-mail can never take the place of time spent in face-to-face connection. Personal connections are made and trust develops when we have the opportunity to spend time with people. This is why as a leader it is so important to go 'on tour', 'walk the floor' and see the staff.

In her case study at **www.coherence-book.com**, Carolyn McCall, who as CEO has brilliantly led easyJet into the FTSE 100, discusses what she did to turn around the airline's fortunes and culture by 'walking the floor', which in turn helped develop productive relationships and foster trust, as Carolyn explains:

> I created an executive leadership team forum almost as soon as I arrived, where the top 50 leaders in easyJet meet every month so we can debate, discuss and shape the strategy before it goes to the plc board, and also it is where we discuss the key issues we face. After establishing that forum, we then created a very effective management conference twice a year with around 150 people

in easyJet. They are our leaders that have the most to do with managing our people... They really buy in because they feel they've been involved in all the key areas... I spend lots of time in the bases. We have 23 bases across Europe where we base aircraft and people. In the beginning, I went out and spoke to people around the airline, particularly the crews, and found out what was wrong. There were loads of issues and problems, but we are now turning things around. For the first six months I was here, I didn't get a single positive customer e-mail – it was all complaints. Now I get 10 positive e-mails to one negative... I continue to get out into the business. I talk to lots of customers and I fly the network all the time. I work on the plane and listen to the crew. I really enjoy working with the teams – I will floor walk, go on the ramp. It means I can really understand how they work. Our staff like to be able to share their views and I want to listen. A big shift that I wanted to make is that I want our people to be open and to tell me the good and bad. I want them to challenge us. If there is a complaint about something, I will always reply. By being out around the business as much as I am, they see my face, we chat informally and I answer questions. They can see that I'm a human being – that I really care. I think the majority of our people would say that I really mean what I say and work hard to deliver what I promise.

Understand motives

It is virtually impossible to trust someone we don't understand. We need to understand the other person's point of view, motives and mindset. Where are they coming from? What's it really all about for them? When we come across an individual whose motives are different from ours, it is harder for us to trust them.

The more we can understand someone's motives and values, the more we can trust them – even when we don't necessarily share those motives and values. This is absolutely essential in successful relationship building, especially when we are seeking to develop high-performing teams. When everyone in the team can at least appreciate where someone is coming from and understand their motives, they can let down their defences and true collaboration is possible. At Complete Coherence we often accelerate the understanding of motives and values in teams by using our Leadership Values Profile (LVP). This online instrument allows everyone to understand their own and everyone else's values and how those values show up in the business. By understanding each other's value system we become more conscious of the benefits their value system brings to the table, while also being more aware of the potential pitfalls and how to successfully navigate around them. Understanding values, which will be unpacked in much more detail later in the chapter, is critical for trust development because it often determines how we connect with each other.

Consistent delivery

In order for us to trust others or for others to trust us, we need to deliver what we say we will deliver when we say we will deliver it. Strategy expert Thras Moraitis talks about the importance of 'Transparency and integrity – doing what you say you will' in his case study at **www.coherence-book. com**. The reality is that if people consistently let us down, eventually we stop trusting them. If we constantly let others down, then eventually they will stop trusting us too.

This happens all the time in business. People agree to things they have no intention of delivering just so they can get out of the meeting or they want to look good, so they over-promise and then under-deliver. If we want to build trust and develop positive working relationships we must do the opposite: under-promise and over-deliver. Whatever we might say and however society and personal and moral expectations may change, a promise is still a promise and if people don't deliver on a promise, then trust is eroded and reputation is damaged.

Our corporate brand is nothing more than a consistently delivered promise. If our brand promises something and we don't deliver on that promise, we lose customers' trust and eventually their business and loyalty.

Working style

Personal connection, an understanding of motives and consistent delivery are all things we can improve and therefore we can learn to build more powerful, trusting relationships. Style is a little more difficult. Even if we spend time with someone, we understand their values and motives and they consistently deliver what they promise, we may still have trouble trusting them because of their working style.

Sometimes we meet people we just don't get on with that well, we don't 'click' with them or we don't resonate with the way they behave, work, play or interact with others. It's difficult to have trusting relationships with these people, although it is possible if you master the second part of the appreciation skill, covered later in this chapter. When we are highly socially intelligent it is possible to work with anyone regardless of style. It's even possible to trust and work effectively with people we actively dislike.

If we think about the key business relationships we have and consider each one from the four cornerstones of trust, the best relationships will be strong in at least three of these areas and the worst ones will exhibit none of the component parts of trust.

Trust and communication are the two essential components of relationship building and they are absolutely critical for people leadership and team development.

People leadership and the development of powerful teams

Enlightened Leadership is only possible when a leader and his or her executive team are coherent and develop vertically across the separate but connected lines of adult development. Unfortunately most leaders are so immersed in short-term commercial performance that they don't get time to address anything other than the top left-hand quadrant of the Enlightened Leadership model (Figure 6.2).

Leaders are in effect so busy managing the commercial performance and occasionally thinking about market leadership that they almost never have time or inclination to look over their left shoulder to personal performance or their right shoulder to people leadership. They might know theoretically that these aspects of leadership are important, especially people leadership, but the noise created around shareholder value has a tendency to drown out almost everything else.

FIGURE 6.2   The Enlightened Leadership model

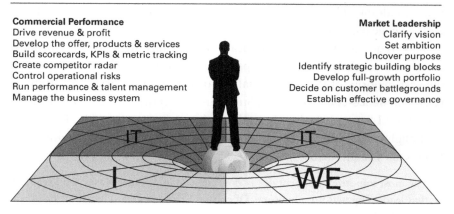

Commercial Performance
Drive revenue & profit
Develop the offer, products & services
Build scorecards, KPIs & metric tracking
Create competitor radar
Control operational risks
Run performance & talent management
Manage the business system

Market Leadership
Clarify vision
Set ambition
Uncover purpose
Identify strategic building blocks
Develop full-growth portfolio
Decide on customer battlegrounds
Establish effective governance

Personal Performance
Step-change quality of thinking
Develop boundless energy
Uncover personal purpose

People Leadership
Identify organizational 'Way' & evolve organizational culture
Develop executive fellowships & high-performing teams
Clarify personal leadership qualities

At Complete Coherence, we believe that the opportunities for business transformation, elevated performance, increased success and influence lie almost exclusively outside commercial performance and in the 'I', 'WE' and long-term 'IT' of business.

In Chapters 2, 3 and 4 we dissected the 'I' of the Enlightened Leadership model and explored the commercially relevant aspects of personal performance and how to create and maintain internal energetic, emotional and cognitive coherence. For us to improve results in any aspect of life we must always start with self. Or as Gandhi said, 'Be the change you wish to see in the world.'

When we vertically develop our physiology, emotion, cognitive, maturity and values lines we are significantly more capable of driving improved performance, not to mention increased energy levels, health, happiness, better-quality thinking and an expanded perspective. We understand ourselves better, which in turn helps us to understand others better. This internal coherence ultimately impacts our commercial performance or the short-term 'IT' of business life. This is especially true when we add to the cumulative power of internal coherence by vertically developing our behaviour line.

But if we really want to make a massive impact on our business, create a legacy and transform results in the long term, then we need to make ourselves almost redundant in the top left-hand quadrant. By doing so, we liberate ourselves to reap the massive rewards inherent in the other three quadrants. Real business transformation will only really emerge when we do the personal inner developmental work ('I'), step-change the top right-hand quadrant ('IT') and also truly attack the bottom right-hand quadrant with a vengeance ('WE').

This requires us to develop leadership teams into high-performing units or even executive fellowships that we trust enough to take care of the vast majority of the commercial performance. In his brief case study at **www.coherence-book.com**, Iman Stratenus, one of the most globally attuned executives I have worked with, explores the importance of 'WE'. Reflecting on Enlightened Leadership and his time as Managing Director with TNT Express in China, Iman explains:

> The most important moment of my development as a leader was when I realized that leadership was not about me. Of course it matters greatly what I do and how I lead – my energy, my intentions and my actions – but the goal is not me, nor is it me who is judged. All that matters is the strength of the connections in the team and the impact we have through our collective efforts. For me, that shift was liberating. All my interactions – interviewing candidates, coaching conversations, leading team discussions, interacting with customers and

suppliers – became a lot more worthwhile and satisfying when I could shift my interest from me to the other person.

Understanding the recipe for trust can certainly help facilitate that process, and we'll unpack how to develop such potent teams later in this chapter. We must also develop the culture and values of the people within the business, and their ability to communicate and connect effectively with each other, all of which will also be covered in this chapter.

Having a big ambition and a brilliant strategy will count for nothing if the executive teams are not pulling together and the culture is dysfunctional. Senior executives need to focus on leading the people in their organizations as well as building companies that can lead their markets.

People leadership occurs at three levels. First of all leaders need to know what personal qualities they possess or need to inspire their top teams and invigorate their organization.

Most leaders haven't spent much time reflecting on what qualities may be required of them, how to create followership or achieve lasting personal impact (Goffee and Jones, 2006).

Secondly, very few leaders understand the stages of team development or know what is required to take a team from one level of team maturity to the next. Consequently very little time is dedicated to building deep trust, high-quality relationships or a 'high-performance culture' within executive teams. In fact many executives have never experienced being part of a truly high-performing team and therefore may not even know what 'great' team-work looks like. We have found that the qualities that characterize truly high-performing teams are not actively cultivated in most businesses. The occasional team away-day tends to focus on commercial performance, not the interpersonal capabilities of the team.

Thirdly, at the organizational level there is a poor understanding of how to measure culture or effect cultural change. As one leader recently put it, 'I have been here for 31 years, seen five cultural transformation programmes come and go and I can tell you the culture has not changed one bit.' Despite the fact that many leaders know that 'culture trumps strategy' and 'you can have the best strategy in the world but if the culture isn't right you won't deliver it,' there is a poor understanding of the key concepts of culture. To successfully drive the business forward, leaders need to be able to transform all three levels – their personal leadership qualities, team development and the corporate culture. But before we can do that we need to know the current connectivity that exists in the business so we know what to focus on for maximum benefit.

The stages of team development

Most leaders come up through the ranks, having managed teams of various sizes. They have learnt on the job how to work with others. Some have developed an ability to get the best out of others; some have simply learnt how to tell people what to do. Very few leaders have been formally trained in the stages of team development or even know much about this topic beyond some generic clichés about 'norming, storming and performing'.

Despite this, many leaders still take their team 'off-site' for a 'team-building session' once in a while. Most leaders have become pretty cynical about such events. Experience has shown them that the best they can hope for is that such events will make no difference; otherwise they may reinforce prejudices or cause the team to go backwards.

That's not to say that team development is a waste of time. Far from it, we think it is absolutely critical. But we must accept that teams take time. Remember, the first critical component in building the trust necessary for high-functioning teams is 'personal connection'. We need to spend time together; it's simply not possible to foster the trust and develop exceptional teams without personal connection. As a consequence, when working with CEOs and senior executives we always advise that if they are not prepared to invest a minimum of two days per quarter in developing their teams, then they probably shouldn't even start because it's a waste of time and money. They would be better off giving the money they were about to spend on the team event to a deserving charity.

After a questionable outward-bound programme or a strained supplier site visit, many leaders conclude that teams are not cost effective and they may as well continue in their command and control approach, meeting separately with the heads of the various business units and having individual meetings with each silo.

The truth is that building a successful relationship between just two people is hard enough, so when we add a third person to the mix the challenge more than doubles. Add 10 more executives, each with his or her own agenda, and the level of complexity and dynamism goes off the charts. No wonder it's difficult to get an executive board to work well together. The reality inside business is that high-functioning coherent executive teams are pretty rare. And this task is significantly hampered by an absence of understanding of the stages of team development.

The lack of knowledge about the inner workings of a team stems from two things. Firstly, few organizations reward their leaders for working well cross-functionally or building a coherent team. Rewards are largely based on individual contribution. As a result most leaders engage in 'symptom thinking' not 'systems thinking' (Cockerill, 1989). Secondly, there is scant technical understanding of the stages of team development, how these stages can be measured and how to guide teams through the stages to much higher levels of performance. Research done at Princeton University and Southern Illinois University looking at hundreds of task-orientated teams over several months has helped to identify highly consistent ways in which teams evolve.

As with all the developmental models shared in this book, it's not possible to skip a stage of development. Teams who put in the work can progress through the levels, and those that don't invest time and effort in the process or are poorly guided will simply slip back to a more primitive stage of functioning. Experience has shown us that once a leader has a deeper appreciation of the stages of team development and has mastered the behaviours, practices, methodologies and disciplines required to achieve more advanced levels of team performance, then they can facilitate more rapid development when they join a new team.

Making a strategic decision to properly invest in team development is one of the three most commercially important moves a leader can make in the 'People Leadership' quadrant of the Enlightened Leadership model and such investment can create a strong competitive advantage.

The issue is how to build and bind teams together. Better teamworking cannot be mandated. In fact leaders who demand team engagement will actually have the opposite effect and inhibit team development. There are certain conditions that, if present, increase the likelihood of genuine team coherence. They are:

- *Interdependency*: it can help to make one person's success dependent on another team member's input, thereby creating interdependency across functions.

- *Common purpose*: teams are united by a common objective. This can be broken down into the team's vision or dream, their purpose, their ambition and their strategy. If a team has made the effort to build a shared version of any one of these, it can serve as a unifying force. If there is alignment across all of these differentiated concepts then team coherence is likely to be significantly higher, and such things can be defined at every level of an organization.

- *Authority*: every team needs a degree of autonomy and the ability to determine its own destiny within the limits of authority given to it. A team that is clear around what delegated authority it has and what it can change is able to cohere around such authority.

- *Team size*: as far as teams are concerned, size is important. With increased size comes increased complexity. Larger teams, of say 18 people, can work extremely effectively but the governance and discipline required is much greater. The optimal size of a team really depends on a number of factors, such as the team's purpose and the range of capabilities required in delivering its purpose. Many organizations think six is the magic number but we have seen dysfunctional teams of four people and highly effective teams of 18 people.

- *Commitment to development*: most executives' experience of team-development events is pretty mixed and there is a justifiable scepticism about 'team away-days'. However, a shared commitment to improving the team's effectiveness and enhancing the team spirit, dynamics and interpersonal relationships can itself be a powerful cohering force. This has to be a sincere commitment, not lip service or 'box ticking'.

- *Leadership*: in our experience a leader's commitment to developing a team is the single biggest determinant of that team's success. This leadership can be supported or enhanced by other team members but if the leader is not behind the 'Team Journey' then the team will never really develop.

- *One boat*: one of the most vital aspects of team success is the idea that we are 'all in this together', one team, one boat (Figure 6.3). Rowing is the most widely used corporate metaphor for teamwork, partly because it illuminates the point that no one member of the team is any more important than any other. The 'stroke' in the stern of the boat sets the rhythm and is the equivalent of the CEO or team leader who is responsible for direction and injecting pace. But everyone in the boat has their role and that role is no more significant than any other. Everyone must play their part and if someone tries to 'be a hero' in their function then actually they will usually slow the boat or team down. Organizational status or hierarchy is irrelevant; what matters is the team result, not anyone's individual expertise. Often leaders who are keen to exercise their own power or authority are the primary reason why the team does not develop beyond the third stage of team development.

If the conditions for the team journey are largely in place, then the stage is set and it is possible to coach and facilitate the team through the seven stages of team development. Passively leaving teams to develop themselves

FIGURE 6.3   Executive team – 'one boat'

Bow Pair (2 & bow)	Engine Room (6,5,4, & 3)	Stern Pair (stroke & 7)
Balance the boat	Power the boat along	Set up the boat
Read conditions & competition	Provide the energy & muscle	Set the speed, cadence & rhythm
Fine-tune the direction	Keep things moving	Make the calls
Communicate	Get through rough water	Adjust the direction
HRD – CIO, Legal, Pub Aff	Mkting Dir – Int'nat Dir – Cm'cial Dir – Ops Dir	CFO – CEO

or holding team events that are not integrated into a people leadership strategy may provide short-term improvements but are more likely to keep teams stuck below Stage 3. Such an unstructured approach to development is one of the main reasons why organizations that want to change fail to do so. Successful transformation requires a much more sophisticated understanding of the stages of team development and how to navigate the stages to unlock the true potential teams offer organizations. High-functioning executive teams are often the difference between success and failure in many organizations, and this is becoming increasingly vital as organizations struggle in a VUCA world.

Twenty-five years of research by Cockerill, Schroeder and others (Cockerill, 1989; Bales, 1951; Cartwright and Zander, 1968; Fisher, 1999; Katzenbach and Smith, 1993; Peterson *et al*, 1998; De Dreu and Weingart, 2003) has provided deep insight into the stages of team development most commonly seen in organizations today. It was their work that uncovered the 12 performance-driving behaviours we explored in the last chapter. Their efforts have also provided the foundations for the seven distinct stages of team development (Figure 6.4):

1 Talented individuals.

2 Battling experts.

FIGURE 6.4 The stages of team development

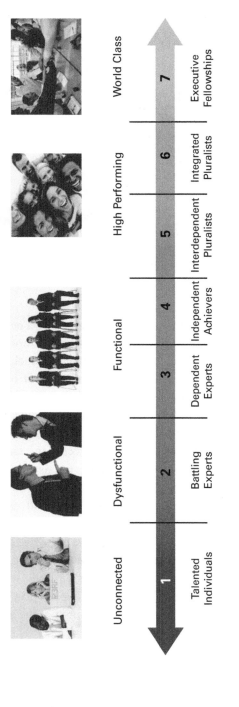

Unconnected	Dysfunctional		Functional		High Performing	World Class
1	2	3	4	5	6	7
Talented Individuals	Battling Experts	Dependent Experts	Independent Achievers	Interdependent Pluralists	Integrated Pluralists	Executive Fellowships

3 Dependent experts.

4 Independent achievers.

5 Interdependent pluralists.

6 Integrated pluralists.

7 Executive fellowships.

Team Stage 1: Talented individuals

The first stage of team development is not really a team. It is a collection of 'talented individuals' who are gathered together under a single leader for organizational reasons. Often this isn't intentional; it's simply the natural consequence of how performance management and people management processes have been set up. The only reason 'talented individuals' come together as a 'team' is for the convenience of a leader who wishes to maintain organizational structures, spans of control and keep wider power hierarchies in place. Thus a leader may be given responsibility for five different areas of the business that have no particular commonality, but the leader is so senior that they must be seen to 'own' sufficient executive responsibility. This sort of 'functional clustering' is relatively common and usually flows from poor organizational design, the fear of senior-talent attrition or empire building. There is usually no clear team purpose and little commitment to a team agenda. Most of the work in these 'teams' occurs at the next level down and the team leader plays a more supervisory or directive role to the individual functional area specialist. Groups of talented individuals are not necessarily dysfunctional because there is little reason for the individuals involved to disagree as there is little overlap in accountabilities. If there is overlap, then this type of 'team' is nearly always dysfunctional.

The only unifying force is the wider organization and possibly the need to manage a talent pool across the various areas of functioning. Such 'teams' are best run as organizational forums rather than as teams, and are represented as a flotilla rather than a single boat.

Team Stage 2: Battling experts

The first real stage of team development is when the collection of talented individuals share a common purpose, even though this may not be explicit or clearly defined. This stage embraces the well-recognized 'storming' and 'norming' phases of team development. The storming occurs because there is a battle for control of the agenda and the team has to sort out its 'pecking order'. Stage 2 normally occurs when the team leader is recently appointed or is promoted, having previously been a peer of the other team members.

The team is largely dysfunctional and this dysfunction is often concealed by a thin veneer of unity or polite professionalism. Underneath this veneer factions form and break as the power struggle ebbs and flows far from sight in corridors and side-bar meetings. Individual team members brief against each other and will often network outside the team to gain support for their own agenda.

At times there is open conflict within team meetings, but that's unusual. There are very low levels of trust, little understanding of each other or even any attempt to understand each other's motives. If there wasn't an organizational reason to stick together this 'team' would probably fragment. Teams of battling experts don't last long and are characterized by a high turnover rate. The ongoing executive churn may keep the team stuck in Stage 2 as 'new arrivals' are thought to be 'the answer' to the team's dysfunction. Unfortunately the new arrival usually gets drawn into the same dysfunction and the turbulence continues.

Signs of disunity are usually visible to people a number of levels down the organization. Such dysfunction is often perceived to be 'part of the executive landscape'. The impaired motivation and reduced staff engagement such senior scuffles cause is often unseen by the battling senior leaders or is not seen as linked to their conflict.

Ultimately a team's dysfunction reflects badly on the individual leader, and if leaders can't bring some semblance of order and performance to their teams they often become the casualty of 'battling experts'. In our work we have seen executive boards stuck at this level and sometimes it is the CEOs who perpetuate the disunity because it enables them to maintain complete control of the agenda and suppress any potential threats to their control.

Team Stage 3: Dependent experts

If the team members manage to resolve some of their differences and enter the 'performing stage' then they reach Stage 3 of team development. Here the team consists largely of a collection of 'dependent experts' who are getting on with each other and doing a professional job. This is perhaps the most commonly encountered stage of team development seen in organizations today. Unfortunately, most executive teams never make it out of Stage 3.

At this level people 'attend' the team meetings and 'report in' what is happening in their function, business unit or silo. The agenda for the team is determined top down and team members look to the team leader to decide what happens and when. Team members often seek guidance from the 'boss' on the goals, objectives and the behavioural norms for the team. Team members often start to unconsciously match the behaviour modelled by the boss in an attempt to fit in and succeed.

At this stage there is often friendliness in the team and members may even enjoy each other's company, but in reality they are still not that much more than a collection of individuals doing their job, held together by the leader in charge (hence dependent). Individual team members will often keep their own agendas hidden for self-protection purposes and only reveal the views that fit with the views of the leader.

There can be significant debate but it is usually individuals passionately advocating their own perspective to 'win' the argument, impress the boss, justify their own position or establish their place in the 'pecking order'. There is little concept building across the team and the debate often feels like 'popcorn' with individuals just making their points while ignoring the previous points, and there is rarely anyone taking responsibility to integrate the various views. The debate amongst dependent experts is often little more than a 'circular stampede', progress is minimal as each individual keeps advocating his or her own position. Alternatively a robust debate or argument breaks out with a winner and a loser, which itself creates a dynamic for future battles and echoes the behaviours seen at Stage 2.

Team learning is low and despite surface goodwill the depth of trust between individual team members is also low. Individual team members will often not trust the commercial judgement of other team members, although this is never made explicit or spoken about directly. Full disclosure rarely happens and 'off-line' 'positioning' conversations in the corridor after the meetings are common.

The leader may be the only integrative force but this often degrades into simple refereeing between debating factions of different 'camps' of opinion. A team at this stage of development is quite resistant to coaching as it is really set up to maintain the status quo and existing power hierarchies. It can work quite effectively, particularly in crisis when directive leadership is required. Stage 3 teams can also succeed in stable environments where there is not much need for speed or adaptive change. However, in a VUCA world a team arrested at this stage will ultimately hold the organization back.

The behaviour of team members at Stage 3 is based on compliance to a set of (often implicit) 'Team Rules' that are largely about reverence or reference to the leader and maintaining the hierarchy. These teams are not traditionally very reflective, which often translates into a tremendous rush to action. They find it difficult to hold concepts and defer decisions to allow learning to take place. Before making any decision, there is often a reference to an external higher authority. So questions are frequently asked about 'what the CEO/Chairman/Board/Shareholders want or think'.

The more top-down interventions the leader makes in the debate, the more the team gets stuck in Stage 3, unable to progress. They get stuck because team members start to believe that they can't change the outcome. Team members become passive because they believe, usually from experience, that the boss will eventually overrule their decisions or impose his or her point of view anyway. The leader who consistently guillotines the debate and decides for the team, however nicely it's done, subtly sustains the team's dependence on the leader's authority.

A 'team' of 'dependent experts' will never progress to Stage 4 until all the team members are willing to have more fierce conversations (Scott, 2002). There has to be a much greater level of frankness and open disclosure of all hidden agendas without fear of the consequences. However, the ability to have such open conversations cannot really occur until the team has developed some very specific capabilities. These capabilities include a significant degree of adult maturity and emotional self-regulation plus the ability to listen at a deeper level. The skills we explored in all the previous chapters of this book can therefore be extremely helpful in facilitating the transition from 'dependent experts' to 'independent achievers'. The transition into Stage 4 is not easy and will not occur without mature support from the team leaders themselves.

Team Stage 4: Independent achievers

The transition into Stage 4 requires team members to connect effectively with each other and openly share their thoughts and feelings. They need to take responsibility for their own energy, their impact on others and their behaviour. They also need to start taking increasing responsibility for the performance of the whole team, not just for their discrete accountabilities. Stage 4 teams are able to operate independently from external authority and team members will proactively drive the future of the team across all four quadrants of the Enlightened Leadership model, although they may not think in these terms. The team takes on the task of pushing the leader out of the day-to-day functioning of the team so the leader can work at the level above. This enables the team to self-organize to a much higher degree. This self-organizing doesn't need the 'permission' or sanction of the leader.

Stage 4 produces a degree of positive independence, empowerment and collective rather than individual authority. Such teams have a much clearer unifying purpose and are often bound by their desire for independence. These teams develop their own capacity to make things happen.

However, 'independent achievers' can be quite fragile and may revert back to 'dependent experts', particularly if the team leader is not comfortable with the team's ability to operate independently of his or her authority. The atmosphere of openness and independence can feel uncomfortable to the team members as the team becomes more vocal and argumentative. This can sometimes be so awkward that the team regresses back to the more congenial Stage 3. In effect, the conflict that arises may spawn a desire to get the team leader back so he or she can referee the debate again. The rebellion that can occur may be either open or hidden, and sometimes both forms exist within the same team.

Open rebellion can start to create very unhelpful dynamics, with the resurfacing of factional divisions, excessive political manoeuvring and perpetual tension within the team. This can result in a heavy-handed autocracy returning to try and reassert some semblance of control and prevent the team from disintegrating. While the new imposed order can appear to suppress the rebellion it often simply pushes it underground. The end result is either a collapse back to Stage 3, constantly simmering undercurrents of tension or an unhealthy team atmosphere that can have a significantly negative impact on motivation and performance.

Stage 4 is fragile and often uncomfortable. It is often the reason that leaders believe that people management is so difficult. Any attempts to develop teams must travel through this stage. It's not easy; it's often uncharted territory for everyone and consequently it can be very demanding on time. As a result leaders can often throw up their hands in horror, step back in and resume the command and control approach of Stages 2 or 3. Any subsequent mention of 'developing teams' is from then on dismissed as a complete waste of time that 'never works anyway'.

Leading a Stage 4 team takes considerable skill, which most team leaders have not developed simply because they have not been trained. So the transition into Stage 4 often requires the support of a good coach who understands the stages of team development and can help the leader manage the complexities of the team dynamics.

Stabilizing a team of 'independent achievers' requires the leader to resist the temptation to reassert his or her authority when the tensions bubble up or the debate becomes more conflicted. Processes must be put in place to help all the team members develop their understanding of each other. We have used the Leadership Values Profile (LVP) to great effect at this point. It provides a common language to allow executives to understand the different perspectives in the team.

With this cultural framework in place, the very thing that caused you to reject the other person's perspective becomes the very thing that now causes you to pull them closer to you. When we see each other through the lens of each other's value system we realize that their point of view, actions and reactions are largely a result of their values and not a personal assault on us as a human being. This can be incredibly liberating for everyone involved. Tensions melt away and instead of clashing, the group finds ways to utilize the strengths that are inherent within each value system so they match the right people to the right roles and tasks within the group. The team comes to understand that these differences are a source of competitive advantage and as such should be embraced not eradicated or stifled. Team members welcome contrary points of view and see the value in bringing a wider perspective as it allows broader insights to be integrated.

In addition to the LVP, the other social and emotional intelligence skills already covered are also very helpful at this stage. Successful Stage 4 development often also benefits from a very direct exploration of trust and a mutual understanding of the ingredients of trust and how each person's trust recipe may differ.

In order to successfully stabilize at Stage 4, each team member needs to consciously avoid reverting back to Stage 3 behaviours such as trying to persuade others to their own 'expert' point of view. The tendency to revert back to Stage 3 behaviours where individuals push their personal agendas is often seen when team members 'grab the pen' or 'play the chairman role' to force through their point of view. If the 'scribe' works to integrate the different perspectives of the team, then genuine 'team think' will emerge and the individual expertise of Stage 3 will give way to the broader achievement focus characterized by Stage 4. When the team members shift their focus from the prowess of the individual or silo to the success of the team, the launch pad is built for Stage 5 development.

Team Stage 5: Interdependent pluralists

When effectively coached into Stage 5, the team members are now able to see and accept each other's unique perspective and successfully integrate those perspectives into the solution. The desire for such integration comes from an understanding of the mutual advantages to be had if the team learns to effectively share and cooperate. Such coherence becomes a pleasure in itself and a pride is taken in the degree of alignment the team now has. Team members start to identify with the team itself and think about how the team can succeed even more. Team meetings become a source of energy and cross-functional stimulation. Ideas are shared with a view to uncovering how they affect each other and the team seeks to identify the synergies so they can benefit the group.

There is a real honesty about silo under achievement and this is shared openly as team members focus on anything that is 'slowing the boat down'.

Rather than flipping into blame or judgement the team welcomes news of underperformance. Such news provides an opportunity to 'make the boat go faster' and improve team performance and impact.

For the first time, genuine team learning starts to occur. Such learning requires the interaction of the team members and cannot be achieved through individual reflection. Shared team concepts emerge and a genuine sense of 'WE' is present. Prior to this, any claims of 'team' are normally lip service, spin or aspiration.

The team leader is seen more as a team member and all team members proactively seek to identify opportunities for cross-functional collaboration. Such fluidity sets the stage for progression to Stage 6.

Individual team members start to meet spontaneously to build a deeper understanding of each other's ideas and to look for connections that can help improve the team and performance. Team interdependency starts to become the *modus operandi* and the ideas generated are more sophisticated because they include more than one and often multiple perspectives. Teams of 'interdependent pluralists' are much more effective at addressing the deep organizational issues and therefore add much more value to organizational performance.

The level of attention paid by all team members to the team spirit, interpersonal dynamics and relationships in the team increases. A much stronger sense of 'WE' is more consistently present; team harmony and coherence become recurring topics for discussion. The team starts to really feel like a high-performing unit and starts to have occasional experiences of 'flow' where team projects or debates become easy and effortless. Quite complex decisions can be made at speed.

Progress into Stage 6 is inhibited when team members, facing the difficulty of working cross-functionally, start arguing for their own silo-specific answers. A second factor that holds teams in the foothills of high performance is an excessive focus on action and implementation. Progress is delayed by inadequate reflection, and insufficient emphasis given to the need to integrate different perspectives. Development is also held back by a tendency to go with the first or early answer rather than parking the initial view and exploring other possible options or concepts. When a leader or team members shoot down an idea prematurely before it has been explored properly or they focus all their energy on all the obstacles to execution, then progress can be stifled. This has been referred to as 'TINA' – 'there is no alternative' – but there are always alternatives and a high performing team knows that.

A lack of conceptual flexibility can cause the team to stall to such an extent it can provoke a return to Stage 3 to break through the knot. To avoid this the team needs to stay positively focused on collaboration and develop the ability to sincerely appreciate each other (See Appreciation skill on page 237).

The transition from Stage 4 to Stage 5 represents a significant leap in team development and marks the shift from a functioning team to a high-performing one. A very quick test of whether a team is at Stage 4 or Stage 5 is to get the team to rate their own level of performance compared with their potential. Stage 4 teams normally rate themselves 7 or 8 out of 10. Stage 5 teams are more likely to rate themselves 4.5 to 6 out of 10. Such scoring is independent of actual performance and reflects Stage 5's clearer understanding of the untapped nature of their potential.

A team of 'interdependent pluralists' is more likely to reject the win–lose mentality common in Stage 4 and below. As a result decisions are often made consensually. While the answers created are certainly more sophisticated, they are not necessarily optimal for the organization. Four key capabilities come on line at Stage 5 of team development:

- There is much greater respect for each other, not just as individuals but as cooperating peers.
- Much greater levels of open sharing occur, which enables team learning to occur.
- Conceptual flexibility kicks in with a greater ability for abstract thought.
- Downward delegation of authority becomes the norm.

With quality team coaching it is possible to shift a team from Stage 3 to Stage 5 within 18–24 months with quarterly team events focused on team development. This can be accelerated with more frequent contact points and a more intense level of investment.

At Stage 5 team members have started to experience the benefits of subjugating their own agenda in the service of the team. They have directly experienced the value, rather than understood the theoretical advantage, of working cross-functionally compared with working in independent, albeit effective, silos. Having come through the challenges of command and control, excessive independence, conflict, passive aggressiveness so as to glimpse the value of collaboration, team members are now ready to move beyond Stage 5 and operate in the more integrated fashion of Stage 6.

Team Stage 6: Integrated pluralists

Very few executive teams make it to Stage 6.

The cohering force at Stage 6 is the persistent desire of all team members to take the organizational perspective in all matters. Enhanced performance of the company becomes the uniting force across interdependent silos. Team members have a high degree of self-regulation and are adept at systems thinking. When 'integrated pluralists' meet, the conversation transcends many of the concerns that occupy teams operating at earlier stages. They are aware of the different levels of the system, move up and down the levels, switching between the complex and the pragmatic as the need arises. The team focus also moves around all four quadrants of the Enlightened Leadership model.

In addition, Stage 6 teams take ownership of the hard questions and bring a more sophisticated mindset to bear on the issues. They seek to understand the multiple interdependencies inside the organization and how these are affected by and influence outside forces. They construct multiple strategic options through leveraging the different perspectives available to them from leaders at all levels of the organization, and also integrate the team's views. They understand that many of the problems faced in complex systems are not problems that can be solved but polarities that must be managed. For example, the team ceases to see short- and long-term or centralized and delegated authority as trade-offs and starts to see them as dependent poles of the same polarity.

Ultimately the team seeks to enhance individual and collective performance across the organization so as to build a more inclusive and successful business.

Team Stage 7: Executive fellowships

True 'executive fellowship' is rarely seen in organizational life. So many things need to be in place for 'executive fellowship' to emerge spontaneously. A fellowship can be developed but it probably takes a minimum of three or more likely five years to really build one in practice. And this is assuming that the motivation for individual and collective development is sustained over that timeframe, despite personnel changes to the team.

'Executive fellowships' build on all the qualities the team developed to achieve exceptional high performance. Those within an 'executive fellowship' have learnt to take a team and company perspective rather than a personal or siloed perspective. They have learnt how to collaborate across different parts of the organization and look for opportunities to build synergy. They are self-managing and self-motivating, and take ownership of the team's performance. They can diffuse conflicts quickly and experience moments of 'flow' when team coherence enables easy and fast resolution of difficult and complex challenges. In an 'executive fellowship' coherence and flow are common qualities and occur consistently.

The transition from Stage 6 to 7 requires more subtle, nuanced development in multiple areas than previous stage transitions. Dave Beresford, the

Performance Director of the amazingly successful GB cycling squad, talks about how they have developed the idea of continuous improvement through integrating a thousand 1 per cent advances. He calls this the accumulation of 'marginal gains'. Building 'executive fellowship' requires such skilful guidance. Most team coaches can spot what's not working and help the team correct that, but it takes real skill to spot what is working and enhance that. We explored this idea in the last chapter in relation to leadership behaviour. A great leader seeks to improve a weakness only to the point where it stops holding that person back, and recognizes that the real gains are made when the focus is on identifying strengths so they can be baked into the business and become a 'Strategic Strength'.

To reach Stage 7 and become an executive fellowship, the team must be prepared to commit time and energy at least every quarter to their own development so as to allow the component parts of trust to flourish. The exact steps that need to be taken on the 'Team Journey' vary depending on the team, their current stage of development, the market conditions and the make-up of the team itself.

Network analysis

In order to facilitate rapid evolution through the stages of team development and to arrive at highly functioning teams and executive fellowships, it can be really helpful to understand the existing networks within an organization. In our work, we help senior leaders to define the current connectivity within an organization using our Leadership Network Analysis (LNA), Team Network Analysis (TNA) and Organizational Network Analysis (ONA) diagnostics. These assessments enable us to precisely define who is connected to whom and why, and identify how strong those connections really are.

One of the interesting paradoxes in modern business is that we have more ways to 'communicate' with each other than ever before but that communication is becoming increasingly shallow, and as such we are actually less connected. We have the tools for greater connectivity but meaningful connection is still rare in most corporations.

It is now clear that top-down traditional 'roll-outs' of initiatives from the 'corporate centre' to the far reaches of the corporate empire are not effective. We encourage organizations to communicate and engage with their people through 'viral' mechanisms, rippling ideas through the existing organizational networks and forums. A nudge, a wave of excitement and an engaging dialogue with staff are much more effective than most traditional 'internal comms' processes. As Nick Warren, Head of Development at First

Quantum Minerals Ltd, pointed out when we interviewed him about his experiences with Enlightened Leadership:

> For us, our culture creates the rules that help us manage the business. You feel it around you. You pick up the signs almost subconsciously and then start to behave in a certain way. We continue to foster that culture by paying attention to the symbols, rituals and stories that make up a culture. Limiting bureaucracy enables the culture to determine the rules of engagement in the business... Culturally driven interventions like storytelling are far greater drivers of behaviour than systems or forms... We want to get away from this Western, McKinsey rationale that it is always about solutions; for us it is much more about listening and ensuring that people feel they are being heard.

Understanding the existing internal network can facilitate high-speed viral infections within the business because it helps to identity who's who in the team and who are likely to be the Connectors, the Mavens and the Salespeople (Gladwell, 2000), as discussed below.

Network analysis is based on complicated social networking theory, but we use a much simpler approach that illuminates some very powerful data in just a few minutes. We ask seven simple questions to define three critical networks:

- *Functional network*: Name the people you typically get work-related information from. Name the people you regularly collaborate with.

- *Emotional network*: Name the people you feel energized by when you interact with them. Name the people you feel personally comfortable sharing sensitive information with. Name the people to whom you turn for support when things are tough.

- *Leadership network*: Name the people you feel personally stretch your thinking. Name the people to whom you turn for leadership or guidance.

The *Mavens*, those who are motivated to educate and help, are usually identified by their dominant functional network. The *Connectors*, those that know and communicate with lots of people, are usually identified by their dominant emotional network. The persuasive, influential *Salespeople* are usually identified by their leadership network.

This analysis can flush out a lot of really critical information about networks within organizations. For example, I worked with a global leadership team where one individual's quality of thinking and innovation abilities were really strong, but his leadership network revealed that very few of his peers turned to him for guidance on the big points where he could have added a lot of value. In addition, his emotional networks were weak despite his having strong functional networks. This was an eye-opener for him and caused him to significantly change his behaviour towards his peers. He realized that he did not have anywhere near the influence he hoped for or needed in order to 'land' his brilliant ideas.

Another executive had very strong emotional connectivity but was moved sideways in a political power reshuffle. This caused significant unrest in the division and a sudden drop-off in performance. This person was emotionally important to the community and the move caused many other people in the division to become very uneasy and lose trust in the leadership.

Because network analysis can also identify hidden talents, when we do this across a whole team, division or company we see all the dendrites that spread out and can easily identify who the key players are. It therefore exposes how the business really functions, rather than how we might want it to function or think it functions. The insights generated can be incredibly useful for succession and driving improved performance.

For example, we did a network analysis across the whole executive team within a company in Eastern Europe. They had appointed two new senior executives to the board, both starting in the business on the same day – a new financial director and a new commercial director. Both candidates had been brought in as potential successors for the CEO position.

After six months we clearly identified that the financial director had become the most highly connected person in the whole executive team – even more so than the CEO. In contrast, the commercial director hardly had any connections at all. It was obvious from the analysis that the financial director was better suited to become the next CEO because he had the stronger network. People turned to him for guidance and leadership; they were energized by him and trusted him with sensitive information. His functional, emotional and leadership connectivity was far better than the commercial director's. He went on to become the CEO in another country sooner than expected and the commercial director was let go not long after.

Spiral dynamics and the evolution of value systems

Trust is the glue that holds teams together. In fact, if we look at the stages of team development, trust is the active ingredient that increases as a team evolves from a collection of 'talented individuals' to an 'executive fellowship'. Understanding another person's motives is a crucial part of the trust recipe, and one of the fastest and easiest ways to understand motives and make serious headway in the development of highly functioning teams is to ensure that everyone in the team knows and understands their own and everyone else's value system.

Numerous authors have written on the development of values and culture. In our work, we have integrated the research of Gert Hofstede, Shalom Schwartz and Clare Graves and a few other academics to enable us to profile how a leader's value systems vary depending on their situation. Of the three main academics mentioned above, Graves's work is perhaps the most commercially useful, not least because it has more of a vertical developmental or evolutionary dimension.

Clare Graves was a psychology professor at Union College in Schenectady, New York. In setting his students various essay assignments he noticed that the student's responses could be grouped into four main types of answers. He concluded that there were four 'world views' that determined the way students wrote their essays and what they emphasized. His model developed over time to identify eight levels or value systems, each emerging from the previous one.

Two of Graves's students, Chris Cowen and Don Beck, went on to build on his work and named the framework 'Spiral dynamics', and it is now one of the most widely used and widely cited cultural assessment tools on the planet (Figure 6.5).

As with all frameworks, when you tell people that it's an upward moving spiral everyone wants to be at the top of the evolutionary spiral. Spiral dynamics is another example of a model that transcends and includes each level. So as we evolve up the spiral we don't lose access to the behaviours or value systems at the lower levels; we simply transcend them and include them in our capabilities. We become more sophisticated as we mature and develop up the spiral because we have access to more perspectives, values and behaviours, but that doesn't mean we are 'better' than those who operate at the lower levels of the spiral and it certainly doesn't mean the higher levels will be happier or more successful. There is clearly more potential as an individual evolves up the spiral, but some of the most effective leaders operate from value systems at a lower level and some who operate further up the spiral can be disastrous in a business setting.

The key consideration is that there are positive and negative aspects of every level, but it is the negative aspect that provides the upward evolutionary force. The impact of each value system is also affected by the maturity of the individual involved. In business we can find mature and immature people operating at every level in the spiral. The only difference is that a mature individual is usually more driven by the upside of the value system whereas an immature individual is usually more driven by the downside of that level.

Each level is depicted by a colour that is relevant to that level, and the focus of each level oscillates between the individual and the collective all the way up the spiral.

What's especially interesting about spiral dynamics is that regardless of scale the model still holds true. Thus you can predict the likely behaviour of an individual, a team, a division, a business, an industry, a nation, a region or the entire population of the planet (Figure 6.5).

FIGURE 6.5   Spiral dynamics

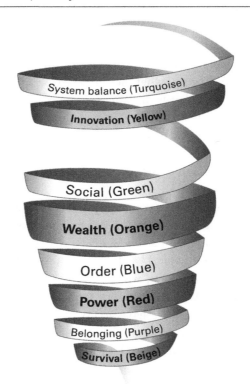

System balance (Turquoise)

Innovation (Yellow)

Social (Green)

Wealth (Orange)

Order (Blue)

Power (Red)

Belonging (Purple)

Survival (Beige)

Beige: survival (individual focus)

Beige is the colour of the sub-Sahara, where the prime focus is on individual survival. This value system was readily apparent when I visited a mining company in Mauritania. It was common to see people sitting by the roadside all day with little or no desire to do anything more than to survive that day. As soon as their basics needs of food and water were met they would stop moving and sit down on the side of the road and simply watch the world go by.

The Beige value system may also still be apparent in certain populations within an industrialized society. For example, it may be present amongst the homeless, the unemployed, the sick or the marginalized. In times of economic hardship it may be possible to witness some very basic Beige-driven behaviour within organizations as survival motives kick in. People may revert to a Beige system when facing bankruptcy or potential redundancy.

What drives people with this value system is their immediate basic need to survive. They are highly attuned to their physical senses, which are often heightened. Satisfaction of basic biological needs tends to stop action and provoke rest until these needs must be addressed again. As such, people at this level tend not to plan at all. They live from day to day.

The best way to help Beige individuals is to bring them together with other Beige individuals so they can start to bond and realize they are not alone. To reach someone who operates from the Beige values system, we first have to directly encounter them. They may not engage with modern communication channels, or if they do it is in a haphazard way because their focus is on their short-term needs first.

The upside of Beige is that the individual survives but the downside is there is very little progress or forward momentum. Eventually people start to cluster together to see if they could survive better as a group, and this is what pushes individuals up the spiral to Purple.

Purple: belonging (collective focus)

Purple is the colour of magic. Magical thinking and a belief in superstition are often rife at this level. Purple emerges when the focus swings to the collective and individuals start to gather together because they realize they are more likely to survive as a group. So the 'tribe' or gang emerges.

Tribal value systems are quite common in business during the early stages of a company's evolution, during mergers and acquisitions, in specific functions or in geographically separate offices. It is for example visible in the sales tribe, the IT tribe or the London or New York tribe, and often the people in those tribes will feel more loyalty to their tribe than they will to the company itself. It is this value system that often reinforces silo behaviour. Membership of the tribe is often reinforced by certain rituals, a special language or a 'uniform'. For example city traders will wear their coloured jackets or celebrate a good week with a mandatory magnum of champagne every Friday (at least they did before the global financial crisis!).

Purple 'gangs' are often small teams for whom their allegiance to the tribe is their main point of connection. Their members can feel somewhat separate from the corporate machine or mission. The sense of bonding with their colleagues keeps them from leaving and they can often be mildly hostile to the company itself. Their analysis of the situation is not that sophisticated and they can easily fall into the victim mode, believing that the business is not working in their interests.

Commercially they are driven by having a safe place to work where no one rocks the boat too much or creates too much change. They are very quick to sense a personal or commercial threat, and they can react strongly to protect their own position and the security of their tribe.

The best way to help Purple individuals move forward is to identify the natural leaders who are trusted by the tribe, promote them and allow them to lead the rest of their colleagues. However, the tribe will need to be reassured that any change will not threaten the tribe. In fact, change must be sold as a way of protecting the tribe. They will engage as a group and can be inspired by a charismatic presentation. It is vital to allow time for the tribe to debate the suggested change and reach a collective agreement.

On the upside of Purple there is a great sense of belonging and life is easier, safer and more comfortable in a collective. The downside is reactive, poorly thought-through behaviour without much direction. And this lack of direction eventually spawns the evolution up the spiral to Red.

Red: power (individual focus)

Red is the colour of power and passion, and the focus swings back to the individual. This level is characterized by individuals who take charge. In fact the military actively flush out Red individuals by dropping recruits into uncertain situations and waiting. They know that the Purple lack of direction will push someone to step up and take the reins – that is the Red leader. The same happens in business: out of the group steps a Red leader who takes the reins and doesn't let go, often going all the way to the top.

Red leaders are one of the two commonest value systems we see in the executive suite of global multinationals, and many companies have unconsciously chosen Red as their corporate colour. This value system is particularly prevalent in the early stages of a company's evolution or in divisions that are opening up new territories. Certain functions, such as sales and PR, are often stuffed with people operating from the Red value system.

Many CEOs and leaders drive their business forward from a Red value system. They are often charismatic, 'larger than life' individuals with a great deal of energy who often have a great sense of humour. However, they can also lead by fear, intimidation or strength of will. Leadership by 'just do as I say' is common. They tend to operate a 'hub and spoke' command-and-control model of leadership. They are good at taking charge and great at simplifying and clarifying the priorities.

Red leaders are fantastic at making things happen, so they are absolutely the best type of leader if you are opening a new market or going into a new country. Red leaders always want to be Number 1 in their market. They are restless, relentless and resilient, with a strong sense of urgency. They move fast to get control and dominate by dint of their status, power or authority. They are good in a fight, an emergency or in a turnaround, where they can be the hero in the hunt for glory.

The best way to help Red leaders develop is to show them how, with a little more structure, they can celebrate an even greater victory. The knack is to help them work smarter not harder; a little more skill and a little less speed is often what's required. It must always be made very clear to Red leaders how they can personally contribute. The battle must remain exciting or fun if their interest is to be maintained. They prefer short, to-the-point communications – 'keep it simple stupid' is their mantra.

The real benefit of Red leadership is their passion and desire to make things happen. However, the downside is that progress is often dependent on the individual leaders themselves. The Red leader can become a bottleneck for decisions, and the excessive responsibility taken by a Red leader can create passivity in those around him or her as the team start to believe there is no point in making a decision themselves as the leader is likely to overrule it anyway. This excessive ownership of every item on the agenda has been called a 'responsibility virus' (Martin, 2002) and can itself stifle growth. The intoxicating nature of ultimate power can fuel a sense of omnipotence in the Red leader and start to drive a whole range of unhelpful behaviours or egomania. It is this power lust that starts to create unrest in the collective, which then begin to gang together to curb the excesses of Red leadership and the next level, Blue, emerges.

Blue: order (collective focus)

Blue is the colour that represents order, conservatism and loyalty, and it illustrates a swing back to the collective. Doing the right thing is important to someone operating from a Blue value system. Meaning emerges for the first time, and the search for a higher principle or authority, be it government or God, becomes important at Blue. Those with a Red value system are often too busy enjoying themselves to wonder too much about what things may mean.

Government departments, bureaucracies and public-sector partnerships often have a Blue culture. These are systems built on rules and order. All businesses must go through a Blue phase to build some infrastructure and a stable platform for growth. It is often insufficient discipline or sloppy methods that prevent large companies from achieving their potential. Good organization and high-quality processes can make a massive difference to most companies.

CEOs and leaders operating from a Blue value system are often highly principled: they seek to do the right thing in the right way at the right time according to their 'rules' of how business should be run. The Blue value system is more common in specialist functions such as finance, accounting or IT.

In an attempt to create order, Blue often puts a whole raft of rules and regulations in place designed to instil some discipline and prevent the Red excesses from derailing the organization. So infrastructure and process start to emerge.

People with a Blue value system are comfortable following the rules of a higher authority, whether that be the company, their boss or God. They are accurate, crisp and want to deliver to a high quality. They consider the meaning of their work and have a desire to bring stability.

Trade unions are often a classic example of crystallized Blue organizational value system. They can often bring much needed stability and fairness to an industry. But they can also become rigidly constrained by their own rules and processes, and drift into unhealthy 'jobsworth' thinking, as evidenced by the UK public-sector strikes in 2012. The fact that public-sector pensions far outstripped the average private-sector worker's and the country just couldn't afford them didn't matter to the offended principles of the Blue value system and the people striking. They couldn't see that a small reduction now might help to secure jobs and pensions in the long term. And it's possibly worse in the United States. In 2008, the city of Vallejo, California, declared bankruptcy under the weight of the escalating pay and benefits of public safety workers. Police and fire-fighters refused to accept that the city simply could not afford their massive pay and pensions; they, like so much of society, believed they were entitled to be rich and refused to negotiate a compromise. Rather than agree to reduction they refused and lost everything (Lewis, 2011).

The best way to develop Blue individuals out of their tendency to get stuck in the rules is to encourage them to experiment and show individuals how this could benefit the collective. This will succeed if it is perceived as the right thing to do and does not contravene Blue's sense of justice and fair play.

All communication must be structured, tidy and be well presented. Meetings must be well managed, stick to time and follow a disciplined process. Blue people tend to be diplomatic and avoid conflict, and are efficient completer-finishers who like to take the moral high ground.

The upside of Blue is stability. But too much Blue and the business can become rigid and inflexible. Like all levels, it is the inflexibility dysfunction of Blue that eventually creates the conditions for the evolutionary push up into the next level and Orange emerges.

Orange: wealth (individual focus)

Orange illustrates a swing back to an individual focus. Interestingly, orange is an extremely popular business colour and it is over-represented for corporate livery – think easyJet, Orange, TNT, ING, etc.

Most businesses are run by leaders from a Red or Orange value system. In many ways the Orange leaders represent a more mature version of the Red leader because they've acquired an understanding of the importance of process and principle and are less inclined to 'shoot from the hip' than the Red leaders.

Free from the stifling constraints of too many Blue rules, the Orange leader looks to build on the best parts of the Blue infrastructure and system whilst being more flexible in order to compete, grow the business and deliver results. The ultimate goal of Orange is wealth.

Whether you loved her or hated her, Margaret Thatcher almost single-handedly broke the Blue union mindset of the 1970s in the UK and her policies pushed the country into an Orange flourish. She relaxed the financial rules, deregulated the markets, sold off some of the state-owned assets and encouraged share ownership in these newly privatized companies. She encouraged people to buy their own council houses, which enabled millions of people to own property for the first time. This had a significant cultural impact in the UK and many people became wealthier.

It has been suggested that most CEOs are professional managers rather than leaders (Tappin and Cave, 2010). The minority who have made the transition from managers to leaders are often commercial executors or corporate entrepreneurs. Both types operate from the Orange value system and focus on delivering short-term commercial performance while leveraging the resources available to them. They take a pragmatic, no-nonsense view of the world and they are happy to do whatever it takes to achieve the targets they set for themselves.

Orange individuals want to make money and win. They are highly competitive on many fronts. They have a slightly more mature ambition than Red individuals and are often better equipped to take advantage of other people's abilities to achieve their own goals. They are very rational and like to understand how things work so they can make the 'machinery' of business deliver its profits.

To help those in an Orange value system out of their tendency to be excessively rational, too materialistic or too self-interested, it can often benefit them to cultivate the ability for reflection. They may also find it useful to work on their emotional intelligence and ability to take people with them.

When communicating with the Orange value system it is vital to be outcome-focused and make it clear how the plan will work to deliver the desired result. There also has to be an opportunity for the individuals to work through the issue and make changes. They will also need to know how it works financially.

Many people consider Orange to be the pinnacle of success. This is the ultimate destination and wealth is the ultimate prize. Needless to say Orange, like every other level, has a dark side – greed and avarice. When we deregulate markets and sweep away too many rules, then we start to create the conditions that foster extreme Orange behaviour. People start to 'play the system' for their own personal benefit. The whole banking-driven economic disaster can be traced back to some extreme Orange people on the bond desks of a few banks in New York who saw the chance to 'game' the whole mortgage market and knowingly sold 'toxic assets' to naïve purchasers because the system allowed them to (Lewis, 2010).

As a result an increasing number of people, particularly Generation Y, have spotted the flaw in this value system and many have begun to seriously wonder or explore what lies beyond (Tapscott, 2009). They seek a way of moving forward that doesn't favour the few at the expense of the many, that doesn't worsen the already considerable gap between the haves and the have-nots. Whilst the upside of Orange is wealth creation, it is polluted by the excessive greed of the few, which acts as the next evolutionary stimulus and Green emerges.

Green: social (collective focus)

Green illustrates a swing back to the collective. Green businesses or Green leaders often emerge as an antidote to Orange excess. They are motivated by finding a more caring, inclusive way of proceeding that benefits the many not just the few. Such businesses are rarely in the FTSE 100, although there are companies whose internal culture has a strong Green orientation. The importance of the Green perspective is increasing as a result of social networking.

Green leaders have realized that the 'winners and losers' mindset is ultimately a zero-sum game. Exploitation detonates strong forces that eventually cause a tsunami of suffering, recrimination and a backlash. If the perpetrators personally escape the wreckage of their companies, colleagues, careers or professions often don't. Green leaders make a different choice. They take a more caring approach. And this care extends from people to the planet. They are interested in their carbon footprints, fair trade, local produce, sustainability and the whole green agenda. They are also much more sensitive to the needs of the collective.

Green CEOs and leaders are often ambassadorial in style. They are generally more emotionally intelligent and are driven by a desire to help. They attempt to include a wide section of opinion and have an intense dislike of hierarchies.

As at all the previous levels before them, the Green leader thinks his or her perspective and approach is the right one and will argue vocally to that effect. In fact every leader in the first tier (Beige to Green) thinks s/he is right and everyone else is wrong. Many team or cultural tensions are rooted in this mistaken belief that 'I am right' and 'they are wrong'. A great deal of time is wasted in team meetings as each leader works hard to persuade other team members that their view is correct. The trouble is that they are all at it.

Green is particularly conflicted around this point. They want to make everyone correct and equally valid. All are welcome, all are included; there is no 'better/worse'. Green abhors better/worse suggestions and is the most likely to reject the vertical nature of development. Green thinkers seek to bring everyone to the same level playing field. But in doing so the Green value system is blind to its own hierarchy and belief that the horizontal ('we are all equal') is better than a vertical hierarchy. Such blindness typifies the Green contradiction. On the one hand very caring and inclusive, and on the other hand myopic and judgemental.

Green leaders focus on taking people with them and will slow down to make sure no one is left behind. They try to achieve win–win relationships and will often 'go the extra mile' to make sure people are able to contribute. They are motivated by human contact and achieving results through the team. Being liked is often more important than competitive advantage.

One of the downsides of Green leadership is that leaders are so busy being inclusive that no one gets anything done and the business loses momentum. The key distinction between a Blue leader and a Green leader is that the Blue leader is guided by principles and doing the right thing, whereas the Green leader seeks to keep everyone on board and leads by consensus.

Green is the last level in 'Tier 1'. And, according to Ken Wilber, it is the main stumbling block for widespread evolution and progress – especially in business (Wilber, 2003). Most leaders don't make it past the Green swamp and stay firmly rooted in the Orange reality, or below.

Ironically individuals who operate with a Green perspective can polarize people. They can slip into negative judgement if their attempts to help or care are thwarted. They may need help to see more than their own perspective. They may also benefit from developing greater flexibility and becoming more decisive if they truly want to create benefits for the many.

When communicating with Green leaders, it is important to be customer-focused and sensitive to minorities. They respond well to sincerity and heartfelt expressed emotion moves them. They want to feel involved and will welcome the opportunity to participate and say their piece. They can react badly to assertive leaders with simple answers.

The upside of Green is collaboration and care, but ultimately the failure of the Tier 1 value systems, of which Green is the last, to adequately deal with the VUCA world has provided a stimulus to accelerate a greater emergence of the 'Tier 2' value system, the first of which is Yellow.

Yellow: innovation (individual focus)

Yellow is a swing back to the individual. When Yellow emerges, it grows out of the understanding that all of the previous perspectives have some validity but that they are all flawed in some way. If you take the inclusivity of Green and the creativity that such inclusivity enables and put it 'on steroids', the result is Yellow innovation.

Yellow is disruptive. Not in a Red maverick way but in a much smarter, more sophisticated way.

Yellow businesses are innovation engines coming up with smart solutions to complex problems. They succeed by changing the game, creating a paradigm shift or establishing clear blue water (Kim and Mauborgne, 2005). Yellow businesses are usually small, or if large they are organized on a small scale. They are competitive because they are fast, agile and able to 'hack' around older, less optimal structures.

Globally only 1 per cent of the population is operating at Yellow (Wilber, 2001). However, amongst the more senior population of ~2,000 business leaders whose value systems we have assessed in the last few years, this figure is closer to 10 per cent.

The Yellow value system is much more common in Generation Y. People of that generation are characterized by high Yellow and high Red values. Mark Zuckerberg is likely to be an off-the-charts Yellow leader and there is no doubt that Facebook is having huge disruptive influence on the planet. He was helped by fellow Yellow innovators such as Sean Parker – the man behind Napster and widely cited as the person who almost single-handedly disrupted the music industry. The Yellow mavericks in organizations do not follow a traditional career path. If it is not working they will often leave and try their hand elsewhere.

Barack Obama is probably also Yellow – a sophisticated president offering something very different from the Red leadership of George Bush (or Bush senior). Bush's values were announced to the world when he stated, 'You're either with us or against us in the fight against terror,' and whilst this statement made clear his perspective it was ultimately insufficiently nuanced to deal with the complex geopolitics that he was facing.

Yellow leaders know that the world is not black and white and they accept that they may be simultaneously part of the problem and part of the solution. To paraphrase business consultant and author Jim Collins, the first six levels of Tier 1 'look out the window' for the source of the problem and someone to blame, and Tier 2 leaders 'look in the mirror' (Collins, 2001).

Yellow leaders don't wait to be asked, they take responsibility for the solution. They see multiple perspectives and can easily handle conflicts of interest. They are drawn to complex problems and see them as challenges. They are excited by new ideas and want to have an impact beyond their company.

To help Yellow individuals achieve their impact it is often necessary to help them with the way that they language their ideas. They can over-complicate things or wrongly assume that people follow the sophistication of their thought processes. They can appear dispassionate and aloof, and this may impair their ability to connect and land their views.

To engage effectively with Yellow individuals, it is vital to lay out the conceptual frame for the conversation first. Then there has to be sufficient substance to the message, otherwise Yellow individuals will perceive it as lightweight, not serious and not worthy of consideration.

The upside of Yellow leaders is that they take personal responsibility; they are innovative, disruptive, very focused on learning and their own development. On the downside the Yellow leader can be way too conceptual, far too complex for most people to understand, and can consequently appear 'aloof', dispassionate or even detached. And it is this apparent disconnection that fosters the emergence of the final value system that has emerged – Turquoise. (Some authors (eg Wilber, 2001) have suggested that Coral is beginning to emerge beyond Turquoise but this is still unclear.)

Turquoise: system balance (collective focus)

Turquoise signals a swing back to the collective again. Turquoise organizations tend to be movements rather than formal businesses. Their focus tends to be evolutionary and long term.

Such movements look for ways to create cultural and social change for the benefit of all people without falling into the trap of being too prescriptive or patronizing. A Turquoise leader is therefore much more interested in a social mission and the greater good.

Turquoise CEOs and leaders are very rare, and when found they are normally at the helm of social or public enterprises. For example Iman Stratenus, ex-Managing Director at the World Business Council for Sustainable Development, a CEO-led organization of forward-thinking companies that galvanizes the global business community to create a sustainable future for business, society and the environment, is a Turquoise leader. You can read Iman's case study at **www.coherence-book.com**, where he reflects,

> 'It is great to know that the "Turquoise" way of leadership can work. When I discovered it and experimented with it in China [as MD for TNT Express], we achieved a lot of things.'

Turquoise leaders can often appear distracted because they are much more attuned to the long term and the unintended consequences of their decisions rather than the short-term result. They are able to compute a massive number of moving variables and look for patterns and balance within complex data sets. Such live calculations and assessments can be baffling for others as it is not always clear what their motivations are or if they are just sitting back and allowing things to happen.

A Turquoise leader can show up as many different colours, since Turquoise transcends *and* includes all previous levels. They can be strongly commercial or global missionaries and normally do not see their role as constrained by the businesses they may run, and may appear unorthodox in their approach. For example, Turquoise leaders may appear to tolerate poor performance whereas what they are really doing is allowing the individual or group to fail because the learning from that experience, whilst it may impact short-term results, will bear greater fruit for the long-term prosperity of the business. A Red or Orange leader is much less likely to allow this and would step in to stop the loss of revenue in the short term.

Globally, only 0.1 per cent of the population operate from a Turquoise value system. This means that less that 2 per cent of the global population are operating from a Tier 2 value system of either Yellow or Turquoise (Wilber, 2001). We only have two Turquoise CEOs in our database of some 2,000 leaders.

Turquoise leaders are not afraid to turn a profit if this helps the cause. They are also interested in being of service and living their lives as an example. System harmony, increasing maturity and natural emergence all invigorate their actions. They are focused on leading beyond their authority and look for ways to be of service to everyone (Middleton, 2007).

To help Turquoise individuals succeed in the world, it can help them to connect with the less sophisticated perspectives that they may have less familiarity with. They may also struggle with being fierce when they need to be. They often prefer to be tolerant, loving and allowing. They may suffer from excessive humility, which can often be misperceived as a lack of resolve. To engage Turquoise individuals, it often helps to highlight any social or evolutionary dimension to the work.

Spiral dynamics in action

We have found that helping a team understand its own value systems can significantly enhance its members' ability to understand other people's motives. When we understand our own values and the values of those people on our team, then exploring our different perspectives on the key issues becomes much less personal. Difficulties that seemed intense and complex dissolve when each person realizes their 'argument' is little more than a reflection of their individual value system and the way that value system plays out within the team.

In addition, built into the Leadership Values Profile are various sub-scales that reveal how people's value systems vary depending on the task they are engaged in. For example, when leaders are working on strategy their profile may be Yellow, suggesting that they are innovative and can contribute new ideas. The same leaders may then shift to Orange or Red for implementation, with low Yellow suggesting their approach is much more pragmatic.

Similarly the gravity within the team can shift depending on what they are doing. How we turn up when we are conceptualizing can be quite different from how we turn up when we are executing the plan or when we are managing people according to the plan. In other words, the LVP can give an individual an understanding of the value system s/he tends to operate from in each of the four quadrants of the Enlightened Leadership model. We can determine what values are at play when the leader is conceptualizing in the top right-hand, market-leadership quadrant; what value is dominant when the leader is executing in the top left-hand commercial-performance quadrant; what values are in operation when the leader is managing others in the bottom right-hand, people-leadership quadrant; and who is the leader personally and how he or she shows up in the bottom left-hand personal performance quadrant. We profile around all four quadrants and our gravity shifts depending on what quadrant we are operating in.

So when we have a much deeper understanding of the subtlety of our own strengths and values we can explain ourselves better to others. So in a meeting we are able to say, 'Look, I can talk the back legs off a donkey when it comes to ideas and strategy but I know you are more Red, which means you will get frustrated by that, so why don't we compromise and agree on a set timeframe for strategic discussion before we get into action?' That way the other person doesn't get so frustrated and we collectively agree a plan that both honours strengths and mitigates weaknesses. This mutual understanding and value-specific language alone can massively improve the quality and output of relationships, and a lot of the arm wrestling and power struggles just disappear.

The values spiral also helps explain why conversations work and don't work, and it can also explain how to make more conversations work more of the time. So, say we are having a strategy conversation; I know that I'm Red so I tend to shoot from the hip, but that you are Yellow and are great with ideas and concepts. I need to hold back and let you get your ideas out. So we might get five or six good ideas. Then, depending on how much Orange we both have, we can convert those ideas into something workable. Once we've decided on the best idea and how it might work in the business, we need to build a process that can deliver the strategy. If neither of us have any Blue, then we have a gap and we need to find a Blue person to add to the team who can help us to thrash out a detailed plan and build it into the business. That's why so much strategy fails: because the team doesn't have all the necessary skills to deliver that strategy effectively and we don't for one minute consider asking others to get involved. So once the Blue person has worked out the best process, other people in the business need to buy in to the strategy for successful execution, and that's a Green strength. If there is Green in the strategy group, then that person can then determine how to get everyone engaged with the strategy the team has created. If there is no Green in the group, we must find someone who is Green and get them to manage that part and sell it to the troops, otherwise we are forced to rely on whoever has the most Green in the room. If we are spending too long debating the finer details, then my Red restless impatience brings the passion and drive back in to make it happen. This is incredibly useful within teams, and all of this detail is unpacked by the LVP so that everyone in a senior executive team knows what values they have when building a strategy, implementing the strategy of managing others. They also know this information about everyone else in the team too.

And the more sophisticated the leader, the more options he or she has in dealing and working with his team. Take Barack Obama for example.

He probably operates at Yellow most of the time. He's really sophisticated conceptually but he can also operate effectively at any of the lower levels. So when the BP-operated Deepwater Horizon oil rig started to spill oil in April 2010, Obama became very Red. He took a very 'strong man' approach, playing to Texas and the southern states that were most affected. He constantly referred to British Petroleum instead of BP. So much so that the UK government ended up having a word! What he was doing however was very smart – he descended the values spiral to play to the home crowd and make the problem a British one, not a US problem. He did the same thing in the contest to win the Democrat nomination for the White House against Hilary Clinton. Both Obama and Clinton are fantastically high-functioning, Yellow and Orange respectively, but in a contest, the more sophisticated individual on the values spiral will usually outgun the other and that's exactly what happened. There was a moment when they were neck and neck and the Orange mindset is do whatever it takes, so Clinton started negative campaigning. As a result Obama simply descended the values spiral and matched her negative campaigning blow for blow, cancelling its impact. Hilary Clinton had played all her cards and had nowhere to go whilst Obama moved back up the spiral to statesmanlike Yellow and became the first African-American President in US history. Remember we can move down the spiral at will in order to match the values of the people around us, but we have to work our way up the spiral through vertical adult development.

The value system that human beings operate from, beautifully described by Clare Graves's spiral dynamics model, offers profound insights about human nature, and the individual, team and organizational benefits of being able to accurately profile this are massive.

A few years ago we did some work with an Australian logistics company, who were trying hard to win a large account from their main rival. They had tried everything to lure the customer using incentives, buy one get one free, 5 per cent off, 15 per cent off, free Fridays. This business was very Orange in its approach and the fact that Orange financial inducements did not work was baffling to them. 'We are cheaper than the competitor, why aren't they switching?' was the question they just couldn't answer.

The customer didn't respond – they weren't persuaded by 'cheaper'. So we explored what the customer's values system was and concluded that it was probably Purple. And Purple companies are not remotely interested in Orange messages. What matters to Purple is safety and maintaining the status quo. Purple is about group survival and security (the customer was actually an IT security company) so the most important thing to them was to avoid change. All our client's messages were focused on what they did differently from their competitor, when really they should have been saying how similar they were. And that's exactly what they did; they explained their similarities first but then added that, unlike their competitor, they could guarantee the security of the parcel to the destination in ways that their competitor could not match. As security was critical for the customer, the disruption was suddenly relevant and our client won the business. They even made more money than they had assumed they could from the account.

The evolution of decision making

Spiral dynamics can also help illuminate how human beings have accumulated power and how groups, teams, organizations or societies make decisions. This understanding can also have a profound impact on how we run corporations today. In particular it helps define a new model of governance for businesses that can step-change organizational speed, the ability to deal with a VUCA world and to transform people engagement (Figure 6.6).

At the start of the evolutionary journey Beige is not powerful and there is no real decision-making system. This evolutionary level is characterized by anarchy. It's 'every man for himself' – do whatever it takes to survive.

At Purple, decision making is still relatively simplistic and decisions are often made by 'tribal elders', or more commonly by the 'mob'. Often no one is really in charge and the mob lurches from one reactive decision to another. There is, as yet, no sophisticated understanding of how the world works. There is a ritualistic and superstitious approach to the events and circumstances of life, which are often seen as magical. Mob rule (ochlocracy) and tribalism characterize the decision-making process in Purple, and the mob tend to stick with tradition and what has worked in the past. Ochlocracy is Greek for 'rule by the general populace', which is democratic 'rule of the people' corrupted by demagoguery or 'tyranny of the majority'. Strength in numbers wins over reason in Purple.

Eventually a Red leader will emerge from the Purple mob and that leader will operate a '1v9' autocratic system – one CEO 'debates' with nine senior executives for a few minutes and then tells them what needs to happen and who's going to do it. Autocracy is of course a significant step forward from mob rule but it's not enough. This approach is excellent when very fast decision making is needed or there are extremely clear lines of accountability, which is why it is still common within the military. However, within global companies seeking to operate successfully in a VUCA world, Red leadership can cause as many problems as it solves.

FIGURE 6.6   The evolution of power and decision making

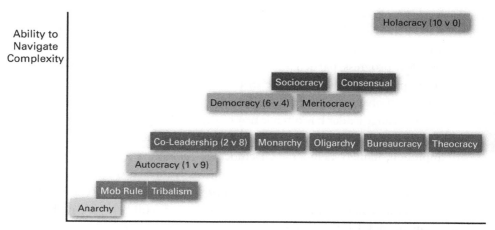

Twenty years ago, Red leaders could manage a business very effectively and there were some stand-out 'celebrity' leaders that were incredibly good at it – Steve Ballmer, Ken Morrison etc. Their command and control, Theory X, reward and punishment, drive the business hard, make sure everyone is clear what is required of them worked and created large successful businesses. But as the business world has become increasingly complex and uncertain, such a leadership approach is under intense pressure to deliver growth across many fronts. It looks less likely that a leader operating with an autocratic approach can be effective across a global business.

Realizing the limitations of a single all-powerful CEO, some organizations started to develop more sophisticated processes that shifted the absolute power of the Red leader and put it in the hands of boards, committees (such as a remuneration committee) or non-executives. And so the Blue decision-making system emerged. Blue decision making is very different from the autocratic directive or the overrule that characterizes Red value systems. Blue decision making is much more likely to be done collectively through co-leadership or by bureaucratic committee rules. So instead of one autocratic leader there might be two Blue co-leaders – a CEO and CFO calling the shots. Thus the decision-making process at executive board level often shifts from 1v9 to 2v8. A constitutional monarchy, oligarchy or theocracy are examples of this Blue co-leadership approach. Two heads are often better than one in making decisions as it often widens the perspective and wisdom available.

Blue can bring elegance, efficiency and stability. The UK monarchy is an example of the stabilizing effect of this approach. The ideas of lean manufacturing, *kaizen* and *Vorsprung durch Technik* also take hold at this level. Bureaucracy is a Blue variant where decisions are made based on rules. This approach can also potentially make more informed decisions but often it can slow progress, particularly in the business world. The rigidity of bureaucratic process or the stalemate of co-leadership can end up triggering the drive to evolve further.

An Orange leader has often learnt to value other people's perspectives and this has changed how they make decisions. They move to a more inclusive approach, namely democracy. Democracy represents a huge leap forward because the decision-making process moves from 1v9 or 2v8 seen at Red and Blue to 6v4. As such it is much more powerful and more informed. It carries the majority, and that's why democracy is still held out as the most sophisticated decision-making framework on the planet.

Autocracy, bureaucracy and some form of democracy are still by far the predominant decision-making frameworks alive and well in modern business. There are still plenty of autocrats running large multinationals but they tend to be very seasoned, high-functioning professionals with a bucket of charisma, a barrow-load of passion and boundless energy. The old-style commercial dictator has largely gone, although the autocratic survivors can still lean on the side of aggression and black and white perspectives, which makes their longevity less likely. There are a handful of examples of co-leadership, usually with a strong CEO–CFO pairing, but this tends to be an accident of two personalities gelling rather than a developed approach to leadership, and whilst there are still examples of executive bureaucracies the predominant model in most businesses is democracy.

However, despite people's advocacy of democracy there are some significant difficulties with this decision-making model. One problem is that it bakes dissent into the business. When you operate a system of democratic governance you always have some people who are 'offside'.

If you have a senior team of a CEO and nine executives, the democratic approach will mean that on any given decision up to four senior executives may not agree with the decision yet they are expected to disseminate that decision and 'hold the line', take 'cabinet responsibility' and not 'brief' against it. All too often this fails, and the four executives who were outvoted can get drawn into corridor discussions and political manoeuvring as they seek to overturn or unpick the decision and seize the power themselves.

Clearly we need a more sophisticated model, otherwise the four are always attacking the six and trying to quietly, or not so quietly, put some spanners in the works so they can turn around and say: 'See I told you it wouldn't work.'

In government the same problem exists where you have the political power flip-flopping between Democrat and Republican or Conservative and Labour. Democracy therefore means that there is always a section of the people who are not happy. For example, on the night of his inauguration for his first term, a group of prominent Republicans met in a hotel and agreed a plan to stop Barack Obama (Draper, 2012). That plan was to 'show a united and unyielding opposition to the president's economic policies', 'Begin attacking vulnerable Democrats on the airways' and 'win the spear-point of the house in 2010, jab Obama relentlessly in 2011, win the White House and the Senate in 2012'. It was not about the greater good and what was best for the American people, but it was a full-on assault against anything that Obama proposed. The fact that they just managed to avoid the fiscal cliff in the beginning of 2013 was testament to just how determined they were to deliver on that agenda. Even though, if no agreement was reached, everyone would have faced significant tax increases the Republicans resisted any compromise to increase tax only for the very wealthy. It stopped being about what was right for the country, but was just how best to thwart any plans for recovery so the Republicans could blame Obama and wrestle back power.

The governance and decision-making models that business or societies hold dear are coming under increasing pressure in a VUCA world. The decision-making systems prevalent in most businesses and governments are insufficiently sophisticated to deal with the level of complexity that exists in the world.

The Green leader seeks to address this by involving others in the decision-making process, which then results in leadership by consensus or a sociocracy. An example is David Cameron's 'Big Society' – helping people to come together to improve their own lives and take a more active role in society – which represented 'a massive transfer of power from Whitehall to local communities' (Conservative Party, 2013). But any attempt to shift from the 6v4 democratic model to a consensual, aligned 10v0 doesn't usually work. What happens is that everyone just goes around in circles in the collaborative Green swamp and the inclusive approach often fails. This failure then reinforces the belief that democracy really is the most sophisticated decision-making process on the planet. It's not.

We need a constructive way to move forward together, but not through consensual agreement because that rarely works. So how do we get 10v0 to work? Fortunately there is a Yellow model of decision making that can deliver rapid and complete alignment within a team even on the VUCA issues or the more thorny issues of government.

That approach is called Holacracy™.

Holacracy™

Arthur Koestler (1967) coined the term Holon (from the Greek *holos*, meaning whole) to describe something that is itself a whole and simultaneously a part of some other whole. So everything that exists, from a neutron to a nation, is not only a whole entity in its own right but it is also a part of something greater, and this greater whole is itself part of something greater again. This whole–part relationship holds true up and down the scale of all things and is very relevant to business. A business unit or department is a complete entity but it is also part of the larger business, which in turn is part of a larger industry. Holacratic process therefore offers a complete and practical system for evolving organizations, management and leadership that acknowledges and utilizes this duality so that business process honours the whole and the part.

Holacracy™, a term coined and trademarked by colleagues of mine at Holacracy One in the United States, is a:

> comprehensive practice for structuring, governing, and running an organization. It replaces today's top-down predict-and-control paradigm with a new way of distributing power and achieving control. It is a new 'operating system' which instils rapid evolution in the core processes of an organization.

When a business evolves to incorporate holacratic processes, it embeds dynamic steering principles into the core of the organization and installs a more organic structure of semi-autonomous, self-organizing teams. It distributes governance across all teams to maximize alignment, and adds bi-directional feedback loops to disseminate knowledge, insight and wisdom across all the organizational layers. It distributes authority using an integrated decision-making process that gives everyone a voice, without the tyranny of consensus, while still allowing for autocratic control and individual action. It reframes operational processes around rapid action and dynamic responsiveness in tight feedback loops, with regular tactical meetings focused on quickly identifying next actions and removing obstacles. And it aligns the organization around a larger evolutionary purpose beyond ego, anchored at the board level and then broken down and distributed throughout the company and its culture. Each aspect of holacratic process supports and is supported by the others. Taken together they offer not just an incremental improvement but a fundamental transformation, a vertical leap to a new tier of organization that fully activates all four quadrants of the Enlightened Leadership model, thus creating Enlightened Organizations.

The Enlightened Organization

There are very few organizations in the world that have even heard of holacracy, never mind organizations that are embracing any type of holacratic process. Since 2010 we have been selectively introducing some of the key ideas, decision-making processes and governance frameworks to enable businesses to operate more holacratically.

For example, we have introduced, 'integrative decision making' – a holacratic decision-making process – to some executive teams, and we have witnessed incredible transformations in their ability to reach genuinely collective, mutually agreed upon 10v0 decisions. Using this process 100 per cent alignment was achieved, with no need for 'cabinet responsibility' and there was very little time and energy wasted trying to neutralize the effects of 'the four' who would have been rendered offside by a democratic vote. As a result the team was able to process gnarly issues they had been stuck on for months – in a matter of minutes. At times the speed and ease of the decision making rendered senior executives virtually speechless.

Holacratic process is, however, more than just a decision-making process; it is a comprehensive practice (not an approach or a theory) for governing and dealing with the incredibly complex dynamics at play inside and outside many modern multinational organizations. It necessitates a much greater level of feedback within the system, and novel operational processes can then take advantage of this new-found agility and decision-making speed to deliver a step-change in results.

Effective holacratic process requires people to:

- clarify purpose;
- clarify all decision-making forums and any new sub-forums;
- define remit and limit of authority of all forums;
- define reporting process, frequency and quality standards;
- establish clear accountabilities;
- create new roles;
- assign new accountabilities to existing roles;
- establish new policies or changes to existing policies;
- define ways of working within teams 'the company way';

- establish meeting discipline and ways of interacting in meetings: 'team rules'.

Make no mistake, moving from leadership to Enlightened Leadership is one thing, moving a group of senior leaders to Enlightened Teams is another and moving an organization to an Enlightened Organization is quite another still. Like all the theoretical models in this book we can't skip forward to the good bits – we have to do all the work. In the same way that we can't strike oil without building the platform, we can't unleash the riches of Enlightened Organizations without building the platform. First we must become coherent leaders, then we must create coherent senior teams and then from that stable platform we can become coherent Enlightened Organizations and reap the rewards.

Holacratic process represents a quantum leap in organizational evolution. And whilst it delivers breathtaking results, it's not for the faint-hearted. It requires a level of open-mindedness that may not be familiar for many leaders and senior executives. So to prevent it all falling apart in a clash of egos, the organization will need a compelling purpose that invites everyone to serve something larger than themselves, and a purpose-driven board to anchor it. Sustaining this over time will require new language and meaning-making in the culture, to help uproot deeply-entrenched mental models (such as predict and control) that are limiting the organization's potential.

Beyond predict and control

Most modern leadership and management techniques are based on a predict-and-control paradigm. This mindset asks those in leadership roles to anticipate the future and design the best path to achieve pre-defined goals in advance. They are also required to control for any deviations to the prescribed plan. This approach matured through the first half of the 20th century and worked well enough in the relatively simple and static pre-VUCA world. Today our predict-and-control techniques are struggling to keep up with the agility and innovation required in a landscape of rapid change and dynamic complexity. They're also failing to ignite the passion and creativity of a new generation of workers who demand greater meaning. In today's environment, steering an organization with predict-and-control methods is akin to riding a bicycle by pointing in the right direction, then holding the handlebars rigid and pedalling, eyes closed.

Holacratic processes help an organization find more dynamic methods for steering its work, to gradually shift the company from predict-and-control through 'experiment-and-adapt' to a 'sense-and-respond' mindset. A sense-and-respond approach is much closer to the 'dynamic steering' we actually use when we ride a bicycle. We have a general aim and adapt continuously in the light of real data that we sense as we progress.

Organizationally, dynamic steering means establishing tight feedback loops and frequent steer points throughout the company's operations. This allows planning and decision-making processes to focus on quickly reaching a workable decision and then letting reality inform the next step. This stops us agonizing about what 'might' happen and stops us trying to conjure up the theoretical 'best' possible decision. Dynamic steering frees teams to move swiftly from excessive planning to actually testing decisions in reality and rapidly adapting them as the results come in. Plans that start out imperfect become well-aligned with actual needs through a continuous process of facing reality and incorporating feedback.

This mindset shift is critical; however, actually transitioning from static control to dynamic steering takes quite a bit more than just new principles. It is necessary to embed this shift into the core of an organization by installing a more organic structure, along with new decision-making and management processes that embody dynamic steering principles. This provides several immediate benefits, such as ultra-efficient meetings, and it sparks a process of organizational evolution that generates deeper learning and transformation over time.

Holacratic governance

In the last chapter I suggested that whilst governance was a widely used and frequently talked about principle in business, what we currently consider to be governance is little more than legal compliance and operational oversight. What is really required is holacratic governance – a series of detailed and robust mechanisms and processes that are thoroughly understood and actioned across a business, which can then continuously improve organizational efficiency and the quality of decision making on complex issues as well as precisely clarifying accountabilities so as to generate greater executive alignment.

In every organization, on virtually every team, there are questions that must be answered for the members to work together effectively. For example: What activities are needed to achieve the group's goals, and who will perform them? How much autonomy will each team member have, and within what limits or requirements? How will various decisions facing the team get made? How will tasks be defined and assigned? What overarching guidelines or policies will be followed?

These are all questions of governance, about how the group will organize their work together – their answers define authorities and expectations within the group. An explicit governance framework to answer these questions only exists, if it exists at all, at the top of an organization, but these questions are just as relevant on the shop floor as they are in the board room. Without an explicit governance process for each team at every level, the opportunities to improve organizational patterns will remain unresolved or largely stuck at the top.

Governance meetings

The way the game of business is currently set up means that most executive teams spend 80–95 per cent of their time focused on short-term commercial performance and operational issues in the top left-hand quadrant of the Enlightened Leadership model (Figure 6.2). What time is left is usually consumed by strategic debate and the occasional cursory nod to 'governance'.

For most organizations their decision-making and accountability agreements are not properly defined. In some cases we have found some to be partially defined but even if they are, which is rare, they are never universally understood and applied up and down the business.

If you ask leaders to make a list of the top 15 most difficult, complex and endemic problems that they are always struggling with, 10 or 12 of them are usually governance issues. As a result leaders are constantly wrestling with issues that are fundamentally caused by a lack of clarity around who makes what decision and why, where these decisions get made and who is really accountable for delivering certain aspects of the business plan. In addition to setting up the necessary decision-making forums and establishing the limits of executive authority, it's also necessary to fully define the feedback loops. What are leaders and executives expected to communicate and to whom? Are they expected to circulate minutes, everything or just the decisions? These issues are no longer 'something to discuss informally at the off-site if we have time'. They are fundamental to business survival in a VUCA world. Successful businesses are no longer run by a few people at the top; globalization, technology, the nature and speed of change, not to mention the increasing complexity, mean that the rules of the game need to be redefined, clarified and aligned behind robust holacratic governance.

Most businesses already realize that they need to address operational, strategic and governance issues but most will try to have all three conversations simultaneously. One of the core principles of holacratic governance is therefore to establish separate meetings, frequencies and meeting disciplines for operations, strategy and governance. In his case study at

www.coherence-book.com, Chris Hope, Head of Operations Strategy and Change for easyJet, explains the profound impact greater meeting discipline had on meeting time and productivity:

> [We] mapped out all the meetings that involved two or more senior managers from the team. This also established how much time we spent in meetings and showed that even a small improvement in our efficiency and effectiveness in those meetings would deliver a significant benefit to the business... We looked at all our meetings to decide which were working well, which needed to be improved and which didn't really need to happen at all... Having set out the structure for the meeting and being clear about what we were trying to achieve, we then focused on behaviours by adapting ground rules for each section. In one section of the meeting, which involves going through action items, it could take us an hour just to check if the items were open or not. We found ourselves having the same discussions again and again. By setting ground rules for that section of the meeting, we could avoid those behaviours.

And the outcome was significant – cutting meeting time by half – and best practice has started to spread throughout the business.

The reason that meetings are such a bone of contention for most business leaders is that they can often take hours without any resolution. What we find when we work with leaders and their executive teams is that often those involved in the meetings are not individually or collectively clear about what conversation they are having.

For example, in the middle of an operational meeting someone will raise a point that has strategic implications, so the team diverts off to discuss strategy for 20 minutes before someone realizes that they have drifted off the original issue. A few moments later someone mentions a governance issue and the same thing happens, largely because there is insufficient differentiation of the three types of meetings. Once people appreciate the distinction and can differentiate between the different types of conversation, they can maintain focus and park things in the right place. Meetings that used to take three hours are wrapped up in 30 minutes because as soon as someone raises a strategic issue at an operational meeting or a governance issue at a strategic meeting the team reminds that individual to raise the issue at the appropriate meeting and the agenda stays on course. What we've found is that just by clarifying these distinctions companies leap forward in productivity and results can improve almost immediately.

Once these meetings are separated, most executive teams benefit from some guidance on the structure and process of each type of meeting, parti-cularly governance. In real governance meetings the team refines its operating model based on new information and experiences that arise while getting the work done. Governance meetings should happen regularly, and can completely replace the all-too-familiar need for large and disruptive 're-organizations' that often reflect poor alignment and sub-optimal performance. Proper governance meetings offer much more agile adaptation in light of real data.

On a human level, regular governance meetings can also transform the emotional tone of a team. Lack of clarity around governance leaves everyone with implicit expectations about who should be doing what and how they should be doing it. Without a defined governance process the tendency is to make up negative stories about others or blame each other when these unspoken assumptions clash, neither of which helps move the organization forward.

With governance meetings introduced, team members now have a forum for channelling the frustration of misaligned expectations into organizational learning and continual improvement. Playing politics loses its utility, and personal drama gives way to a more authentic discussion of how to consciously evolve the organization in light of its goals and broader purpose in the world.

Roles and accountabilities

One of the key early outputs of holacratic governance is the detailed clarification and definition of roles and accountabilities. Again this sounds obvious and most executive teams believe this is already done well enough or covered in their job description. However, in our experience, when we look at executive accountabilities in detail it is possible to identify a number of gaps where no one is clearly responsible as well as a number of role overlaps. I am continually surprised by how much we are able to improve a team's clarity around their accountabilities even when they have already spent a lot of time working on their 'RACI' (responsible, accountable, consulted and informed) frameworks.

In defining roles and specifying accountabilities, it is critical that this is done regardless of who is available to fill such roles and whether they have the skill set to deliver. Many organizations try to fit the role to the person rather than deciding what the business really needs and then recruiting and training people to that requirement.

A purpose-driven board

As the 'war on talent' becomes ever fiercer, it is increasingly apparent that the financial ambition of a company is insufficient to attract, retain and motivate the best people. Similarly, mission statements outlining 'visions of future desired states' are often seen as too abstract. Companies and boards need to uncover a more emotive cause if they want to truly motivate their talent and unlock discretionary effort. A corporate cause should draw on the evolutionary purpose of the organization, ie what purpose does the world need that business to serve. Why does that company really exist?

Profit is a metric not a purpose. But with a board composed entirely of shareholder representatives, profit is very likely to get mistaken for a purpose. Holacratically-run organizations are first and foremost cause-driven, with all activities designed to deliver the organization's purpose.

What does the world need this organization to be, and what does it need to be in the world? What is its unique purpose, its contribution to bringing something novel to life, to furthering creativity and evolution? The needs of shareholders and other stakeholders remain important constraints, but with holacratic processes installed it is this deeper evolutionary purpose or cause that ultimately rules and pulls the organization forward. Although we've only explored a small part of holacratic process, it's important to appreciate that each aspect dovetails with the others to create exceptionally strong organizations, able to adapt in real time, make faster, better informed and aligned decisions so as to embody Enlightened Leadership – not just at an individual leadership level but as a collective force for good in the world.

How to be more influential

When we have created more personal coherence though physiological, emotional and cognitive coherence our behaviour also becomes more coherent and performance and results improve. We become more successful. We also feel younger, healthier and happier, and the quality of our thinking improves. When we can take others with us so we can create potent relationships and powerful teams, then astonishing things are possible within business; and when we implement holacratic process to bake those astonishing things into the business then anything is possible.

Building on all the physical and personal skills from previous chapters, the skills in this chapter are focused on other people and culminate in elevated emotional social intelligence (ESQ).

According to a 1995 *Time Magazine* article, IQ gets you hired, but EQ (emotional intelligence) gets you promoted. Of course we all know individuals have got to the top without either! But, if we wish to succeed in a VUCA world we will need social intelligence. It is social intelligence that unlocks discretionary effort and makes legacy leadership possible.

Although some people are more naturally gifted socially than others, social intelligence is a natural consequence of internal vertical development. When we have access to more energy, when we become aware of our emotions and can self-manage and regulate their impact, we therefore have constant access to our very best thinking, which in turn makes us more socially intelligent. When we mature as adult human beings and expand our perspectives so that we understand our own and other people's value systems, then we become even more socially intelligent. And when we learn the last two interpersonal skills of Enlightened Leadership our ESQ is significantly increased, which in turn facilitates the development of high-functioning teams and executive fellowships.

The MAP skill (discussed below) helps us to tap into our social intuition, empathy and rapport, enabling us to become more deeply aware of others. And when we learn how to appreciate others, we develop positive working relationships more easily, even with those we wouldn't normally gravitate to.

In the good old days it may have been possible to rise through the ranks on IQ, business smarts and aggression without any regard for social or emotional intelligence, but today it is impossible to build a great company without ESQ. The coherent Enlightened Leader is distinguished by the application of emotional and social intelligence to sustain positive relationships, drive success and create genuinely brilliant future-proofed organizations.

Relationships coherence – social intuition, empathy and rapport: MAP skill

As I said at the start of this chapter, the problem with 'communication' as we currently understand it is that as soon as someone transmits a message we don't receive that message – we get ready to transmit our own message back. For most of us, when someone says something, we start thinking. Their input triggers thoughts in us – we think: 'That's a good idea – I love talking to him, he has such great ideas,' or 'Here we go again, that's a terrible idea – usual ill-thought-out rubbish.'

This thinking about what the other person is transmitting or what they're saying starts almost immediately. We then start chasing our own thoughts rather than processing what the other person said. As a result, we think we are in dialogue with someone when actually what's really happening is that two people are in dialogue with themselves. We see this in business in the form of endless circular meetings. Part of the reason meetings go on so long and nothing gets resolved is that no one is actually listening to each other.

Everyone is just having a conversation with themselves: 'I just said that!' 'Did you? Oh I wasn't listening.' We even say that to each other!

Not only that but we are often so desperate to get our point across before someone else does or before we forget it that we interrupt the original transmission. Men tend to do this more than woman and it's usually a control play or a tool to manipulate the conversation to get primary positioning, so we hear things like, 'Let me stop you there ...'. Even if the interruption is for good reasons, to clarify the message, it's still a break in the transmission and therefore often sets up confusion and miscommunication.

The MAP skill for high-quality listening

The MAP skill is an acronym for the process you go through to ensure that you are really listening at the deeper meaning Level 3.

- **M**ove your attention away from your own thinking and drop into the body and BREATHE.
- **A**ppreciate the speaker.
- **P**lay back the underlying meaning.

Rather than immediately focusing on what you are going to say or interrupting the other person when a transmission starts, move (M) your attention away from the noise in your own head. So consciously and deliberately move your attention away from your own thoughts, your own preconceived ideas, your own judgements about yourself, the meeting, the pile of work you have still to do on your desk, and shift your focus to the centre of your chest and your breath. Using the BREATHE skill from Chapter 2, breathe rhythmically, evenly and through the heart. Stop thought-chasing.

When I first teach this skill to executives they think they won't hear if they're not thinking or fully consciously engaged with the words. But considering that only 7 per cent of the communication is determined by the words we use anyway, it's not necessary to 'actively listen' to every word transmitted. Even when we are not actively listening our brain still processes most of the words anyway, so we really don't need to concentrate that hard. The MAP skill can save us all a lot of energy that we waste in having to concentrate intensely.

Next you activate a state of appreciation (A) for the transmitter. This is the critical step. Influential psychologist Carl Rogers referred to this state as an 'unconditional positive regard' (Rogers, 1967). Turn on a warm, glowing feeling of acceptance and support for the person communicating to you, regardless of what they say or do. Rogers believes that unconditional positive regard is essential to healthy development, and when we do this properly the transmitter feels it – they feel a sense of grace and acceptance that can be extremely moving.

When I'm teaching this skill it's usually one-on-one or to a group of tough, hard-nosed business executives and leaders, so it can be quite funny. To help break down their initial resistance and discomfort I usually go overboard in the instruction and ask them to 'bathe each other in the warm glow of appreciation'. It's such an unusual request and one that is never heard in business that eventually everyone starts laughing and we can move on without any resistance. What is remarkable is that once leaders put down their prejudices around this process and just try it – without exception, they feel the difference it makes to the depth and authenticity of the interaction and communication.

Both as the person doing the 'bathing' and the person receiving the unconditional positive regard, we instinctively feel more peaceful, less resistant, all the judgements slip away and we feel supported and nurtured. When we do this two really profound things happen.

First, it changes the transmitter in two fundamental ways. As a result of the warm acceptance and lack of judgement that is radiating toward them, they often open up and tell us things they hadn't planned to tell us and we get much more information. If we do this with a customer or a supplier or a client, they will tell us all sorts of things that they had no intention of divulging. Plus when the other person feels encouraged and appreciated the quality of their transmission also improves. So not only do we get more information but the information we get is also transmitted much more clearly, more precisely and more succinctly. We get to the heart of the issue much faster using appreciation than we ever would with impatience, interruption or restlessness.

When we radiate impatience or negativity, which is often what happens in business, the opposite is true. Our frustration or judgement simply closes the transmitter down. We get less information than we need and the quality of that information is poor. When the transmitter doesn't feel listened to or is frequently interrupted, he or she starts to mumble, stumble over words and become hesitant. This in turn can make the receiver even more frustrated and negative, which shuts the transmitter down still further.

The second incredible thing to occur when receivers put themselves in a state of appreciation is that it completely changes the capability of the receiver. The reason this happens is because at a biological level the fluctuations in our heart rate variability change from chaotic to coherent. Think of it like manually tuning into a radio station; when we are in a negative incoherent emotional state there is too much interference and static in the connection so we can't fully make out what is being transmitted. Once we tune in to exactly the right frequency and create coherence at a biological level, the transmission becomes crystal clear and we can start to perceive meaning at a much deeper level.

With a coherent internal signal the receiver starts to hear things that would have been impossible to hear from a place of frustration or judgement. When we do this well, it enables us to hear things that the other person didn't even say! It feels to the transmitter that we're reading their mind – but we're not, we're just tuning into them so brilliantly that it feels like we're reading their mind.

I remember coaching a guy who managed a number of well-known professional golfers for a sports management company. I explained how there is always more going on in every conversation than just the words, tonality and body language. There is always, even in the most fleeting conversations, a deeper level. He didn't believe me. He was adamant that in some conversations there was no deeper meaning, and gave me the example of one of his golfers who had called him to give him flight information and ask him to organize taxis to and from the airport. The manager said, 'He told me he was landing at Terminal 2 at 10 o'clock, and needed a taxi back the next morning to get a flight to the Copenhagen Open in time for practice rounds. That was it.' He believed the conversation was a straightforward information download. I disagreed.

What this golfer was really saying was, 'take care of me', and beneath that what he actually meant was, 'you're not taking care of me.' I shared this insight with the manager. I said that at an even deeper level still the golfer thought the manager was taking better care of the other golfers in his stable and the player was pretty upset about it. I suggested that he call his client the next day and make a real fuss of him because 'take it from me he is really upset.'

The manager didn't believe me and did nothing. Within a week the problem was all over the back pages of the national press. The golfer was threatening to leave the management group and it took the manager months to repair the damage. If he'd just listened properly in that first conversation he would have saved everyone time and stress.

Once you've detected what's going on at a deeper level, you then have to play back (P) what you've received. Until you get good at this you can't be sure that what you think is going on is actually what is really going on.

Often we mistakenly assume we have accurately detected the meaning, but often what we have detected is just our own internal noise. Quality playback is vital. It must be distinguished from just repeating, summarizing or précising what the other person said. And it absolutely is not about providing our own view or answer. It's about playing back what we feel the other person meant at the deeper level.

There are two rules to playback to make sure it achieves the desired quality:

- When playing back what you believe the receiver meant by their communication, you need to play back as a subjective 'felt' sense rather than an objective observable fact. In other words play back in terms of 'I' rather than 'it'. So you could preface your playback with: 'You said a lot of things, but it feels to me that what you really meant was ...' or 'I got the sense that this is about ...'. Playing back to someone, 'I get the sense that this is about your boss' is a lot less confrontational than asserting, 'This is obviously about your boss.' When you play back your subjective sense of the transmission, the transmitter can't argue with you because he or she can't dispute what you are feeling. Plus even if you are right in your assertive 'it' statement, being so direct can often simply push the receiver into a defensive stance and no real progress will be possible. But if the statement is about what it feels like to you, they can't disagree – you're not saying it is something, you're just saying it feels like it might be something to you.

- For playback to be successful it must always be presented as an offer or a question. It is not an assertion. Offering it as a question for them to confirm or deny is much more inclusive and allows you to mutually decide if your subjective sense was accurate or inaccurate. This approach therefore invites them into the interpersonal space with you, and your question creates a connection that they can choose to engage with or not. If your subjective sense was accurate, the transmitter will usually confirm your assertion; if not, they will deny it and give you more information so that you can fine-tune your playback. In the moment of confirmation you are suddenly aligned in the same place of understanding. The transmitter knows for certain you understand them: you've played back and they've confirmed. This can be profoundly moving for the receiver who can feel genuinely heard and listened to – often for the first time. It is also the moment when the transmitter's view of you, the receiver, is suddenly transformed. It is a moment of supreme influence because the transmitter feels that you have taken the time to understand them and that you have almost read their mind. When you as the receiver play back something so insightful and accurate that the transmitter wasn't even aware of it until you said it – that's the moment your relationship is transformed and you have established profound influence.

This is the ultimate goal of the MAP skill – to create an experience for the transmitter of being completely understood. This is such a rare experience that it can be incredibly motivational to the transmitter and can unlock a huge amount of discretionary effort. They feel seen, heard and understood, often for the first time in what could be years: 'Finally my boss gets me,' 'someone is listening,' 'he (or she) finally understands me.' When employees and members of your senior team experience this with you, it is likely they'll do anything for you.

The MAP skill is a simple yet deceptively powerful technique that can transform interpersonal dynamics. But it does come with a warning. This technique allows us to understand what's really going on for someone – even when they themselves may not be sure what the issue really is. As a result we must always share any insights we may perceive with the utmost care and consideration.

One of the big advantages of this technique is that when we realize the dynamic between two people or two opposing groups we have a choice about how to resolve the conflict, and that's incredibly powerful.

We used this MAP skill in negotiations between management and the unions to break through months of stalemate with one client. Every year, prior to our involvement these groups would negotiate on terms and conditions, and every year it would be fraught, protracted and both sides would emerge feeling bruised. Eventually some compromise would be agreed upon, but neither side was that happy and the process would be repeated the following year. Both sides were taught the MAP skill, which meant that everyone fully understood and recognized each other's position. By installing a foundation of common understanding, management were able to facilitate a negotiated settlement that the union was happier about in much less time and with a fraction of the angst. That's the power of the MAP skill.

Imagine being able to go into any meeting and immediately grasp the meaning behind all the exchanges; it would be like seeing the code in the Matrix. The MAP skill allows us to defocus a bit on what is actually being said, focus on our breathing, appreciate the other person – and out pops the real meaning of what the person is really communicating. When we have that level of insight, meetings take a fraction of the time, they are less fraught and everyone feels valued, listened to and acknowledged.

I remember teaching this technique to the whole senior team at Hewlett-Packard (HP). Before learning the MAP skill their meetings would go on for hours and they would never get through the whole agenda; after they learnt the technique, they got through the entire agenda in half the time. When we get a whole team listening this way, interaction can be super-clear, super-productive and super-fast.

Plus when you play back really accurately what's going on for another person it reflects well on you – they look at you as though you are a genius and your 'stock' goes through the roof with them. They look at you with new eyes. That's really the moment of influence when the relationship transforms. And when I teach this in a group session I can get people to experience this in about two and a half minutes! It may be simple but it is one of the most profound developmental skills we teach because it builds influence; and when a whole team uses it, it can cut down meeting times by 50 per cent and it can reduce energy spent by about 50 per cent too.

Relationship coherence – social intelligence: appreciation of others' skill

We explored how to create an optimistic outlook using the appreciation skill in Chapter 5. This skill is also fundamental to social intelligence because it allows us to appreciate someone else.

When we sincerely appreciate something in another human being that is also meaningful to them, it can be profoundly motivational and this exchange can unlock the vast reservoir of discretionary effort.

I remember speaking to a main board director of a top retailer one day about appreciation, and he could remember the day when the CEO of that company said something nice to him. In the same way that everyone remembers where they were when Princess Diana was killed or when John Lennon got shot, this moment was so significant and so rare that he remembered the date. They had worked together for 25 years!

Unfortunately, appreciation in any form is not common in most organizations.

This skill is however especially useful when we meet and must work with someone we would not normally or naturally resonate with.

For us to really connect with another human being, we have to shift our own perception and find something about that person that we can sincerely appreciate. When we like someone or naturally gravitate to them or feel as though they are 'on the same wavelength', that process is easy and largely unconscious. We instinctively trust them. Or at least trust is made possible by that initial acceptance and connection. It's a virtuous cycle. Remember the four component parts of trust – personal connection, understanding motives, consistent delivery and working style. If we can appreciate someone then we are much more likely to spend time with them and personally connect; if we do we are more likely to understand their motives; we already resonate with their working style so as long as they deliver consistently, trust is likely to develop and the relationship will prosper.

On the other hand, if we find it difficult to appreciate someone we won't want to spend time with them and will instead avoid them. We therefore won't get to understand their motives, and as we don't like their work style it actually won't matter much whether they deliver or not because there is little trust and almost no relationship. This creates a barrier that effectively stops the relationship working before it's even begun. And that barrier can therefore be a serious hindrance to the development of trust and the creation of an effective working relationship. The appreciation skill can therefore make a massive difference to building successful working relationships.

Highly socially intelligent leaders are able to find something to appreciate about everyone they meet, not just the ones they naturally resonate with. With elevated ESQ we can learn to connect with anyone and create a productive relationship. Even if the only thing we can appreciate is that the individual in front of us isn't twins!

The appreciation process

We have to find some quality within the other person that we can sincerely appreciate, because if we can't appreciate them then we can't make an effective connection. And if we can't make an effective connection we can't be an influential Enlightened Leader.

Many leaders are so busy focusing on the tasks they have to complete to deliver their quarterly targets that they can easily forget that their success is entirely dependent on others. Learning to notice what is special and magnificent about other people can be a very valuable practice to sustain our balance and motivation throughout the day.

Create a list of the people and the things about them that you can learn to appreciate in your life (Table 6.1).

Make sure you take the time to notice at least one of these every day and talk to the person about it.

It's a general principle that all positive emotion is transformative. This is why the SHIFT skill from Chapter 4 is so useful, because it allows us to induce positive emotions and alter brain function and the way we see things. Appreciation is a powerful antidote to judgement or any negative emotion and can radically influence your ability to create strong working relationships.

TABLE 6.1　Appreciation list

Who	What (specific quality)	When (it shows up)	Where (it shows up)	How (exactly it shows up)
Fred	Determination	When it's difficult	Team meetings	To hold a line
Tracey	Attention to detail	On the big points	In documents	Adds clarity
Angela	Warmth	Most of the time	With most people	Welcoming
Doug	Wit	When its tense	Before presentations	Self-deprecation

Developing social intelligence starts with breathing skills and the emotional awareness to recognize that someone is irritating us. When we are more emotionally skilled, we can then actively move into a different more constructive emotion such as patience. When we are in a more appropriate emotional state we ensure that we keep our frontal lobes on and don't become reactive. Instead we take a more expanded perspective and seek to understand the other person's motives and values. Social intelligence therefore builds on all the skills that we talked about in previous chapters together with the MAP skill and learning how to appreciate someone we don't like or have anything in common with.

Relationship coherence facilitates complete coherence

Enlightened Leadership emerges when we develop coherence across all the various critical internal and external lines of development (Figure 6.7) –

FIGURE 6.7   Lines of development

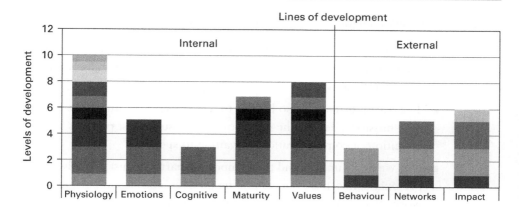

each one strengthening and facilitating the next. In this chapter we have explored the last two external lines of development – networks and impact as well as more thoroughly unpacking the values line of development.

Relationship coherence is the final piece of the Enlightened Leadership puzzle. And it is deliberately positioned that way because relationships and connections inside and outside work are the biggest determinants to a happy, successful and fulfilled life. Success of any type without people to share that success with, and without people to take with us, is pretty hollow.

When experienced palliative-care nurse Bronnie Ware started to document what people in the last weeks of their life really felt remorse over, she discovered five common themes – 'I wish I'd had the courage to live a life true to myself, not the life others expected of me,' 'I wish I hadn't worked so hard,' 'I wish I'd had the courage to express my feelings,' 'I wish I had stayed in touch with my friends' and 'I wish that I had let myself be happier' (Ware, 2011).

When we have developed physiological and emotional coherence, we have more energy and can experience any emotion we wish – including courage. We will by definition find it easier to express our feelings and let ourselves be happy. When we embrace the power of relationships and build cohesive high-performing teams or executive fellowships, we won't need to work so hard. The efforts of the many toward a common purpose finally liberate us all from the tyranny of short-term materialism so that we refuse to lose touch with friends and neglect loved ones. Add to that cognitive coherence, better-quality thinking and elevated maturity, and then improved performance and abiding deep-rooted success – professionally and personally – is finally possible.

Summary of key points

If you don't remember everything in this chapter, remember this:

- Most people's experience of personal and professional relationships is patchy at best, because relationships are the hardest thing we do as human beings.

- The reason listening is so hard is that we were only taught the transmission side, not the reception. As a result, most people's definition of communication is 'waiting to speak'.

- Plus we don't understand the component parts of trust, namely personal connection, understanding motives, consistent delivery and work style. Trust is therefore absent, lost or eroded, and we don't really know why.

- Without communication and trust, strong, enduring relationships – inside and outside work – are virtually impossible.

- This can be transformed through people leadership.

- Real business transformation will only really emerge when we do the personal inner developmental work ('I'), step-change the top right-hand long-term quadrant ('IT') and also truly attack the bottom right-hand quadrant of people leadership ('WE').

- It is possible to develop leadership teams into high-performing units or even executive fellowships that we trust enough to take care of the vast majority of the commercial performance.

- The first step is to assess and establish the existing connections and use those insights to guide team development.

- There are seven stages of team development from a collection of 'talented individuals' that is largely inert or dysfunctional to 'executive fellowships' that can radically alter the business and the results.

- Spiral dynamics offers a profound insight into personal and collective value systems that can allow everyone in a team to understand their own and each other's motives which in turn can radically improve productivity and performance.

- Spiral dynamics also sheds light on the power struggles in business and the unsatisfactory and dysfunctional decision-making and governance dilemmas that so often hamstring business and hold it back. The solution to that is Holacracy™. Holacracy™ offers a new, more effective, approach to governance in a VUCA world.

- Holacratic process is more than just a decision-making process; it is a comprehensive practice (not an approach or a theory) for governing and dealing with the incredibly complex dynamics at play inside and outside many modern multinational organizations.

- It represents a quantum leap in organizational development because it offers not just an incremental improvement but a fundamental transformation, a vertical leap to a new level of organization that fully activates all four quadrants of the Enlightened Leadership model, thus creating Enlightened Organizations.

- The final skills of Enlightened Leadership are the interpersonal skills that, when combined with the physical and personal skills, facilitate superior ESQ and complete coherence.

- Enlightened Leadership is achieved when the leader is physiologically coherent, emotionally coherent, cognitively coherent, behaviourally coherent and able to create successful coherent relationships in all areas of his or her life. This is complete coherence.

Conclusion

Most business leaders are under enormous pressure and are therefore fully immersed in their industry and rarely have time to reach out beyond it or read books on subjects that are not directly and obviously relevant to their industry or their results. There is however a vast treasure trove of science and research-based knowledge that could radically alter the performance of their organizations, if only it were known and applied. The critical problem is that most of this knowledge is not 'commercial knowledge', neatly packaged and applied to organizations via business or leadership books, an MBA course or a management journal. It is knowledge of the human system, biology, brain function, adult development, behaviour or human relationships, and it's usually delivered in a range of dry, dull academic or scientific papers contained in obscure journals that are almost incomprehensible to anyone who is not also an academic, scientist or medical professional. This book is therefore the presentation of some of the key secrets that can, if properly applied, consistently elevate performance and results, leading to nothing short of a complete transformation of the lives of leaders, their organizations and the wider world. Coherence and Enlightened Leadership is an invitation to re-imagine a new future. A future that is not just measured by materialistic rewards but one that redefines the very purpose of business itself so as to support humankind and human evolution. We need a new way of keeping score in business, a new bottom line that accounts for the return on financial capital and also the return on natural, social and human capital. Only then can we really know the true value of a business.

The reason I know about any of this research is that I originally trained as a medical doctor and before leaving the profession I spent 11 years in many of the front-line medical trenches around the world in hospital-based roles, general practice and ultimately academic medicine. As a medical doctor first and businessman second, I soon realized that I was in the unique position of spanning two very different worlds that rarely meet except through the prescription of blood pressure medication, depression pills or post-operative care following a heart-attack! In Chapters 2, 3 and 4, we explored how one of those worlds – neuroscience – has a profound implication on the other.

One of the reasons I decided to leave medicine was my inability to make a big enough dent in the scale of human suffering I was seeing. For example, the average GP may have 2,000 patients on his list, but 1,800 of those he never sees because they are largely healthy. So he only sees about 200 patients each year and usually it's the same 200 people! And although I found working as a cardiologist, oncologist or obstetrician was, for me at least, more engaging, I still wasn't able to reach *enough* people. I wanted to work with people whose actions affected the lives of thousands if not more. That meant working with big multinational corporations. Some of the big, multinationals employ hundreds of thousands of people, and if we extend their reach to include family, friends and customers then big business has the potential to affect many millions of lives. I don't say this for reasons of grandeur. I say this from a sincerely held belief that all of our lives could be so much more fulfilling. We could significantly reduce the scale of human suffering if we encouraged people to apply the advances in understanding of the human condition across the globe. I believe, for example, that Coherence and Enlightened Leadership can help us to finally solve many of the so-called 'wicked problems' currently facing society (see free bonus chapter at **www. coherence-book.com**).

I have had the great good fortune to meet and work with some great teachers. In this book I have attempted to share with you some of their key insights. In examining the many, largely agreed upon 'facts' from multiple, often obscure fields of science and medicine, as well as the research from business schools and leadership journals, some astonishing conclusions become clear, conclusions that, extraordinary as they may seem, consist of no more than pre-existing knowledge. But when these insights are taken together something remarkable emerges about us that is simply breathtaking. The complexity of the human condition and the potential inherent in that sophistication inspired me from an early age, and I hope that some of what I have shared has inspired you. One or two insights may turn out to be untrue. But I hope that you embrace most of it, find time to practise a few of the skills that resonate most strongly with you, and apply the knowledge in this book to your life for real world benefits. These insights, which I have accumulated over many years of study, have certainly helped me to understand that we are all so much more than we realize or have been led to believe. And they also made me realize that if enough organizations change then it *is* possible to reduce human suffering on a grand scale, because when applied these insights can transform our experience of ourselves, how we relate to each other and the very nature of the lives we live.

REFERENCES

Achor, S (2010) *The Happiness Advantage: The seven principles that fuel success and performance at work*, Crown Business (Random House), New York, NY

Alexander, F (1939) Psychological aspects of medicine, *Psychosomatic Medicine*, **1** (1), pp 7–18

Anglo American Corporate Website (2013a) About us/Our approach [online] www.angloamerican.com/about [accessed 10 July 2013]

Anglo American Corporate Website (2013b) About us/What we do [online] www.angloamerican.com/about [accessed 10 July 2013]

Antonovsky, A (1987) *Unraveling The Mystery of Health: How people manage stress and stay well*, Jossey-Bass, San Francisco, CA

Antonuccio, D O, Danton, W G and DeNelsky, G Y (1995) Psychotherapy versus medication for depression: challenging the conventional wisdom with data, *Professional Psychology, Research and Practice*, **26** (6), pp 574–85

Ariely, D (2008) *Predictably Irrational: The hidden forces that shape our decisions*, HarperCollins, London

Ariely, D (2010) *The Upside of Irrationality*, HarperCollins, London

Ariely, D, Gneezy, U, Lowenstein, G and Mazer, N (2005) *Large Stakes and Big Mistakes*, Federal Reserve Bank of Boston Working Paper 2005 series, No 05–11

Aristotle (4th Century BC) *De motu animalium*

Armour, J A and Ardell, J L (eds) (1994) *Basic and Clinical Neurocardiology*, Oxford University Press, Oxford

Arnetz, B B and Ekman, R (eds) (2008) Stress in Health and Disease, *Yale Journal of Biology and Medicine*, **81** (1), pp 53–54

Attenborough, D (1979) *Life on Earth*, episode 13, BBC, 10 April 1979

Bales, R F (1951) *Interaction Process Analysis: A method for the study of small groups*, Addison-Wesley, Cambridge, MA

Barton, D (2011) Capitalism for the long term, *Harvard Business Review*, March

Bass, B M (1999) Two decades of research and development: transformational leadership, *European Journal of Work and Organizational Psychology*, **8** (1), pp 9–32

Berman, S (2010) *Capitalizing on Complexity: Insights from the Global Chief Executive Officer Study*, IBM Global Business Services, Somers, USA

BHP Billiton Annual Report (2010) www.bhpbilliton.com/home/investors/reports [accessed 10 July 2013]

BHP Billiton Corporate Website (2013) About us/Our company [online] www.bhpbilliton.com/aboutus [accessed 10 July 2013]

Birchal, A (2011) Worked to death, *Management Today*, December

Bly, R (2001) *Iron John: A book about men*, Rider, London

Bolletino, R and LeShan, L (1997) Cancer, in *Mind–Body Medicine*, ed A Watkins, pp 87–109, Churchill Livingstone, New York, NY

Boneva, R S, Decker, M J, Maloney, E M, Lin, J M, Jones, J F, Helgason, H G, Heim, C M, Rye, D B and Reeves, W C (2007) Higher heart rate and reduced heart rate variability persist during sleep in chronic fatigue syndrome: a population-based study, *Autonomic Neuroscience: basic & clinical*, **137**(1–2), pp 94–101

Boyatzis, R E (1982) *The Competent Manager: A model for effective performance*, London, Wiley

British Heart Foundation (2012) Gabby Logan encourages women to love their hearts [online] http://www.bhf.org.uk/media/news-from-the-bhf/september/women-and-heart-disease.aspx [accessed 10 July 2013]

Brown, B (2013) *Daring Greatly: How the courage to be vulnerable transforms the way we live, love, parent, and lead*, Penguin, New York, NY

Buckingham, M and Coffman, C (1999) *First, Break All the Rules: What the world's greatest managers do differently*, Simon and Schuster, London

Burton, W N, Conti, D J, Chen, C Y, Schultz, A B and Edington, D W (1999) The role of health risk factors and disease on worker productivity, *Journal of Occupational and Environmental Medicine*, **41** (10), pp 863–77

Campbell, J (2012) *The Hero with a Thousand Faces*, Novato, New World Library

Campbell, J and Moyers, B (1988) *The Power of Myth*, Doubleday, New York, NY

Cantin, M and Genest, J (1986) The heart as an endocrine gland, *Clinical and Investigative Medicine*, **9** (4), pp 319–27

Cartwright, D and Zander, A (1968) *Group Dynamics: Research and theory*, Harper and Row, New York, NY

Carver, C S, Scheier, M F and Weintraub, J K (1989) Assessing coping strategies: a theoretically based approach, *Journal of personality and social psychology*, **56** (2), pp 267–83

Centers for Disease Control and Prevention USA (2013) Deaths and mortality statistics [online] http://www.cdc.gov/nchs/fastats/deaths.htm [accessed 10 July 2013]

Childre, D and Martin, H (2000) *The Heartmath Solution: The Institute of Heartmath's revolutionary program for engaging the power of the heart's intelligence*, HarperCollins, London

Christensen, C M (1997) *The Innovator's Dilemma: When new technologies cause great firms to fail*, Harvard Business School Press, Boston, MA

Christensen, C M, Allworth, J and Dillon, K (2012) *How Will You Measure Your Life? Finding fulfilment using lessons from some of the world's greatest businesses*, HarperCollins, London

Christensen, C M, Alton, R, Rising, C and Waldeck, A (2011) The big idea: the new M and A playbook, *Harvard Business Review*, March

Coates, J (2013) *The Hour Between Dog and Wolf: Risk taking, gut feelings and the biology of boom and bust*, Fourth Estate, London

Cockerill, A P (1989a) *Managerial Competence as a Determinant of Organisational Performance*, Unpublished doctoral dissertation sponsored by the National Westminster Bank, University of London

Cockerill, A P (1989b) The kind of competence for rapid change, *Personnel Management*, **21**, pp 52–56

Cockerill, A P, Schroder, H M and Hunt, J W (1993) *Validation Study into the High Performance Managerial Competencies*, London Business School, unpublished report sponsored by National Westminster Bank, Prudential Corporation, Leeds Permanent Building Society, the Automobile Association, the UK Employment Department and the UK Civil Aviation Authority

Collins, J (2001) *Good to Great: Why some companies make the leap and others don't*, Random House, London

Colvin, G (2010) *Talent Is Overrated: What really separates world-class performers from everybody else*, Penguin, New York, NY

Conservative Party (2013) Website/Policy/Where we stand/Big society [online] http://www.conservatives.com/Policy/Where_we_stand/Big_Society.aspx [accessed 10 July 2013]

Cook-Greuter, S R (2004) Making the case for a developmental perspective, *Industrial and Commercial Training*, **36** (7), pp 275–81

Croghan, J H and Lake, D G (1984) Competencies of effective principles and strategies for implementation, *Educational Policy Analysis*, Southeastern Regional Council for Educational Improvement, #410 Research Triangle Park, NC

Csikszentmihalyi, C (2002) *Flow: The classic work on how to achieve happiness*, Rider, London

Damasio, A (2000) *The Feeling of What Happens: Body, emotion and the making of consciousness*, Vintage, London

Damasio, A (2006) *Descartes' Error*, London, Vintage

Davidson, R J and Begley, S (2012) *The Emotional Life of Your Brain: How its unique patterns affect the way you think, feel, and live – and how you can change them*, Penguin, London

De Dreu, C K W and Weingart, L R (2003) Task versus relationship: conflict, team performance, and team member satisfaction: a meta-analysis, *Journal of Applied Psychology*, **88**, pp 741–49

Deepu, C J, Zhihao Chen, Ju Teng Teo, Soon Huat Ng, Xiefeng Yang and Yong Lian (2012) A smart cushion for real-time heart rate monitoring, *Biomedical Circuits and Systems Conference*, (BioCAS) 2012 IEEE, pp 53–56

Dekker, J M, Schouten, E G, Klootwijk, P, Pool, J, Swenne, C A and Kromhout, D (1997) Heart rate variability from short electrocardiographic recordings predicts mortality from all causes in middle-aged and elderly men: the Zutphen study, *American Journal of Epidemiology*, **145** (10), pp 899–908

Devan, J, Millan, A K and Shirke, P (2005) Balancing short and long term performance, *McKinsey Quarterly*, www.mckinsey.com/insights/mckinsey-quarterly [accessed 10 July 2013]

Dispenza, J (2007) *Evolve Your Brain: The science of changing your mind*, Health Communications Inc, Deerfield Beach, FL

Dowrick, S (1997) *Forgiveness and Other Acts of Love*, Norton, New York, NY

Draper, R (2012) *Do Not Ask What Good We Do: Inside the US House of Representatives*, Simon and Schuster, New York, NY

Dweck, C S (2007) *Mindset: The new psychology of success, how to learn to fulfil our potential*, Ballantine Books, New York, NY

Elkind, P and McLean, B (2003) *The Smartest Guys in the Room: The amazing rise and scandalous fall of Enron*, Penguin, New York, NY

Ellamil, M, Dobson, C, Beeman, M and Christoff, K (2012) Evaluative and generative modes of thought during the creative process, *NeuroImage*, **59** (2), pp 1783–94

Engel, G L (1968) A life setting conducive to illness: the giving-up–given-up complex, *Annals of Internal Medicine*, **69** (2), pp 239–300

Ericsson, K A, Krampe, R T and Tesch-Römer, C (1993) The role of deliberate practice in the acquisition of expert performance, *Psychological Review*, **100** (3), pp 363–406

Everson, S A, Kaplan, G A, Goldberg, D E, Salonen, R and Salonen, J T (1997) Hopelessness and four-year progression of carotid atherosclerosis: the Kuopio ischemic heart disease risk factor study, *Arteriosclerosis Thrombosis Vascular Biology*, **17** (8), pp 1490–95

Eysenck, H J (1993) Prediction of cancer and coronary heart disease mortality by means of a personality inventory: results of a 15-year follow-up study, *Psychological Reports*, **72** (2), pp 499–516

Fisher, K (1999) *Leading Self-directed Work Teams*, McGraw-Hill, New York, NY

Frankl, F E (1959) *Man's Search for Meaning*, Beacon Press, Boston, MA

Gardner, H (1983) *Frames of Mind: The theory of multiple intelligences*, HarperCollins, London

Gerber, M E (1995) *The E-Myth Revisited*, HarperCollins, New York, NY

Gerritsen, J, Dekker, J M, TenVoorde, B J, Kostense, P J, Heine, R J, Bouter, L M, Heethaar, R M and Stehouwer, C D (2001) Impaired autonomic function is associated with increased mortality, especially in subjects with diabetes, hypertension, or a history of cardiovascular disease: the Hoorn Study. *Diabetes Care*, **24** (10), pp 1793–8

Gershon, M (1998) *The Second Brain*, HarperCollins, New York, NY

Gladwell, M (2010) *What the Dog Saw and Other Adventures*, Penguin, London

Gladwell, M (2000) *The Tipping Point: How little things can make a big difference*, Little Brown, London

Gladwell, M (2005) *Blink: The power of thinking without thinking*, London, Penguin

Glassman, A H and Shapiro, P A (1998) Depression and the course of coronary artery disease, *American Journal of Psychiatry*, **155** (1), pp 4–11

Goffee, R and Jones, G (2006) *Why Should Anyone Be Led by You? What it takes to be an authentic leader*, Harvard Business School Press, Boston, MA

Goleman, D (1987) Research affirms power of positive thinking, *New York Times*, 3 February

Goleman, D, Boyatzis, R E and McKee, A (2002) *The New Leaders: Transforming the art of leadership*, Little Brown, London

Goleman, D and Dalai Lama (2004) *Destructive Emotions: And how can we overcome them*, Bloomsbury, London

Grant Thornton (2012) Grant Thornton's International Business Report: Women in senior management: still not enough [online] www.internationalbusinessreport.com/reports/2012/women.asp [accessed 10 July 2013]

Graves, C (1981) Summary statement: the emergent, cyclical, double-helix model of adult human biopsychosocial systems, presented in Boston, May 1981

Grossarth-Maticek, R (1980) Psychosocial predictors of cancer and internal diseases: an overview, *Psychotherapy and Psychosomatics*, **33** (3), pp 122–28

Haidt, J (2006) *The Happiness Hypothesis: Putting ancient wisdom and philosophy to the test of modern science*, Arrow Books, London

Hameroff, S and Penrose, R (2003) Conscious events as orchestrated space-time selections, *Neuroquantology*, **1** (1), pp 10–35

Henry, J P (1982) The relation of social to biological processes in disease, *Social Science and Medicine*, **16** (4), pp 369–80

Henry, J P, Stephens, P M and Ely, D L (1986) Psychosocial hypertension and the defence and defeat reactions, *Journal of Hypertension*, **4** (6), pp 687–97

Ho, M W, Popp, F A and Warnke, U (1994) *Bioelectrodynamics and Biocommunication*, World Scientific Publishing, Singapore

Hollenbeck, G P, McCall Jr, M W and Silzer, R F (2006) Leadership competency models, *The Leadership Quarterly*, **17** (4), pp 398–413

Ikai, M and Steinhaus, A H (1961) Some factors modifying the expression of human strength, *Journal of Applied Physiology*, **16** (1), pp 157–63

Johnson, B C, Manyika, J M and Yee, L A (2005) The next revolution in interaction, *McKinsey Quarterly*, **4**, pp 20–33

Jung, R E, Gasparovic, C, Chavez, R S, Flores, R A, Smith, S M, Caprihan, A and Yeo, R A (2009) Biochemical support for the 'threshold' theory of creativity: a magnetic resonance spectroscopy study, *Journal of Neuroscience*, **29** (16), pp 5319–25

Kahneman, D (2011) *Thinking, Fast and Slow*, Penguin, New York

Kahneman, D and Deaton, A (2010) High income improves evaluation of life but not emotional well-being, *PNAS*, **107** (38), pp 16489–93

Kaipa, P and Radjou, N (2013) *From Smart to Wise: Acting and leading with wisdom*, Jossey-Bassey, San Francisco

Katz, D, MacCoby, N and Morse, N C (1950) *Productivity, Supervision and Morale in an Office Situation*, Institute for Social Research, University of Michigan, Ann Arbor, MI

Katzenbach, J R and Smith, D K (1993) *The Wisdom of Teams*, Harvard Business School Press, Boston, MA

Kegan, R and Lahey, L (2009) *Immunity to Change: How to overcome it and unlock the potential in yourself and your organisation*, Harvard Business School Press Boston, MA

Kiecolt-Glaser, J K, Stephens, R E, Lipetz, P D, Speicher, C E and Glaser, R (1985) Distress and DNA repair in human lymphocytes, *Journal of Behavioral Medicine*, 8 (4), pp 311–20

Kim, W C and Mauborgne, R (2005) *Blue Ocean Strategy: How to create uncontested market space and make the competition irrelevant*, Harvard Business School Press, Boston, MA

Kleiger, R E, Miller, J P, Bigger, J T Jr and Moss, A J (1987) Decreased heart rate variability and its association with increased mortality after acute myocardial infarction, *American Journal of cardiology*, 59 (4), pp 256–62

Koestler, A (1967) *The Ghost in the Machine*, Macmillan, New York, NY

Kohlberg, L (1981) *The Philosophy of Moral Development: Moral stages and the idea of justice*, Harper & Row, London

Kohn, A (1993) *Punished by Rewards: The trouble with gold stars, incentive plans, A's, praise and other bribes*, Houghton Mifflin, New York, NY

Kounios, J, Frymiare, J L, Bowden, E M, Fleck, J I, Subramaniam, K, Parrish, T B and Jung-Beeman, M (2006) The prepared mind: neural activity prior to problem presentation predicts subsequent solution by sudden insight, *Psychological Science*, 17 (10), pp 882–90

Kubzansky, L D, Kawachi, I, Spiro, A I, Weiss, S T, Vokonas, P S and Sparrow, D (1997) Is worrying bad for your heart? A prospective study of worry and coronary heart disease in the Normative Aging Study, *Circulation*, 95 (4), pp 818–24

Landau, E (2009) Landau study: experiences make us happier than possessions, February 2009, CNN.com [online] http://edition.cnn.com/2009/HEALTH/02/10/happiness.possessions/ [accessed 10 July 2013]

Langer, E J (2010) *Counter Clockwise: A proven way to think yourself younger and healthier*, Hodder and Stoughton, London

Lazarus, R S and Folkman, S (1984) *Stress, Appraisal, and Coping*, Springing Publishing Company, New York, NY

Le Fanu, J (1999) *The Rise and Fall of Modern Medicine*, Little, Brown and Company, London

LeShan, L (1977) *You Can Fight for Your Life*, M Evans, New York, NY

Levitin, D J (2006) *This is Your Brain on Music, The science of a human obsession*, Dutton, New York, NY

Levy, S M, Lee, J, Bagley, C and Lippman, M (1988) Survival hazards analysis in first recurrent breast cancer patients: seven-year follow-up, *Psychosomatic Medicine*, 50 (5), pp 520–28

Lewis, M (2010) *The Big Short*, Penguin, London

Lewis, M (2011) *Boomerang: The Biggest Bust*, Penguin, London

Limb, C J and Braun, A R (2008) Neural substrates of spontaneous musical performance: an FMRI study of jazz improvisation, *PLoS One*, 3 (2), p 1679

London School of Economics (2009) When performance-related pay backfires, *Financial*, www.finchannel.com [accessed 10 July 2013]

L-Xufn, Hy, Loevinger, J and Le Xuan, Hy (1996) *Measuring Ego Development: Personality and clinical psychology*, 2nd edn, Lawrence Erlbaum Associates, Inc, Hillsdale, NJ

Lynch, J L (2000) *A Cry Unheard: New insights into the medical consequences of loneliness*, Bancroft Press, Baltimore, MD

Lyubomirsky, S (2007) *The How of Happiness*, Penguin, New York, NY

MacLean, P D (1990) *The Triune Brain in Evolution: Role in paleocerebral functions*, Plenum Press, New York, NY

Malik, M and Camm, A J (1995) *Heart Rate Variability*, Wiley-Blackwell

Maltz, M (1960) *Psycho-Cybernetics*, Simon and Schuster, New York, NY

Marmot, M (1991) *The Whitehall Study*, Professor Sir Michael Marmot, Department of Epidemiology and Public Health, London, University College London

Martin, R (2002) *The Responsibility Virus: How control freaks, shrinking violets – and the rest of us – can harness the power of true partnership*, Basic Books, New York, NY

Martin, R L (2011) *Fixing the Game: How runaway expectations broke the economy, and how to get back to reality*, Harvard Business School Press, Boston, MA

Mayor, D F and Micozzi, M S (eds) (2011) *Energy Medicine East and West: A natural history of Qi*, Churchill Livingstone Elsevier

McGregor, D (1960) *The Human Side of Enterprise*, McGraw Hill, New York, NY

McVeight, K (2011) Facebook 'friends' did not act on suicide note, *Guardian*, 6 January

Mehrabian, A (1972) *Silent Messages: Implicit communication of emotions and attitudes*, Wadsworth Publishing Company, Belmont, CA

Michaels, E, Handfield-Jones, H and Axelrod, B (2001) *The War for Talent*, Harvard Business School Press, Boston, MA

Middleton, J (2007) *Beyond Authority: Leadership in a changing world*, Palgrave MacMillan, New York, NY

Murray, C and Lopez, A (1996) *The Global Burden of Disease: A comprehensive assessment of mortality and disability from diseases, injuries, and risk factors in*

1990 and projected to 2020: summary (Global burden of disease and injury series), Harvard University Press, Cambridge, MA

Muslamova, I, The Power of the Human Heart [online] http://hypertextbook.com/facts/2003/IradaMuslumova.shtml [accessed 10th July 2013]

Nabi, H *et al* (2008) Does personality predict mortality? Results from the GAZEL French prospective cohort study, *International Journal of Epidemiology*, 37 (3), pp 591–602

Neilson, J P and Mistry, R T (2000) Fetal electrocardiogram plus heart rate recording for fetal monitoring during labour, *Cochrane Database of Systematic Reviews*, (2) CD000116

News Medical website (2012) First sign of coronary heart disease in men could be death [online] www.news-medical.net/news

Norretranders, T (1998) *The User Illusion: Cutting consciousness down to size*, Penguin, New York, NY

Ornish, D (1998) *Love and Survival: The scientific basis for the healing power of intimacy*, HarperCollins, New York, NY

Pennebaker, J W (1997) *Opening Up: The healing power of expressing emotions*, Guilford Press, New York, NY

Pereira, V H, Cerqueira, J J, Palha, J A and Sousa, N (2012) Stressed brain, diseased heart: A review on the pathophysiologic mechanisms of neurocardiology, *International Journal of cardiology*, 166 (1), pp 30–37

Pert, C B (1997) *Molecules of Emotion: the science behind Mind-Body medicine*, Simon & Schuster, New York

Peterson, R S, Owens, P D, Tetlock, P E, Fan, E T and Martorana, P (1998) Group dynamics in top management teams: groupthink, vigilance, and alternative models of organisational failure and success, *Organisational Behavior and Human Decision Processes*, 73, pp 272–305

Petrie, N (2011) *A White Paper: Future trends in leadership development*, Center for Creative Leadership, First issued December 2011

Pettingale, K W, Philalithis, A, Tee, D E and Greer, H S (1981) The biological correlates of psychological responses to breast cancer, *Journal of Psychosomatic Research*, 25 (5), pp 453–58

Phipps, C (2012) *Evolutionaries: Unlocking the spiritual and cultural potential of science's greatest idea*, HarperCollins, New York, NY

Piaget, J (1972) *The Psychology of the Child*, Basic Books, New York, NY

Pink, D H (2009) *Drive: The surprising truth about what motivates us*, Penguin, New York, NY

Plutchik, R (1967) The affective differential: emotion profiles implied by diagnostic concepts, *Psychological Reports*, 20 (1), pp 19–25

Prochaska, J O, Norcross, J C and Diclemente, C C (1994) *Changing for Good*, Avon Books, New York, NY

Purcell, H and Mulcahy, D (1994) Emotional eclipse of the heart, *British Journal of Clinical Practice*, 48 (5), pp 228–29

Reported in July 2006, the *Journal Liaowang Eastern Weekly* (Liaowang Dongfang Zhoukan) and mentioned in the August 2006 China Labour Bulletin

Rio Tinto (2012) *Group Strategy Annual Report 2012* [online] www.riotinto.com/annualreport2012 [accessed 10 July 2013]

Rio Tinto (2013) Corporate Website, About us/Strategy [online] www.riotinto.com/about-us-ID8.aspx [accessed 10 July 2013]

Rogers, C R (1967) *On Becoming a Person*, Constable, London

Rooke, D and Torbert, W R (2005) Seven transformations of leadership, *Harvard Business Review*, 1 April 2005

Roosevelt, E (1960) This is my story, *Catholic Digest*, August

Rosch, P (1995) Perfectionism and poor health, *Health and Stress Newsletter Issue 7 (Newsletter of the American Institute of Stress)*, pp 3–4

Rosenman, R H (1993) The independent roles of diet and serum lipids in the 20th-century rise and decline of coronary heart disease mortality, *Integrative Physiological and Behavioral Science*, 28 (1), pp 84–98

Rowland, W (2012) *Greed Inc: Why corporations rule the world and how we let it happen*, Arcade Publishing, New York, NY

Schroder, H M (1989) *Managerial Competence: The key to excellence*, Kendall Hunt, Dubuque, IA

Scott, S (2002) *Fierce Conversations*, Piatkus Books, London

Seamark, M (2011) Lloyds boss goes sick with 'stress': Shock departure eight months into job *Daily Mail*

Sheldon, K M and Kasser, T (1995) Coherence and congruence: two aspects of personality integration, *Journal of Personality and Social Psychology*, 68 (3), pp 531–43

Sinek, S (2011) *Start With Why: How great leaders inspire everyone to take action*, Penguin, New York, NY

Society for Heart Attack Prevention and Eradication (2013) What you should know [online] http://www.shapesociety.org/about-shape/what-you-should-know [accessed 10 July 2013]

Society of Women's Health Research (nd), Fact sheet: cardiovascular disease, SWHR, Washington, DC

Stogdill, R M and Coons, A E (1957) *Leader Behaviour: Its description and measurement*, Bureau of Business Research, Ohio State University, Columbus, OH

Strogatz, S (2004) *Sync: The emerging science of spontaneous order*, Penguin, London

Talbot, M (1991) *The Holographic Universe*, HarperCollins, New York, NY

Taleb, N N (2007) *The Black Swan: The impact of the highly improbable*, Penguin, London

Tappin, S (2012) *Dreams to Last*, Beijing University Press, Beijing

Tappin, S and Cave, A (2010) *The New Secrets of CEOs: 200 global chief executives on leading*, Nicholas Brealey, London

Tapscott, D (2009) *Grown Up Digital: How the net generation is changing the world*, McGraw Hill, New York, NY

Thomas, L (1986) *The Incredible Machine*, National Geographic Society, Washington

Tiller, W A, McCraty, R and Atkinson, M (1996) Cardiac coherence: A new, non-invasive measure of autonomic nervous system order, *Alternative Therapies in Health and Medicine*, 2 (1), pp 52–65

Todaro, W (2003) Want to be a CEO? Stay put, *Forbes* [online] www.forbes.com [accessed 10 July 2013]

Tolle, E (2005) *The Power of Now*, Hodder & Stoughton, London

Townsend, N, Wickramasinghe, K, Bhatnagar, P, Smolina, K, Nichols, M, Leal, J, Luengo-Fernandez, R and Rayner, M (2012) *Coronary Heart Disease Statistics*, British Heart Foundation, London

Treanor, J (2011) Lloyds chief Horta-Osório takes time off with fatigue, *Guardian*, 2 November

Tsuji, H, Larson, M, Venditti, F, *et al* (1996) Impact of reduced heart rate variability on risk for cardiac events: The Framingham heart study, *Circulation*, 94, pp 2850–55

Tsuji, H, Venditti, F, Manders, E, *et al* (1994) Reduced heart rate variability and mortality risk in an elderly cohort, *Circulation*, 90, pp 878–83

Umetani, K, Singer, D H, McCraty, R and Atkinson, M (1998) Twenty-four hour time domain heart rate variability and heart rate: relations to age and gender over nine decades, *Journal of the American College of Cardiology*, 31 (3), pp 593–601

Wallis, C (2005) The new science of happiness: what makes the human heart sing? *Time Magazine*, 17 January

Walsch, N D (1998) *Conversation with God, Book 3*, Hampton Road Publishing Company, Vancouver

Ware, B (2011) *The Top Five Regrets of the Dying*, Hay House, London

Watkins, A D (2011) Chapter 24: The Electrical Heart – *Energy in Cardiac Health and Disease* in Energy Medicine East and West: A Natural History of Qi Churchill Livingstone Elsevier (eds Mayor, D F and Micozzi, M S)

Watkins, A D and Cobain, M (2013) The effects of breath control and emotional management training on neuroendocrine and cardiovascular markers of stress in the workplace (manuscript in preparation)

Watkins, A D, Young, K and Barren, D (2013) Improving Energy Levels in Retail Executives, manuscript in preparation

Watkins, A D, Young, K and Barron, D (Submitted 2013) The biological impact of compassion meditation in Tibetan monks, *International Journal of Psychophysiology*

Watkins, A D, Young, K, Barron, D and Sikder, O (2013) The biological impact of leadership development coaching, manuscript in preparation

Watkins, A D (1997) *Mind–body medicine: A clinician's guide to psychoneuroimmunology*, Churchill Livingston, New York, NY

Wilber, K (2001) *A Theory of Everything: An integral vision for business, politics, science and spirituality*

Wilber, K (2003) *Boomeritis: A novel that will set you free*, Shambhala, Boston, MA

Wilber, K (2012) Excerpt C: the ways we are in this together, excerpt from forthcoming book the *Kosmos Trilogy*, Vol 2 [Online] http://integrallife.com/integral-post/ways-we-are-together [accessed 10 July 2013]

Wolf, M M, Varigos, G A, Hunt, D and Sloman, J G (1978) Sinus Arrhythmia in acute myocardial infarction, *Medical Journal of Australia*, 2 (2), pp 52–3

World Federation for Mental Health (2012) *Health Depression: A global crisis; Depression: A Global Public Health Concern*, pp 6–8

World Health Organization (2011) *Global Status Report on Noncommunicable Diseases 2010*, Geneva, World Health Organization

Yerkes, R M and Dodson, J D (1908) The relation of strength of stimulus to rapidity of habit-formation, *Journal of Comparative Neurology and Psychology*, 18, pp 459–82

INDEX

CPSIA information can be obtained at www.ICGtesting.com
Printed in the USA
BVOW09s1524151014

370960BV00009B/234/P

9 780749 470050